THE ACKERMAN

MARTELL

GUIDE

to the best
restaurants and hotels
in the British Isles

Selected by
Roy Ackerman

ALFRESCO
LEISURE PUBLICATIONS PLC

Alfresco Leisure Publications PLC, 35 Tadema Road, London SW10 0PZ

First published 1991
Copyright © Alfresco Leisure Publications PLC, 1991

Produced and edited by
Alfresco Leisure Publications PLC
with Pilot Productions Ltd

Illustrations, cover illustration and cover design by Chris Ackerman-Eveleigh
Design by Malcolm Smythe
Page make-up by Keith Shannon
Photography by Leigh Simpson
Colour origination by TPS Graphics, Cardiff CF3 0EG
Made and printed in Great Britain by Butler and Tanner Ltd,
    Frome, Somerset BA11 1NF
Typeset by Dorchester Typesetting Ltd, Dorchester, Dorset DT1 1UA
Text film by MRM Graphics, Winslow MK18 6BY

Contents

At Martell we have been making fine Cognac since 1715. Our unrivalled success is derived from a 'savoir-faire' that has been handed down through the years from father to son. First established by Jean Martell, the traditions of the family business have been sustained through eight successive generations.

A leading Cognac House earns its status by skilful selection, ageing and inspired blending of eaux-de-vie. Martell demand standards of the highest quality, and our Head Taster selects only the finest Cognacs for inclusion in the blends which are deemed both worthy and representative of our unique House style.

Creating the right blend takes great care, patience and an exceptional palate. Out of this union comes a fine end-product; Martell Cognac is renowned for its unique, smooth flavour.

Like Martell Cognac, this *Guide* is the end-product of a fine union, and Martell is delighted to be associated with it once again.

Roy Ackerman has been as discerning as our Head Taster in his selection of fine eating places. There is something here to suit everyone's palate – more so than ever – since in addition to traditional restaurants and country house hotels in this country, there is a colourful exploration of Europe.

We are confident that you will find the 1991/92 edition of *The Ackerman Martell Guide* a useful and enjoyable kaleidoscope of gastronomic delights.

Bon Appétit!

The Art of Martell Cognac

The making of Cognac is an art form, and at Martell we like to think it is one we have mastered. Every bottle of our Cognac is the result of a long, careful production process, which includes the art of marrying different blends.

By the distillation of natural wines from the Grande Champagne, Petite Champagne, Borderies and Fins Bois, we create blends which are unique to the oldest of the major Cognac Houses.

To arrive at this stage, our Head Taster will first experiment with the Cognacs in miniature. Once he is satisfied, the different Cognacs will be taken from the warehouses into the blending room, known as the salle de coupe or the salle de mariage. When blended and filtered, the Cognac will at first lose its fine quality, and will require time to recuperate. It may be left in a vat for up to 24 hours, during which time it is turned continuously by a paddle. After regular tastings it will either be despatched for bottling, or blending once more.

The making of Cognac is an art in itself – but there is an art to *savouring* it to the full. The beauty of what we at Martell like to refer to as the 'Martell Moment', is that it is an art which can be appreciated by the enthusiast and connoisseur alike.

The Art of Drinking Cognac

Across the world, people drink Cognac in different ways. In parts of the Far East, for example, water is added and Cognac is drunk as an accompaniment to a meal. In France, it is popular as a refreshing apéritif, served with orange juice or tonic water. In Britain, the preference is for Cognac served on its own.

The Art of Appreciating a Fine Cognac

The beauty of Martell Cognac is not just to be found in its taste – there are several key stages to the art of Cognac appreciation:

★ The Art of Capturing that Golden Spirit ★

Once you have poured a measure into a glass, take a good, long look at it. Hold it up to the light, and appreciate its rich amber tones – these are the results of years spent ageing in oak barrels.

★ The Art of Releasing the Bouquet ★

Warmth is the key to releasing the bouquet of Cognac, but do not be tempted to heat the glass over a flame – harsh heat actually impairs the flavour. Instead, cup your hands around the glass, and you will gently warm the Cognac. As you do this, the bouquet will be released, allowing you to appreciate the full nose of the blend.

You will then start to notice the fine, flowery fragrance of the grapes from the Charente region, together with the vanilla from the oak barrels, and the special nuttiness of the Borderies: a delightful combination.

★ The Art of Savouring the Taste ★

The final stage to the art of appreciation lies with the taste. Martell Cognac has a subtle complexity of flavours, which should be savoured to the full. Drink in small sips and feel the Cognac warming on your tongue. Slowly, all the delicious aromas will be released.

Martell Cognac

Martell Cognac offers a wide range of Cognacs for your appreciation:

Martell VS 3★★★
`A blend of Cognacs from the four finest growth areas. Grande and Petite Champagne give the blend its vigour, Borderies bring a touch of mellowness, and the Fins Bois a lightness.

Martell VSOP Medaillon
Martell's Very Special Old Pale. This mature blend has a high proportion of Grande Champagne, which provides its bouquet and body. Fins Bois its characteristic taste, with Borderies mellowing the flavour.

Martell Cordon Bleu
This blend has the classic Martell hallmark, Grande and Petite Champagne add strength, body and finesse, while rare old Borderies – some more than a generation old – add a special mellowness, and give this Cognac the unique nutty taste of Martell.

Martell XO Supreme
Every eau-de-vie in this blend had been aged to absolute perfection – a long, long process, requiring great patience. This is an extremely high quality Cognac, containing rare eaux-de-vie – taken mainly from the Martell family vineyards – which are reserved cxclusively for the most special of blends.

Martell Extra
The top of our range, this is made in limited quantities, and is a blend of Grande and Petite Champagne giving vigour and body, combined with very old mellow Borderies to round off the taste. Martell Cognac at its best.

Santé!

Château de Chanteloup
Cognac

Introduction

by ROY ACKERMAN

Business Trends

There is no question that 1990 and 1991 will go down as two of the most difficult years for restaurateurs and hoteliers in Great Britain. An extraordinary number of places have either changed hands or ceased trading altogether. Some went down simply to re-appear in a different guise (such as 36 on the Quay at Emsworth), others were new and just didn't make it (like Snaffles in London). Many that have changed hands are country house hotels – 1990 has seen new faces at Flitwick Manor, Hintlesham Hall, and Homewood Park; the Castle at Taunton has had its drawbridge rattled but has repelled invaders (the Chapmans are staying). Among restaurants with rooms there have also been changes: sadly, Sonia Stevenson is no longer at the Horn of Plenty.

Some closures have brought increased pleasure elsewhere, as at Sharrow Bay, to which Colin White has returned after running his own place in the Cotswolds. Sometimes those who have benefited are yet farther afield – Cliff and Kay Morgan have decamped from La Chaumière in Cardiff to Le Résidence in northern Cyprus! Some shuffles (unlike Cabinet ones) take a while before everyone is settled into their new positions – following Ruth and David Watson's departure from Hintlesham Hall, they have at last re-emerged at the Fox and Goose at Fressingfield.

Surprisingly, casualties in London have been fewer than one might have expected – only about a dozen among last year's listings have failed to survive, such as 51-51, Liaison, Le Mazarin, Les Trois Plats, and Rochfords; but set against the calamities there are some notable newcomers to the scene who should weather the current storm. These include Bryan Webb's Hilaire – hardly a newcomer, but new in that Bryan Webb now owns and runs his own establishment thanks to a small group of shareholders; and 190 Queen's Gate, a BES scheme which has a large number of leading chefs, hotel managers and restaurateurs as its shareholders.

As far as the Guide is concerned, the problem with great flux is inaccuracy. While we undertake to be correct with our information at the time of going to press, please check at the time of booking any details that are particularly important to you, in case there has been subsequent change. In particular, we have made a positive decision not to refer, in a review, to any rumours we may have heard about an establishment possibly coming on to the market.

Getting It Wrong

In many respects restaurants and hotels represent a microcosm of the world at large. Besides having a modicum of common sense, dealing with people successfully is one of the essential abilities for a restaurateur, and if only one other was permitted for either a chef, restaurateur or hotelkeeper, I would choose foresight: be prepared, for without adequate preparation of staff, food, and room, you will be in trouble.

I have cooked with otherwise talented chefs who, because of lack of *mise en place*, have found themselves in the most disastrous of situations quite unnecessarily.

Roy Ackerman and Martell wish you 'Bon Appétit'

MARTELL

Similarly, failure to prepare a restaurant adequately doubles the work of its staff. Simple, obvious, but I am constantly surprised by the people who get it wrong – regularly!

Irritating Habits

The waiter who has been trained to walk through the room, blithely ignoring everyone's frantic gestures or empty plates with a degree of superciliousnous that displays complete contempt for his customers.

Staff preparing for the next service, oblivious to the fact that present customers still require theirs.

The receptionist who willingly takes an incoming call from a sales representative whilst you, the paying customer, are kept waiting at the desk desperate for the bathroom, telephone, food, etc.

Enough of getting it wrong. Taking a wider view, food and service in this country have dramatically improved in Britain over the last twenty years and, encouragingly, we now have a generation of nationally and internationally known young British chefs and restaurateurs who are helping to lift the traveller's attitude to food in Britain, to help us compete in the world of international tourism.

No Place for Food in National Culture

Among those establishments who are finding business difficult, far from all are of indifferent quality. Higher interest rates and an accompanying downturn in business have taken their toll on some promising places. It is always sad when a place with an inspired chef who is cooking well, disappears. And the question has to be asked, would such establishments survive if they were on the continent? By and large my feeling is that they would.

One of the problems we still have in Britain is that eating out is not a meaningful part of our culture. Indeed I'd go as far as to say that eating well anywhere – even in the home – remains beyond most people's expectations. I appreciate that saying this will offend many people but, outside a dedicated group of people who love cooking or are interested in food and in the enjoyment of food, the mass of people in Britain appears to be indifferent to quality food in any shape or form.

In this (as, perhaps, in other ways) this country seems to be moving far more towards the United States of America than the United States of Europe. 1992 seems set to herald a rash of fast food, call-order restaurants, ready-prepared meals and convenience foods – a trend that threatens to stamp out what little cooking of quality is enjoyed in the home at the present time. When I criticise fast food and burger restaurants, invariably the riposte is – where else can you eat out for £2.50/£3.00 etc? There is no denying that's true; there are very few restaurants (proper) that offer a meal for similar money. But you could certainly eat a very decent meal at home for that amount. I maintain that it is just as easy and less expensive to buy the ingredients and prepare a simple stew or soup than it is to buy a 'convenience' meal prepared at your local supermarket.

Sadly, for many homes, the dining table is a thing of the past. The dining room as such has become a spare room or is used only for the special occasion. Even the kitchen has become a place for a quick snack. It is rare, today, for a family to meet around the table because everyone is following his or her own pursuits elsewhere or is simply mesmerised by the TV. Corny as it may sound, I feel that a great number of social problems in our country are caused by lack of family communication around the table. Even the traditional once-a-week family meal seems in many cases to have gone by the board.

Likewise, the brief revival of pride in national cuisine, which came to the fore a few years ago, seems to be tailing off. So few restaurants offer the local specialities of the area where they are situated. Why? Almost every place you visit in France, Italy or Germany is proud of its local speciality, or local indigenous ingredients. Surely we in Britain could put together a movement to save what is left of our national food culture, and to encourage families to appreciate both the aesthetic, health-giving, and social functions of good food.

Good fresh food can be cheaper than food packaged and marketed through the supermarket. The skills required to cook it are really very straightforward, but gone are the days when mothers taught them to their children. Absent, too, is the much-mocked domestic science lesson from the curriculum, except as an insignificant aspect of the Technology course, yet what insight into the world of food it once offered young people.

Is it now the time to introduce into the national curriculum food education in some form? On the health issue, think of the advantages in old age and the cost saving to the country in health bills if children were taught the nutritional values of food, and the pros and cons of alcohol. Perhaps a part of the vast amount of money presently spent in the food sector on advertising could be switched to developing an informative educational policy for young people. Yes, I am talking about sponsored education, because I see no alternative – (what government will be prepared to apportion the amount of money that would be required?) – and at the end of the day it has to be good for the food and drink industry as well as for the people of Britain.

A hope for the future is the newly-formed Academy of Culinary Arts, which is backed by the Government and leading organisations in the restaurant, hotel and catering industry. The Academy aims to teach its students the very top skills in cooking and service. As well as permanent lecturers it will call on the resources of the leading chefs of Britain who are devoting their time free of charge for Master Classes. Hopefully these skills will filter down and help lift standards not only at the top establishments but also the middle and pub/restaurant end. This can only benefit the consumer.

As we go to press we are carrying out a survey in France and Britain among a variety of social groups to guage and compare attitudes on eating out and eating in the home. If you would like to know the results of this survey, please phone (0898) 866966. (Calls are charged at 34p per minute at cheap rate and 45p per minute at other times.) No-one has yet given a satisfactory explanation as to why there is such a difference between the British and French attitudes to food. What is it that makes these attitudes so different and what can we do to improve the British attitude? I have my own opinions as to how the survey might work out, but I could be wrong and I wait with knife and fork poised to digest the results when they have been fully analysed.

How to Use this Guide

Main Reviews
This year we have chosen a simpler format for the reviews, taking the best of our previous versions. The main reviews are set out very simply: London is arranged alphabetically by establishment name. Reviews in England, Scotland, Wales, Northern Ireland and the Republic of Ireland are arranged alphabetically by location, then by establishment name.

Some reviews are longer than others. The length of a review does not necessarily indicate the relative importance of an establishment – some have been covered more fully in previous editions of the Guide, which are available from Alfresco.

I have used a small team of reviewers who have worked with me for some years and whose judgement I trust, and who understand what I am seeking in standards of cuisine, atmosphere and service.

Clover Award Winners
Special colour sections feature the majority of our Clover Award winners, London in one section (pages 17 to 64) and the rest of the country in the second (pages 145 to 240). A few Clover Award winners (late decisions!) are not featured in colour; they appear in alphabetical order within their appropriate section.

Listings
Where we are unsure about an establishment, or have visited it only once, or there has been a change of some significance since our last visit, we list it without a review. These listings appear at the end of each section.

Ethnic Restaurants
As we made a special feature of London's ethnic restaurants in last year's guide, this year most will be found in the London Listings section. We are once again indebted to Fay Maschler for providing the information.

Vital Statistics
These have been compiled from information supplied to us by the establishments themselves, in response to our questionnaires. They have been checked and we have done our best to ensure that all information contained in this book is accurate. However, it is perfectly feasible that a restaurant or hotel may choose to change its 'last order' time or the day of the week that it is closed. Similarly, an owner, manager or chef may well move on. Even the style of food might be changed. We assume that in most cases you will book before going to a restaurant or hotel, and if you feel that any detail is especially important, we suggest you check it at the time of booking. When we have quoted particular dishes in a review, we cannot guarantee that they will be available on your visit – this is obviously true if you visit in a different season. In most cases, menus will be far more comprehensive than the extracts we have chosen.

Price
The price shown is the average cost of dinner for two people, without wine, but including coffee, service and VAT. Where possible, we have

quoted a set price dinner menu, which in some cases might be four or even five courses; otherwise the figure relates to a typical three-course meal.

Vests
As before, I have used the 'vested interest' symbol to indicate restaurants in which I have a personal investment.

Major investment

B.E.S. Shareholder
Minor investment

Europe
Our Special Feature this year is a photo-montage of a trip through Europe I was fortunate to make during the summer of 1990. I hope you enjoy reading this section as much as I enjoyed researching it!

Food and Restaurant Styles

Bistro: normally smaller establishments, checked or paper tablecloths, bentwood chairs, cluttered decor, friendly informal staff. Honest, basic and robust cooking, possibly coarse pâtés, thick soups, casseroles served in large portions.

Brasserie: large-ish, styled room, often with long bar, normally serving one-plate items rather than formal meals (though some offer both). Often possible just to have a drink, or coffee, or just a small amount to eat. Traditional dishes include charcuterie, moules marinières, steak frites. Service generally by waiters in long aprons and black waistcoats.

Farmhouse cooking: usually simply cooked with generous portions of basic, home-produced fare using good, local ingredients.

Country house hotel cooking: can vary from establishment to establishment but usually modern English style with some influence from classic or even farmhouse style.

Classic/haute cuisine: the classic style of cooking evolved through many centuries, best chronicled by Escoffier. Great depth of flavour. Style does not necessarily mean the most expensive ingredients – can include simply poached and boiled dishes such as chicken, tongue and offal. Classical presentation can be served at table or plated.

Cordon bleu: derives from the cookery school of the same name, perhaps normally associated with dinner party or private house cooking.

New or modern English/French/European/eclectic: draws from classical style but with new style saucing and the better aspects of nouvelle presentation. Plated in the kitchen, allowing the chef the final responsibility for presentation.

Nouvelle cuisine: at its best a distinctive style and presentation with a lighter and more innovative approach to some standard dishes. Concentrates on subtle flavours and unusual combinations. Plated, often referred to as 'art on the plate'. Has gained an unfortunate reputation for offering inadequate portions and concentrating more on presentation than content, but at its best is exceptionally good.

The Four-Leaf Clover

The four-leaf clover has been chosen because it is a symbol of luck and also a rare find. There is always a degree of luck involved when good ambience, excellent food, wine and service and the response of the customer combine to make the perfect occasion. A White Clover means that in my opinion, this is a very special place for many reasons, and made for a memorable experience. A Black Clover represents excellence in **all** aspects of food, service and decor, and these establishments are the very best in Great Britain in the Republic of Ireland. The Ackerman Martell Guide Clover Leaf Awards for 1991 are given to:

LONDON

Alastair Little
L'Arlequin
Bibendum
The Capital Hotel
Le Caprice
Cavaliers
Chez Nico
Claridge's (*N*)
Clarke's
The Connaught Hotel
The Dorchester (*N*)
Four Seasons Restaurant
Le Gavroche
The Gay Hussar (*N*)
Harvey's
Hilaire (*N*)
L'Incontro
Kalamaras
Kensington Place
Langan's Brasserie
Mosimann's
The Oak Room
190 Queen's Gate (*N*)
The Ritz Hotel
River Café
Rue St Jacques
The Savoy
Le Soufflé Restaurant
Stephen Bull (*N*)
Sutherlands
La Tante Claire
Turner's

ENGLAND

(outside London)

Adlard's, Norwich
Les Alouettes, Claygate
Amberley Castle, Amberley
Bath Spa Hotel, Bath (*N*)
Bilbrough Manor, Bilbrough
Bishopstrow House,
    Warminster (*N*)
The Box Tree, Ilkley
Brown's, Worcester
Calcot Manor, Tetbury
The Carved Angel, Dartmouth
The Castle Hotel, Taunton
Chewton Glen, New Milton
Chez Nous, Plymouth
Cliveden, Taplow (*N*)
Clos du Roy, Box
Corse Lawn House,
    Corse Lawn
Croque-en-Bouche,
    Malvern Wells
Epicurean, Stow-on-the-Wold
Fischer's, Baslow
Gidleigh Park, Chagford
Gravetye Manor,
    East Grinstead
Hambleton Hall, Hambleton
Hartwell House, Aylesbury (*N*)
Hope End, Hope End
Lucknam Park, Colerne
Lynwood House, Barnstaple
Manleys, Storrington
Le Manoir aux Quat'Saisons,
    Great Milton

McCoy's, Staddlebridge

Melton's, York (*N*)

Michael's Nook, Grasmere

Middlethorpe Hall, York

Miller Howe, Windermere

Morel's, Haslemere

Normandie Hotel, Birtle

Oakes, Stroud

Old Beams, Waterhouses

Old Plow, Speen

Old Woolhouse, Northleach

Old Vicarage, Ridgeway

Old Manor House, Romsey (*N*)

L'Ortolan, Shinfield

Paris House, Woburn

Pebbles, Aylesbury

Pool Court,
    Pool-in-Wharfedale

Le Poussin, Brockenhurst (*N*)

Read's, Faversham (*N*)

Redmond's, Cheltenham

Restaurant Nineteen,
    Bradford (*N*)

Roger's Restaurant,
    Windermere

Rosers Restaurant,
    St Leonards-on-Sea (*N*)

Seafood Restaurant, Padstow

Sharrow Bay, Ullswater

Sloan's, Birmingham

Stane Street Hollow,
    Pulborough

Stapleford Park,
    Melton Mowbray

Stock Hill House, Gillingham

Ston Easton Park,
    Ston Easton

Sundial, Herstmonceux

Swallow Hotel, Birmingham (*N*)

Le Talbooth, Dedham

Thornbury Castle, Thornbury

Twenty One Queen Street,
    Newcastle-upon-Tyne (*N*)

Waterside Inn,
    Bray-on-Thames

Whitechapel Manor,
    South Molton

SCOTLAND

Altnaharrie Inn, Ullapool

Atkins Restaurant, Aberfeldy (*N*)

Champanay Inn, Linlithgow

The Cross, Kingussie

Inverlochy Castle,
    Fort William

Martin's, Edinburgh (*N*)

One Devonshire Gardens,
    Glasgow

Peat Inn, Peat Inn

La Potinière, Gullane

WALES

Bodysgallen Hall, Llandudno

Walnut Tree, Llandewi Skirrid

NORTHERN IRELAND

Ramore, Portrush (*N*)

REPUBLIC OF IRELAND

Adare Manor, Adare (*N*)

Ballymaloe House, Shanagarry

Mustard Seed, Adare

Park Hotel, Kenmare

Park Restaurant, Blackrock (*N*)

Restaurant Patrick Guilbaud,
    Dublin (*N*)

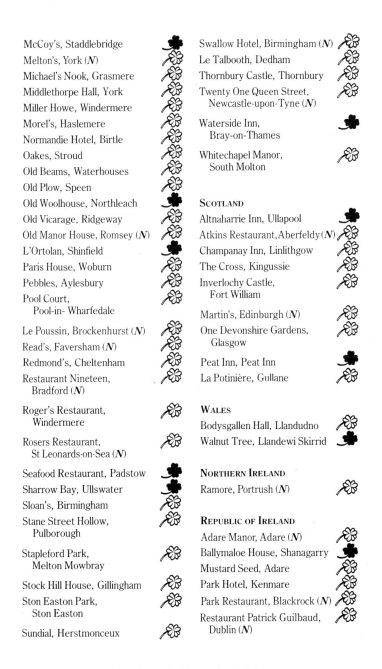

New clovers for this year marked (*N*).

OP PRESS : STOP PRESS : STOP PRESS : STOP PRESS : STOP PRESS : STOP P

Late Changes

Just after we had gone to press with all but these pages, there were a number of major changes announced, particularly in the area of hotel groups. Pavilion Leisure, the holding company for Select Hotels, went into receivership. This affects the following hotels and readers may wish to check when booking:

The Howard Hotel, Edinburgh; The Priory Hotel, Bath; Rookery Hall, Nantwich; and The White Hart, Coggeshall.

Other last minute changes that came to our attention:

The Royal Oak at Yattendon was sold at the beginning of March 1991; Blinkers French in Manchester ceased trading; Columbus in London ceased trading; and The Mansion House restaurant in Dartmouth ceased trading.

Update Hot-line

Since sudden changes now seem to be a feature of life for restaurants and hotels, we have set up an Update Hot-Line which you can telephone for the latest information on establishments featured in this edition of *The Ackerman Martell Guide*. The information will be updated monthly.

This number is (0898) 334329. Calls are charged at 34p per minute cheap rate, and 45p per minute at all other times.

Discount Offers

And now the good news. A number of restaurants and hotels have kindly agreed to offer special discounts exclusively to readers of *The Ackerman Martell Guide*. These offers are available for a variety of restaurants and hotels, on meals, wines and accommodation, and means that readers of the Guide have even more opportunity to enjoy good value at our leading establishments around the country.

You must claim your discount at the time of making the booking — the establishment may ask you to bring either your copy of the Guide or the voucher page along with you for endorsement. All offers are subject to availability.

Turn to page 461 for a full list.

Bishopstrow House

ALASTAIR LITTLE   London W1

49 Frith Street, London W1
Telephone: 071-734 5183
Open: lunch Mon-Fri, dinner Mon-Sat (closed Bank Holidays, 1 wk
    Christmas)
Last orders: lunch 2.30pm, dinner 11.30pm

£70

Alastair Little
a very talented young chef. At his restaurant, where Alastair cooks
with assistance from Juliet Peston, there are none of the swags and
finery that many find rather intimidating; instead, you'll find a simple
converted shop with wooden floor, cream walls, bare tables and
(surprisingly comfortable) wooden chairs. On the plate, the quality of
the raw ingredients shines through: strips of squid, slices of scallop
and shelled prawns appear in a clear seafood broth made as pretty as
a rock pool with strands of carrot, cucumber and fennel, and
garnished with a tiny baby octopus. Mullet, which was plump, moist
and cooked to the second, needed only char-grilling. Main course
portions tend to be generous. Finish off, perhaps, with some cheese
– a good excuse to order more pain poîlane! The wine list is short and
includes a couple of wines available by the glass. The bar downstairs
serves 'lighter' food at lunch and dinner – which is not to imply that
the food upstairs is in any way heavy! Rather that the menu
downstairs does not draw so distinct line a between starters and main
courses, with the result that a quicker or shorter meal may be taken.

Downstairs at Alastair Little (below), *and, right, the ground floor restaurant. Here you
will find, quite simply, some of the best food on offer in London.*

L'ARLEQUIN	**London SW8**

124 Queenstown Road, London SW8 3RJ
Telephone: 071-622 0555   *Fax:* 071-498 7015
Open: lunch + dinner Mon-Fri
Last orders: lunch 2.00pm, dinner 10.00pm

£85

The solid foundation of French cuisine is perfectly illustrated at L'Arlequin. Chef/patron Christian Delteil has no time for food fads. His cooking is consistently creative, but he always keeps one eye firmly on the traditions of his native south-west France. Regulars know the standard of excellence they can expect, and are never disappointed. Notable among his creations are noix de ris de veau vigneronne and rosette d'agneau en tapenade. Genevieve Delteil – graciously and apparently effortlessly – supervises the service from a team as skilful as any in town. This quietly decorated Battersea dining room would hold its own with many of its Parisian equivalents. The wine list travels through France before making a brief trip across the rest of the world, and exploring on a separate journey the world of dessert wines.

Christian Delteil, whose cooking reflects his own origins in south west France. His creations have a fine pedigree – there's no place for fads. Left: *Loup au vin rouge.*

BIBENDUM   London SW3

Michelin House, 81 Fulham Road, London SW3 6RD
Telephone: 071-581 5817   *Fax:* 071-623 7925   **£70**
Open: lunch + dinner daily (closed 4/5 days Christmas)
Last orders: lunch 2.30pm (3.00pm Sat + Sun), dinner 11.30pm (10.30pm
        Sun)

New-found assertiveness in both the kitchen and at front-of-house
creates the impression that this, one of London's top restaurants,
has been around a lot longer than barely 4 years. This is undoubtedly
a tribute to the skills of designer Sir Terence Conran and of chef
Simon Hopkinson's excellent cooking, which he describes as 'cuisine
de grand-mère'. The style ranges over the classics, and finds its
inspiration and ingredients on both sides of the Channel: soupe des
poissons, grilled aubergines with pesto, roast best end of lamb with
basil and tomato, grilled pigeon with shallots, sherry vinegar, olive oil
and parsley, and equally, you may be offered deep-fried cod and
chips, with tartare sauce, or roast grouse with bread sauce.
Vegetables (listed separately) may include roast onions and braised
endives. The wide-ranging wine list takes in some lesser known
areas alongside the better-known wines.

Barely four years old, yet Bibendum has established itself with confidence among London's leading venues. Perhaps one should not be surprised, as Bibendum is the product of Terence Conran's design and Simon Hopkinson's 'cuisine de grand-mère'.

THE CAPITAL HOTEL   London SW3

22-24 Basil Street, Knightsbridge, London SW3 1AT
Telephone: 071-589 5171   *Fax:* 071-225 0011
Open: lunch + dinner daily
Last orders: lunch 2.30pm, dinner 11.00 pm

£85

The award of two Egon Ronay stars and a Michelin rosette to chef Philip Britten proves once again David Levin's ability to pick winners. The restaurant, with its elegant new decor, is at the centre of the London hotel dining scene, and enjoys a regular clientele of local residents and businessmen. It's appropriate that Philip worked in his early days with Richard Shepherd, who as chef at the Capital gained its first star in 1974. He is a quiet technician whose aim is quite simply to provide good food. Try a salad of black sausage with green beans, some brill and olive lasagna with confit potatoes, and an understated orange tart (from an £18.50 set lunch menu) – the simple descriptions belie the depth of flavour achieved. On the wine list, look out for the introduction, later this year, of wines imported direct from David Levin's recently acquired Loire vineyard.

Elegant new decor at the Capital, where chef Philip Britten has collected two Egon Ronay stars and a Michelin rosette. But despite public success his dishes often reflect the demeanour of a quiet technician – especially on the lunch menu.

CAVALIERS   London SW8

129 Queenstown Road, London SW8 3RH
Telephone: 071-720 6960   £75
Open: lunch + dinner Tue-Sat (closed 3 wks Aug, Christmas)
Last orders: lunch 2.00pm, dinner 10.30pm

Cavaliers has had a facelift to bring its decor up to the standard of its
cuisine. (Last year David Cavalier was awarded his first Michelin
rosette, and this year an Egon Ronay star.) There's a smart new
navy blue painted exterior with ivory lettering, a changed logo and
menu design, and a new interior. A soft and warmly-decorated
sitting-room in terracotta and peach now leads into a dining room
done in pale lemon, cream and terracotta. Try the scallop tart with
lemon oil, or red mullet with olives and basil to start; partridge
Souvaroff, or fillet of beef with foie gras and a truffle sauce as main
courses; and a grand marnier soufflé with caramelised oranges, or
simply chocolate desserts to conclude. The carefully thought out
wine list represents vineyards across the world, and has a good
selection of half bottles.

Cavalier's reputation grows with an Egon Ronay star added to his Michelin rosette.

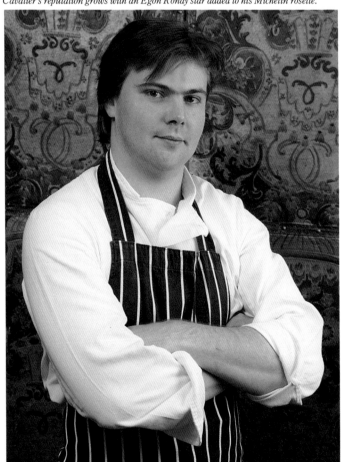

The new decor at Cavaliers.

LE CAPRICE   London SW1

Arlington House, Arlington Street, London SW1A 1RT
Telephone: 071-629 2239   *Fax:* 071-493 9040

£60
Open: lunch + dinner daily (closed 1 wk Christmas)
Last orders: lunch 3.00pm (3.30pm Sun), dinner midnight

Chris Corbin and Jeremy King have transferred chef Tony Howarth
to their new acquisition, The Ivy. Nevertheless, Mark Hix's menu at
this fashionable, black-and-white decorated brasserie remains as
eclectic and up-to-date as ever. Foccaccia of avocado, anchovy and
parmesan, risotto nero, grilled lamb cutlets with salsa verde and
polenta, magret de canard with celeriac and lentils ... plus old
favourites such as soups, bang-bang chicken, and salmon fishcake.
The literary, media and art personalities who haunt Le Caprice
appreciate its discreet staff and competent service. Now in its tenth
year, Le Caprice will no doubt be as packed out in its fifteenth!

CHEZ NICO   London W1

35 Great Portland Street, London W1N 5DD
Telephone: 071-436 8846
Open: lunch + dinner Mon-Fri (closed 10 days Christmas, 3 wks summer)
Last orders: lunch 2.15pm, dinner 11.00pm

£110

Nico Ladenis is now firmly entrenched as one of the leading lights of the London culinary world. Already crowned by both peers and critics (including 3 Egon Ronay stars and 2 Michelin rosettes), Nico does not, however, rest on his laurels, but continually strives for perfection. If it's available, try a ravioli de homard au beurre de truffes, or tartine briochée de foie gras chaud et d'orange caramelisée avec sa petite salade, or pigeonneau de Bresse au chou et au foie gras, or tian de volaille aux artichauts et aux morilles. At two courses for £40 lunch (or dinner) here is not cheap, but it does afford you an opportunity to eat some of the best food in the country.

Everything is at its best at Chez Nico: exquisite, nothing overblown or overstated.

CLARIDGE'S   London W1

Brook Street, London W1A 9JQ
Telephone: 071-629 8860   *Fax:* 071-499 2210
Open: lunch + dinner daily
Last orders: lunch 3.00pm, dinner 11.30pm

£85

Claridge's still has that special 'something' which is difficult to define; it has a lot to do with the professionalism of Ron Jones as General Manager and Marjan Lesnik as Maître Chef des Cuisines. Over the years I have noticed that receptions or cocktails parties at Claridge's are invariably fully attended, an indication of the affection and esteem in which the grand old hotel is held. Whether you choose a simple roast or a speciality such as partridge pot-roasted with truffles and a leek sabayon sauce, a meal at Claridge's is always a pleasure. The wine list is at the top end of the price range, in keeping with a hotel of Claridge's stature.

CLARKE'S   London W8

124 Kensington Church Street, London W8 4BH

Telephone: 071-221 9225   *Fax:* 071-229 4564   **£70**
Open: lunch + dinner Mon-Fri (closed Bank Holidays, 1 wk Easter, 2 wks
      Aug, 2 wk Christmas)
Last orders: lunch 2.00pm, dinner 10.00pm

Clarke's continues to win awards, including an Egon Ronay star, which is gratifying recognition of the success of Sally Clarke's bold and unusual approach. Her dinner menus offer no choice, but you can confidently trust the judgement of this very capable and charming restaurateur. With sympathy for those who shy from surprises, dinner menus are planned a week ahead, and at lunch a short menu offers just three choices at three courses. A recent, excellently balanced dinner offered proscuitto ham with fig, grilled peppers and aubergine, marinated olives, goat cheese and rocket leaves; then breast of pigeon grilled and served over potato-apple cake with cider glaze, served with broccoli and chestnuts; British cheeses with grapes; and to finish, prune and armagnac ice cream with a wafer cone.

The shop next door stocks, amongst other things, the full range of Sally's amazing breads (studded either with olives, or with parmesan, or walnuts, or made from cornmeal) as well as wines chosen from California, the source of much of Sally's inspiration.

Sally Clarke's no-choice menu confidently expresses her sound and thorough judgement. Dishes are a cross between modern French, modern English and Californian.

THE CONNAUGHT   London W1

Carlos Place, London W1Y 6AL
Telephone: 071-499 7070   *Fax:* 071-495 3262

£80
Open: Restaurant: lunch + dinner daily; Grill Room: lunch + dinner Mon-Fri
(closed Bank Holidays)
Last orders: lunch 2.30pm (2.00pm Grill Room), dinner 10.15pm (10.30pm
Grill Room)

Ultimately, it is attention to little details that makes The Connaught
stand out. Take their pastry for example: they wanted the best, so
they installed a new pastry kitchen, which now produces some of the
best croissants this side of the Channel. In the main kitchen Michel
Bourdin's brigade produces the sort of food that remains a perennial
favourite to the habitués, British and foreign, of the impeccable
dining-room. Try the petit pilaw de crabe, homard et langoustines
thermidore, or consommé en gelée Cole Porter to start; then
perhaps roast sirloin of Scottish beef 'Old England', panaché de
tubercules saisonniers, or carré d'agneau du Kent forestière; and to
finish fraises et framboises Romanoff or marquise au chocolat et
cointreau. With all its elegance of a bygone era, The Connaught is
one of the clubbiest of London hotels.

FOUR SEASONS RESTAURANT　　　London W1

The Inn on the Park, Hamilton Place, Park Lane, London W1A 1AZ
Telephone: 071-499 0888　　*Fax:* 071-493 6629
Open: lunch + dinner daily
Last orders: lunch 3.00pm, dinner 11.00pm

£90

Chef Bruno Loubet is a very good cook, and his bordelais upbringing has undoubtedly influenced his approach to food. He prefers the honesty of 'cuisine du terroir' – a style which he has adapted into a modern rendering of classic regional cuisine. He likes dishes to have definite textures and strong flavours of the ingredients themselves. His talent is ably demonstrated in his first course suggestions of tarte tatin de céléri aux truffes du Périgord, or the ravioles de navets et champignons sauvages; and in the main course offerings of tournedos de thon aux arômates, or the carré d'agneau en croûte, petite moussaka, son jus simple. Finally, from the pudding menu, a pyramide de chocolat praliné, crème vanille epitomises the level of his skills. Bruno is determined to give The Four Seasons its own identity, so that people think of it first as a restaurant rather than as a hotel facility. The wine list, however, clearly benefits in sheer depth of choice from the restaurant being part of an international hotel of stature. The standards of housekeeping in the hotel itself are excellent, making it a luxurious place to stay and take advantage of The Four Seasons.

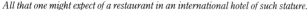

All that one might expect of a restaurant in an international hotel of such stature.

Bruno Loubet's cooking is a modern rendering of cuisine de terroir. His dishes have definite textures and flavours that express the essential character of ingredients.

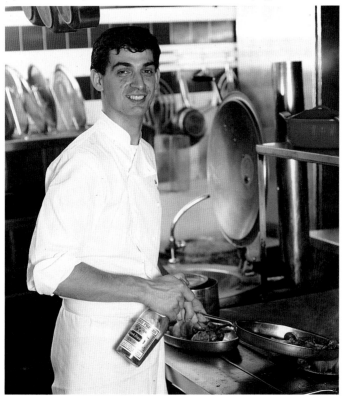

LE GAVROCHE   London W 1

43 Upper Brook Street, London W1Y 1PF
Telephone: 071-408 0881
Open: lunch + dinner Mon-Fri (closed Bank Holidays, Christmas
    & New Year)
Last orders: lunch 2.00pm, dinner 11.30pm

£125

Albert Roux has now handed over control of the kitchen to his son Michel, who had been working alongside his father for some time. Michel is the fourth generation of Rouxs to follow the family tradition, and he is cooking as well as his father. Indeed, the succession has brought fresh energy to the famous Gavroche team. Albert himself still looks in, most days, and the cooking remains true to his style. Traditional favourites abound, such as boudin blanc de volaille Jocelyne, mousselin de homard au champagne, filet de bar rôtie au poivre, la marmite bretonne, poulet fermier en cocotte aux lentilles et thym, rognons de veau aux trois moutardes, omelette Rothschild, and a sablé aux fraises to finish.

The mostly French wine list has an incredible range of regions, châteaux, vintages – and prices! – but then Le Gavroche is a restaurant to be taken seriously: serious dining deserves serious wine. In the dining room, Silvano Giraldin was recently named as the Maîtres d'Hôtels' Maître d'Hôtel for his thorough professionalism and capability in attending to his customers' every need, from arrival to departure.

The family that has done so much for gastronomy in this country enters upon its fourth generation of cooks. Michel Roux Jr has brought fresh energy to the Gavroche team, but there was never a sense of his needing to prove himself: the Roux style is a tradition constantly in the making.

THE GAY HUSSAR London W1

2 Greek Street, London W1V 6NB
Telephone: 071-437 0973
Open: lunch + dinner Mon-Sat
Last orders: lunch 2.30pm, dinner 11.00pm

£50

It's many years since the Gay Hussar first opened its doors to become one of London's most famous rendezvous for writers and politicians. T.S. Eliot was an early habitué, and customers have included Princess Alexandra, Michael Foot, writers, publishers, and politicians from both sides of the house. It is still a favoured spot particularly at lunch. Regulars appreciate the excellent, discreet service led by John Wrobel and Lazlo Holecz's traditional Hungarian cooking. Favourite dishes include the famous cherry soup, pressed boar's head, cold pike and beetroot sauce and cucumber, roast saddle of carp with new potatoes, minced goose with pungent smoked beans, roast duck with red cabbage and apple sauce, and for pudding sweet cheese pancakes. poppy seed strudel, or dobos torta.

A cheerfully warm welcome.

Robust cooking.

HARVEY'S   London SW17

2 Bellevue Road, London SW17 7EG
Telephone: 081-672 0114
Open: lunch + dinner Tue-Sat (closed Bank Holidays, 2 wks Aug, 2 wks
     Christmas)
Last orders: lunch 2.00pm, dinner 11.15pm

£75

Harvey's is now well and truly established with Marco Pierre White
concentrating much more on his kitchen than on adverse publicity.
This talented, unorthodox chef can turn out some staggering
combinations, and is not only the second British chef to be awarded
two Michelin rosettes (in addition to three Egon Ronay stars), but at
age twenty-eight, is also the youngest. His sure touch is demonstrated in such dishes as brandade of morue with langoustines, sauce
gazpacho, or roast sea scallops with spices, pigeon en vessie with
thyme or best end of lamb with tapenade. The extensive wine list
repays careful attention.

   True to fashion, Marco Pierre White's book *White Heat* is as
different from anything else as the rest of his style. I can think of
no-one else who would have dared, certainly not in the last decade, to
have published a cookery book mostly in black & white.

   As we were going to press (and just after our photographer took
the pictures!) Marco has informed us that he was completely
transforming the interior of the restaurant – walls and artwork
particularly.

Harvey's may be undergoing a transformation but happily the unorthodox talent in the kitchen remains. Left: Roger Pizey, one of the team.

HILAIRE   London SW7

68 Old Brompton Road, London SW7 3LQ
Telephone: 071-584 8993
Open: lunch Mon-Fri, dinner Mon-Sat (closed Bank Holidays, 1 wk
        Christmas, 1 wk Easter, 2 wks Aug)
Last orders: lunch 2.30pm (3.00pm Sun), dinner 11.00pm

£75

Chef Bryan Webb and his wife Jenny have bought this small, individualist restaurant from Trusthouse Forte, and Bryan, who has been head chef here since 1987, has restructured the menus.

Lunch is priced at £14.50 for two courses (£18.00 for three); dinner is £23.00 for two courses, with a fish course at £6.50 and cheese or dessert at £4.50. A new wine list offers interest with something to suit most pockets. From the new menus enjoyable dishes have been a tartlet of calves' sweetbreads and fresh cèpes, salad of grilled red mullet, potato salad and caviar, deep-fried oysters and laverbread with Thai dip as starters, then as main courses rabbit en crepinette with wild rice and celeriac chips, grey-leg partridge with port, brandy and grapes, and grilled sea-bass with lentils and salsa verde. For pudding try some ricotta tart with cinnamon ice cream, or apple parfait with apple fritters, or a selection from the cheeseboard.

Bryan Webb has made Hilaire indelibly his own.

L'INCONTRO   London SW1

87 Pimlico Road, London SW1 8PH
Telephone: 071-730 3663
Open: lunch Mon-Sat, dinner daily (closed Bank Holidays)
Last orders: lunch 2.30pm (3.00pm Sat), dinner 11.30pm

£70

From a vase of beautiful white lilies to the mirrors and colour scheme
– cool greys punctuated by the brash bright blue and red of the
armchairs – the long modern dining-room is as modish as its clientele.
This is a fashionable restaurant that rose on the crest of the new
Italian wave and which is still riding the swell. The food is modern in
style, taking its inspiration from the area around Venice, and might
include baccala mantecato – fish mousse served with polenta, and
scallops served Venetian-style. Other areas are equally well represented, however, with dishes such as a warm salad of scampi,
prawns and cannelini beans, or roast partridge with peverada and
blueberry sauce. All pasta is freshly made on the premises, and might
come with a wild mushroom sauce, fresh clam sauce, or as vegetarian
pasta parcels. Service is slick and very Italian. The wine list is also
naturally mostly Italian, in the middle-to-upper price bracket.

KALAMARAS	London W2

76-78 Inverness Mews, London W2 3JQ
Telephone: 071-727 9122
Open: dinner Mon-Sat (closed Bank Holidays)
Last orders: midnight

£40

This is one of my favourite places to go when I've had a surfeit of modern, art-on-the-plate meals. Stelios Platanos' straightforward genuine Greek cooking is down-to-earth and wholesome. The menu, written in Greek, lists appetising dishes which will be explained to you by a waitress. Try the fasolakia, some garides, horta, maybe arnaki spanaki lemonato, or barbounia. Finish off with coffee and loukoumia, and perhaps a glass of Metaxa.

Tables elbow-to-elbow in the true noisy taverna style.

KENSINGTON PLACE   London W8

201-205 Kensington Church Street, London W8 7LX
Telephone: 071-727 3184   **£60**
Open: lunch + dinner daily (closed 3 dys Aug, 3 dys Christmas)
Last orders: lunch 3.00pm (4.00pm Sun), dinner 11.45pm (10.15pm Sun)

Rowley Leigh consistently validates the critics' acclaim that this fashionable brasserie-style restaurant has earned. Roux-trained, his cooking is high on style as well as inventiveness, and has that other essential virtue: it is *reliably* good. Whether you choose cannelini bean soup with pesto, or braised squid with boletus mushrooms, or game terrine with quince chutney and brioche you can be sure of an interesting starter, and the main courses too are likely to please, be they braised coquelet with salt pork, zampone and cabbage, or stuffed breast of veal with spinach and garlic, or steamed John Dory with chanterelles and mint, or roast haunch of hare with chestnut purée. Kensington Place, its decor stark and bright, is trendy and noisy, vibrant with success – it's been open three years now. We could do with a few more like it.

Rowley Leigh, Roux-trained chef of this fashionable brasserie.

LANGAN'S BRASSERIE	London W1

Stratton Street, London W1X 5FD
Telephone: 071-491 8822
Open: lunch Mon-Fri, dinner Mon-Sat (closed Bank Holidays)
Last orders: lunch 2.45pm, dinner 11.45pm (12.45am Sat)

£65

Who would have believed that in the 1990s you could get away with black pudding on a sophisticated menu, but get away with it Richard Shepherd does, serving it with kidneys and bacon. This is a tremendously good value item, value for money being one of the reasons for Langan's perennial popularity. The other reasons are its decor, with its wealth of paintings, and the sheer buzz of this huge establishment (it serves some 400 meals a day), and the way the whole enterprise is backed up by the zip of the serving staff. The vast turnover of the place also allows the food to be produced fresh on a daily and seasonal basis. The result is a menu on which I defy anyone not to find something to his or her liking: from the famous soufflé aux épinards, sauce anchois, and petits tournedos au poivre vert, to roast grouse with game chips and bread sauce. A recent good meal was calves' liver and bacon followed by a crêpe with almonds and honey. It's honest food based on traditional values but above all Langan's wants to please the customers.

Richard Shepherd's classical and brasserie cooking remains ever popular at Langan's.

MOSIMANN'S   London SW1

11b West Halkin Street, London SW1 8JL

Telephone: 071-235 9625   **£90**
Open: lunch + dinner Mon-Sat (closed Bank Holidays)
Last orders: lunch 2.30pm, dinner 11.00pm

1990 saw Anton Mosimann consolidating the success of his elegant
and exclusive private dining club. Head Chef Ray Neve has a calendar
full of special club dinners and events. A top wine producer from
Piedmont presents his wines alongside regional specialities; a
traditional dinner marks the opening of the grouse season; a
gastronomic tour of Beaujolais is arranged – and consolation for those
who couldn't go is a Beaujolais luncheon at the Club. The kitchen, still
very much under Anton's eye, continues to turn out some very good
food, such as winter leaves with Scottish lobster and scallops, rack of
lamb with a herb crust and ratatouille, crab cakes with endive and
watercress sauce, and an orgie des sorbets to finish!

Anton Mosimann (right), *whose contribution to British gastronomy may be seen in the work of many of his former chefs and apprentices (now with restaurants of their own up and down the country), pulls together all the strands of his talents at this elegant private dining club.*

ONE NINETY QUEEN'S GATE   London SW7

190 Queen's Gate, London SW7 5EU

Telephone: 071-581 5666   £70
Open: lunch + dinner daily (Bistrot 190 open all day, daily)
Last orders: lunch 3.00pm (4.00pm Sun) dinner 11.30pm (10.00pm Sun);
        (Bistrot 190 12.30am at present)

Amongst the Board of Directors and shareholders of One Ninety are such well-known names as Michel Roux, Richard Shepherd, Terence Holmes, Raymond Blanc and Brian Turner. In the kitchen, Antony Worrall-Thompson provides the energy and creativity. With such a formidable array of names and faces it is hardly surprising that the restaurant is such a success. However, rather than write about it myself (and be accused of promoting my own interests!), I have included some extracts of what other people have written about One Ninety.

'I had to make way for the Duchess of York. It's that sort of place. A feuilletée of asparagus and artichokes with a powerful olive oil and basil dressing was a knock out'. Tim Cottrell (*Daily Telegraph*)

'. . . by far the plushest restaurant I have visited since I first kidnapped this column. The puddings were so delicious that we happily ate ourselves into the ground'. Craig Brown (*The Times*)

'. . . a corn-fed pigeon wrapped in a poultice of savoy cabbage and popped inside a string vest of puff pastry . . . made me laugh and tasted very good.' Tom Sutcliffe (*The Independent*)

. . . marvellous, strong-flavoured gutsy food.' Lindsey Bareham (*The Sunday Telegraph*)

I'll just add that the new Bistrot 190 next door is proving a very popular extension to the club's repertoire, open to non-members.

Gourmet membership is available at One Ninety to non-industry members.

The elegant interior of One Ninety sets the tone.

OAK ROOM RESTAURANT   London W1

Le Meridien Hotel, Piccadilly, London W1V 0BH
Telephone: 071-734 8000   *Fax:* 071-437 3574
Open: lunch Mon-Fri, dinner Mon-Sat (Bank Holidays)
Last orders: lunch 2.30pm, dinner 10.00pm

£85

The Oak Room offers a combination all too rarely found in a hotel dining room, namely well-spaced tables in an elegant Edwardian baroque setting, professional service and some very good food. Chef David Chambers works in close collaboration with consultant chef Michel Lorain of Côtes St Jacques at Joiguy. Some chefs might find this rather daunting. Not so David Chambers, who views the partnership as an opportuntity to maintain an awareness of the latest ideas in France, whilst still developing his own individual cuisine. The result is a menu balanced between cuisine traditionelle and cuisine créative, and a menu gourmand. Some excellent dishes have included a ravioli of wild mushrooms in a light sauce flavoured with soft herbs, sautéed fresh foie gras on a bed of noodles garnished with crayfish tails and whole sea scallops on fresh truffles and sautéed potatoes. The style of the wine list matches the menu. For a light lunch, the Terrace Garden offers good value.

THE RITZ   London W1

150 Piccadilly, London W1V 9DG
Telephone: 071-493 8181   *Fax:* 071-493 2687
Open: lunch + dinner daily
Last orders: lunch 2.30pm, dinner 11.30pm

£90

'Putting on the Ritz' – the song conveys a 'frisson' of anticipation and indeed the hotel has somehow always been slightly more risqué than some of its more stately counterparts. With countless celebrities entering its portals, the Ritz is used to dealing with all kinds of situations and people. The beautiful dining room is justly famous, and on warmer summer days, the Italian Garden offers outside dining for a lucky few. A staff of character are led by Terry Holmes, a man of immense personality. The dishes of the day offer traditional favourites such as a daily roast, poached fish, sautéed calves liver and bacon, or their modern interpretations such as terrine of smoked salmon and leeks with a truffle vinaigrette, roast sea-bass with root vegetables and a red wine sauce, and a warm fig and raspberry filo parcel on a fresh mint cream sauce to finish.

Inimitable, the Ritz occupies a unique position in our culture. Yet, however magnificent its style, its culinary success often resides in traditional favourites – the roast, the poached fish – offered daily in the beautiful dining room.

THE RIVER CAFÉ   London W6

Thames Wharf Studios, Rainville Road, London W6 9HA
Telephone: 071-381 8824   £75
Open: lunch Tue-Sun, dinner Mon-Fri (closed Bank Holidays, 10 dys
　　　Christmas)
Last orders: lunch 2.30pm (3.00pm Sat + Sun), dinner 9.00pm

To paraphrase a recent remark, The River Café is the sort of amateur success story that might have many a professional gnashing his teeth! Opened as a canteen for husband Richard Rogers' architectural practice, Ruthie Rogers' restaurant (run with her partner Rose Gray) quickly rose to success when its doors were opened to the public, and it is still in the forefront of the new-wave Italian cooking. A November menu might offer amongst the starters char-grilled red and yellow peppers with red anchovies, capers, fresh basil, slivers of garlic and bruschetta; or polenti di quattro formaggi – wet polenta (harvested the month before in Alba) served with taleggio, mascarpone, parmesan and gorgonzola; then, as main courses, grilled, marinated, butterflied leg of lamb with salsa verde and celeriac baked with cream and fresh red chilli; or pan-fried calves' kidneys with pancetta, radicchio, fresh sage, blue lentils, red wine and mascarpone. Puddings might include fresh pear and almond tart, or bread and butter pudding made with pannetone. Portions are substantial, flavours are good, but, despite amateur origins, the restaurant has a professional feel to it. There is usually a 'guest wine' offered on the menu, although the whole wine list is full of interesting finds from Italy. The River Café is always packed, so booking ahead is essential. Decor remains as you would expect an architectural practice's canteen to look.

Ruthie Rogers' and Rose Gray's River Café, like no other canteen you ever ate in.

RUE ST JACQUES   London W1

5 Charlotte Street, London W1P 1HD
Telephone: 071-637 0222   *Fax:* 071-637 0224   **£80**
Open: lunch Mon-Fri, dinner Mon-Sat (closed Bank Holidays, Christmas +
   New Year)
Last orders: lunch 2.30pm, dinner 10.00pm

Mirrors reflect walls in deep burgundy hung with large old portraits in
oils. Large white-clothed tables are well-spaced. There's sober
elegance all around, but it's neither stuffy nor 'whispery'. Classical
music plays in the background. Service is French and very
professional. Silver domes are used but without theatricality.
Gunther Schlender's food is classic and consistent, well presented
and of a high standard: feuilleté St Jacques with a saffron sauce; roast
pheasant with beautifully light truffled dumplings in a rich red wine
sauce; caramelised pears with honey ice cream and eau-de-vie sauce.
Wines include some reasonably priced choices.

Go there for Günther Schlender's modern French cuisine.

THE SAVOY   London WC2

The Strand, London WC2R 0EU
Telephone: 071-836 4343   *Fax:* 071-240 6040
The River Restaurant   £75
The Grill   £85
Open: The River Restaurant: lunch + dinner daily; The Grill: lunch Mon-Fri,
    dinner Mon-Sat
Last orders: lunch 2.30pm, dinner 11.30pm

A part of Britain's heritage, The Savoy is now under the guidance of
Herbert Striessnig. A worthy successor to Willy Bauer, Striessnig
handles the stately ship in a firm but sympathetic manner, ever
conscious of his customers' needs. The Savoy management is equally
attentive to the need of the catering industry to introduce new
recruits to its ranks. It is to be commended therefore for its series of
roadshows, touring around catering colleges encouraging young
people to become involved not just with The Savoy but with the
catering industry as a whole.

The Savoy kitchens, under the eye of Maître Chef des Cuisines
Anton Edelmann, continue to excel in both classic and modern styles,
the very good food prepared, of course, from fresh daily supplies. In
addition to the usual menus, growing demand has led to the
introduction of a vegetarian menu de régime naturel. The menu
offers dishes such as a risotto with morilles and parmesan cheese and
a delicate maize-flavoured broth with sorrel and fried croûtons.
Anton himself looks after The River Room, while The Grill Room
Maître Chef is David Sharland. Service (led by Luigi Zambon and
Angelo Maresca respectively) is exemplary throughout.

Left: *Afternoon tea at the Savoy.*
Top: *The Savoy Grill.*
Above left to right: *the Honeymoon Suite, the Sitting Room.*
Below: *'Upstairs' at the Savoy.*

LE SOUFFLÉ RESTAURANT	London W1

Inter-Continental Hotel, 1 Hamilton Place, Hyde Park Corner,
London W1V 1QY

Telephone: 071-409 3131   *Fax:* 071-493 3476   £85
Open: lunch Sun-Fri, dinner daily
Last orders: lunch 3.00pm (3.30pm Sun), dinner 11.30pm

Peter Kromberg and his brigade of over sixty continue to maintain Le Soufflé's position in the top rank of London hotel dining rooms. Peter is a highly skilled technician thoroughly at home with the challenges of a big hotel kitchen (he has been with the group for twenty-four years) and a meal here rarely disappoints. However, there is more on offer at the Inter-Continental than just formal dining. We've said a lot over the years about the soufflés, so this year we offer some examples from the Sunday Brunch menu, which is divided into starter, main course and dessert sections. Depending on your appetite at this increasingly popular mealtime, you might choose crispy golden potato pancakes with slices of Scottish smoked salmon, creamed cheese and chives, followed by sautéed veal escalope with buttered new dill potatoes and a bundle of fresh asparagus, then finish with a freshly baked thick waffle, sprinkled with cinnamon sugar and served with strawberries, ice cream and strawberry whipped cream. Whatever the mealtime, the food is backed by a wine list to match, a pleasant, comfortable dining room and excellent service headed by Joseph Lanser.

Peter Kromberg, a man at the top of his profession, oversees a wide range of fare at Le Soufflé, and whatever the meal, the food is backed by a wine list to match and excellent service.

THE ART OF SOUL SEARCHING.

SUTHERLAND'S RESTAURANT	London W1

45 Lexington Street, London W1R 3LG
Telephone: 071-434 3401
Open: lunch Mon-Fri, dinner Mon-Sat (closed Bank Holidays)
Last orders: lunch 2.15pm, dinner 11.15pm

£85

Despite a fall-off in business from some of the advertising and PR companies in the Soho area, Sutherland's continues to be fully patronised by a knowledgeable set of customers who enjoy the consistent but imaginative cooking of Garry Hollihead. The kitchen is well backed up by the front of house staff – everyone seems as keen as if they had a piece of the action! Breads, as good as ever, set the tone for dishes such as oxtail and quail consommé with wild rice and oxtail ravioli, or charlotte of John Dory wrapped in leaf spinach with a light stock flavoured with vermouth, or fresh pasta noodles with a cream sauce of wild cèpes, pine kernels and chervil from a selection of starters; then as main courses perhaps saddle of roe deer with red cabbage, dauphinoise potatoes and a dark pruneau jus, or sautéed fillet of brill with a brioche crust and braised endives, or a tart of morels, baby spinach and jerusalem artichokes with a soft herb sauce. Desserts too live up to expectations – if it's available try a whole poached pear with a soup of autumn fruits. The simply set out wine list is a good accompaniment to Garry's cooking, priced in the middle range.

Garry Hollihead's red mullet with ravioli of cèpes and a light veal stock.

LA TANTE CLAIRE   London SW3

68 Royal Hospital Road, London SW3 4HP
Telephone: 071-352 6064   *Fax:* 071-352 3257   **£115**
Open: lunch + dinner Mon-Sat (closed Easter, 3 wks Aug, Christmas)
Last orders: lunch 2.00pm, 11.00pm

1990 saw the launch of Pierre Koffmann's excellent book *Memories of Gascony*. It's the sort of cookery book I want to read at one sitting! The book follows the seasons with a rhythmical text of recollections of a rural upbringing in 1950s' Gascony. Evocative text is illustrated with equally evocative and beautiful photographs, colourful paintings and of course recipes. These are clear and easy-to-follow and include one for Koffmann's renowned pig's trotter.

The point about this book, though, is that it is a useful insight into the culinary influences upon a great chef. After reading his book, I feel I know Pierre Koffmann better. The next time I eat in this restaurant it will, I am sure, be with a new dimension of appreciation of dishes such as gigotin d'agneau des pyrenées au thym with a gratin landais, ris de veau croustillant with oignons confits, and a croûstade de pommes caramelisée. Assured service by Jean-Pierre Durantet adds to the pleasure of a meal at La Tante Claire.

Left: *Pierre Koffmann, whose classic cuisine is as successful as ever at his stylish and comfortable restaurant.*

TURNER'S   London SW3

87-89 Walton Street, London SW3 2HP
Telephone: 071-584 6711
Open: lunch Sun-Fri, dinner daily (closed Bank Holidays, 1 wk Christmas)
Last orders: lunch 2.45pm, dinner 11.00pm (10.00pm Sun)

£75

Brian Turner seems to be one of the few chefs who has not produced
a cookery book this year! Instead you'll find him in the heart-and-heat
of things, that is, in the kitchen. Here he is breaking a new chef into
the Turner mould. Over the years Brian has evolved his own style of
cooking, classically-based, strong on flavours and modern in presentation. Try a warm pigeon salad with a lentil dressing, or red
mullet with an orange butter sauce and braised fennel, or fillet of veal
wrapped in a cabbage leaf with a fresh foie gras mousse, and finish
perhaps with chestnut cream in a shell. Decor is characteristically
uncluttered, and Brian likes to pop out into the dining room to advise
and greet customers – many of whom are regulars.

Below: *Chef/patron Brian Turner.* Above right to left: *Sea-bass on a bed of red cabbage
with a light fish-based sauce; Scallops with a tagliatelle of cucumber.*

London Establishment Reviews

ALASTAIR LITTLE   London W1

See page 18 – our Clover Award Section.

ALBA   London EC1

107 Whitecross Street, London EC1
Telephone: 071-588 1798   **£45**
Open: lunch + dinner Mon-Fri (closed Bank Holidays)
Last orders: lunch 3.00pm, dinner 11.0pm

Alba draws its inspiration, not surprisingly, from the eponymous area of Piedmont, so dishes from that area figure strongly on the menu. The famous white truffles can, in season, be shaved over appropriate dishes such as risotto, but such luxury does cost £9.50 or so! The central part of the menu is given over entirely in fact to Piedmontese dishes, including carne all'Albese (thinly sliced raw beef with olive oil and lemon), fresh pasta with wild porcini mushrooms, and monkfish with a white wine, lemon, butter and parsley sauce. The rest of the menu comprises antipasti, soups, pasta, meat and fish dishes that are more in a traditional/trattoria style.

Another source of inspiration for the restaurant is the personality of Carla Vaschetto, who comes from near Alba. She presides at front-of-house with grace and gusto over an uncontrived, modern interior – a long, narrow room painted pink, grey floor tiles, glass and chrome up-lighters, white clothed tables and black chairs. This is a welcome venue in the Barbican.

ANNA'S PLACE	London N1

90 Mildmay Park, London N1
Telephone: 071-249 9379   **£45**
Open: lunch + dinner Mon-Fri (closed 2 wks Christmas, 2 wks Easter,
        4 wks Aug)

Anna Hegarty bought this former tobacconists and general store in 1979, and the old enamelled cigarette ads, that are part of the bric-à-brac on the walls, attest to this former use. In the decade since then Anna's has proved constantly popular, and it's easy to understand why. The welcome from Anna and her staff is warm and the atmosphere is convivial. Recent extensions (recorded in a photomontage on the stairway leading down to the loos) have meant a larger bar area at the rear. An attractive paved courtyard is also made available in summer.

   Anna Hegarty herself is now more often to be seen at front of house, although her Swedish practicality is still in evidence in the kitchen: the massive red Aga not only looks good but keeps the bread and mulled wine warm too! The menu has evolved now that Anna has assistance from two other cooks. Gone are the deep-fried brie and Swedish meatballs in favour of more experimental dishes. Among them are sill tallrik – two, or perhaps even three, kinds of marinated Swedish herrings; potkes – Swedish potted cheese with akvavit and herbs; fillets of brill wrapped around nuggets of salmon and ginger and then steamed; and especially lör biff med lök ringar och klyt potatis – 'leaf beef' (escalloped fillet of beef) with onion rings, raw egg yolk and sautéed spiced potatoes. It may sound odd but is in fact quite delicious; it consists of strips of grilled steak with deep-fried onion rings, and the egg yolk is served in a hollowed-out tomato. Anna tells you how to pour the egg over the hot beef, which cooks the yolk. If you have room for pudding (portions are generous!) you might try some waffles with blueberry conserve and whipped cream, or Swedish apple cake with a creamy vanilla sauce. A short wine list from Europe and the New World is reasonably priced; akvavit is also a popular choice. Leave your car at home and enjoy this one-off, unpretentious, neighbourhood restaurant.

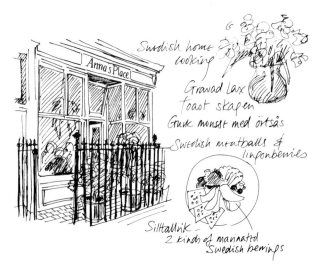

Swedish home cooking
Gravad Lax
Toast skagen
Gruk monsst med örtsås
Swedish meatballs & linponberries
Silltallrik – 2 kinds of marinated Swedish herrings

L'Arlequin   London SW8

See page 20 – our Clover Award Section.

L'Artiste Assoiffé   London W11

122 Kensington Park Road, London W11 2EP
Telephone: 071-727 4714   **£40**
Open: lunch Sat, dinner Mon-Sat
Last orders: lunch 2.00pm, dinner 11.00pm

Things have changed since 1968 when this popular bistro first opened its door; bargains are rather harder to find round the corner at Portobello market! Console yourself with a meal here. The decor, centred around a Victorian fairground carousel, is characterful and well-worn but comfortable, with open fires in winter and a terrace in summer. The food is based on plain French cooking – just right after a hungry Saturday morning at the market! Book.

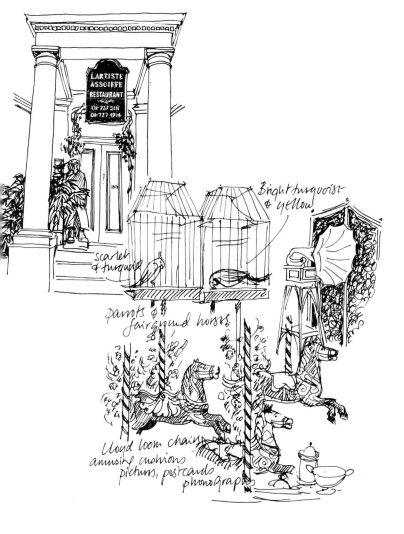

Au Jardin des Gourmets   London W1

5 Greek Street, London W1V 5LA
Telephone: 071 437 1816   *Fax:* 071-437 0043   **£60**
Open: lunch Mon-Fri, dinner Mon-Sat (closed Bank Holidays)
Last orders: lunch 2.30pm, dinner 11.15pm (11.30pm Sat)

The team of Nicolas Picolet in the kitchen and Franco Zoia providing excellent service at front of house goes from strength to strength at this popular Soho restaurant, although neither of them has been here quite as long as the restaurant itself (sixty years old in 1991). Another great asset, of course, is the cellar, personally selected by Joseph Berkmann, resulting in one of the best restaurant cellars in the capital, if not the country. There is particular strength in the bordeaux and burgundy sections, as well as among the champagnes and Californians. Nicolas' bourgeois French cooking is very reliable. He uses excellent beef for an entrecôte marchand du vin, good fish stock as the base for fish soup with rouille, and proffers a well-kept cheeseboard. Some roast or grilled dishes are only available for two people. Private rooms have recently been enlarged.

One of a pair of bronze Art Nouveau sculptures that hold flowers in 'Au Jardin des Gourmets'

Au Jardin des Gourmets.

L'Aventure   London NW8

3 Blenheim Terrace, London NW8 0EH
Telephone: 071-624 6232   **£50**
Open: lunch Mon-Fri + Sun, dinner daily (closed Bank Holidays)
Last orders: lunch 2.30pm, dinner 11.00pm

This is a good local restaurant with the particular advantages of a charming owner, Catherine Parisot and a terrace for alfresco summer eating. From the daily menu, you might opt for a good fish dish such as coquilles St Jacques florentina. Follow it with some well-kept cheese and one of the tempting puddings.

AVOIR BAR AND GRILL   London SW3

332-334 King's Road, London SW3 5UR
Telephone: 071-352 4071   **£50**
Open: all day, daily
Last orders: 11.45pm

If the writing on the menu at the new-look Avoir Bar and Grill looks familiar, that's because the consultant chef is Antony Worrall-Thompson. And if the cooking tastes familiar, that's because the chef is Nick Rochford, who was at the Village Restaurant in Wimbledon, then Rochford's in Putney, and most recently at the Castle in Taunton. However, those who like the familiar will be reassured by the black and red decor, which remains. Lighting is artful, background music tasteful and discreet, and service is slick.

The menu is definitely in the modern bistro vein, and features starter dishes such as spinach and arugola with poached egg and croutons, baked oyster mushrooms, pan-fried artichoke with parma ham, salad of grilled vegetables (perhaps aubergine, leek and fennel). Main courses could be a simple steak frites, or confit of duck with butter beans and bacon, chargrilled calves' liver with bacon, some grilled haddock with mustard and breadcrumbs, or a delicious warm goose carpaccio on wilted spinach. Vegetables (ordered separately) range from bubble and squeak, or cabbage with bacon to French beans, while salad choices are unusual: rocket, lettuce hearts, chicory and watercress, tomato and basil. Good puddings – pear and ginger crumble, deep-fried ice cream with raspberry and almond sauce, lemon tart. The concise wine list is moderately priced.

THE BASIL STREET HOTEL   London SW3

Basil Street, Knightsbridge, London SW3 1AH
Telephone: 071-581 3311   **£55**
Open: lunch Mon-Fri + Sun, dinner daily
Last orders: lunch 2.30pm, dinner 9.45pm

Behind the clamorous tinselled fringe of Knightsbridge is a retreat of Edwardian tranquillity. Courteous, helpful staff greet and usher you to your room – immaculate and traditionally furnished, and now with softer colours than before. In the public areas, Persian rugs cover polished wooden floors, and comfortable chintz sofas blend with antiques.

LA BASTIDE   London W1

50 Greek Street, London W1V 5LQ
Telephone: 071-734 3300   **£55**
Open: lunch Mon-Fri, dinner Mon-Sat (closed Bank Holidays, Christmas to
New Year)
Last orders: lunch 2.30pm, dinner 11.30pm

La Bastide is another Soho institution, and long may Susan Warwick at this gracious Georgian house continue to welcome a loyal and discerning clientele. The establishment's main tenet is value for money – they seem genuinely more concerned with pleasing their customers than with getting rich, a refreshing attitude these days. The cooking aims to be simple and healthy, and combines ingredients with a natural affinity to one another rather than experimenting for the sake of it. The cooking updates and lightens French traditional fare. It seeks to delight rather than dazzle, and is well described as 'honest'. The regions of France are visited on a monthly basis, and a Loire menu included sautéed pigeon with a quince purée, wild mushrooms wrapped in cabbage, scallops gratinated in a butter sauce, and puff pastry filled with cream and grapes. (This was priced at £21 for four courses.) The regular carte is thus quite short, and might offer a soup of mussels and fennel, then saddle of venison with calvados and apples. The French wine list is well laid out with an eye to the regional menu, and includes a separate list of half bottles. Red burgundies and bordeaux are particularly well represented.

THE BERKSHIRE HOTEL   London W1

350 Oxford Street, London W1W 0BY
Telephone: 071-629 7474   *Fax:* 071-629 8156   **£65**
Open: lunch Sun-Fri, dinner daily
Last orders: lunch 2.30pm, dinner 10.30pm

Edwardian Hotels' Berkshire aims to provide every modern amenity but with the decor and ambience of an English country house. Right in the heart of London, its gracious public rooms are filled with period furniture, and there's an open fire in the drawing room where you can relax to the sound of a harp being played or browse through the bookshelves. The bar, too, has a clubby feel, and the 147 bedrooms continue the theme, while still managing to incorporate modern comforts such as full air-conditioning. Ascots Restaurant serves chef Stephen Leus's cuisine inspirationale – a 2-course dinner for £16.00 or three courses for £19.95. Ascots also offers a pre-theatre menu at £25.00 per person (a 3-course set menu, changed daily, with two choices at each course), and a complimentary car service to the theatre.

BIBENDUM   London SW3

See page 22 – our Clover Award Section.

BLAKES HOTEL   London SW7

33 Roland Gardens, London SW7 3PF
Telephone: 071-370 6701   *Fax:* 071-373 0442   **£140**
Open: lunch + dinner, daily (closed Christmas Day + Boxing Day)
Last orders: lunch 2.30pm, dinner 11.30pm

Anouska Hempel Weinberg's celebrated paean to luxurious and slightly decadent good taste continues to appeal to the travelled connoisseur of elegance and style, yet the hotel also manages to dispense convenience and efficiency to many satisfied international businessmen and women. The fifty-two glamorously appointed bedrooms are as impressive, though less often written about, as the mostly-black, mirrored, basement restaurant. But there's one thing you can't escape at Blakes: it is expensive, and there's no point pretending otherwise. If you're counting pennies, go somewhere else. Otherwise go to Blakes to relax and really be involved in the mood of the place. Chef David Wilson contributes to the ambience with his precise cooking and well defined flavours, using top grade ingredients such as beluga caviar, foie gras, black truffles, or more modest ones such as those in an inkfish risotto, steamed cumin scallops with fried seaweed and turmeric, noisettes of venison with blueberries, chicken and crab Fabergé with garlic and ginger sauce. For dessert there's Malmesbury berry flan, or even avocado with mint, vanilla, coconut or bitter chocolate ice creams (or probably all four flavours if you really want!). Naturally, the wine list is not cheap either, with house wine starting at £13.50 a bottle.

BLUEPRINT CAFÉ   London SE1

Design Museum, Shad Thames, Butlers Wharf, London SE1 2YD
Telephone: 071-378 7031   **£45**
Open: lunch daily, dinner Tue-Sat (closed Bank Holidays)
Last orders: lunch 3.00pm (3.30pm Sun), dinner 11.00pm

The Blueprint Café is a stylish restaurant, even though its location is a little off the beaten track. The room, which seats about eighty, is long and sleek with circular tables and a bar area by the entrance. A window runs the length of the river walls, giving spectacular views around Tower Bridge. Banquette seating faces this view. Table tops are either red or white laminate. Service is attentive, friendly and efficient. The menu changes daily and is Italian influenced – Mediterranean in the broadest sense. Pasta is freshly made on the premises and might be served as black taglietelle with squid and spicy sauce; and there are also soups, rillettes, taramasalata, grilled tuna, baked sea-bass, braised rabbit with bacon, mushrooms and mashed potato, grilled calves' liver with fried onions and pancetta. Desserts might include tarte tatin, espresso ice cream, or an unusual Jack Daniels sorbet with apple. A concise wine list is reasonably priced.

LE BOUCHON LYONNAIS   London SW8

---

38 Queenstown Road, London SW8 3RY
Telephone: 071-622 2618   £30
Open: all day daily (closed Christmas)
Last orders: 11.00pm

Battersea's version of a Lyonnais bistrot or bouchon. Simple hearty
food, reasonable wines and noisy, exuberant atmosphere. Get here
early to be sure of one of the elbow-to-elbow tables. Another branch
(parent restaurant is La Petite Auberge) is Le Bouchon Bordelais at 9
Battersea Rise, SW11.

BOULESTIN   London WC2

Garden Entrance, 1a Henrietta Street, London WC2E 8PS
Telephone: 071-836 7061   £90
Open: lunch Mon-Fri, dinner Mon-Sat (closed Bank Holidays, 1 wk
    Christmas)
Last orders: lunch 2.30pm, dinner 11.15pm

A change of ownership at Boulestin means that hotel chain Queens
Moat Houses is now the proprietor, but since chef Kevin Kennedy is
still at the stove, the transition has been a smooth one. The feeling of
elegance and grandeur in this plush basement dining room continues
unabated, the wine list is as extensive and expensive as before, and
Kevin's confidence with his menu is as bold as the decor. Strong
flavours throughout but a carefully balanced result in a carte full of
luxury ingredients, excellent sauces and pleasing presentation on the
plate. Service here is an extra plus – the staff really seem to enjoy
what they are doing, and are solicitous and professional; and there
are two very knowledgeable wine waiters.

Sumptous warm decor
terracottas & golds
marble columns
& chandeliers

The entrance facing out
market piazza

LA BRASSERIE — London SW3

272 Brompton Road, London SW3 2AW
Telephone: 071-584 1668 £45
Open: all day daily
Last orders: midnight (11.30pm Sun)

Open all day from 8.00am, this 150-seater brasserie – with its 1930s' Parisian decor and flexible menu – looks as authentic as a brasserie can on this side of the Channel. Try coffee and croissants or oeuf sur le plat for breakfast, an omelette as a snack, or, for a full meal, perhaps rillettes de lapereau followed by poussin grillé (with frîtes, naturally!) or gigot aux haricots. Very French, zippy service and a buzzing atmosphere.

BROWN'S HOTEL — London W1

Albemarle Street, London W1A 4SW
Telephone: 071-493 6020 £75
Open: lunch + dinner daily
Last orders: lunch 2.30pm, dinner 10.00pm

It's a quintessentially English establishment, its hallmarks being old-fashioned standards of service and luxury. The elegant panelled lounge has almost become synonymous with English afternoon tea. That jacket and tie are required wear is taken as a matter of course by Brown's customers. There's a clubby feel, many regular guests are greeted by name. Traditional English food is served in the traditional English restaurant, cooked by executive chef Martin Davies and his brigade. Bedrooms reflect a mix of tradition and modernity, and impeccable housekeeping.

BUBB'S — London EC1

329 Central Markets, London EC1A 9NB
Telephone: 071-236 2435 £60
Open: lunch Mon-Fri (closed Bank Holidays, 1 wk Christmas, 2 wks Aug)
Last orders: lunch 2.15pm

Perhaps the best possible praise of Bubb's, a converted butcher's shop in Smithfield, is that it is always full. The downside is that it is incredibly difficult to get a booking. But for those who are tenacious, the reward is a typical French bistro meal – moules, pâté, salade de chèvre, sardines grillées, coq au vin, poussin grillé. Short, reasonable wine list.

LE CADRE	London N8

10 Priory Road, Londn N8 7RD
Telephone: 081-348 0606 **£60**
Open: lunch Mon-Fri, dinner Mon-Sat (closed Bank Holidays, 5 days
     Christmas, 2 wks Aug)

David Misselbrook and Marie Fedyk have appointed a new chef, Simon Wills. The modern French menus continue to be reasonably priced – two courses for £13.50 or three for £16.50 at lunch; at dinner they rise to £21.00 and £25.00 respectively. Dishes might include a terrine of confit of duck with a hazelnut sauce, a salad of artichokes, lobster and garlic croûtons with a saffron vinaigrette, calves' liver with onion confit and jus of lemon thyme, pheasant with walnuts and madeira, followed by passion fruit crème brûlée or gratin of grapefruit and orange with lemon sorbet. The wine list is short, reasonably priced and French.

THE CAFÉ DELANCEY	London NW1

3 Delancey Street, London NW1 7NN
Telephone: 071-385 1985   *Fax:* 071-383 5314 **£45**
Open: all day, daily (closed some Bank Holidays)
Last orders: 11.30pm

The Café Delancey is now a regular institution in this part of Camden, and is approaching its seventh birthday. It has a free-and-easy feeling to it, so that you can go and sip coffee and read the papers for a while and not feel rushed, or have a three-course dinner party for up to forty people and be equally sure of enjoyment. Popular dishes include warm chicken liver salad, char-grilled steak with a green peppercorn sauce and rösti potatoes, their own recipe smoked pork sausages served with horseradish sauce and red cabbage, croque monsieur with salad, crème brûlée, café liegois – the list is almost as long as the menu! The concise wine list retains a bistro pricing, with champagnes alone exceeding £25. This is a café in the true French sense of the word, and it still amazes me that there are not more like this in London. I'm therefore delighted to see that a second branch has opened in Holborn, at 32 Proctor Street, WC1, with a similar menu and ambience; but for the third you'll have to go to Manhattan (corner of 73rd and 1st Avenue).

Le Café du Marché

LE CAFÉ DU MARCHÉ   London EC1

22 Charterhouse Square, Charterhouse Mews, London EC1M 6AH
Telephone: 071-608 1609   **£40**
Open: lunch Mon-Fri, dinner Mon-Sat (closed Bank Holidays)
Last orders: lunch 2.30pm, dinner 10.00pm

The marché is Smithfield, the café is tucked down a cobbled alley off a corner of Charterhouse Square. There's a warm welcome as you dive into a bustling, bistro-style room animée, as the French say, with live jazz centred on a piano (the back of which doubles as a dessert trolley!). The £11.00 prix fixe dinner menu may offer oeuf mayo, boudin noir grillé, fromage ou dessert. £17.50 buys more choice including perhaps a good fish soup served with croûtons, grated cheese and rouille, salmon in a cream and saffron sauce, calves' liver with wild mushrooms and red wine sauce. Good, hot vegetables. Very French service and a great atmosphere. Good local restaurant.

CAFÉ FLO   London NW3

205 Haverstock Hill, London NW3
Telephone: 071-435 6744   **£30**
Open: all day, daily (closed Bank Holidays, 5 days Christmas)
Last orders: 11.30pm (11.00pm Sat+Sun)

This is the original Café Flo which spawned the rest, having opened in 1987 in a useful location for visitors to the Screen on the Hill. The authentic café atmosphere never fails to pack them in for breakfast, lunch, tea, dinner or supper, and it is especially crowded at weekends. The formula which proved so popular began here – incredibly reasonably priced bistro food, set menus from as little as £5.95 – and it is little wonder that the group now includes four Cafés Flo: in Hampstead, the West End and Richmond, with the Bar and Grill also in Hampstead (see separate entries).

CAFÉ FLO   London WC2

51 St Martin's Lane, London WC2
Telephone: 071-836 8289   **£30**
Open: all day, daily (closed Bank Holidays, 5 dys Christmas)
Last orders: midnight (11.00pm Sun)

The second Café Flo offers the same menu as the first, but in a West End setting – a narrow room in St Martin's Lane which, surprisingly, seats sixty. It is endlessly popular with cinema and theatre-goers, who take advantage of fixed price menus ranging from an amazing £5.95 (for two courses and coffee) to £10 (for three courses and coffee). Classic bistro cooking includes daily specials in addition to a regular printed menu; you might find confit de canard, moules farcies, soupe des poissons, cassoulet, entrecôte frites, and of course salade Flo. Wines are very reasonably priced, and service is friendly and efficient.

CAFÉ KENSINGTON   London W8

Lancer Square, Kensington Church Street, London W8 4EH
Telephone: 071-938 2211   *Fax:* 071-937 8071   **£50**
Open: all day, daily
Last orders: 11.30pm (11.00pm Sun)

Peter Goodwin, the man beind La Brasserie at Brompton Cross, has opened this modern, Californian-influenced version of it in a new shopping development just off Kensington Church Street. The chef is Sybil Kapoor who has worked alongside Jonathan Waxman in New York and Sally Clarke in London, and her menu is a derivative of their styles: lots of grills, eclectic, and making a virtue of simplicity. An all-day menu is available from 9.00am on weekdays and 10.00am on Sundays. You could conceivably work your way through the day from a light breakfast (muesli, a plate of fresh fruit, cinnamon toast) to an after-cinema snack (multi-coloured peppers and spicy lamb sausage on a pizza), via a couple of full meals. Try a warm salad of spinach, mint, feta and black olives, risotto with shiitake and oyster mushrooms, roast loin of lamb with a thyme-flavoured jus and a salad of rocket and crisps, and then baked figs with crème fraîche to finish. The wine list visits Europe and the New World, and is reasonably priced. Café Kensington is not a serious rival to its neighbours Clarke's and Kensington Place; rather, it fills a separate niche by being a functional and very stylish café.

CAFÉ ROYAL GRILL ROOM   London W1

68 Regent Street, London W1R 6ER
Telephone: 071-439 6320   **£75**
Open: lunch Mon-Fri, dinner Mon-Sat
Last orders: lunch 3.00pm, dinner 11.00pm

In an era when minimalist is more the norm, the rococo decor of the
Grill Room – ornate gilt mouldings, mirrored walls and painted ceiling
– seems almost decadent. The food, wisely, doesn't try to compete
with such extravagance – have a simply grilled salmon cutlet, or a
steak and a good bottle of wine, and just enjoy the turn-of-the-
century atmosphere! Smooth, professional service led by Carlo
Ambrosini.

CANNIZARO HOUSE   London SW19

West Side, Wimbledon Common, London SW19 4UF
Telephone: 081-879 1464   *Fax:* 081-879 7338   **£65**
Open: lunch + dinner daily
Last orders: lunch 2.30pm, dinner 10.30pm

Changes at Cannizaro House in 1990, but it's still billed as London's
first country house hotel, and new chef, Nigel Couzens, continues
the vein of modern English cooking with dishes such as poached
quail's eggs served in a pastry barquette, filled with a julienne of
leeks and glazed with hollandaise sauce, fillets of red mullet garnished
with mussels and served with a cream and chablis sauce, fillet of beef
with sage sauce topped with oysters, almond and walnut slice on a
strawberry coulis. The wine list is in the upper price bracket. There
is a trend here towards conference customers, who will enjoy the
gracious public and bedrooms just as much as the leisure visitor.

THE CAPITAL HOTEL   London SW3

See page 24 – our Clover Award Section.

LE CAPRICE   London SW 1

See page 27 – our Clover Award Section.

CARRARO'S   London SW8

32 Queenstown Road, London SW8 3RX
Telephone: 071-720 5986   **£50**
Open: lunch Mon-Fri, dinner Mon-Sat (closed Bank Holidays, 2wks Aug)
Last orders: lunch 2.45pm, dinner 11.00pm (11.30pm Sat)

Most evenings will find live music in some form at Carraro's, an
elegant restaurant smartly decorated with Tuscan frescoes, and laid
out with first class linen and glassware. Service is attentive but never
obtrusively so. The menu has several Tuscan and Venetian overtones – try a refreshing salad of rucola, radicchio, mushrooms,
mozzarella with flaked parmesan and lemon dressing, or prosciutto di
cinghiale (wild boar ham), or risotto with either fresh leeks and wild
mushrooms, or prawns, cuttlefish, clams and mussels. Cuttlefish
appears again amongst the main courses, this time with polenta,
which can also be served with calves' liver Venetian style. The
attractive wine list has regional maps and is reasonably priced:
there's a good selection of half bottles and a more expensive
selection from Carraro's Chosen Cellar, from which the top notch is
£395 for a bottle of Brunello di Montalcino 1964. Both menu and wine
list are updated seasonally.

CASALE FRANCO   London N1

(rear of) 134-137 Upper Street, London N1 1PQ
Telephone: 071-226 8994   **£40**
Open: lunch Fri-Sun, dinner Tue-Sun (closed Christmas Day +
        New Year's Day, 2 wks Sep)
Last orders: lunch 2.30pm, dinner 11.30pm (11.00pm Sun)

Bookings are not accepted at this new, popular addition to the Italian
restaurant scene in Islington, but it's location (in a yard off the main
road) makes waiting no hardship, especially in summer, and if you
don't mind sharing tables, space is usually found swiftly. The decor is
spartan but interesting, dominated by brick walls and lots of copper
tubes and wires. Tables are closely packed and the atmosphere
buzzes with people having a good time. And well they might as the
food is good, and very reasonably priced. The pizzas are around £4,
other main courses don't top £9, so you could try a crab and seafood
salad, grilled polenta, grilled vegetables, tomato, mozzarella and basil
salad. This is a good local place, especially for a quick meal before or
after the cinema.

CAVALIERS   London SW8

See page 26 – our Clover Award Section.

LE CHAUSSON   London SW11

35-37 Parkgate Road, London SW11 4ND
Telephone: 071-223 1611/924 2462   **£60**
Open: lunch Mon-Fri, dinner Mon-Sat (closed Christmas + Easter)
Last orders: lunch 3.00pm, dinner 11.00pm

Chef/patron Eric Marin is a brave man, launching another French
restaurant in Battersea, but his pedigree (Le Gavroche in London, La
Tour d'Argent in Paris), should equip him well for the task. The menu
suggests some quite ambitious combinations – sweetbreads with
lobster and vanilla sauce, cotelette of wild boar with cinnamon sauce;
some are themed – raspberries en chausson (a puff pastry case).
Other dishes hit the target more accurately, such as beef consommé
with marrow, steamed turbot, chartreuse of pheasant, apple and fig
tart for pudding, as well as the small cheese tartlets offered as
appetisers, the olive bread, and the home-made petits fours – almond
tuiles, palmiers and raisin biscuits. The wine list is mostly French and
moderately priced.

THE CHELSEA HOTEL   London SW1

17-25 Sloane Street, London SW1X 9NU
Telephone: 071-235 4377   *Fax:* 071-235 3705   **£45**
Open: lunch + dinner daily
Last orders: lunch 2.30pm (2.00pm Sun), dinner 11.00pm (10.30pm Sun)

The 225-bedroomed Chelsea Hotel is now firmly established on this
site so convenient for Knightsbridge shoppers, who along with
business people make up a large proportion of its clientele. The
interior decor – simple, modern yet lavish (Philippe Starck chairs)
confirms its bid to be a leading London hotel for the 1990s. The
restaurant and bar, called At The Chelsea, is situated beneath a huge
glass atrium with an amazing '30s-style chrome staircase just aching
to support an entrance! Chef de cuisine Mark Gregory, from New
Zealand, aims to offer balanced and appetising dishes using only the
freshest ingredients, and will cook food as plainly as personally
desired, though it would be a brave diner who would eschew the
combinations on offer. Try, for instance, Japanese scallops coated
with bonito flakes, deep fried and served with a pickled ginger dipping
sauce, or, from closer to home, rack of Welsh lamb, roasted, and
served with a lentil and roasted garlic jus. To finish, you might like
Belgian chocolate fondue with marshmallows, fresh fruit and cointreau profiteroles. The wine list is concise and reasonably priced,
with – not suprisingly – a good sprinkling from the New World.

CHEZ MOI   London W11

1 Addison Avenue, Holland Park, London W11 4QS
Telephone: 071-603 8267   **£60**
Open: lunch Mon-Fri, dinner Mon-Sat (closed Bank Holidays,
        1 wk Christmas)
Last orders: lunch 2.00pm, dinner 11.00pm   *– good local restaurant*

Richard Walton's popular, classic restaurant maintains a strong local
following. He is proud to call his style 'solid and almost old fashioned',
based on the classics but with a spirit of adventure in the background!
On the set lunch menus you might find some experimentation with
Thai flavours alongside such sturdy British favourites as hindle wakes
(boned chicken stuffed with almonds, prunes and herbs) or Glamorgan sausages (a vegetarian sausage of leeks and Caerphilly cheese).
The à la carte menu tends towards France, as does the wine list.

CHEZ NICO   London W1

See page 28 – our Clover Award Section.

CHINON   London W14

25 Richmond Way, London W14 0AS
Telephone: 071-602 5968   **£55**
Open: lunch Tue-Fri, dinner Tue-Sat (closed 2 wks Aug-Sep, Bank Holidays)
Last orders: lunch 2.00pm, dinner 10.30pm (11.00pm Fri + Sat)

 Ring the bell for admission. It's a small restaurant decorated with
pale terracotta walls and some good paintings, a cream fabric-draped
ceiling and tapestry-covered chairs. Cooking is imaginative, skilled in
execution and beautifully presented. If available, try the toasted
scallops plump and moist, with vegetable spaghetti and a thin buttery
sauce. Quail stuffed with haggis, and served with green lentils and a
cardamon flavoured jus, makes a deliciously unusual starter. Fillet of
beef cooked rare, set on potato dauphinoise, surrounded by French
beans comes in a man-sized portion, with a rich sauce and tasty wild
mushrooms. Game of the day might be breast of pheasant stuffed
with boudin noir, served with a thin sauce and a necklace of
cranberries. There's no choice for dessert, just an assiette of,
perhaps, raspberry sorbet, white chocolate parfait, tarte au citron,
and an almond tuile filled with sweetened cream and fresh fruits.
Details, from bread to vegetables and petits fours, are good. Well
chosen wine list with a good selection of ½-bottles. Book.

CHRISTIAN'S   London W4

Station Parade, Burlington Lane, London W4 3HD
Telephone: 081-995 0382   **£50**
Open: lunch Tue-Fri, dinner Tue-Sat (closed 2 wks in winter, Christmas)
Last orders: lunch 2.00pm, dinner 10.15pm

Christian's is the sort of restaurant that everyone would like in the
neighbourhood, and few have! Having closed its offshoot, Le Bistro,
Christian Gustin is now firmly back in control here, competently
cooking more modern but still classically based short monthly menus:
goat's cheese soufflé, pork with apple and armagnac sauce, chocolate
terrine. The cats still snooze on the banquettes that line grey striped
walls covered with pictures, and the staff are unfailingly pleasant.

CIBO   London W14

3 Russell Gardens, London W14 8EZ
Telephone: 071-371 6271   *good local restaurant*   **£65**
Open: lunch daily, dinner Mon-Sat
Last orders: lunch 2.30pm, dinner 11.00pm

Cibo has quickly become one of the most fashionable Italian
restaurants in town – a popular haunt of media people. The
restaurant is modern and clean-lined with some exuberant pictures.
Gino Taddei is at front of house, while partner Claudio Pecorari does
the cooking. Fish dishes are popular, as is the home-made pasta.
Good espresso, affordable Italian wine list.

CIBOURE   London SW1

21 Eccleston Street, London SW1W 9LX
Telephone: 071-730 2505   **£55**
Open: lunch + dinner Mon-Fri (closed 3 wks Aug-Sep, Bank Holidays)
Last orders: lunch 2.30pm, dinner 11.00pm

This starkly modern, black and white themed, designer restaurant
continues to draw a strong regular following. The food provides the
colour here – and very enjoyably so. Short menus offer well-executed
dishes in modern French style with some southern overtones: an
aubergine stuffing for roasted red pepper, fresh thyme with a dish of
chicken. French regional wines accompany professional service.

CLARIDGE'S   London W1

See page 29 – our Clover Award Section.

CLARKE'S   London W8

See page 30 – our Clover Award Section.

COLUMBUS   London SW3

8 Egerton Garden Mews, London SW3
Telephone: 071-589 8287   *Fax:* 071-823 9118   **£55**
Open: lunch Sun-Fri, dinner daily (closed 10 days Christmas, Easter)
Last orders: lunch 3.30pm, dinner 11.30pm (11.00pm Sun)

Neal Grossman's Knightsbridge restaurant has proved popular with
residents, shoppers and the media world, as befits its location. Chefs
Paul Hughes and Camilla Kennedy offer (as the name implies) New
World cooking, also described as 'high energy modern cooking' –
whether that refers to the kitchen brigade or the effect of the food is
up to you! Influences come from the south west of the States as well
as Italy and Thailand – specialities include spiced bruschetta, corn
masa blinis, fettucini with sun-dried tomatoes, and barbecued
chicken. Good Sunday brunch.

THE CONNAUGHT   London W1

See page 32 – our Clover Award Section.

CORNEY AND BARROW   London EC4

44 Cannon Street, London EC4N 6JJ
Telephone: 071-248 2700   *Fax:* 071-382 9373   **£60**
Open: lunch Mon-Fri (closed Bank Holidays)
Last orders: lunch 3.00pm

This branch of Corney and Barrow has a '30s feel to it with pastels
and chrome dominating a stylish decor. Each table has a host service
button, an electronic bell-push enabling the host of table to summon
waiting staff discreetly. Up-to-date financial information is available
via VDUs, and if you only have one hour for lunch (and remember to
tell them as you go in!) they guarantee that you can have your meal in
that hour. Paul Magson's menus include several dishes designed with
healthy eating in mind, such as courgette soup with a hint of curry,
then grilled mahi-mahi with ginger butter and pickled seaweed, or a
hearty (but not too hearty) bean casserole with pimento, sultanas and
cous-cous. None of the puddings tagged as healthy, but is all sound
delicious, from bread and butter pudding made with fresh egg custard
to fruit terrine with seasonal berries. Corney and Barrow's wine list
prevails.

CORNEY AND BARROW — London EC2

118 Moorgate, London EC2M 6UR
Telephone: 071-628 2898   *Fax:* 071-382 9371   **£60**
Open: lunch Mon-Fri (closed Bank Holidays)
Last orders: lunch 3.00pm

This restaurant, champagne bar and wine shop caters for the city power-lunch brigade. Chef Robin Stewart might offer pancakes filled with crab, ginger and coriander, or tartare of salmon with sour cream, followed by fillet of red skin bass with spiced okra, or steak and kidney pie. Treacle tart or rice pudding are contrasted on the pudding menu with a simple selection of fresh fruits, sliced prettily onto a plate. The choice of teas is longer than the choice of coffees, and the Corney and Barrow wine list is available in all its glory.

CORNEY AND BARROW — London EC2

109 Old Broad Street, London EC2N 1AP
Telephone: 071-638 9308   *Fax:* 071-382 9373   **£60**
Open: lunch Mon-Fri (closed Bank Holidays)
Last orders: lunch 3.00pm

This is the most traditional-looking of Corney and Barrow's three city wine bar/restaurants, targetted firmly at the square mile's managing directors, chairmen and senior executives who flock to this 28-seater establishment to be greeted by a copy of the Financial Times and a hot towel. The atmosphere is tasteful and exclusive, the service (led by Valerie Lambert) discreet and professional, and Lorcan Cribbin's menus are creative with a strong leaning towards healthy food, as demanded by his work-stressed clientele! There is a carte, and set menus at £19.95 or £24.95 for two courses with coffee. The carte might offer a salad of French beans, quails' eggs and avocado with a walnut dressing, then medallions of venison with poached pear and a redcurrant jus, and, to finish, a white chocolate mousse with a passion-fruit sauce. There is also a vegetarian choice, and several teas (including Japanese) as alternatives to coffee. The wine list has all the depth and variety you would expect from one of the capital's leading wine merchants.

CROWTHER'S RESTAURANT London SW14

481 Upper Richmond Road West, London SW14 7PU
Telephone: 081-876 6372 £55
Open: lunch Tue-Fri, dinner Mon-Sat (closed Bank Holidays)
Last orders: lunch 2.00pm, dinner 10.30pm

Shirley Crowther serves in the small rather country-style dining room, while Philip cooks modern dishes with good saucing and baking. Try, for example, a very fresh ballotine of duck with orange and kumquat confit; or flavoursome loin of pork in filo pastry with a fine garlic and juniper sauce. Well-kept farmhouse cheeses and tarte au citron are as good as ever. Some decent ½-bottles on a good short wine list.

DAPHNE'S RESTAURANT London SW3

110-112 Draycott Avenue, London SW3 3AE
Telephone: 071-589 4257 £50
Open: lunch Mon-Fri, dinner Mon-Sat (closed Bank Holidays)
Last orders: lunch 2.30pm, dinner midnight

Daphne's continues to fulfil its role as a reliable, comfortable neighbourhood restaurant. Since the neighbourhood in question includes Sloane Square, it tends to attract a lot of Sloanes – or at least their mothers! An abundance of plants and tiled floors set the tone here. The international menu offers competent, classical cooking: prawn mousse with cognac-flavoured sauce, saddle of rabbit roasted with garlic and rosemary. Good dessert soufflés. Smooth, courteous service.

THE DEPOT   London SW14

Tideway Yard, Mortlake High Street, London SW14
Telephone: 081-878 9462   *Fax:* 081-392 1361   **£35**
Open: lunch + dinner daily (closed 3 days Christmas)
Last orders: lunch 3.00pm, dinner 11.00pm (10.30pm Sun) (open all day,
            daily, for lighter meals)

The Depot is a popular place to enjoy a snack, a meal, or just a glass
of wine in an attractive setting – a comparatively recent riverside
redevelopment overlooking the Thames at Mortlake. There are
some tables (with green umbrellas) in an ivy-clad terrace within
Tideway Yard itself, but the main body of stripped pine tables and
chairs are inside, where you'll find bare brick walls, mirrors, big
picture windows facing the river, and the happy buzz of people
enjoying themselves. In the evening it is essential to book, though
they do keep a couple of tables unbooked, and you can queue for
these.

The food is reasonably priced and plentiful, and is based around
freshly made pasta and sauces. Inspiration here is largely northern
Italian, and there are also several café-style dishes such as stir-fried
prawns, lamb chops with tarragon, fish pie and good salads. There's a
blackboard of daily specials. The light menu (available during the
mornings and afternoons) comprises filled, freshly baked baguettes,
and cakes from the dessert menu. The wine list is very reasonably
priced and offers several house choices by the glass – top bottle price
in 1990 around £12 for Rothbury Chardonnay.

Service is by cheerful youngsters in green polo shirts, and staff
loyalty seems high. Success has not gone to proprietor Mark Milton's
head, he has simply opened two more branches: Gavin's in Putney
and Ciao in Fulham (see listings). Both operate to the same formula
but naturally with different settings.

DON PEPE RESTAURANT   London NW8

99 Frampton Street, London NW8 8NA
Telephone: 071-260 3834   *Fax:* 071-724 8305   **£50**
Open: lunch + dinner, Mon-Sat
Last orders: lunch 2.30pm, dinner 12.15am

Jose Garcia's tapas bar and restaurant is one of the originals of the
genre, and is still considered by many to be the best. The restaurant
is at the rear with the tapas bar at the front of the room, and you can
enjoy specialities such as lubina a la sal, chuleton Don Pepe, and
vieiras a la Gallega. Live music and a television screen add to the
bustle and atmosphere.

LA DORDOGNE   London W4

5 Devonshire Road, London W4 2EU
Telephone: 081-747 1836   *Fax:* 081-994 9144   £45
Open: lunch Mon-Fri, dinner daily (closed Bank Holidays)
Last orders: lunch 2.30pm, dinner 11.00pm

La Dordogne is a warm neighbourhood French restaurant with a
friendly ambience. Cooking is essentially traditional but more modern
in terms of sauces (which are light) and presentation. They now
serve oysters as a seasonal speciality – natives from Ireland and rock
oysters from Brittany – and offer a separate lobster menu. The carte
offers familiar favourites such as a salade gourmande of foie gras,
cured duck and quail egg, or a vegetable terrine. Scallops might be
served grilled with a red pepper sauce, chicken breast is stuffed with
mushrooms, sliced and served on a ginger sauce, while duck magrets
might be interleaved with slices of pear and served on a lime sauce.
Desserts range from îsle flottante, via marquise au chocolat, to gratin
de pommes, sauce caramel. An all-French wine list is reasonably
priced.

DUKES HOTEL   London SW1

35 St James's Place, London SW1A 1NY
Telephone: 071-491 4840   *Fax:* 071-493 1264   £85
Open: lunch + dinner daily
Last orders: lunch 2.30pm, dinner 10.00pm (9.45pm Sun)

In the heart of St James's, Dukes Hotel offers a friendly atmosphere
with elegance and privacy – one of London's most charming small
hotels (only thirty-six rooms). It is ideally located for business and
pleasure visits, and the mere mention of the name of the owners,
Cunard Hotels, is enough to conjure up an image of luxury. The
restaurant lives up to this reputation, and chef Anthony Marshall who
has been at the helm for over five years is well in tune to his
customers' tastes. Thus you will find on his menus smoked salmon,
or parma ham with summer fruits, or tomato consommé with cheese
dumplings, and fresh asparagus in season, scallops steamed gently in
elderflower wine and served on a bed of wild rice, stuffed breast of
quail on a potato cake with a champagne sauce, grilled double lamb
cutlets, and a choice of cheese, pudding, or savoury to complete a
meal. The extensive, international wine list appeals to an international clientele, with prices to match.

THE DORCHESTER HOTEL   London W1

Park Lane, London W1A 2HJ
Telephone: 071-629 8888   *Fax:* 071-409 0114
The Grill Room   £60
Open: lunch + dinner, daily
Last orders: lunch 2.30pm, dinner 11.00pm (10.30pm Sun + Bank Holidays)
The Terrace Restaurant   £105
Open: dinner Mon-Sat
Last orders: dinner 11.30pm
The Oriental Restaurant   £60
Open: lunch + dinner Mon-Sat
Last orders: lunch 2.30pm, dinner 11.00pm

The long-awaited re-opening of The Dorchester occurred on 19th November, 1990, to intense media coverage and much public excitement. By the time our Guide comes out this will of course be old news, but for the record, I can tell you that £100m was spent on restoration and refurbishment during the 23-month closure. Renovation, to preserve and heighten the traditional opulence of the hotel, was the key word for such areas as the Promenade, the Bar, the Grill and Terrace restaurants, the Penthouse, Pavilion and Oliver Messel Suites. All the bedrooms were redecorated, with bathrooms being remodelled in Italian marble (and possibly the biggest deepest baths in London). The entire hotel is now air-conditioned. The kitchen and service areas, including staff facilities, have been remodelled. So, the overall impression to returning customers is of a familiar face, but with its levels of glamour and luxury heightened considerably.

However, there are some new features. There's a new restaurant, the Oriental Restaurant, offering predominantly Cantonese cuisine but with other oriental specialities too; a private club, called the Dorchester Club, for late night dinner and dancing in a Georgian townhouse atmosphere; a Boardroom Suite catering to an international business clientele; and the Dorchester Health Club satisfying beauty and fitness requirements in a relaxed atmosphere created by fountains, statues and engraved glass.

With an extra restaurant (as well as the traditional banqueting and room service facilities) to accommodate, executive Chef Willi Elsener will be a very busy man (he was busy even during the closure, for the kitchen was done to his specification). His own concept of food for the '90s, cuisine légère, with its emphasis on nutrition using low fat and wholemeal products, and plenty of fresh fruit and vegetables, will be featured strongly in the Terrace. Each restaurant also has a Premier Sous Chef (Peter Auer in the Terrace, Mark Kirk in the Grill – continuing to specialise in contemporary and traditional British cooking, Simon Yung in the Oriental); and likewise each has its own Manager: Peter Buderath, John Curry, and Dino Kwan, respectively.

Peter and John are just two of the familiar faces who have returned to the Dorchester – over 30% of the staff have in fact done so. The management are confident that a large percentage of their guests will also return – the Dorchester breeds strong loyalties – and it would seem that both existing and new guests will not be disappointed.

THE ENGLISH GARDEN   London SW3

10 Lincoln Street, London SW3 2TS
Telephone: 071-584 7272   *Fax:* 071-581 2848   **£70**
Open: lunch + dinner daily (closed Christmas Day + Boxing Day)
Last orders: lunch 2.30pm (2.00pm Sun), dinner 11.30pm (10.00pm Sun)

In the various shuffles that Malcolm Livingston has operated amongst
the chefs in his restaurants, Brian Turner has remained at the
English Garden, the fashionable local Chelsea restaurant decorated in
swagged English country-house style. In common with the other
outlets, Turner follows the Michael Smith policy of modern British
cooking: traditional base with a 1990's interpretation – collops of beef
with oysters and stout sauce, roast rack of lamb with a hazelnut
crust, home-made sausages with blackcurrant relish, treacle tart
with butterscotch custard.

THE ENGLISH HOUSE   London SW3

3 Milner Street, London SW3 1QA
Telephone: 071-584 3002   **£75**
Open: lunch + dinner daily (closed Christmas Day + Boxing Day)
Last orders: lunch 2.30pm (2.00pm Sun), dinner 11.15pm (10.00pm Sun)

Malcolm Livingston appointed a new chef, Andy Bailey, during 1990,
but the transition was a smooth one and the traditional/modern
English menus continue to attract praise. Home-smoked chicken
breast and purple fig salad tossed with mixed leaves and an aniseed
dressing, followed by baby lamb wellington with prune forcemeat and
prune brandy sauce, then Michael Smith's 18th-century chocolate
pye (rich chocolate mousse with a crisp almond crust) all bear
testimony to the continuing tradition. The English country house
decor, too, remains a tribute to the late Michael Smith, to whose
taste it was created. A new face at front-of-house, Dieter Turgen-
sen, adds to the sense of change within a context of continuity, and
the moderately priced wine list remains a comfort to those who
peruse and imbibe it.

LE FIDÈLE   London SW12

4 Nightingale Lane, London SW12 8XS
Telephone: 081-675 6771   **£70**
Open: lunch + dinner Mon-Sat
Last orders: lunch 2.30pm, dinner 11.30pm

Le Fidèle is the new-look Yours Faithfully, from the fair hand of designer and owner Delva Simunovitch. The decor is a stunning mixture of modern materials, warm colours and classic table settings. Chef Patrick Pavageau's subtle modern French cooking finds a good outlet here – he has a particularly sure touch with fish and duck dishes. Good value set lunches, moderately priced French wine list.

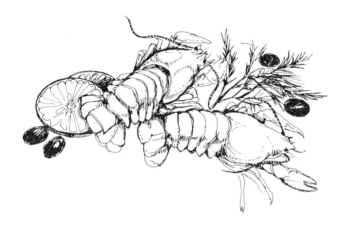

FOUR SEASONS RESTAURANT   London W1

See page 34 – our Clover Award Section.

FREDERICK'S RESTAURANT   London N1

Camden Passage, London N1 8EG
Telephone: 071-359 2888   **£65**
Open: lunch + dinner, Mon-Sat (closed Bank Holidays)
Last orders: lunch 2.30pm, dinner 11.30pm

Frederick's came of age on 22nd November 1990, celebrating twenty-one years on Thanksgiving Day, the day that Mrs Thatcher announced her intention to resign! We did not manage to secure a table for that particular party evening, so over-subscribed was Louis Segal's idea of serving both lunch and dinner from that opening day and at 1969 prices (plus VAT). Presumably it was as resounding a success as all Louis' enterprises. The kitchens underwent refurbishment in 1989. Head chef Jean-Louis Pollet has been at Frederick's for 14 years, changing his menu every fortnight but still cooking to the same basic format – a carving trolley at lunch times, a 3-course shoppers' lunch on Saturdays at just £10.95. The wine list remains competitively priced.

FRITH'S RESTAURANT   London W1

14 Frith Street, London W1V 5TS
Telephone: 071-734 7535/071-439 3370   **£65**
Open: lunch Mon-Fri, dinner Mon-Sat (closed Bank Holidays)
Last orders: lunch 2.30pm, dinner 11.15pm

Carla Tomasi's popular Soho restaurant goes from strength to strength. 1990 saw the addition of Frith's Vegetarian Café in the basement below the main restaurant, seating just twenty-five lucky customers. Carla also offers a local delivery service during the day, and sometimes gives jars of her famous chutneys to favoured customers.

A November meal comprised an excellent wild mushroom risotto, the rice creamy and perfectly cooked with an abundance of funghi; breast of chicken stuffed with leeks and porcini with a roasted garlic and walnut cream, accompanied by a first-class salad of varied leaves and a dressing redolent of truffle oil. Delicious home-made breads. Other offerings on the same menu included a salad of raw porcini with pine nuts, radicchio, rocket and pecorino, braised quails with polenta and pancetta, and steamed turbot with three salsa: verde, rossa and bianca. Excellent espresso to finish, and a largely Italian wine list is reasonably priced. This is a restaurant that is under-used in the evening.

Friths, Soho

LE GAVROCHE   London W1

See page 36 – our Clover Award Section.

GAVVERS London SW1

61 Lower Sloane Street, London SW1W 8DH
Telephone: 071-730 5983 **£65**
Open: lunch Mon-Fri, dinner Mon-Sat
Last orders: lunch 2.30pm, dinner 11.00pm

Ironically, the Roux brothers' umbrella seems to have caused some misconceptions about this commendable restaurant. Don't go expecting the brillance of Le Gavroche or The Waterside; simply go for a well-prepared enjoyable meal. At dinner, if you stick to the house wine included in the fixed price menu (£27.50), there are no extras, from kir and nibbles right through to coffee. There's almost a bistro atmosphere, with tables jammed together and brisk French service.

THE GAY HUSSAR London W1

See page 38 – our Clover Award Section.

GILBERT'S RESTAURANT London SW7

2 Exhibition Road, London SW7 2HF
Telephone: 071-589 8947 **£50**
Open: lunch Mon-Fri, dinner Mon-Sat (closed Christmas to New Year)
Last orders: lunch 2.00pm, dinner 10.15pm

Ann Wregg and Julia Chalkley are now well established in their friendly neighbourhood restaurant. Ann Wregg's friendly attitude at front-of-house goes a long way towards ensuring a strong and loyal following, while Julia Chalkley's cooking does the rest. Her menus, which change every two weeks, are imaginative rather than elaborate, home-made and seasonal, and she aims to provide food that is nourishing, substantial and delicious. The word is that she succeeds. Lunch menus are priced at £8.50 for one course, £12.50 for two or £14.50 for three, and dinner at £18.50 for two courses or £21.50 for three. Choices are similar at both meal times, but portions are larger in the evening; all options include home-made bread, vegetables or salad, and coffee. You might choose a wild rabbit terrine with damson chutney, or some marinated smoked cod with ginger and soy, then a daube of beef cooked provençale-style, or tagliatelle with mussels and a pineau des charentes sauce, and, to finish, a walnut and lemon tart, or figs baked with honey and served with crème fraîche. The wine list is arranged by grape varieties with extensive tasting notes, a page of house recommendations available by the glass or bottle, and a good sprinkling of halves on the remainder of the list.

THE GORE HOTEL   London SW7

189 Queen's Gate, London SW7 5EX
Telephone: 071-584 6601   *Fax:* 071-589 8127   **£50**
Open: all day, daily (closed Christmas Day + Boxing Day)
Last orders: 11.30pm

All change at The Gore in 1990. Proprietor Peter McKay has wisely taken full advantage of being next door to the headquarters of the Restaurateurs' Association of Great Britain headquarters and the industry's own club, One Ninety Queen's Gate. He has allowed part of his own premises to be used by One Ninety and chef Antony Worrall-Thompson as Bistrot 190, much vaunted and more accessible to the public than the club restaurant. The decor in this corner, street-level room is more casual than the club, with masses of pictures and swags of dried flowers and hops. A corner of the bar is occupied by enormous vats of olives, from which your portion comes when you order. Portions are enormous and mostly the combinations work well. Amongst the dishes that have been enjoyed recently are char-grilled squid with frites and arugola, char-grilled calves' liver and bacon with creamed polenta and tortellini, wild mushroom ravioli gratin, beef carpaccio with char-grilled vegetables, gnocchi with parma ham, lemon and tomatoes, Toulouse sausages with mash and fried apples – this is not food for those with bird-like appetites! The lemon tart is a particular hit amongst the desserts. The wine list changes monthly, being compiled by a guest wine shipper each time, issuing a strong challenge to anyone who wishes to drink his (or her) way through the wine list!

What of the hotel itself? A hotel of mellow charm is the line on the brochure. It has its roots firmly in the Victorian era, as do so many of the architectural features of Kensington, and is richly decorated with mahogany and walnut, oriental rugs on the floors, fine prints on the walls, and antique furniture throughout. There are fifty-eight comfortably-appointed bedrooms, currently being refurbished in the same style as the rest of the hotel.

THE GREENHOUSE RESTAURANT — London W1

27a Hay's Mews, London W1X 7RJ
Telephone: 071-499 3331 **£65**
Open: lunch Mon-Fri, dinner Mon-Sat
Last orders: lunch 2.30pm, dinner 11.00pm

The Greenhouse is approached through a garden, then there's a small entrance hall, cleverly enlarged with mirrors, which leads to the bar and restaurant. Chef Gary Rhodes has joined the Greenhouse from The Castle in Taunton, and his English menu reads well. If it's available, try a fillet of smoked haddock with a Welsh rarebit on a tomato and chive salad, or the excellent chicken liver parfait with home-made grape chutney and toasted brioche. Main courses might include baked cod with a parsley crust on creamed potatoes, leg of chicken filled with onions, garlic, bacon and wild mushrooms served on a bed of Mediterranean vegetables, a very good calves' liver and bacon with onion gravy, pasta in mushroom cream sauce with spicy tomatoes. Puddings could be a burnt lemon meringue tart, pear crumble with home-made ice cream and custard sauce, sticky toffee pudding, or apple and almond flan with a calvados sauce and apple sorbet. The wine list is concise – only sixteen bins, and reasonably priced, given the location.

GREEN'S RESTAURANT AND OYSTER BAR — London SW1

36 Duke Street, St James's, London SW1Y 6DF
Telephone: 071-930 4566   *Fax:* 071-930 1383 **£65**
Open: lunch daily, dinner Mon-Sat (closed Bank Holidays)
Last orders: lunch 3.00pm, dinner 11.00pm

Green's offers a sophisticated, club-like atmosphere with traditional mahogany panelling and prints on the walls, and green leather banquette seating on two floors; the downstairs room is usually the quieter. Service is professional and discreet, but friendly. The clientele comprises loyal regulars including representatives from royalty, show business, the art world and captains of industry, mixed with a good sprinkling of theatre-goers and tourists. The food too is traditional and based on tenets of simplicity and quality. Beth Coventry continues to turn out a lengthy menu of traditional favourites, such as fresh asparagus in season or miniature Raj fishcakes with spicy mayonnaise, roast rack of lamb with mint and onion sauces, traditional fish pie with leeks and prawns, and, for desserts, treacle tart, sticky toffee pudding (lifted out of the ordinary by the addition of dates), fruit crumble and custard, or champagne syllabub.

GRILL ST QUENTIN   London SW3

2 Yeomans Row, London SW3 2AL
Telephone: 071-581 8377   *Fax:* 071-584 6064   **£50**
Open: all day, Mon-Sat (closed Christmas to New Year)
Last orders: 11.30pm

The Grill St Quentin, part of the St Quentin group (owned in turn by
the even more famous Savoy group) is a useful, all-day spot in the
heart of Knightsbridge, offering a traditional French menu in a bright
dining room. The atmosphere is lively and the staff are very much on
their toes! Some of the best pommes allumettes in London can be
enjoyed with steaks (the menu helpfully explains the French degrees
of steak rareness), grilled salmon, or good choucroûte. Desserts are
not to be missed, especially anything that comes from their own
patisserie, Les Specialités St Quentin at 256 Brompton Road. Back at
the Grill, the set lunch of three courses for £11.90 is excellent value,
as is the reasonably priced French wine list. (See also separate entry
for the restaurant, St Quentin.)

Shining brass
& pin lights

Huge central
flower
arrangement
on circular waitis
station

Soft green mottled pillars

intense blue (old medicine
bottle) glass uplighters.

Fresh
crusty
french
baguettes

Grill St. Quentin

THE HALCYON HOTEL London W11

81 Holland Park, London W11 3RZ
Telephone: 071-727 7288   *Fax:* 071-229 8516 **£60**
Open: lunch + dinner daily
Last orders: lunch 2.30pm, dinner 11.30pm

A sympathetic conversion of two large Victorian houses. The ornately elegant reception with stunning flower arrangements serves also as a lounge. The twenty-one spacious suites boast beautiful fabrics, wide deep sofas and polished period furniture. Extras include safe deposits. Marble bathrooms have bidets, some jacuzzis, and good toiletries. Patio doors leading to a small garden lend daylight to the stylish Kingfisher Restaurant on the lower floor. The menu reads well and includes some up-to-date Italian dishes; and results on the plate live up to expectations. Balance and flavour are, in particular, successful in the breast of guinea fowl with apples and calvados butter with a good dauphinois, preceded by a salad of fresh anchovy fillets. Pleasant efficient service and a wine list of depth and price to match the setting.

THE HAMPSHIRE HOTEL London WC2

31 Leicester Square, London WC2 7LH
Telephone: 071-839 9399   *Fax:* 071-930 8122 **£80**
Open: lunch + dinner daily
Last orders: lunch 2.00pm, dinner 11.00pm

An unpromising location (in the former dental hospital right in the heart of Leicester Square) hides a surprising find: the Hampshire Hotel is an oasis of tranquillity and comfort. Once behind the elegant doors the country house feel envelopes you completely. You can take tea in the panelled drawing room, a cocktail in the bar (strains of Cole Porter from the piano), and pre- and post-theatre customers make good use of Celebrities Restaurant, where chef Colin Button shows his skills. From butcher's boy to Buckingham Palace, he has now found the right niche – and an appreciative audience for such delights as langoustine and mushroom lasagna, boiled slipper of bacon with pease pudding, dumplings and parsley sauce, and warm winter fruits with their own sorbets. Wine list in the upper price bracket.

HARVEY'S   London SW17

See page 40 – our Clover Award Section.

HIDERS   London SW6

755 Fulham Road, London SW6 5UU
Telephone: 071-736 2331   £45
Open: lunch Mon-Fri, dinner Mon-Sat (closed Bank Holidays,
    1 wk Christmas)
Last orders: lunch 2.30pm, dinner 11.30pm

A pleasantly decorated, popular local restaurant which offers
straightforward cooking. The menus change every couple of weeks,
and are in the traditional-to-modern British vein. Try the cucumber
and mint soup, if it's available. Desserts are a strong point, especially
the tulipe of sorbets, and the marzipan biscuit of fresh fruits. Concise
French wine list, reasonably priced.

HILAIRE   London SW7

See page 42 – our Clover Award Section.

HOTEL CONRAD   London SW10

Chelsea Harbour, London SW10 0XG
Telephone: 071-823 3000   *Fax:* 071-351 6525   **£70**
Open: lunch + dinner daily
Last orders: lunch 2.30pm (3.00pm Sun), dinner 10.30pm

The Hotel Conrad is one of the more recent additions to the London
hotel scene. Conrad International Hotels is a division of the Hilton
group, and this establishment is the first purpose-built, all-suite hotel
in Europe, as well as being the first newly-built 5-star standard hotel
to open in London for about a decade. There are 160 suites of which
twenty-two are guaranteed to be no-smoking, with daily rates from
around £200 to around £1,000! With views over the new harbour
complex and marina, it is perhaps not surprising that the hotel's
decor (by David Hicks) recalls a cruise liner during the 1920s – the
Art Deco answer to a brief that called, apparently, for 'international
elegance with a laid-back quality'. The lounge has a stunning
strongly-patterned carpet in green, cream and scarlet, and a similar
geometric design is to be found in the predominantly gold and scarlet
dining room, called the Compass Restaurant. Here, Andrew Ben-
nett's cooking draws inspiration from around the globe, and you
might start a meal with sashimi of scallops with lime and olive oil,
moving on to a nage of lobster with cous-cous and fennel, or
medallions of beef with black truffles and duck foie gras, served with
crisply cooked vegetables. Desserts from the trolley complete the
meal. There are some separate choices for vegetarians. The lunch
menu offers some of the same choices as the evening carte, but also
includes a set menu which at around £16 (in 1990) offered amazing
value considering the setting. One such English-themed meal
comprised consommé of beef celestine, then trio of English game
with blueberries, and Yorkshire treacle tart with hot lemon cream to
finish. Coffee is also included in this price. The wine list offers
something to suit most of the wide range of clientele that the hotel
attracts.

Hotel Conrad.

L'HOTEL AND LE MÉTRO   London SW3

28 Basil Street, London SW3 1AT   **£50**
Open: lunch + dinner, Mon-Fri (closed Bank Holidays)
Last orders: lunch 2.30pm, dinner 10.00pm

L'Hotel and its ground floor wine bar, Le Métro, are owned by David
Levin of the adjacent Capital Hotel adjacent, and the kitchens
therefore come under the control of the Capital's chef, Philip Britten.
The concept at L'Hotel was to create an ambience of quietness and
discretion, with personal touches in the decor and furnishings. It is
tiny – only twelve twin-bedded rooms and one double-bedded suite,
but all are individually designed with well-appointed bathrooms.
Unusually, breakfast (residents only) lunch and dinner are served in
the wine bar. A short menu of familiar favourites – warm chicken liver
salad, croque monsieur, confit de canard, steak with maître d'hotel
butter, crème brûlée and mousse au chocolat. The now famous
cruover machine enables an ever-changing selection of bottles of
wine to be offered for tasting by the glass, although there are many
bargains to be found by the bottle on David's all-French wine list.

THE HYATT CARLTON   London SW1
TOWER HOTEL

2 Cadogan Place, London SW1X 9PY
Telephone: 071-235 5411   *Fax:* 071-245 6570   **£70**
Open: lunch + dinner daily
Last orders: lunch 2.45pm (2.30pm Sun in Rib Room), dinner 10.45pm
         (10.30pm Sun) Chelsea Room, 11.15pm (10.45pm Sun)
         Rib Room.

The modern Hyatt Carlton Tower has 159 rooms, comfortably
appointed to cater to their international clientele, and the management team was strengthened in 1990 by the appointment of Michael
Gray as general manager. Of the two restaurants, the Rib Room is
the more traditional and the Chelsea Room more nearly avant garde,
though both come under the watchful eye of Bernard Gaume who has
been here since 1968. With Jean Quero in place as maître d'hotel
since 1960, the Hyatt Carlton is clearly a hotel that breeds loyalty in
both staff and customers. In the Chelsea Room, overlooking Cadogan
Square, there is often live music and the decor – light wood panelling
and lots of greenery in the conservatory area – gives a relaxed feel to
the room. Fish and seafood are Bernard's strengths and these are
well treated and well received. An international wine list with prices
to match.

The Hyde Park Hotel . London SW1

Knightsbridge, London SW1Y 7LA
Telephone: 071-235 2000 **£70**
Open: lunch + dinner daily
Last orders: lunch 2.30pm, dinner 10.00pm

The grand marbled entrance hall with its glittering chandeliers, ornate ceiling and gilded pilasters can hardly fail to impress. To complete the picture, take a full suite, furnished with antiques, and with private balcony overlooking Hyde Park. More modestly, the individually decorated bedrooms feature polished traditional furniture with every modern comfort from satellite TV to a phone in the bathroom. The spacious chandeliered Park Room restaurant offers some good modern Italian cooking, such as duck breast, borlotti beans and black truffle in balsamic vinegar. The Grill Room offers more traditional cooking. General Manager Paolo Biscioni leads the smart attentive hotel staff.

L'Incontro London SW1

See page 43 – our Clover Award Section.

The Ivy London WC2

1 West Street, London WC2H 9NE
Telephone: 071-836 4751 *Fax:* 071-497 3644 **£55**
Open: lunch + dinner daily (closed Christmas)
Last orders: lunch 3.00pm (3.30pm Sun), dinner midnight

Christopher Corbin and Jeremy King from Le Caprice re-opened The Ivy in the summer of 1990, and brought chef Tony Howarth onto the team too. The Art Deco interior recalls the hey-day of The Ivy (when it was the haunt of such luminaries as Lloyd George and Noel Coward), and it makes a restful setting for Tony's eclectic, international food. The menu is laid out in a refreshingly simple way, with headings for seafood, hors d'oeuvres, soups, eggs and pasta, fish, roast and grills, cold dishes, entrées, vegetables and salads, desserts and savouries, enabling you to put together as complex or as simple a meal as you wish. Try the shaved, sugar-cured tuna with avocado and lime, black mushroom soup, sauté of lamb's kidneys and sweetbreads, shrimp gumbo, rice pudding with armagnac-flavoured prunes, and sour cherry sorbet. The wine list is as easy on the eye as it is on the palate, and the wallet need not suffer too badly either. The range is mostly European with a few from the New World. Service is polite and efficient.

JOE ALLEN   London WC2

13 Exeter Street, London WC2E 7DT
Telephone: 071-836 0651   **£50**
Open: all day, daily (closed Christmas)
Last orders: 12.45am

Joe Allen is still packing them in. A proportion of the staff is still
'resting' actors and actresses, the customers are still mostly
theatre-goers and tourists, and the burgers are still off the menu,
although they are one of the restaurant's best sellers! The eyes take
some adjustment to the level of light if you go in from a blisteringly
hot London summer afternoon – but it's a good place to escape to,
then, as it's air-conditioned. Spinach salad, grilled chicken, burgers,
cocktails, Californian wines, pecan or apple pie, and ice creams are
the staples of the menu.

Joe Allen's Jukebox. Fast, noisy, fun!

KALAMARAS   London W2

See page 44 – our Clover Award Section.

KENSINGTON PLACE   London W8

See page 45 – our Clover Award Section.

LANGAN'S BISTRO   London W1

26 Devonshire Street, London W1N 1RJ   *good local bistro*
Telephone: 071-935 4531   **£50**
Open: lunch Mon-Fri, dinner Mon-Sat (closed Bank Holidays)
Last orders: lunch 2.30pm, dinner 11.30pm

Plus ça change, moins ça change … and here they haven't changed at
all! It's still a charming and useful neighbourhood bistro with a regular
clientele who appreciate the competent and often imaginative cooking
in dishes such as monkfish with tomato fondue and anchovies. Puds
are more traditional and there's a simple wine list.

LANGAN'S BRASSERIE   London W1

See page 46 – our Clover Award Section.

LAUNCESTON PLACE RESTAURANT   London W8

1a Launceston Place, London W8 5RL
Telephone: 071-937 6912   *Fax:* 071-376 0581   **£50**
Open: lunch Sun-Fri, dinner Mon-Sat (closed 2 days August Bank Holiday,
        3 days Christmas)
Last orders: lunch 2.30pm (3.00pm Sun) dinner 11.30pm

A good local restaurant with comfortable, uncluttered dining rooms in
the style of an English town house – rich cream walls, gilt mirrors,
carpeting. (For a more intimate dîner à deux ask for a table in the
inner room.) The cooking, like the Italian-inspired art on the walls,
looks southwards for its ideas: you might be offered tiny grilled squid
with roquette and a ginger dressing, or some grilled endive, red,
yellow and green peppers, courgettes and tomatoes. These last
came with a dish of sour cream and a type of sambal with chopped red
onion and diced tomato – a redundant embellishment since the
vegetables were sweet and tasty. Salmon fillets were served on a
watercress and orange salad, while a breast of corn-fed chicken was
grilled and served with some excellent rice and a little jus. Bread is
good: small, foccaccia-style warm rolls. There's a reasonably priced
wine list. Service is courteous and friendly.

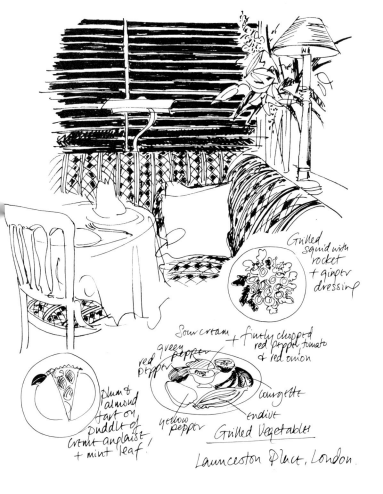

Grilled squid with rocket + ginger dressing

Sour cream + finely chopped red pepper, tomato & red onion

green pepper
red pepper
yellow pepper
courgette
endive
Grilled Vegetables

Plum & almond tart on puddle of crème anglaise + mint leaf!

Launceston Place, London.

LEITH'S RESTAURANT — London W11

92 Kensington Park Road, London W11 2PN
Telephone: 071-229 4481 £80
Open: dinner daily (closed 4 days Christmas, 2 days Aug)
Last orders: dinner 11.30pm

Prue Leith has been an influence on the British catering scene for over twenty years and her star continues to rise. Recently appointed to the Chair of the Restaurateurs' Association of Great Britain (as if she were not already busy enough), she still finds time to run her restaurants. Although new influences, particularly from the east, are appearing, the famous duckling with almonds, orange and celery is still a best seller, and Prue has also been at the forefront of restaurants catering for the increasing number of vegetarians.

THE LINDSAY HOUSE — London W1

21 Romilly Street, London W1V 5TG
Telephone: 071-439 0450   *Fax:* 071-581 2848 £70
Open: lunch + dinner daily (closed Christmas Day + Boxing Day)
Last orders: lunch 2.30pm (2.00pm Sun), dinner midnight (10.00pm Sun)

Once past the heavy front door of this 17th-century house (ring for admittance), there are comfortable sofas and armchairs for drinks and nibbles. Upstairs, the main dining room is decorated in elegant period country house style. The menu offers a good range of well-executed dishes of British inspiration: veal and ham terrine served with a madeira and truffle jelly or collops of South Downs lamb in a red wine sauce. Good coffee and chocolate fudge. Useful for before or after the theatre.

LOU PESCADOU — London SW5

241 Old Brompton Road, London SW5 9HP
Telephone: 071-370 1057 £50
Open: lunch + dinner daily
Last orders: lunch 2.30pm, dinner midnight

You still can't book, so arrive early, or late, or wait in the small bar. (Ring the bell for admittance.) It's invariably busy, slightly scruffy. Service can be brusque, but the fish and shellfish is absolutely fresh. Simply cooked is best; follow it with apple tart or chocolate mousse.

LUC'S RESTAURANT & BRASSERIE   London EC3

17-22 Leadenhall Market, London EC3V 1LR
Telephone: 071-621 0666   **£50**
Open: lunch Mon-Fri
Last orders: lunch 3.00pm

Book to enjoy straightforward French brasserie dishes served by
friendly young French staff in an authentically French brasserie,
situated at the heart of Leadenhall Market. Robust plats du jour and
daily specials supplement the carte, and if you're pressed for time
you can just order a main course. Animated and busy.

First floor brasserie
very Gallic, great
        charm.

Leadenhall
    market
amazing
Victorian ironwork
painted in red,
    blue & cream
        silver 'dragons'

MAGNO'S BRASSERIE   London WC2

65A Long Acre, London WC2E 9JH
Telephone: 071-836 6077   **£40**
Open: lunch Mon-Fri, dinner Mon-Sat (closed Christmas, New Year, Easter)
Last orders: lunch 2.30pm, dinner 11.30pm

Restaurateur Magno Coliadis is celebrating ten years' service to a
regular clientele. The £16.50 menu (including coffee and dessert) is
good value for money and might include a creamy carrot soup
flavoured with coriander, followed by pan-fried fillet of pork with a
honey and hazelnut sauce. The carte is also available, of course, and
features specialities such as thin slices of salmon marinated in
aromatic herbs, olive oil and lime juice and served with a salmon
tartare, and roast rack of lamb served with a fresh rosemary sauce.
The predominantly French wine list is good value, and usually
features a wine of the month.

THE MARKET BAR   London W11

240 Portobello Road, London W11
Telephone: 071-229 6472   *Fax:* 071-221 9796   **£50**
Open: lunch + dinner, daily (closed Bank Holidays, 4 dys Christmas)
Last orders: lunch 3.00pm, dinner 11.30pm (10.30pm Sun)

A former pub in Portobello Road with a medieval but eclectic style of
decor might be a surprising place to find Dorchester-trained chef
Andy Eastick, but there he is, cooking very competently. The
Market Bar is run by architect Adrian Forsyth and designer Tony
Weller. Downstairs is primarily a bar with food, while the restaurant
is upstairs. The dinner carte (minimum charge of £10 per head) might
offer seafood tortellini with poached oysters and mussels in a light
saffron sauce, or game terrine with a cranberry and red onion
marmalade; main courses might be sea-bass with a confit of spring
onion, horseradish and tomato with a piquant lime sauce or sautéed
fillet of beef on a provençale tart with a basil sauce. There's usually a
vegetarian option, such as a feuilleté of wild mushrooms and spinach
with a light Jerusalem artichoke sauce. Puddings include home-made
vanilla ice cream, warm pancakes filled with apple purée in a calvados
sauce, tiramisu, gratin of peaches. There's also a set menu at £22.50
for three courses – no choice except between vegetarian and regular.
Largely French, moderately priced wine list. An interesting addition
to the Portobello culinary scene.

The Market Bar, Portobello Road

MARTIN'S RESTAURANT · London NW1

239 Baker Street, London NW1 6XE
Telephone: 071-935 3130/0997   **£50**
Open: lunch Mon-Fri, dinner Mon-Sat (closed Bank Holidays)
Last orders: lunch 2.30pm, dinner 10.30pm

Martin Coldicott runs this comfortable, fifty-five seater restaurant very professionally. Food, wines, clientele and service are all taken seriously but no-one involved takes him or herself too seriously. The restaurant, a conservatory-style room, offers a relaxed atmosphere, pleasing to both business and private customers alike. Brendan McGee's cooking offers modern British food, but it's a style firmly rooted in the classical. The result includes dishes such as steamed mussels with pickled ginger; sautéed supremes of gurnard with yellow pepper and saffron sauce, or simple grilled lamb cutlets with tomato and tarragon coulis; ravioli of wild mushrooms; breast of pheasant with pease pudding. The vegetables and potatoes are invariably organically grown, and vegetarians are specifically catered for. Desserts might include an elderflower and lime parfait, or prune and almond tart. The cheeseboard usually includes a number of unpasteurised cheeses. A concise wine list has plenty of New World choices, and is reasonably priced.

MÉNAGE À TROIS · London SW3

15 Beauchamp Place, London SW3 1NQ
Telephone: 071-589 4252   **£60**
Open: lunch Mon-Fri, dinner daily (closed 25+26 Dec)
Last orders: lunch 3.00pm, dinner 12.15am

Still the same formula of starter-sized portions. Best value is the 3-course lunch priced at £15.00. Trios of pastry parcels may be filled with anything from cheese to fruit. Inventive ideas include a black walnut crust for seafood in a warm salad. Good bread. The softly lit basement setting is comfortable: white painted brick walls, wood panelling, mirrors and live piano music.

MESON DON FELIPE   London SE1

53 The Cut, London SE1 8LF
Telephone: 071-928 3237   **£35**
Open: lunch Mon-Fri, dinner Mon-Sat (closed Bank Holidays)
Last orders: lunch 3.00pm, dinner 11.00pm

Phil Diment and his Spanish wife, Ana, run Meson Don Felipe as a
typical Spanish bar; they offer a range of tapas (small dishes of
appetisers traditionally served with drinks) and raciones (larger
dishes). You can put together as large or as small a meal as you wish.
Given the location (just opposite the Young Vic theatre), it is quite
usual to find people having a snack before a play and something more
substantial later. What to choose? Well, there's quite a range of more
than forty meat, fish and vegetable combinations. Favourites are
fresh marinaded anchovies (a revelation if you only know the oily
salty tinned fillets!), shell-on prawns with garlic mayonnaise,
deep-fried stuffed mussels, snails in spicy sauce, hot spicy sausages,
a broth of ham and vegetables, pickled baby aubergines, spinach with
pine nuts and garlic, as well as more familiar dishes like paella and
Spanish omelette. For pudding try the almond and pastry cream tart,
or vanilla ice cream with dark sherry. With an extensive, Spanish,
reasonably priced wine list, live flamenco guitar every evening and an
incredibly lively atmosphere, Meson Don Felipe is a good port of call.

The same menu is available at other branches of the group –
Meson Doña Ana at 37 Kensington Park Road, W8, and Meson Don
Julian at 125-127 Dawes Road, SW6 (see listings).

Le Mesurier   London EC1

113 Old Street, London EC1V 9JR
Telephone: 071-251 8117   **£55**
Open: lunch Mon-Fri (closed Bank Holidays, 1 wk Christmas, 3 wks Aug)
Last orders: lunch 3.00pm (only party bookings of 15-26 people taken for
        dinner)

Chef/patron Gillian Enthoven's little restaurant (seating 20) is mostly used by business-people, but can also be the location for a more leisurely lunch. Whatever the occasion, guests can be assured of some reliable cooking in the modern French style with traditional overtones. Inspiration may also be drawn from holidays in Turkey, as in the lamb en croûte with fresh figs and ginger. Soufflés are a speciality; you can have one made from sea-bass served with a langoustine sauce for a main course, or a hot raspberry soufflé for dessert. A popular starter is oysters on the shell, covered with a cream and shallot sauce, topped with gruyère cheese and glazed under the grill. The wine list is concise and reasonably priced.

Mijanou   London SW1

143 Ebury Street, London SW1W 9QN
Telephone: 071-730 4099   *Fax:* 071-823 6402   **£65**
Open: lunch + dinner Mon-Fri (closed 2 wks Christmas, 1 wk Easter,
    3 wks Aug)
Last orders: lunch 2.00pm, dinner 11.00pm

Neville and Sonia Blech run a small, personal restaurant, working and cooking (as they say) for people, not for restaurant critics! However, both groups seem well pleased with their efforts (customers return time and again from far-flung points of the globe), and this is largely because Neville and Sonia follow their own instincts rather than fashion. Sonia describes her cooking as 'artisanale' – everything is done by hand on the premises, including the bread and the ice cream. The emphasis is on lightness and subtlety. Sauces are neither thickened nor over-reduced. Everything tastes of itself, and anything artificial is avoided. You can choose with confidence from a menu that might include amongst its starters mousse of vegetables and fromage blanc served warm in puff pastry with a tomato and green bean coulis, and fresh foie gras served on a black Muscat wine and grape jelly; and for main courses medallions of venison served with an elderberry and juniper gin sauce, or a marmite – various fish and seafood cooked very lightly in a consommé of vegetables and noodles. Desserts are equally delightful, and you could try an arlequinade of various home-made sorbets served with tropical and seasonal fruits, or a white chocolate bavarois with Tia Maria and coffee sauce. An excellent wine list (Neville Blech's personal selection) has plenty of wines at under £20 a bottle.

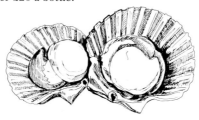

MIMMO D'ISCHIA   London SW1

61 Elizabeth Street, Eaton Square, London SW1
Telephone: 071-730 5406
Open: lunch + dinner Mon-Sat (closed Bank Holidays)
Last orders: lunch 2.15pm, dinner 11.15pm

excellent local Italian **£55**

Twenty-one years on and Mimmo d'Ischia is still going strong, appealing to loyal regulars and newcomers alike. The recent hot summers have led to the installation of air-conditioning, so that you can now enjoy traditional and regional Italian cooking in even greater comfort. Try the sea-bass, the spare ribs, penne arrabbiata and the mixed hors d'oeuvres. The wine list includes a useful notation of strength by volume.

MON PETIT PLAISIR   London W8

33 Holland Street, London W8
Telephone: 071-937 3224   **£55**
Open: lunch + dinner Mon-Fri (closed Bank Holidays)
Last orders: lunch 2.15pm, dinner 10.45pm

Mon Petit Plaisir is one of Mon Plaisir's little brother (see listings). Alain Lhermitte's second restaurant, seating just twenty-five, has been going for about two years now, offering a mixture of modern and traditional French dishes, all freshly cooked. The carte might include a seafood feuilleté with a lobster sauce, or a goat's cheese salad, then medallions of pork with a bitter orange sauce, or Scottish salmon with an onion confit. There is a daily set lunch at around £14.50, and a concise French wine list on which the top priced bottle is under £30 – even champagne!

MONSIEUR THOMPSON'S   London W11

29 Kensington Park Road, London W11 2EU
Telephone: 071-727 9957   **£60**
Open: lunch Mon-Fri, dinner Mon-Sat (closed Bank Holidays)
Last orders: lunch 2.30pm, dinner 10.30pm

Dominique Rocher has won awards for the refurbishment of his Notting Hill restaurant. He wanted to get away from a chintzy, English look and has certainly succeeded with an interesting blend of classic and modern: high ceilings, frescoes and heavy curtains, plus murals by Eric Sharp – the overall design was created by Alex Stubbs. In this setting you can enjoy typical French bistro fare – crudités with tapenade, rillettes or confit de canard, entrecôte de boeuf.

MOSIMANN'S   London SW1

See page 48 – our Clover Award Section.

MOTCOMBS   London SW1

26 Motcomb Street, London SW1X 8JU
Telephone: 071-235 9170   *Fax:* 071-245 6351   **£50**
Open: lunch + dinner, Mon-Sat (closed Bank Holidays)
Last orders: lunch 3.00pm, dinner 11.15pm

Philip Lawless's pretty establishment with its club-like atmosphere, ground-floor wine bar and restaurant below is fully air-conditioned, which has increased its popularity ever more during the last two summers! There is a suite available for private parties, and Philip Lawless has now acquired additional premises around the corner in Halkin Arcade, which he is operating as The Club (originally opened by Mario and Franco, those two famous restaurant names from the '60s). Membership details are available from the restaurant, where James Peake continues to turn out food that is acceptable and consistent. There are usually several starters, a separate list of warm salads, another list of soups, a separate list again for oysters and game (in season), vegetables and salads, entrées and grills. The speciality of the house is roast crispy duckling with apple sauce, for two people.

LE MUSCADET   London W1

25 Paddington Street, London W1M 3RF
Telephone: 071-935 2883   **£60**
Open: lunch Mon-Fri, dinner Mon-Sat (closed 3 wks Aug, 2 wks Christmas,
    Bank Holidays)
Last orders: lunch 2.30pm, dinner 11.00pm (10.00pm Sat)

Set in a small converted modern shop, this neighbourhood bistro with
close packed tables exudes a vibrant French atmosphere. Owner
François Bessonnard recites the day's blackboard menu: moules,
parfait de foie de volaille, Dover sole with champagne sauce, duck
with wine and cream sauce. Cheeses may include three chèvres and
an outstanding brébis. House muscadet is £8.10 and there's fine old
calvados for a trou normand. Book. Good local restaurant.

THE NEAL STREET RESTAURANT   London WC2

26 Neal Street, London WC2 9PH
Telephone: 071-836 2368   *Fax:* 071-497 1361   **£75**
Open: lunch + dinner, Mon-Fri (closed Bank Holidays,
    1 wk Christmas/New Year)
Last orders: lunch 2.30pm, dinner 11.00pm

Chef/proprietor Antonio Carluccio is becoming increasingly familiar
to television viewers, but his regular customers over the past ten
years in Neal Street know already that this unassuming, friendly man
is also a very good chef. The surroundings of the restaurant, Sir
Terence Conran's sleek design, are a perfect foil to his cooking,
which he describes as 'clean and served to give comfort to the
body…with no snobbery'. He admits to erring on the conservative
side but this only underlines how well he understands his clientele.
They – and any newcomers – can enjoy modern Italian food, the best
ingredients treated with care and combined in dishes like Sardinian
gnochetti with broccoli and peperoncho, or smoked mozzarella and
sun-dried tomato salad, or some porcini risotto – there's a waiting
time of twenty minutes while this quintessential dish is cooked to
order, but it's well worth it. Move on to grilled marinated eel, Roman
style, or medallions of venison with funghi and polenta. Vegetables,
too, excite the palate – Tuscan beans with virgin olive oil, broccoli
with ginger, creamed spinach, carrots with coriander. The puddings
prolong the happy experience – try baked barolo pear with vanilla ice,
a green apple sorbet with calvados, or vin santo with cantuccini. As
you would expect, espresso is excellent, and the wine list matches
the food in region, price and quality.

NEW SERPENTINE RESTAURANT   London W2

Hyde Park, London W2 2UH
Telephone: 071-402 1142   **£35**
Open: all day daily for snacks (closed 3 days Christmas)
Last orders: lunch 3.00pm, dinner 10.30pm

In the hot summer of 1990, Prue Leith's contributions to feeding the
tourists and residents of London found another outlet, this time in the
Serpentine Restaurant on the waterfront in Hyde Park (she already
provides a similar service at Hampton Court). The initial temporary
building is rather like an octagonal tent, but serves her purposes
admirably. The menu changes quite frequently, but as it happens, and
in company with most other reviewers, we enjoyed our meals here in
the balmy days of summer. Particularly popular was a chilled
courgette and mint soup served with poppyseed sticks; warm
sesame chicken on a mixed leaf and spring onion salad (goujons of
breast meat, chargrilled and dusted with sesame seeds and sesame
oil); spinach and sorrel roulade filled with cream cheese, tomato and
basil with new potatoes and salad; olive and artichoke pie with tomato
and black olive salad (more brownie points for taking care of
vegetarians!); and puddings such as chocolate bavarois with fruit
sauce, a plate of fruit and sorbets, or Eton mess. There are separate
menus for morning coffee and afternoon tea.

NINETY PARK LANE   London W1

Grosvenor House Hotel, Park Lane, London W1
Telephone: 071-409 1290   **£115**
Open: lunch Mon-Fri, dinner Mon-Sat
Last orders: lunch 2.45pm, dinner 10.45pm

Louis Outhier acts as consultant chef here. The dishes that emanate
from menus drawn up by himself and his protégé Jason Riches
(several with oriental influences) are certainly imaginative. The
3-course lunch at around £25 offers the best value. Especially
enjoyable dishes this year included a Thai chicken and coconut soup,
best end of lamb with lyonnaise sausage and lemon balm, and
asparagus brochettes of scallops and turbot. The wine list is all that
you would expect of Trusthouse Forte's flagship hotel. The very
professional Sergio Rebecchi oversees the service. The long
panelled dining room with its sofa seating is plush but elegant – this is
an expensive restaurant and looks like one.

OAK ROOM RESTAURANT   London W1

See page 51 – our Clover Award Section.

ODETTE'S RESTAURANT   London NW1
AND WINE BAR

130 Regent's Park Road, London Nw1 8XL
Telephone: 071-586 5486/8766   **£55**
Open: lunch Mon-Fri, dinner Mon-Sat (closed Bank Holidays, 10 days
      Christmas, 2 wks Aug)
Last orders: lunch 2.30pm, dinner 11.00pm

Simone Green's restaurant with its cheerful green awning is
customer-led and has been so for fourteen years. Service is friendly
and efficient, the ambience warm and welcoming in a mirror-lined yet
intimate dining room that overflows into a conservatory area. In
summer, tables even spill onto the pavement outside. There's also a
wine bar below and some private rooms. Each part of the operation
has a slightly different feel. The style of cooking moves with the
times, and has recently evolved to embrace the modern style of
young chef Dan Evans, who recently joined Odette's from Alastair
Little, where he was sous chef for three years. His autumn menus
bear testimony to this pedigree, with offerings such as a winter broth
of lamb, smoked bacon and cabbage, contrasting with a roulade of
fresh crab with a ginger and orange dressing; or roast saddle of rabbit
in a gin and lime sauce accompanied by a fricassée of the legs with
cream and wild mushrooms, or pan-fried fillets of salt cod with
mussels and a cumin sauce. The wine bar menu is more casual, with
terrines, salads, sausages and mash, omelettes and pasta. The wine
list of some seventy bins is well travelled and has useful tasting notes
and a good selection of halves. Simone looks forward to another
fourteen years!

A ravioli of wild mushrooms
  made with Beetroot pasta   5.95
A chilled 'Capucino' soup of
cucumber, fennel & dill   3.75
Hot fenillets of Pigeon &
    Venison   5.95

Roast Poussin stuffed
with leeks & a light chicken
mousse   11.00
Supreme of Salmon, roast in
its skin on a bed of samphire
    & red butter sauce 12.00
A tournedos of Beef with a coast grain mustard Sabayon,
served on a bed of grated carrot & courgette & a red wine & basil
                    reduction 13.50

ODIN'S RESTAURANT   London W 1

27 Devonshire Street, London W1N 1RJ
Telephone: 071-935 7296   **£80**
Open: lunch Mon-Fri, dinner Mon-Sat (closed Bank Holidays)
Last orders: lunch 2.30pm, dinner 11.30pm

As in the other Langan restaurants, the pictures which cover almost
every inch of space on the walls, provide the backcloth to a meal
here. Soft lighting, smooth service and some enjoyable food
complete the picture. Enjoyable starters include a salad of crab with
peppers and cucumbers, or chilled celeriac mousse with apple
chutney. For a main course, you might choose pan-fried calves' liver
with peppercorn sauce, or roast best end of lamb with artichoke,
flageolet beans and tomato. Lighter main courses such as steamed
monkfish with a prawn and black pepper sauce leave room for a date
and ginger or chocolate pudding, or sweet wine Bavarian cream.
Good claret on a well-chosen wine list.

ONE NINETY QUEEN'S GATE   London SW 7

See page 50 – our Clover Award Section.

ORSO RESTAURANT   London WC2

27 Wellington Street, London WC2E 7DA
Telephone: 071-240 5269   *Fax:* 071-497 2148   **£60**
Open: all day, daily (closed Christmas)
Last orders: midnight

Orso, which is part of the same group which owns Joe Allen, serves by contrast regional Italian cooking. Set in a basement, the restaurant has a simple tiled decor which offsets well the pretty crockery. The menu (in Italian on the left, English on the right) includes such starters as arugola, parma ham and parmesan salad, cuttlefish cooked in ink with spinach and polenta, small pizzas, or wild mushroom risotto. Main courses of roast sea- bass with artichokes and new potatoes, or sliced calves' liver with pancetta, might be accompanied by broccoli with olive oil and lemon, or grilled courgettes. Fruit, cheese and desserts are listed separately, though they can be taken together. The concise Italian wine list is moderately priced.

PELICAN DU SUD   London SE1

Hays Galleria, Tooley Street, London SE1 2HR
Telephone: 071-378 0096   **£50**
Open: all day, daily (closed Christmas)
Last orders: 9.45pm (5.30pm Sat + Sun)

The setting for the second Café Pelican is a glass-covered atrium in Hays Galleria, and perhaps even more appealing than the original in St Martin's Lane. The menu concept is the same – modern French food in good portions, chosen either from a carte or a set menu at around £16, with a choice of two dishes at each of three courses. From this you might enjoy a chilled cucumber and mint soup, then leg of lamb steak with flageolets, with a warm, light gooseberry tart to finish. The all-French wine list is concise and reasonably priced.

POLLYANNA'S RESTAURANT London SW11

2 Battersea Rise, London SW11 1ED
Telephone: 071-228 0316 **£60**
Open: lunch Sun, dinner Mon-Sat (closed Christmas Day, Boxing Day +
New Year's Day)
Last orders: lunch 3.00pm, dinner midnight

Norman Price's restaurant, Pollyanna's, is a 35-seater, cosy neighbourhood restaurant offering modern French-style cooking in comfortable surroundings. The chef, however, is English – Richard
Aldridge, and his menu is written in English too (though the daily
specials are in French!). Any confusion ends at the stove, however,
for Richard's touch is sound in starters like quail mousse served on a
potato salad, or fillet of beef and bacon terrine, or boudin de fruits de
mer; and main courses like rack of lamb served with a herb crust on a
madeira sauce, blue parrot fish filled with a seafood mousse, steamed
and served on a fresh basil sauce, or caille farçie aux épinards et à la
mousse de roquefort. Puddings might be a light orange and passion
fruit mousse, or dark and white chocolate marquise, or tarte aux
poires. The wine list is extensive, French, well annotated and very
fairly priced – a real labour of love from Norman Price.

POMEGRANATES London SW1

94 Grosvenor Road, London SW1V 3LF
Telephone: 071-828 6560   *Fax:* 071-828 2037 **£65**
Open: lunch Mon-Fri, dinner Mon-Sat
Last orders: lunch 2.15pm, dinner 11.15pm

Patrick Gwynn-Jones continues in great style in his popular, small,
private and club-like restaurant-by-the-river in Pimlico. He describes
it as comfortable and non-trendy, and is proud that it has remained
unchanged during his sixteen years' proprietorship. The clientele is a
good mix of city, showbusiness, restaurant industry and visitors to
London who come to relax and enjoy Patrick's affable hosting. Mark
Orr is given plenty of credit for his five-year input to the kitchen,
although the restaurant is nevertheless firmly in the chef/patron
category. Patrick says his menus offer cosmopolitan peasant food,
though I envy the peasant who can regularly partake of Jamaican fish
tea (a red mullet broth made with rum!), or burek (feta cheese,
spinach and mint in filo pastry) with a Sudanese pepper sauce, then
moving on to Tennessee oyster stew, or murg makhani (chicken in
butter and tomato sauce). Try the home-made honey and cognac ice
cream, in particular. Such a varied menu demands a strong,
wide-ranging wine list to accompany it, and this is what Patrick
proffers, at very reasonable prices.

PORTERS   London WC2

17 Henrietta Street, London WC2
Telephone: 071-836 6466   **£35**
Open: all day, daily
Last orders: 10.30pm

The Earl of Bradford's London outpost (see also Weston Park at
Shifnal in the England section) has been going strong for about fifteen
years. Named after the porters of Covent Garden, the menu
specialises in pies of beef, chicken or vegetables under puff or
wholemeal pastry, salads, and English puddings and ices. The setting
is a large, glazed room with ceiling fans and friendly young staff.

THE PORTMAN   London W1
INTER-CONTINENTAL HOTEL

22 Portman Square, London W1H 9FL
Telephone: 071-486 5844   *Fax:* 071-935 0537   **£60**
Open: lunch Sun-Fri, dinner daily (closed Bank Holidays)
Last orders: lunch 2.30pm (3.30pm Sun), dinner 10.30pm

The Portman Inter-Continental celebrates twenty years in 1991, and
was the first of the group to be opened in London. The 272 rooms are
luxuriously appointed. The executive chef in charge of the Portman's
kitchens since 1984 is David Dorricott, who serves innovative and
creative cuisine in the hotel's Truffles Restaurant. There's an almost
bewildering array of menu options: a 3-course lunch or dinner for
around £27 including coffee, taking choices from the carte, a
fixed-price no-choice 3-course lunch at around £20, a special
5-course dinner for around £30 (to live piano music), and a 3-course
Brunch on Sundays for around £20 with live jazz! But whatever you
choose, you can be assured of interesting food, such as a supreme of
warm hickory-smoked pigeon with freshwater crayfish, then perhaps
roast guinea fowl with wild rice, goose liver and spinach, and
strawberry millefeuille. The wine list has all the depth and range you
would expect at an international hotel, with prices to match.

LE POULBOT   London EC2

45 Cheapside, London EC2V 6AR
Telephone: 071-236 4379   **£65**
Open: lunch Mon-Fri (closed Bank Holidays)
Last orders: lunch 3.00pm

Le Poulbot comprises a restaurant downstairs and a brasserie
upstairs where you can have breakfast from 7.30am to 10.00am on
weekdays. Part of the Roux Brothers' stable, this one has had Nick
Reade in the kitchen for just over a year now, and features Susan
Thompson at front of house. It is geared very much to its city
clientele: red plush high button-backed banquettes characterise the
booth seating in the restaurant itself. Again in the Roux mould, the
fixed price menu includes an aperitif as well as coffee, petits fours and
service. You might choose a ballotine of foie gras served on toasted
brioche, then filet d'agneau en croûte à l'estragon with good crisp
vegetables, the lamb enclosing a light tarragon mousse, all wrapped
in a crisp pastry. The wine list is in the middle price range.

LE QUAI ST PIERRE   London W8

7 Stratford Road, London W8 3JS
Telephone: 071-937 6388   **£70**
Open: lunch Tue-Sat, dinner Mon-Sat (closed Christmas)
Last orders: lunch 2.30pm, dinner 11.30pm

Another of Pierre Martin's successful group of restaurants, Le Quai, just south of Kensington High Street, offers the same formula as the others, including the famous plateau de fruits de mer. The aim remains the provision of top quality seafood at reasonable prices in pleasant surroundings, and the stated objective is to maintain the high reputation currently enjoyed. Thus, all manner of fish and shellfish can be found on Alain Patrat's menu, cooked simply and to order. As before, some fish is priced per 100g, and this branch has more meat dishes than some of the others. White and rosé wines, together with champagnes, dominate a reasonably priced wine list.

QUINCY'S   London NW2

675 Finchley Road, London NW2 2JP
Telephone: 071-794 8499   **£50**
Open: dinner Tue-Sat (closed Bank Holidays, 2 wks Christmas, 2 wks Aug)
Last orders: dinner 10.30pm (11.00pm Sat)

The team of proprietor David Wardle and chef Roy Kilner is clocking up seven years' service in their friendly, neighbourhood restaurant, and they are proud to call their regular customers friends. They succeed in serving a mixture of French and British food (the menu changes monthly), cooked with care and concentrating on true flavours. There is always one choice at each course for vegetarians, and a September menu offered – from six starters – veal and smoked oyster terrine with spiced tomato coulis, from six main courses – breast of duck with nutmeg and calvados, and from six desserts and cheeses – rhubarb crumble. The £19.50 set price includes coffee but not service. The concise wine list of some forty bins is French and very reasonably priced. This is a good, local restaurant.

REBATO'S   London SW8

169 South Lambeth Road, London SW8 1XW
Telephone: 071-735 6388   **£40**
Open: lunch Mon-Fri, dinner Mon-Sat (closed Bank Holidays)
Last orders: lunch 2.30pm, dinner 11.100pm

One of the first tapas bars in London, and still one of the best. Flowers are used lavishly in the decor to give a feeling of vibrancy and colour, while Spanish music and lively customers complete the picture. The tapas themselves range from grilled fresh sardines, fresh anchovies, salt cod and squid to chorizo sausages, olives, tripe, tortilla and paella. You can have a full meal in the restaurant area at the rear – here too, fish is a strength. The wine list is extensive – and Spanish!

THE RITZ   London W1

See page 52 – our Clover Award Section.

RIVA   London SW13

169 Church Road, London SW13 9HR
Telephone: 081-748 0434   **£45**
Open: lunch Sun-Fri, dinner daily (closed Bank Holidays)
Last orders: lunch 2.30pm, dinner 11.00pm (11.30pm Sat, 10.30pm Sun)

Andrea Riva has opened his new-wave Italian restaurant on a site formerly occupied by a branch of The Ark. Walls are a pale ochre (one is covered by a mirror), tables (set quite close together) have white linen undercloths, paper slips and linen napkins, set with white china and plain glassware. The formula and food are successful: ciabatta and olive breads are brought as soon as you sit down, with unsalted butter and a bottle of olive oil. Good bruschetta with plum tomatoes, garlic, black olives and herbs, buffalo mozzarella salad with anchovies and basil, parma ham with rucola and grana, grilled vegetables (aubergines, zucchini and peppers) marinated in extra virgin olive oil, green chilli and mint, creamed salt cod on grilled polenta, gnocchi with ricotta and gorgonzola (available as a starter or as a main course), black risotto with baby cuttlefish and shallots, grilled baby calamari, pan-fried calves' liver with garlic-flavoured creamed polenta and wild mushrooms. Desserts are equally delicious, and range from tiramisu to wild fruit cake, via espresso with vanilla ice cream to vin santo dessert wine served with cantuccini (Tuscan almond biscuits). Cheeses may also be taken with polenta. The concise northern Italian wine list is moderately priced with some interesting choices.

Ochre ragged walls
soft greens in the
paintwork
+ tiny flying
spotlights

huge glass cube
of tables reflected
in the long
mirrored wall

Hard wooden
school-type chairs

CAFE RESTAURANT
RIVA

deep golden
olive oil on
table + flat
moist Italian breads

THE RIVER CAFÉ   London W6

See page 53 – our Clover Award Section.

RSJ RESTAURANT   London SE1

13A Coin Street, London SE1 8YQ
Telephone: 071-928 4554   **£40**
Open: lunch Mon-Fri, dinner Mon-Sat (closed Bank Holidays)
Last orders: lunch 2.00pm, dinner 11.00pm

RSJ is now something of a Coin Street institution: in 1990 Nigel Wilkinson celebrated his first decade in this converted warehouse. He has expanded the operation to include a wine brasserie on the lower floor; it opened in September 1990. It's a chance to indulge Nigel's passion for wines, particularly those of the Loire. There are some unusual reds from that area on the list which offers the opportunity to taste most of his bin selections by the glass. Chef Ian Stabler continues to produce his modern style of cooking which brings value for money (sensible portions) to nouvelle cuisine. At £13.25 for two courses or £14.75 for three, there are few who would argue with that, and many who enjoy his smoked fish mousseline, loin of lamb pan-fried and served with a courgette and tomato flan and a rosemary sauce, and thin slices of apple tart on a puff pastry base served with caramel sauce to finish. Vegetarians might choose an artichoke, broccoli and carrot gateau, seasoned with herbs and spices and served with summer vegetables, and 'demi-veggies' some fresh pasta filled with mushrooms, truffles and herbs, topped with a salad of fine asparagus and sautéed rock shrimps. A well-kept cheeseboard is an alternative to pudding.

RUE ST. JACQUES   London W1

See page 54 – our Clover Award Section.

RULES RESTAURANT   London WC2

35 Maiden Lane, Loncon WC2E 7LB
Telephone: 071-836 5314   *Fax:* 071-497 1081   **£50**
Open: all day, Mon-Sat (closed Christmas Day + Boxing Day)
Last orders: midnight

Rules is a traditional English restaurant. Established in 1798, its Covent Garden location has made for several literary and theatrical associations, such as Dickens, Thackeray, Graham Greene, while signed portraits of the Prince of Wales and Lillie Langtry bear testimony to royal connections, too. So what have people been eating here for nearly 200 years? The finest game, Scottish beef, North Sea fish, oysters, pies and puddings. These might be preceded by mushroom and madeira soup, and followed by apple and blackberry pie with custard. Chef Neil Pass cooks simply and well, and the food is served with panache and efficiency by Josie Davidson's team at front of house.

SAN LORENZO   London SW3

22 Beauchamp Place, London SW3 1NL
Telephone: 071-584 1074   **£50**
Open: lunch + dinner Mon-Sat (closed Bank Holidays)
Last orders: lunch 3.00pm, dinner 11.30pm

A favourite stop for lunch when shopping, or for a more relaxing dinner, and perennially popular with visiting media stars. The restaurant is on two floors, each room decorated in stylish, modern fashion. Traditional Italian cooking might offer the occasional surprise, such as crudités con bagna cauda, and the pasta is always reliable. Good Italian wine list.

SANTINI RESTAURANT   London SW1

29 Ebury Street, London SW1 0NZ
Telephone: 071- 730 8275/4094   *Fax:* 071-730 0544   **£90**
Open: lunch Mon-Fri, dinner daily (closed Bank Holidays)
Last orders: lunch 2.30pm, dinner 11.30pm (11.00pm Sun)

Santini is modern and elegant, and caters for a well-to-do, see-and-be-seen clientele. The business lunch price went up in 1990 to £18.00 for two courses and coffee. The modern Italian cooking is, however, unreservedly popular, featuring such favourites as carpaccio, baked artichokes, grilled langoustines, wild mushrooms with polenta, ossobuco milanese, sea-bass with herbs, baby squid Venetian-style, and desserts from the trolley. The largely Italian wine list is in the middle to upper price bracket.

THE SAVOY   London WC2

See page 56 – our Clover Award Section.

SCOTTS   London W1

20 Mount Street, London W1Y 6HE
Telephone: 071-629 5248   *Fax:* 071-491 2477   **£85**
Open: lunch Sun-Fri, dinner daily (closed Bank Holidays, Christmas to
       New Year)
Last orders: lunch 2.45pm, dinner 10.45pm (10.00pm Sun)

In the centre of Mayfair, the institution that is Scotts goes on. Scotts – a venue for diplomats and businessmen – includes a cocktail bar, oyster and caviar bar, a private room – and virtually doubles as an art gallery with some fine paintings and drawings. John Bertram's cooking combines traditional English with classical French styles, resulting in a menu ranging from nage de poisson à la Scotts (an ensemble of sole, king scallops, langoustines, lobster and turbot with a chablis-based beurre blanc) to a simply grilled Dover sole. Les Royal Natives Nicholas – named for owner Nicky Kerman – are nine selected oysters, gently poached in their own juices, covered with a delicate parmesan sauce and glazed. An extensive, largely French, middle-to-upper price range wine list has a separate Louis Jadot selection.

Sonny's	London SW13

94 Church Road, London SW13 0DQ
Telephone: 081-748 0393   *good local restaurant*   **£40**
Open: lunch Sun-Fri, dinner daily (closed Bank Holidays)
Last orders: lunch 2.00pm (3.00pm Sun), dinner 11.00pm (10.30 Sun)

The decor of Sonny's is unpretentious – plain floors, cream walls with a few prints, white paper slips on the tables, an atmosphere created by the buzz of happy customers. Owner Rebecca Mascarenhas runs her establishment with flair, and commands a high degree of loyalty in her staff. Ellie Link is well in command of her kitchen, with some good dishes and an imaginative knack of combining flavours. Specialities include potato blinis with crème fraîche and salmon caviar, char-grilled duck with braised funghi, and Eton berry mess; other good dishes, tried, include salad of char-grilled squid tossed in peanut and chilli butter, home-made pasta with wild mushrooms, giant prawns on a wilted spinach salad with sesame seeds and sesame oil, char-grilled tuna with lime, black-bean cakes with tomato salsa. Puddings are also good, especially the crème brûlée, blood orange tart, and frozen brazil nut and coffee parfait. Good cheeseboard, and dessert wines by the glass. The wine list is concise and contains a sprinkling of ½-bottles.

An innovation during 1990 was the opening next door of Sonny's Food Shop, usefully open on Sunday mornings. It stocks, amongst many items, breads (olive, parmesan, pain de campagne), pastries, charcuterie, cheeses, sauces (sold in refundable-deposit kilner jars), jars of sun-dried tomatoes in olive oil, pesto, fish soup, sorbets and ice creams, as well as ready-made dishes for dinner parties. With a branch of the restaurant in Nottingham and another in Erpingham, Norfolk, Rebecca is a happy – if busy – lady.

Le Soufflé Restaurant	London W1

See page 58 – our Clover Award Section.

Soulard	London N1

113 Mortimer Road, London N1
Telephone: 071-254 1314   **£40**
Open: lunch + dinner Tue-Sat (closed Bank Holidays, 1 wk Christmas)
Last orders: lunch 2.00pm, dinner 10.30pm

Philippe Soulard is establishing a good niche for his neighbourhood restaurant. Food is traditional French, service is friendly, the setting is simple – a small square green and cream room centred around a brick fireplace. Prices are not high, with a short wine list starting at £6.25. If available, try the confit de canard or pavé de boeuf à la moëlle.

THE STAFFORD　　　　　　　　　London SW1

16 St James's Place, London SW1A 1NJ
Telephone: 071-493 0111　*Fax:* 071-493 7121　　　　　**£70**
Open: lunch + dinner daily (closed Christmas)
Last orders: lunch 2.30pm, dinner 10.30pm (9.30pm Sun)

In the heart of clubland the Stafford is well camouflaged, complete
with long-serving staff and a long-standing regular clientele. Deep
leather chesterfields, picture-clad walls, antiques and fresh flowers
set the scene. By contrast, the American Bar has a baseball theme!
Another unexpected touch – there's a tiny private garden.

STEPHEN BULL　　　　　　　　　London W1

5-7 Blandford Street, London W1H 3AA
Telephone: 071-486 9696　　　　　　　　　　　　　**£60**
Open: lunch Mon-Fri, dinner Mon-Sat (closed Christmas)
Last orders: lunch 2.30pm, dinner 11.15pm

Stephen Bull is now firmly established in his clean-cut, Marylebone
premises, and has enjoyed much critical and customer acclaim. In a
simple setting, the friendly and efficient front-of-house staff serves
what has been described as Stephen's up-market bistro food. He has
a sure touch, and robust flavours sing out in such dishes as pumpkin
and orange soup, or terrine of rabbit and duck with a fig compote
(both starters from an autumn menu). Equally delicious were
mackerel fillets with garlic flageolets and a red wine sauce, and
sautéed breast of guinea fowl with red cabbage and a purée of apple
and celeriac. Puddings might include a delicious lime tart made with
coconut pastry, or a raspberry sablée. The wine list is reasonably
priced.

ST JAMES'S COURT HOTEL　　　　　London SW1

41 Buckingham Gate, London SW1E 6AF
Telephone: 071-821 1899　*Fax:* 071-630 7587　　　　**£80**
Open: lunch Mon-Fri, dinner Mon-Sat (closed Christmas to New Year)
Last orders: lunch 2.30pm, dinner 11.00pm

The St James's Court Hotel has 390 luxurious and well-equipped
bedrooms and apartments. There's also a business centre, aimed at
international business clientele. The Auberge de Provence is one of
three restaurants in the hotel, the others being the Inn of Happiness
(offering a Chinese menu) and the Café Mediterranée (with an
international menu). Executive chef Prem Kumar is Indian, but each
restaurant also has its own head chef. Olivier Massart heads the
brigade for the Auberge, taking over from Yves Gravelier. His menus
continue to offer modern French cooking, attractively presented,
with some regular selections for vegetarians. The largely French
wine list is in keeping with the status of the hotel, the wines coming
directly from L'Oustau de Baumanière, home of Jean-André Charial
who is consultant chef to the Auberge.

St Quentin   London SW3

243 Brompton Road, London SW3 2EP
Telephone: 071-581 5131   *Fax:* 071-584 6064   **£50**
Open: lunch + dinner daily
Last orders: lunch 3.00pm (4.00pm Sat + Sun), dinner midnight
              (11.30pm Sun)

The restaurant arm of the St Quentin group offers a similar menu to
the grill but in a slightly more formal atmosphere. The menu here is
thus still quintessentially French, and whether you want a steak
frites, or some foie gras, or a simply grilled Dover sole, you can be
certain of consistency from chef Stephen Whitney who joined in 1990.
A recent addition to the group is the Café St Quentin at 215
Brompton Road, as well as the charcuterie-traiteur at 10 Egerton
Gardens Mews.

-St. Quentin-

Sud-Ouest Restaurant   London SW3
and Café

27-31 Basil Street, London SW3
Telephone: 071-584 4484   *Fax:* 071-581 2462   **£45**
Open: restaurant: lunch Mon-Sat (closed Bank Holidays), café: open all day,
       Mon-Sat
Last orders: restaurant: lunch 3.00pm, café: 11.00pm

Sud-Ouest is run on the principle of serving good food in relaxed
surroundings by professional staff without the trappings of exclusiv-
ity, such as high prices and formal dress. Nigel Davis's cooking draws
its inspiration primarily, though not exclusively, from south west
France. You might enjoy a terrine of aubergines or a salad of green
beans and foie gras to start, with cod basquaise or roast rack of lamb
with a garlic and shallot confit to follow. Finish with baked figs with
almonds and honey, or prune and armagnac mousse. The wine list is
not restricted to France, and has some good New World selections.
The shorter café menu offers lighter options, such as grilled goat's
cheese sald, or Toulouse sausage with lentils, or sandwich made
from ciabatta bread or croissant filled with parma ham. Good
espresso and cappuccino, as well as herb teas and wines by the glass.

Le Suquet   London SW3

104 Draycott Avenue, London SW3 3AE
Telephone: 071-581 1785   **£55**
Open: lunch + dinner daily
Last orders: lunch 2.30pm, dinner 11.30pm

To my mind still the best of Pierre Martin's group of restaurants, Le
Suquet has not really changed its format or style since its inception,
and is no less popular for that. It is a breath of southern France in
Chelsea, and Jean-Yves Darcel continues to produce plateaux de
fruits de mer, sea-bass, fillet of turbot, coquilles au safran and all
manner of other fish dishes (plus a daily meat dish for carnivores).
Chablis is still a popular choice on the short wine list.

Sutherland's Restaurant   London W1

See page 60 – our Clover Award Section.

Sweetings   London EC4

39 Queen Victoria Street, London EC4N 4SA
Telephone: 071-248 3062   **£45**
Open: lunch Mon-Fri (closed Bank Holidays, 1 wk Christmas/New Year)
Last orders: lunch 3.00pm

Graham Needham's Sweetings is a city institution, a quality fish
restaurant catering to business-people who enjoy oysters, dressed
crab, fish pie, brill, turbot and wild salmon cooked in traditional
British fashion. The simple bill of fare lists separately the cold table,
vegetables, and savoury alternatives to sweets such as baked jam
roll, baldji figs, steamed syrup pudding, or bread and butter pudding.
Wines – some available by the glass and some by the bottle – are
reasonably priced. The house selection is a Muscadet de Sèvre et
Maine at £9.00. No credit cards.

Tall Orders   London SW6

676 Fulham Road, London SW6 5SA
Telephone: 071-371 9673   **£40**
Open: all day, daily
Last orders: 11.30pm (11.45pm Sat, 10.30pm Sun)

Tall Orders was relatively new when we compiled last year's guide,
but now a second branch has been opened in the West End. Nick
Gill's concept is executed from the kitchen by Bruce Ward, and the
team has built up a strong local following. The menu has not changed
substantially since the start – you still put your meal together as a
tower to be served in chinese bamboo steamer baskets, and the food
draws its inspiration generally from the Mediterranean. Bread, a
ciabbatta roll, is served with black olives and pesto, and a ragoût of
beans is spiced with harissa and puntalette. Puddings can also be
ordered as a tower if you feel unable to choose between, say, fresh
summer berries with crème fraîche, hazelnut meringue with lime
caramel, or espresso mousse with cappuccino cream. Wines and
other drinks are reasonably priced in this busy restaurant with its
tables packed closely together.

LA TANTE CLAIRE   London SW3

See page 62 – our Clover Award Section.

THIERRY'S   London SW3

342 King's Road, London SW3
Telephone: 071-352 3365   £45
Open: lunch + dinner, Mon-Fri (closed Bank Holidays, 2 wks Aug)
Last orders: lunch 2.30pm, dinner 11.00pm

Chef Richard Blades cooks a menu of regional French dishes, served
at reasonable prices. The set lunch at £9.90 for three courses is good
value. On the carte, you might find soufflés, terrines, a feuilleté of
quails' eggs, soupe à l'oignon gratinée, then as main courses perhaps
a marmite de pêcheur, or a confit de canard aux échalottes. Desserts
are good, particularly a pithiviers aux poires belle hélène. A very
reasonably priced wine list. A cheerful, bistro decor (red checked
cloths with white paper slips, terracotta walls, blackboard menu).

TIRAMISU RESTAURANT   London NW6

327 West End Lane, London NW6
Telephone: 071-433 1221   £50
Open: lunch Sun-Fri, dinner daily (closed Christmas)
Last orders: lunch 2.30pm, dinner 11.30pm

Tiramisu is located in an arcade of shops just opposite West
Hampstead Green, and comprises a small, white room, lined with
brown banquettes, white-clothed tables, bentwood chairs, and a
terracotta-tiled floor. Lunchtimes tend to be quiet but evenings busy
at this modern Italian restaurant which prides itself on the quality of
its raw ingredients. The menu bears two notations – CN for natural
cooking, and CV for vegetarian cooking. In the latter category is a
simple but well-handled starter of grilled oyster mushrooms with
rucola salad, in the former a warm salad of salt cod and fagioli beans.
A delicious CV main course is risotto with mozarella and peas, while
CN fans could choose escalopes of salmon steamed with vinegar and
spring onion. On Sundays there is a set lunch at £15 for two courses
but including vegetables, dessert and coffee. The wine list has some
intriguing offerings that repay several visits.

TURNER'S   London SW3

See page 64 – our Clover Award Section.

LE VAGABOND   London SW18

11 Alma Road, London SW18 1AA
Telephone: 081-870 4588   **£45**
Open: lunch Mon-Fri, dinner Mon-Sat (closed Bank Holidays, 2 wks Jan, 2
    wks Aug)
Last orders: lunch 2.00pm (3.30pm Sun), dinner 10.30pm

On the site formerly occupied by Liaison there is now Le Vagabond, a
small, friendly neighbourhood restaurant which aims to offer quality
food at reasonable prices in a warm and welcoming ambience. Grills
are very much in evidence in main course dishes such as grilled fillets
of red mullet. Starters might include pan-fried livers and croûtons on
a mixed salad, or tartlet of spinach and quail eggs in a béarnaise
sauce. There are always three vegetarian main dishes, one of which
is often vegan as well – an autumn menu in this section offered fried
eggplant, basted with mushroom and sesame seeds and served with a
sauce of tomato and basil. Puddings might be a tulipe of fruits on a
mango sauce, poached pear on chocolate served in a pastry cage, or a
terrine des sorbets. A concise wine list is reasonably priced, and
French.

VERONICA'S RESTAURANT   London W2

3 Hereford Road, London W2 4AB
Telephone: 071-229 5079/221 1452   *Fax:* 071-229 1210   **£50**
Open: lunch Mon-Fri, dinner Mon-Sat (closed Bank Holidays)
Last orders: lunch 2.30pm, dinner 11.30pm

A grey awning with Veronica Shaw's name emblazoned across it
heralds your arrival, and the colour scheme inside is also grey –
mottled on the walls, lightened with bright yellow trimmings and blue
and white striped tablecloths. There's a frequently changing range of
pictures for sale.
    The menu at Veronica's changes monthly and is themed, so that in
November it was 'gunpowder, treason and plot', using 17th-century
recipes. The menu even incorporated a 'newsletter' of the era,
featuring that novelty food item, the potato! Dishes are annotated as
being of a high fibre, low fat or vegan nature, so that you might
choose a salamagundy – a high fibre salad of lettuce, spinach,
watercress, herbs, currants, olives, capers, beetroot, almonds,
gherkins and radishes, tossed in walnut oil and vinegar, or fresh
lemon and cayenne dressing as a low fat version. A main course in the
same category was beef casserole with almonds and grapes,
attributed to Hannah Woolley, likewise the vegetarian option: a rich
barley pot of barley, thyme, sage, raisins and root vegetables, with a
touch of sherry and rosewater. For pudding, try orange butter of
1683 and pineapple sticks – a sabayon of orange, eggs and honey with
sticks of pineapple to dip. (Pineapples were first imported to this
country in the 17th Century.) A concise wine list is very reasonably
priced, and includes an organic cognac!

VERY SIMPLY NICO   London SW1

48a Rochester Row, London SW1 1PJ
Telephone: 071-630 8061   **£55**
Open: lunch Mon-Fri, dinner Mon-Sat (closed Easter, 3 wks summer,
        10 days Christmas)
Last orders: lunch 2.15pm, dinner 11.00pm

Nico Lademis has moved Andrew Jeffs, his second chef at Chez Nico,
to head the team at his bistro. A refurbishment has also made
concessions – the plastic cloths being replaced by linen. Warm potato
salad with cod and mayonnaise, chicken and mushroom vol-au-vent –
reports say that the standard of cooking has gone up a notch.

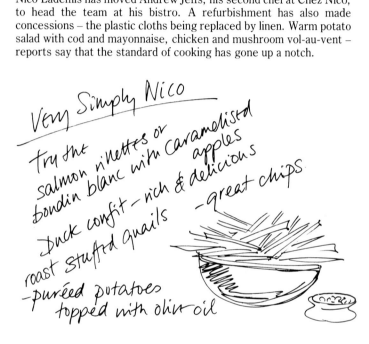

Very Simply Nico

try the salmon rillettes or boudin blanc with caramelised apples

Duck confit – rich & delicious

roast stuffed quails – great chips

– puréed potatoes topped with olive oil

VILLAGE TAVERNA   London SW10

196-198 Fulham Road, London SW10
Telephone: 071-351 3799   **£40**
Open: dinner daily (closed 4 days Christmas)
Last orders: dinner 1.00am

Still my favourite local Greek, family run, good value for money, a
place to relax. Yannis and Christine have been in Fulham Road for
sixteen years now – fifteen years ago Christine stepped into the
kitchen to help out on a particularly busy night, found that she liked
being there and the customers liked her food, and there she has been
ever since. Long may she continue there. You don't have to have the
kleftiko (although I invariably do) as they have the full range of Greek
favourites (sheftalia, souvlakia, lamb fasolaki or bizeli, avgolemono,
grilled haloumi), and kateifi or baklava to go with your coffee. A lively
atmosphere.

WALTONS   London SW3

121 Walton Street, Chelsea, London SW3 2HP
Telephone: 071-584 0204   *Fax:* 071-581 2848   **£100**
Open: lunch + dinner daily (closed Christmas Day + Boxing Day)
Last orders: lunch 2.30pm (2.00pm Sun), dinner 11.30pm (10.00pm Sun)

This long-established restaurant has undergone a complete overhaul,
with a new chef and new decor – but the luxurious style of the yellow
and grey decor remains. Service is now more professional and does
justice to the accomplished cooking of Paul Hodgson. The new menu
mixes traditional with some more creative dishes such as our
enjoyable breast of duck with a honey flavoured armagnac sauce,
served on hazelnut flavoured noodles. The after-theatre supper, at
£19.50 for two courses with coffee, and the traditional Sunday lunch,
at £16.50 for three courses with coffee, remain excellent value.
Classic wine list.

WILTONS   London SW1

53 Jermyn Street, London SW1Y 6LX
Telephone: 071-629 9955   **£65**
Open: lunch Mon-Fri, dinner Mon-Sat (closed Bank Holidays)
Last orders: lunch 2.15pm, dinner 10.15pm

Wiltons' many regulars appreciate the restrained, formal service and
traditional straightforward cooking. You'll find oysters, in season,
lobster, salmon and Dover sole (best simply prepared, as is the
traditionally roasted seasonal game). High prices accentuate the
clubby atmosphere and decor. This is a popular spot with Cabinet
Ministers: I wonder if the new regime will join the club?

WODKA RESTAURANT — London W8

12 St Alban's Grove, London W8 5PN
Telephone: 071-937 6513   **£45**
Open: lunch Mon-Fri, dinner daily (closed Bank Holidays)
Last orders: lunch 2.30pm, dinner 11.00pm

Wodka is a small restaurant just south of Kensington High Street, and the owners are keen to point out that they are a restaurant that happens to serve Polish food, as opposed to being a Polish restaurant. In effect they take basic Polish or other Eastern European ingredients and adapt them to more Western tastes. The menu offers, as starters, barszcz, herring fillets with dill pickles, apple and sour cream, pierogi filled with sauerkraut and mushrooms, and of course blinis topped with herring, smoked salmon, aubergine mousse, cream cheese and herbs, or caviar (beluga or keta). Main courses are equally substantial – stuffed cabbage, kulebiak, shashlik with kasza, venison with a mixed berry sauce. The wine list covers France, the New World and Chile (amongst other countries), but not surprisingly the main items on the list are the flavoured vodkas – cherry, bison grass, lemon, or warm honey being the most popular.

ZUMA — London SW3

Chelsea Cloisters, Sloane Avenue, London SW3
Telephone: 071-225 1048/9   *Fax:* 071-581 3259   **£45**
Open: lunch + dinner daily (closed 3 dys Christmas)
Last orders: lunch 3.00pm (3.30pm Sat + Sun), dinner 11.30pm

Zuma aims to provide contemporary, mostly American, food at reasonable prices and also doubles as a gallery for young artists' work (photographs from the Special Photographers' Company, art prints from the Delisle Gallery). The glass-fronted ground floor area allows ample scope for the see-and-be-seen elements of its clientele. The food is in keeping with the setting, leaning towards California but with tastes from Tuscany too. It includes, as starters, roasted pepper soup with sour cream and chilli, carpaccio of beef with a cèpe confit and shaved parmesan, deep fried squid with salsa verde, spicy crabcakes with herb mayonnaise, black pepper pappardelle with wild mushrooms, chives and crème fraîche, white and dark chocolate truffle for dessert.

London Listings

The Abbey Court Hotel
20 Pembridge Gardens, London W2 4DU
Tel: 071-221 7518   *Fax:* 071-792 0858
Open: 24-hour room service
One of the first no-restaurant luxury hotels
in London.

Al Bustan
27 Motcomb Street, London SW1X 8JU
Tel: 071-235 8277   **£60**
Open: lunch + dinner daily
Last orders: lunch 2.30pm, dinner 11.00pm
Delicious Lebanese food in light and airy
surroundings.

Al San Vincenzo
30 Connaught Street, London W2
Tel: 071-262 9623
Open: please ring for details
Last orders: please ring for details
London opening as we go to press for
Vincenzo and Elaine Borgonzola's Italian
restaurant, moving into town from
Cheam.

Andrew Edmunds Wine Bar
46 Lexington Street, London W1R 3LH
Tel: 071-437 5708   **£45**
Open: lunch + dinner Mon-Fri (closed Christmas)
Last orders: lunch 2.45pm, dinner 10.45pm
Candles in bottles on bare wooden tables;
mainly young regulars; simple food; new
chef (Paul Croal). Good atmosphere.

The Archduke Wine Bar
Concert Hall Approach, South Bank,
London SE1 8XU
Tel: 071-928 9370   **£50**
Open: lunch Mon-Fri, dinner Mon-Sat (closed Bank
Holidays)
Last orders: lunch 2.15pm, dinner 10.45pm
Elizabeth Philip's useful wine bar at the
South Bank. Cuisine bourgeoise, lively
atmosphere.

Athenaeum Hotel
116 Piccadilly, London W1V 0BJ
Tel: 071-499 3464   *Fax:* 071-493 1860   **£70**
Open: lunch + dinner daily
Last orders: lunch 3.00pm, dinner 10.30pm
Luxurious West End hotel, elegant fur-
nishings, attentive service in the res-
taurant, 112 bedrooms.

Au Bois St Jean
122 St John's Wood High Street, London NW8 7SG
Tel: 071-722 0400   **£40**
Open: lunch + dinner daily (closed Christmas Day
+ Boxing Day)
Last orders: lunch 2.30pm, dinner 11.30pm
Traditional and modern French cooking,
long established local restaurant.

Auntie's
126 Cleveland Street, London W1
Tel: 071-387 1548   **£50**
Open: lunch Mon-Fri, dinner Mon-Sat (closed
Christmas, 2 wks Aug)
Last orders: lunch 2.30pm, dinner 11.00pm
British cooking: as we went to press, Shaun
Thompson was back here after a spell at
Jason Court Restaurant.

Bahn Thai
21a Frith Street, London W1V 5TS
Tel: 071-437 8504   **£35**
Open: lunch + dinner daily (closed some Bank
Holidays)
Last orders: lunch 2.45pm (2.30pm Sun), dinner
11.15pm (10.45pm Sun)
One of the earliest and remaining one of the
best Thai restaurants. Fish and shellfish
are their strength, decor and service
comes second.

Beau Rivage
228 Belsize Road, London NW6 4BT
Tel: 071-328 9992   **£45**
Open: dinner Mon-Sat (closed 2 wks Aug)
Last orders: dinner 11.30pm
Leisurely Mauritian seafood restaurant.

The Bengal Lancer
253 Kentish Town Road, London NW5 2JT
Tel: 071-485 6688   *Fax.* 071-482 5423   **£30**
Open: lunch Sun-Fri, dinner daily (closed
Christmas)
Last orders: lunch 3.00pm, dinner midnight
(12.30am Sat)
Cheerfully inauthentic local Indian res-
taurant with a decor of simulated colonial-
ism. Good fun.

Bentley's in the City
11 Queen Victoria Street, London EC4N 4UJ
Tel: 071-489 8067   *Fax:* 071-248 5145   **£60**
Open: lunch + dinner Mon-Fri
Last orders: lunch (restaurant) 2.30pm, dinner
(champagne & oyster bar) 8.30pm
City branch of famous West End fish and
seafood establishment.

The Berkeley
Wilton Place, London SW1X 7RL
Tel: 071-235 6000   *Fax:* 071-235 4300   **£70**
Open: lunch + dinner daily (closed Restaurant
lunch Sat, Buttery dinner Sun)
Last orders: lunch 2.30pm (2.45pm Sat, 2.15pm
Sun), dinner 10.45pm (11.15pm Sat, 10.15pm
Sun)
Modern hotel with a country house feel,
luxurious and elegant restaurant, 160
bedrooms.

Bintang
93 Kentish Town Road, London NW1
Tel: 071-284 1640   **£25**
Open: lunch Thu + Fri, dinner daily
Last orders: lunch 2.30pm, dinner midnight
A small, family-run Malaysian restaurant,
moderately priced, specialising in seafood
and excelling in vegetable dishes.

Bloom's
130 Golders Green Road, London NW11 8HB
Tel: 081-455 1338   **£40**
Open: dinner Sun-Thu (closed Bank Holidays,
    Jewish Holidays)
Last orders: dinner 9.30pm
Kosher restaurant, eternally popular.

Bloom's
90 Whitechapel High Street, London E1 7RA
Tel: 071-247 6001   **£40**
Open: all day, Sun-Fri (closed Bank Holidays,
    Jewish Holidays)
Last orders: 9.30pm (2.00pm Fri in winter, 3.00pm
    Fri in summer)
The other branch of the same long-serving
    family-run restaurant.

The Blue Elephant
4-6 Fulham Broadway, London SW6 1AA
Tel: 071-385 6595   *Fax:* 071-386 7665   **£55**
Open: lunch Sun-Fri, dinner daily (closed 3 dys
    Christmas)
Last orders: lunch 2.30pm, dinner 12.30am
    (10.30pm Sun)
Astonishing decor, practically a complete
    Thai village with huts, streams, jungles
    and bridges. Flamboyant food and prices.

Bombay Brasserie
Bailey's Hotel, Courtfield Close, London SW7 4QH
Tel: 071-370 4040   **£60**
Open: lunch + dinner daily (closed 2 dys
    Christmas)
Last orders: lunch 2.30pm, dinner 11.30pm
The glories of the Raj made manifest: an
    astounding looking restaurant with huge
    conservatory. Regional specialities which
    make up the menu are prepared with
    varying degrees of success.

Boucha's
3 North End Parade, North End Road,
    London W14
Tel: 071-603 0613   **£45**
Open: dinner Mon-Sat (closed Bank Holidays)
Last orders: dinner 11.00pm
Careful, bistro-style cooking. Friendly staff,
    only twenty-four covers.

Boyd's Glass Garden Restaurant
135 Kensington Church Street, London W8 7LP
Tel: 071-727 5452   **£55**
Open: lunch + dinner Mon-Fri (closed 1 wk
    Christmas)
Last orders: lunch 2.30pm, dinner 10.30pm
Pretty conservatory-style restaurant, mod-
    ern English food.

La Brasserie Highgate
1 Hampstead Lane, London N6 4RS
Tel: 081-341 9736   **£45**
Open: lunch + dinner daily (closed Christmas Day)
Last orders: lunch 3.30pm, dinner midnight
Highgate branch of the Fulham Road
    original.

Brinkley's Champagne Bar
17c Curzon Street, London W1Y 7FE
Tel: 071-493 4490   **£55**
Open: all day, Mon-Fri (closed Bank Holidays)
Last orders: midnight
Up-market Mayfair wine bar and res-
    taurant.

Bu San
43 Holloway Road, London N7
Tel: 071-607 8264   **£20**
Open: lunch Tue-Sat, dinner daily
Last orders: lunch 3.00pm, dinner 11.00pm
Tiny (six tables) family-run Korean res-
    taurant with great charm. Long Korean
    menu divided by cooking methods. The
    stir-fries are particularly good. Also some
    Japanese dishes at less than Japanese
    restaurant prices.

Burt's
42 Dean Street, London W1V 5AP
Tel: 071-439 0972   **£55**
Open: lunch Mon-Fri, dinner Mon-Sat (closed Bank
    Holidays)
Last orders: lunch 2.30pm, dinner 11.30pm
Particularly strong on vegetarian food; cool,
    modern decor.

Café des Amis du Vin
11-14 Hanover Place, London WC2
Tel: 071-379 3444   **£60**
Open: lunch + dinner Mon-Sat (closed 1 wk
    Christmas)
Last orders: lunch 3.00pm, dinner 11.30pm (wine
    bar open all day to 11.00pm)
Popular Covent Garden venue, French food
    and wine.

Café Delancey
32 Proctor Street, Red Lion Square, London WC1
Tel: 071-242 6691   *Fax:* 071-383 5314   **£40**
Open: all day, daily (closed some Bank Holidays)
Last orders: 11.30pm
Useful brasserie, offshoot of the Camden
    original.

Café Pelican
45 St Martin's Lane, London WC2N 4EJ
Tel: 071-379 0309   **£45**
Open: all day, daily (closed 1 wk Christmas)
Last orders: 11.30pm (snacks till 1.00am)
Large, busy French-style brasserie, useful
    for a snack and a glass of wine, especially
    pre- or post-theatre or cinema.

La Cage Imaginaire
16 Flask Walk, London NW3 1HE
Tel: 071-794 6674   **£45**
Open: lunch + dinner Tue-Sun (closed Bank
    Holidays)
Last orders: lunch 2.30pm, dinner 11.00pm
    (11.30pm Sat)
Traditional and modern French cooking,
    small popular local restaurant.

Camden Brasserie
216 Camden High Street, Camden Town,
    London NW1
Tel: 071-482 2114   **£40**
Open: lunch + dinner daily (closed 3 dys
    Christmas)
Last orders: lunch 3.00pm, dinner 11.30pm
    (10.30pm) Sun
Owned, together with the Underground
    Café next door, by Sue Miles and Nigel
    Richardson. Friendly atmosphere.

The Canal Brasserie

Canalot Studios, 222 Kensal Road,
London W10 5BN
Tel: 081-960 2732 **£40**
Open: all day, Mon-Sat + lunch Sun
Last orders: lunch 2.30pm, brasserie 11.00pm
Brasserie in a converted chocolate factory!
Menus of modern European food change
regularly.

Le Carapace

118 Heath Street, London NW3 1DR
Tel: 071-435 8000 **£50**
Open: lunch Sun, dinner daily
Last orders: lunch 3.30pm, dinner 11.00pm
(10.30pm) Sun
Set menus at £19.95 or £30.00 for six
courses of modern regional French food.
Friendly, local restaurant.

Caravan Serai

50 Paddington Street, London W1M 3RQ
Tel: 071-935 1208 **£40**
Open: lunch Mon-Sat, dinner daily (closed
Christmas Day + Boxing Day)
Last orders: lunch 2.30pm, dinner 10.30pm
Afghan food, resembling Nepalese in its
spicing and the first course dumplings.
Middle Eastern in its reliance on flat
breads.

Casa Natalina

44 Forest Hill Road, London SE22 0RS
Tel: 081-599 2211 **£30**
Open: dinner Mon-Sat (closed Bank Holidays,
2 wks Aug)
Last orders: dinner 10.45pm (11.00pm Sat)
Recently opened traditional Italian
restaurant, specialising in pasta.

Chada Thai Cuisine

208-210 Battersea Park Road, London SW11
Tel: 071-622 2209 **£30**
Open: lunch Mon-Fri, dinner Mon-Sat
Last orders: lunch 2.30pm, dinner 11.00pm
(11.30pm Fri + Sat)
Some interesting steamed dishes differenti-
ate this neat and pretty Thai restaurant
from many others in South London.

Charbar

2a Pond Place, London SW3 6QJ
Tel: 071-584 4555 **£50**
Open: all day, daily (closed 4 dys Christmas)
Last orders: midnight
Do-it-yourself char-grills in plant-filled sur-
roundings.

Chesterfield Hotel

35 Charles Street, London W1X 8LX
Tel: 071-491 2622 **£60**
Open: lunch + dinner daily
Last orders: lunch 2.00pm, dinner 10.30pm
(10.00pm Sun)
Club-like feel in the public rooms, light and
airy Terrace restaurant, 113 bedrooms.

Chez Solange

35 Cranbourne Street, London WC2H 7AD
Tel: 071-836 5886 **£40**
Open: lunch + dinner Mon-Sat (closed Bank
Holidays)
Last orders: lunch 3.15pm, dinner 12.15am
Long-established French restaurant.

Chez Gerard

31 Dover Street, London W1
Tel: 071-499 8171 **£55**
Open: lunch + dinner Mon-Sat (closed Bank
Holidays)
Last orders: lunch 2.45pm, dinner 11.30pm
Perennial French restaurant, traditional
cooking.

Chez Liline

101 Stroud Green Road, London N4 3PX
Tel: 071-263 6550 **£60**
Open: lunch + dinner Mon-Sat (closed Bank
Holidays)
Last orders: lunch 3.00pm, dinner 11.00pm
Mauritian seafood restaurant.

Chiang Mai

48 Frith Street, London W1V 5TE
Tel: 071-437 7444 **£35**
Open: lunch + dinner daily
Last orders: lunch 3.00pm, dinner 11.00pm
Food from the Northern provinces of Thai-
land with specialities of the long-cooked
dishes and spicy sausage. Service can
give you short shrift.

Cho Won

27 Romilly Street, London W1 5PQ
Tel: 071-437 2262 **£40**
Open: lunch + dinner Mon-Sat
Last orders: lunch 3.00pm, dinner 11.00pm
Friendly Soho Korean restaurant with a
karaoke machine on the first floor. Set
lunches are a bargain.

Christopher's American Grill

14 Garrick Street, London WC2E 9BJ
Tel: 071-836 6456 **£00**
Open: please phone for details
Last orders: please phone for details
New opening after our press deadline on
the site of former Inigo Jones – char-grills
a speciality.

Chutney Mary

535 King's Road, London SW10
Tel: 071-351 3113 **£50**
Open: lunch + dinner daily
Last orders: lunch 2.30pm (4.00pm Sun), dinner
11.30pm (10.00pm Sun)
Meticulously researched Anglo-Indian
dishes plus regional specialities cooked
by chefs brought direct from India: curried nostalgia.

Chutneys

124 Drummond Street, London NW1
Tel: 071-388 0604 **£25**
Open: lunch + dinner daily
Last orders: lunch 2.45pm, dinner 11.30pm
Slick outlet for Indian vegetarian food.
Amazingly good value buffet.

Ciao

222 Munster Road, London SW6 6AY
Tel: 071-381 6137 **£40**
Open: lunch + dinner daily (closed Bank Holidays
+ Sun before, 3 dys Christmas) (open for
snacks all day, daily)
Last orders: lunch 3.15pm, dinner 11.00pm
(10.30pm Sun)
Another branch of Mark Milton's Depot
group of café/brasseries.

City Limits Restaurant & Wine Bar
16-18 Brushfield Street, Spitalfields,
London E1 6AN
Tel: 071-377 9877 **£50**
Open: lunch Mon-Fri (closed Bank Holidays, 1 wk
Christmas)
Last orders: lunch 3.00pm (wine bar open to
11.30pm daily)
Home-made gravadlax, char-grilled steaks
and fish in cosy basement restaurant.

City Brasserie
Plantation House, 9A/9B Mincing Lane,
London EC3M 3DX
Tel: 071-220 7094 **£55**
Open: lunch + dinner Mon-Fri (closed Christmas
Eve to 2 Jan)
Last orders: lunch 3.00pm, dinner 9.00pm
Popular venue, exactly what it says it is!

Classic Thai
111 Turnpike Lane, London N8
Tel: 081-340 6590 **£30**
Open: dinner daily
Last orders: dinner 11.00pm
This North London local restaurant stands
out for the quality of the Thai food at
reasonable cost and the classicism of the
decor.

Connolly's Restaurant
162 Lower Richmond Road,
London SW15 1LY
Tel: 081-788 3844 **£50**
Open: lunch daily, dinner Mon-Sat (closed Bank
Holidays)
Last orders: lunch 2.30pm (4.00pm Sun), dinner
10.30pm
Eamonn Connolly's modern British cooking,
sister Kate's charming service.

La Croisette
168 Ifield Road, London SW10 9AF
Tel: 071-373 3694 **£60**
Open: lunch Wed-Sun, dinner Tue-Sun
Last orders: lunch 2.30pm, dinner 11.30pm
Another of Pierre Martin's popular chain of
fish restaurants.

Dan's Restaurant & Garden
119 Sydney Street, London SW3 6NR
Tel: 071-352 2718 **£60**
Open: lunch Mon-Fri, dinner Mon-Sat (closed Bank
Holidays, 1 wk Christmas)
Last orders: lunch 2.15pm, dinner 11.00pm
Competent cooking; friendly service;
bright, fresh ambience; garden eating in
summer.

Deals West Restaurant Diner
14/16 Fouberts Place, London W1
Tel: 071-287 1001 **£50**
Open: all day, daily
Last orders: 11.30pm (12.30am Fri + Sat, 10.00pm
Sun)
Another branch of Eddie Lim and Viscount
Linley's popular Chelsea diner.

Dragon Inn
63 Westbourne Grove, London W2 4UA
Tel: 071-229 8806 **£30**
Open: dinner daily
Last orders: dinner 11.30pm
The same menu as the Gerrard Street
branch in a more elegant setting, with the
same high standards of food. Stuffed duck
with yam and quick-fried squid with dried
squid are notable.

Dragon Inn
12 Gerrard Street, London W1
Tel: 071-494 0870 **£25**
Open: dinner daily
Last orders: dinner 11.30pm
London's best dim sum. Excellent, authentically earthy Cantonese cooking. Try the
tripe dishes or the pig's trotter with
braised noodles. Service variable.

Dragon's Nest
58-60 Shaftesbury Avenue, London W1
Tel: 071-437 3119 **£35**
Open: lunch + dinner daily (open all day Sat + Sun)
Last orders: lunch 3.00pm, dinner 11.30pm
London's only Chinese restaurant specialising in Taiwanese cooking rather than the
usual Cantonese. Ask the staff's help in
ordering unfamiliar dishes and Taiwanese
dumplings and breads. Gaudy decor.

Eleven Park Walk Restaurant
11 Park Walk, London SW10 0AJ
Tel: 071-352 3449 **£55**
Open: lunch + dinner Mon-Sat (closed Bank
Holidays)
Last orders: lunch 3.00pm, dinner midnight
Friendly service, classic Italian food, cool
modern decor.

Emile's
144 Wandsworth Bridge Road,
London SW6 2UH
Tel: 071-736 2418 **£45**
Open: dinner Mon-Sat (closed Bank Holidays)
Last orders: dinner 11.00pm
The original Emile's, a popular local res-
taurant. Good value, French/English
cooking, warm greeting, friendly service.

Emile's
96/98 Felsham Road, London SW15 1DQ
Tel: 081-789 3323 **£45**
Open: dinner Mon-Sat (closed Bank Holidays)
Last orders: dinner 11.00pm
The second branch of Emile's.

Equities Restaurant
1 Finsbury Avenue, London EC2M 2PA
Tel: 071-247 1051 **£55**
Open: lunch Mon-Fri (closed Bank Holidays)
Last orders: lunch 3.00pm
Sister restaurant to Shares. City clientele,
good cheeses.

The Fenja
69 Cadogan Gardens, London SW3 2RB
Tel: 071-589 7333 *Fax:* 071-581 4958
Victorian house converted into a smart,
comfortable hotel. Residents enjoy access to Cadogan Gardens. Thirteen bedrooms, no restaurant.

La Fin de la Chasse
176 Stoke Newington Church Street,
London N16 0JL
Tel: 071-254 5975 **£40**
Open: lunch + dinner Tue-Sat (closed Bank
Holidays, 2 wks Christmas, 1 wk Easter, 2 wks
Aug)
Last orders: lunch 2.00pm, dinner 10.30pm
Booking essential for French provincial
cooking at this local restaurant.

Fortyseven Park Street
47 Park Street, London W1Y 4EB
Tel: 071-491 7282   *Fax:* 071-491 7291
Fifty-two beautifully appointed suites, part
of the Rouxs 'empire', food brought in
from Le Gavroche. Welcome includes
champagne. Business facilities available
7.00am to 11.00pm.

Fung Shing
15 Lisle Street, London WC2
Tel: 071-437 1539 **£35**
Open: all day, daily (closed 3 dys Christmas)
Last orders: 11.30pm
The favourite amongst most of London's
Chinese population. Consistently excel-
lent Cantonese cuisine and friendly staff.
Order barbecue beef, a hot-pot dish and
any of the special dishes on the menu.

Gardners Restaurant
156 Chiswick High Road, London W4 1PR
Tel: 081-995 1656 **£35**
Open: lunch Sun, dinner Tue-Sun
Last orders: lunch 2.00pm, dinner 11.00pm
(10.30pm) Sun
Unpretentious ground floor restaurant
using free-range, organic and 'real' produce. Bistro in the basement.

Garuda Restaurant
150 Shaftesbury Avenue, London WC2
Tel: 071-836 2644 **£30**
Open: lunch Mon-Sat, dinner daily
Last orders: lunch 2.30pm, dinner 11.30pm
A popular Indonesian restaurant with modern decor, useful in theatreland. The
rijstafel (rice table) is a good way to
sample a range of dishes.

La Gaulette
53 Cleveland Street, London W1P 5PQ
Tel: 071-580 7608 **£60**
Open: lunch Mon-Fri, dinner Mon-Sat (closed Bank
Holidays)
Last orders: lunch 3.00pm, dinner 11.00pm
Another of Sylvain Cheong's Mauritian sea-
food restaurants.

Gavins
5 Lacy Road, London SW15 1HN
Tel: 081-785 9151 **£40**
Open: lunch + dinner daily (closed Bank Holidays)
Last orders: lunch 3.00pm, dinner 11.00pm (open
for snacks all day, daily)
A third Mark Milton café/brasserie, just off
Putney's new shopping centre.

Geale's
2 Farmer Street, London W8 7SN
Tel: 071-727 7969   *Fax:* 071-229 8632 **£40**
Open: lunch + dinner Tue-Sat (closed Bank
Holidays + following Tue, 2 wks Christmas, 1
wk Easter, 2 wks Aug)
Last orders: lunch 3.00pm, dinner 11.00pm
Long-established, very popular fish and chip
restaurant.

Glaister's Garden Restaurant
4 Hollywood Road, London SW10 9HW
Tel: 071-352 0352 **£45**
Open: lunch + dinner daily (closed Bank Holidays,
1 wk Christmas)
Last orders: lunch 3.00pm (4.00pm Sat + Sun),
dinner 11.45pm (10.30pm Sun)
Modern European cooking, large patio
garden.

Gonbei
151 King's Cross Road, London WC1X 9BN
Tel: 071-278 0619 **£30**
Open: dinner Mon-Sat (closed Bank Holidays, 1 wk
Jan, 1 wk Aug)
Last orders: dinner 10.30pm
Small, easy-going Japanese restaurant/sushi
bar frequented and staffed by the young.

Good Food Chinese Restaurant
8 Little Newport Street, London WC2 7JJ
Tel: 071-734 2130 **£30**
Open: all evening and night, daily (closed Christmas
Eve + Christmas Day)
Last orders: 4.30am
Accurately named, tiny Cantonese res-
taurant with Hakka specialities and many
unusual dishes. Worth ordering are the
New Zealand green-lipped mussels in
black bean sauce, and the fish and
shellfish dishes. Helpful service.

Gopal's of Soho
12 Bateman Street, London W1V 5TD
Tel: 071-434 0840 **£30**
Open: lunch + dinner daily (closed Christmas Day
+ Boxing Day)
Last orders: lunch 3.00pm, dinner 11.30pm
(11.00pm Sun)
Indian owner/chef with a CV that includes
the Red Fort and Lal Qila. Soft pink
surroundings. Dum (hot-pot) cooking is a
strength.

The Goring Hotel
17 Beeston Place, Grosvenor Gardens,
London SW1W 0JW
Tel: 071-834 8211   *Fax:* 071-834 4393 **£60**
Open: lunch Sun-Fri, dinner daily
Last orders: lunch 2.30pm, dinner 10.00pm
Mr Goring's hotel was, in 1910, the first to
offer private bathrooms and central heat-
ing. Still in the same family, still the same
high standard. Eighty-six bedrooms.

The Grafton Francais
45 Old Town, London SW4 0JL
Tel: 071-627 1048 **£55**
Open: lunch Tue-Fri + Sun, dinner Tue-Sat (closed
Bank Holidays, 1 wk Christmas, 3 wks Aug)
Last orders: lunch 2.30pm (3.00pm Sun), dinner
11.30pm
French cooking, unpretentious surround-
ings. Good value lunches.

Great Nepalese
48 Eversholt Street, London NW1
Tel: 071-388 6737 **£30**
Open: lunch + dinner daily
Last orders: lunch 2.30pm, dinner 11.15pm
Good use of pulses, dried and pickled vegetables, dumplings and combative cuts of meat typical of Nepalese food. Friendly staff.

Green Cottage
9 New College Parade, Finchley Road, London NW3
Tel: 071-722 5305 **£25**
Open: all day, daily
Last orders: 11.30pm
Inexpensive neighbourhood Cantonese restaurant with Chinatown quality cooking. Excellent roast duck and pork, and one-dish meals and vegetarian dishes. Free tea.

Green's Restaurant & Oyster Bar
Marsham Court, Marsham Street, London SW1P 4LA
Tel: 071-834 9552 *Fax:* 071-233 6047 **£55**
Open: lunch Mon-Fri, dinner Mon-Sat (closed Christmas)
Last orders: lunch 3.00pm, dinner 11.00pm
The former Locket's, now part of Simon Parker Bowles' clubby seafood empire.

Greig's Restaurant
5 White Hart Lane, London SW13 0PX
Tel: 081-876 3335 **£40**
Open: lunch Tue-Fri + Sun, dinner daily (closed Christmas/New Year)
Last orders: lunch 2.30pm (3.30pm Sun), dinner 11.00pm
English menu at this local restaurant near the river.

Guernica
21a Foley Street, London W1P 7LA
Tel: 071-580 0623 **£35**
Open: lunch Mon-Fri, dinner Mon-Sat (closed Bank Holidays, 2 wks Aug)
Last orders: lunch 2.45pm, dinner 10.45pm
Spanish/Basque restaurant offering good value for money.

Gurkha Brasserie
756 Finchley Road, London NW1
Tel: 081-458 6163 **£25**
Open: lunch Sat + Sun, dinner daily
Last orders: lunch 2.30pm, dinner 12.30am
Small, chummy local Indian restaurant notable for its Nepalese dishes including momo, chow chow and tender spiced chicken livers.

The Halkin Hotel
5-6 Halkin Street, London SW1X 7DJ
Tel: 071-333 1000 *Fax:* 071-333 1100 **£100**
Open: lunch + dinner daily
Last orders: lunch 3.00pm, dinner 11.00pm
As we went to press the Halkin had not yet opened, but it was due to do so by publication time. Chef is Paul Gayler, formerly of the much-vaunted Inigo Jones in Covent Garden.

L'Hippocampe
63 Frith Street, London W1V 5TA
Tel: 071-734 4545 **£50**
Open: lunch Mon-Fri, dinner Mon-Sat (closed Bank Holidays, 10 dys Christmas/New Year)
Last orders: lunch 3.00pm, dinner midnight
A new location for this fish restaurant, formerly in Fulham.

Hoizin
72-73 Wilton Road, London SW1
Tel: 071-630 5107 **£45**
Open: lunch + dinner daily
Last orders: lunch 2.30pm, dinner 11.30pm
The management owns a fishmonger's in Chinatown, and fish is the thing to order at this severely decorated Chinese restaurant. Green Jade Delight, a mixture of fish, shellfish, water chestnuts and bamboo shoots that you wrap in lettuce leaves is an exemplary dish.

Ikkyu
67 Tottenham Court Road, London W1
Tel: 071-636 9280 **£30**
Open: lunch Mon-Sat, dinner daily (closed 10 dys Christmas)
Last orders: lunch 2.30pm, dinner 11.30pm
Busy basement restaurant with home-style Japanese food at unusually reasonable prices. Set lunches a bargain.

Jacques
130 Blackstock Road, London N4 2DX
Tel: 071-359 3410 **£60**
Open: lunch Sat + Sun, dinner daily (closed Bank Holidays, 10 dys Christmas, 2 wks Aug)
Last orders: lunch 2.45pm Sat, 2.30pm Sun, dinner 11.00pm
Jacques Herbert's French restaurant, opera in the background, good wines.

Jade Garden
15 Wardour Street, London W1
Tel: 071-437 5065 **£35**
Open: all day daily
Last orders: 11.30pm
Very good dim sum and other Cantonese dishes but service is variable.

Jamdani
34 Charlotte Street, London W1P 1HJ
Tel: 071-636 1178 **£50**
Open: lunch + dinner daily (closed Christmas Day + Boxing Day)
Last orders: lunch 2.45pm, dinner 11.30pm
The chic design (by Rodney Fitch Associates) and the regional food compete for attention. Good vegetable dishes.

Jashan
19 Turnpike Lane, London N8
Tel: 081-340 9880 **£30**
Open: lunch + dinner daily
Last orders: lunch 2.30pm, dinner 11.30pm
Unusually good, painstaking Indian restaurant in the suburbs of North London.

Jason Court Restaurant
Jason Court, 76 Wigmore Street, London W1
Tel: 071-224 2992 **£60**
Open: lunch Mon-Fri, dinner Mon-Sat (closed Bank
Holidays, 2 wks Aug)
Last orders: lunch 2.30pm, dinner 10.30pm
Change of chef at this modern British
restaurant as we went to press – Stephen
Chamberlain still at front of house.

Jin
16 Bateman Street, London W1
Tel: 071-734 0908 **£45**
Open: lunch Mon-Sat, dinner daily
Last orders: lunch 3.00pm, dinner 11.30pm
Slightly more expensive and elegant than
neighbouring Soho Korean restaurants.
It is a good place to start an exploration of
this cuisine with its fiery pickles and
table-top barbecues.

Jin Kichi
73 Heath Street, London NW3
Tel: 071-794 6158 **£30**
Open: lunch Sat+Sun, dinner Tue-Mon
Last orders: lunch 2.30pm, dinner 11.30pm
A bustling yakitori bar with in addition a
comprehensive standard Japanese menu.
It has become a Hampstead hang-out.

Joe's Café
126 Draycott Avenue, London SW3 3AH
Tel: 071-225 2217 **£70**
Open: lunch daily, dinner Mon-Sat (closed 1 wk
Christmas)
Last orders: lunch 3.30pm, dinner 11.30pm (open
for snacks all day, Mon Sat)
Joseph Ettedgui's stylish café/restaurant
near many of his shops at Brompton
Cross.

John Howard Hotel
4 Queen's Gate, London SW7 5EH
Tel: 071-581 3011   *Fax:* 071-589 8403 **£60**
Open: lunch + dinner daily
Last orders: lunch 2.30pm, dinner 10.30pm
Comfortable Kensington hotel, modern
French cooking by Simon Gale.

Julie's
135 Portland Road, London W11 4LW
Tel: 071-229 8331 **£50**
Open: lunch Mon-Sat, dinner daily
Last orders: lunch 2.45pm, dinner 11.15pm
(10.15pm Sun)
Twenty-one years old and still going strong.

Kanishka
161 Whitfield Street, London W1P 5RY
Tel: 071-388 0860 **£30**
Open: lunch Mon-Fri, dinner daily (closed
Christmas)
Last orders: lunch 3.00pm, dinner midnight
(10.00pm Sun)
Ideal Indian restaurant for the carnivore and
vegetarian who wish to dine together.
Two kitchens supply the different modes.

Kaspia
18/18a Bruton Place, London W1X 7AH
Tel: 071-408 1627 **£70**
Open: lunch + dinner Mon-Sat (closed Bank
Holidays)
Last orders: lunch 2.30pm, dinner 11.30pm
Caviar restaurant and shop; also a branch in
Paris.

Khan's
13-15 Westbourne Grove, London W2 4UA
Tel: 071-727 5400 **£30**
Open: lunch + dinner daily
Last orders: lunch 2.30pm, dinner 11.30pm
Sound, inexpensive Indian food served in an
agreeably rackety atmosphere where
sharing tables is the norm.

Khun Akorn
136 Brompton Road, London SW3
Tel: 071-225 2688 **£40**
Open: lunch + dinner daily
Last orders: lunch 3.00pm (2.30pm Sun), dinner
11.00pm (10.30pm Sun)
Here you will find Royal Thai cuisine which
has a gastronomic definition beyond
hyperbole. Surroundings are somewhat
hotel lobby.

Kim Phuong
8 Rocks Lane, London SW13
Tel: 081-878 8105 **£35**
Open: lunch Tue-Sun, dinner Mon-Sat
Last orders: lunch 2.30pm, dinner 11.00pm
Named after the spritely owner, this stylish
Vietnamese restaurant is popular with
locals. The menu is of manageable size
and gives a good entrée into the cuisine.

Lahore Kebab House
2 Umberston Street, London E1
Tel: 071-437 2001 **£20**
Open: all day, daily
Last orders: 11.00pm
Imran Khan and many others gravitate to
this caff for freshly cooked kebabs and
karahi dishes and well-made breads and
salads.

Lal Qila
117 Tottenham Court Road, London W1P 9HL
Tel: 071-387 4570 **£35**
Open: lunch + dinner daily (closed Christmas Day
+ Boxing Day)
Last orders: lunch 2.45pm, dinner 11.15pm
Up-market Northern Indian restaurant
where they would like you to start with a
cocktail, but concentrate on the good
tandoori and karahi dishes.

Laurent Restaurant
428 Finchley Road, London NW2 2HY
Tel: 071-794 3603 **£35**
Open: lunch + dinner Mon-Sat (closed Bank
Holidays)
Last orders: lunch 2.00pm, dinner 11.00pm
Honest local restaurant, specialising in
cous-cous.

Lido
41 Gerrard Street, London W1
Tel: 071-437 4431   **£40**
Open: all day, daily
Last orders: 4.30am
Luxurious, spacious setting for Chinatown.
Good dim sum; stay with the Cantonese
dishes.

London Hilton on Park Lane
22 Park Lane, London W1A 2HH
Tel: 071-493 8000   *Fax:* 071-493 4957   **£100**
Open: lunch + dinner daily
Last orders: lunch 2.45pm, dinner 11.45pm
Windows on the World restaurant on the
28th floor enjoys splendid views. Also
Trader Vic's restaurant. 446 bedrooms.

Malaysia Hall Dining Hall
46 Bryanston Square, London W1H 8AJ
Tel: 071-723 9484   **£10**
Open: lunch + dinner daily
Last orders: lunch 2.30pm, dinner 9.00pm
A subsidised canteen offering authentic and
ridiculously cheap Malaysian food. Used
by Malaysian students but welcoming to
all.

Mandalay
100 Greenwich South Street, London SE10 8UN
Tel: 071-691 0443   **£35**
Open: lunch Sun, dinner Tue-Sat (closed Christmas
+ New Year)
Last orders: lunch 2.30pm, dinner 10.30pm
The only Burmese restaurant in Britain.
The dedicated owner and helpful staff
explain the similarities and contrasts with
other Oriental cuisines. Soup plays an
important role.

Manzi's
1/2 Leicester Square, London WC2H 7BC
Tel: 071-734 0224   **£55**
Open: lunch Mon-Sat, dinner daily (closed
Christmas Day, Boxing Day, Good Friday)
Last orders: lunch 2.30pm, dinner 11.30pm
Long-established fish and seafood res-
taurant, now with a branch also in Dock-
lands.

May Fair Inter-Continental Hotel
Stratton Street, London W1A 2AN
Tel: 071-629 7777   *Fax:* 071-629 1459   **£70**
Open: lunch Sun-Fri, dinner daily (closed Boxing
Day) (coffee shop open all day, daily)
Last orders: lunch 2.30pm, dinner 10.30pm
Luxurious hotel undergoing massive im-
provements. Michael Coaker cooks for
Le Château restaurant. Professional
service.

Mélange Restaurant
59 Endell Street, London WC2H 9AJ
Tel: 071-240 8077   *Fax:* 071-379 9129   **£40**
Open: lunch Mon-Fri, dinner Mon-Sat (closed Bank
Holidays, 1 wk Christmas)
Last orders: lunch 2.30pm, dinner 11.30pm
Bohemian Covent Garden restaurant, sim-
ple well cooked food.

Melati Restaurant
21 Great Windmill Street, London W1V TPH
Tel: 071-437 2745   **£35**
Open: open all day, daily
Last orders: 11.30pm
Long-serving, cheerful café serving authen-
tic Malaysian food with a large selection
of fish and vegetarian dishes.

Meson Dona Ana
37 Kensington Park Road, London W11 2EU
Tel: 071-243 0666   **£45**
Open: lunch Mon-Fri, dinner Mon-Sat (closed Bank
Holidays)
Last orders: lunch 3.00pm, dinner 11.00pm
The second of the Diments' tapas bars.

Methuselahs Wine Bar & Restaurant
29 Victoria Street, London SW1
Tel: 071-222 0424   **£50**
Open: lunch + dinner Mon-Fri
Last orders: lunch 2.45pm, dinner 11.00pm
Sophisticated wine bar menu.

Minang
11 Greek Street, London W1
Tel: 071-287 1408   **£40**
Open: lunch + dinner Mon-Sat
Last orders: lunch 3.00pm, dinner 11.30pm
Pretty, bright Indonesian/Malaysian res-
taurant with the same ownership as
Melati. Sweet service. Rijstafel (rice
table) provides an opportunity to sample
a wide range of dishes.

Ming
338 King's Road, London SW3 5ES
Tel: 071-352 0775   **£30**
Open: lunch + dinner daily (closed Bank Holidays,
4 dys Christmas)
Last orders: lunch 2.30pm (3.00pm Sun), dinner
11.00pm
Cool and elegant Chinese restaurant, good
value set meals.

Miyama
38 Clarges Street, London W1Y 7PJ
Tel: 071-499 2443   **£70**
Open: lunch Mon-Fri, dinner Mon-Sat (closed Bank
Holidays, Christmas/New Year)
Last orders: lunch 2.30pm, dinner 10.30pm
West End branch of this pair of Japanese
restaurants – calm, sophisticated, owner-
run with two teppan-yaki bars. One of the
best and one of the most beautiful ...

Miyama Japanese Restaurant
17 Godliman Street, London EC4V 5BD
Tel: 071-489 1937   **£70**
Open: lunch + dinner Mon-Fri (closed Bank
Holidays)
Last orders: lunch 2.30pm, dinner 10.00pm
. . . and its lovely City sister.

Mon Plaisir du Nord
Camden Passage, London N1
Tel: 071-359 1932   **£45**
Open: lunch Tue-Fri + Sun, dinner Tue-Sat
Last orders: lunch 2.15pm (3.00pm Sun), dinner
11.15pm
New branch of Alain Lhermitte's Mon
Plaisir.

Mon Plaisir

21 Monmouth Street, London WC2H 9DD
Tel: 071-836 7243   *Fax:* 071-379 0121   **£45**
Open: lunch Mon-Fri, dinner Mon-Sat (closed Bank
   Holidays)
Last orders: lunch 2.15pm, dinner 11.15pm
The original outlet for Alain Lhermitte's
   cooking.

Monkeys

1 Cale Street, London SW3
Tel: 071-352 4711   **£50**
Open: lunch + dinner daily (closed Christmas Day
   + Boxing Day, 1 wk Feb, 1 wk Aug)
Last orders: lunch 2.15pm, dinner 11.30pm
Good local restaurant, modern European
   food.

Morakot

11 Berwick Street, London W1V 3RG
Tel: 071-734 5300   **£30**
Open: lunch + dinner Mon-Sat
Last orders: lunch 3.00pm, dinner midnight
Authentic Thai food in peaceful, family-run
   restaurant bordering the Soho food
   market.

Mr Kong

2 Lisle Street, London WC2H 7BA
Tel: 071-437 7341   **£40**
Open: all day, daily
Last orders: 1.45am
Above average Cantonese restaurant with
   friendly service. Try the belly pork with
   preserved cabbage and the stuffed and
   fried bean curd.

The Museum Street Cafe

47 Museum Street, London WC1A 1LY
Tel: 071-405 3211   **£40**
Open: lunch + dinner daily (closed Bank Holidays,
   1 wk Christmas, 1 wk Easter)
Last orders: lunch 2.30pm, dinner 9.15pm
Useful location, appealing short menu,
   specialising in char-grills.

Mustards Smithfield Brasserie

60 Long Lane, London EC1A 9EJ
Tel: 071-796 4920   **£40**
Open: lunch + dinner Mon-Fri (closed Bank
   Holidays, Christmas/New Year)
Last orders: lunch 2.30pm, dinner 11.00pm
   (brasserie open all day, Mon-Fri)
Modern European cooking, useful hours
   include pre- and post-theatre menus.

Myung Ga

1 Kingly Street, London W1
Tel: 071-287 9768   **£45**
Open: lunch + dinner daily
Last orders: lunch 3.00pm, dinner 11.00pm
Young staff and quite elaborate decor
   seemingly based on the style of Charles
   Rennie Mackintosh coaxes this new
   Korean restaurant into the soi-disant
   trendiness of West Soho.

Nakano

11 Beauchamp Place, London SW3
Tel: 071-581 3837   **£60**
Open: lunch Tue-Sat, dinner Tue-Sun
Last orders: lunch 2.30pm., dinner 11.00pm
Is a jaded palate your problem? Try cuttle-
   fish marinated with its own gut and other
   arcane Japanese specialities at this allur-
   ing basement restaurant.

Nanten Yakitori Bar

6 Blandford Street, London W1
Tel: 071-935 6319   **£25**
Open: lunch Mon-Fri, dinner Mon-Sat
Last orders: lunch 2.30pm, dinner 10.30pm
The red lantern outside denotes the possi-
   bility of fast and inexpensive meals. Just
   such a thing is available at the long
   yakitori bar on the ground floor.

Neshiko

265 Upper Street, London N1 2UQ
Tel: 071-359 9977   **£40**
Open: lunch + dinner Mon-Fri (closed Bank
   Holidays)
Last orders: lunch 2.30pm, dinner 11.00pm
The Japanese owner is keen to explain the
   refinements of his country's cuisine to
   Westerners, from home cooking to
   elaborate banquets.

Nikita's

65 Ifield Road, London SW10 9AU
Tel: 071-352 6326   *Fax:* 081-993 3680   **£55**
Open: dinner Mon-Sat (closed Bank Holidays)
Last orders: dinner 11.30pm
Blinis and caviar, flavoured vodkas and jolly
   ambience in this basement restaurant.

Nusa Dua

11-12 Dean Street, London W1
Tel: 071-437 3559   **£35**
Open: lunch Mon-Fri, dinner Mon-Sat (closed Bank
   Holidays)
Last orders: lunch 2.30pm, dinner 11.30pm
Indonesian restaurant serving notably
   generous portions. The bean curd
   omelette is a must. Pleasant decor and
   charming service.

One Nine Two

192 Kensington Park Road, London W11 2JF
Tel: 071-229 0482   **£50**
Open: lunch daily, dinner Mon-Sat
Last orders: lunch 2.30pm, dinner 11.30pm
Daily changing menu at this friendly local
   restaurant.

Oriental Restaurant

The Dorchester Hotel, Park Lane, London W1
Tel: 071-629 8888   **£100**
Open: lunch + dinner Mon-Sat
Last orders: lunch 2.30pm, dinner 10.45pm
Consummately elegant and expensive
   Chinese restaurant. The Cantonese
   cooking here is on a par with Hong Kong.
   Dishes served separately adds to the
   stateliness of the occasion. Deep-fried
   duck with mashed taro, soya marinated
   beef shank, fried eel in cinnamon blossom
   sauce and the E-fu noodles are note-
   worthy.

Palio

175 Westbourne Grove, London W11 2FB
Tel: 071-221 6624 **£35**
Open: all day, daily
Last orders: 11.00pm
Modern Italian restaurant on a Sienese theme.

Park Inn

6 Wellington Terrace, Bayswater Road,
London W2
Tel: 071-229 3553 **£40**
Open: lunch + dinner daily
Last orders: lunch 2.30pm, dinner 11.30pm
Stylish, intimate Peking and Cantonese restaurant, strong on fish and seafood with many original specialities such as crab with green bean noodles in chilli hot pot and fried asparagus with prawn cake.

The Park Lane Hotel

Piccadilly, London W1Y 8BX
Tel: 071-499 6321 **£80**
Open: lunch Tue-Fri, dinner Mon-Sat (closed Bank Holidays)
Last orders: lunch 1.45pm, dinner 10.30pm (Brasserie open all day, daily)
Independent hotel, a 1920s' gem. Palm Court lounge, 323 bedrooms, Bracewells restaurant.

Pavilion

Finsbury Circus Gardens, London EC2M 7AB
Tel: 071-628 8224 *Fax:* 071-628 6205 **£55**
Open: lunch Mon-Fri (closed Bank Holidays)
Last orders: lunch 2.30pm
Booking essential for modern French food at this small popular restaurant.

The Pelham Hotel

15 Cromwell Place, London SW7 2LA
Tel: 071-589 8288 *Fax:* 071-589 8444 **£70**
Open: lunch + dinner daily
Last orders: lunch 2.30pm, dinner 10.30pm
37-bedroomed hotel, the interior designed by owner Kit Kemp.

Penang Satay House

9 Turnpike Lane, London N8
Tel: 081-340 8707 **£25**
Open: dinner Mon-Sat
Last orders: dinner 10.45pm (11.45pm Fri + Sat)
Popular neighbourhood Singapore/Malaysian restaurant with a menu of well spiced dishes. Try the hot king prawn in shrimp sauce.

La Petite Auberge

36 Queenstown Road, London SW8 3RY
Tel: 071-720 2449 **£55**
Open: lunch Mon-Fri, dinner Mon-Sat (closed 3 dys Christmas)
Last orders: lunch 3.00pm, dinner 11.00pm
Bruno Laurent's original Battersea restaurant which spawned Le Bouchon Lyonnais and Le Bouchon Bordelais also.

Pho

2 Lisle Street, London W1
Tel: 071-437 8265 **£15**
Open: all day, daily
Last orders: 11.00pm
A rudimentary Vietnamese café, ideal for a quick meal. Pho (noodle soup) is a speciality. There are many other noodle dishes and light, crisp spring rolls.

Pinocchio's Restaurant

160 Eversholt Street, London NW1 1BL
Tel: 071-388 7482 **£40**
Open: lunch Mon-Fri, dinner Mon-Sat (closed Bank Holidays)
Last orders: lunch 2.00pm, dinner 10.00pm
Traditional Italian cooking. Especially popular at lunchtime.

PJ's

52 Fulham Road, London SW10
Tel: 071-589 0025 **£45**
Open: all day, daily
Last orders: 11.30pm
American-influenced bar and grill near South Kensington.

Poissonnerie de l'Avenue

82 Sloane Avenue, London SW3 3DZ
Tel: 071-589 2457 **£45**
Open: lunch + dinner Mon-Fri (closed Bank Holidays, 10 days Christmas, 4 days Easter)
Last orders: lunch 3.00pm, dinner midnight
Classically prepared seafood served in oak-panelled dining room of this long-established restaurant. Owner-operated.

Poons Restaurant

4 Leicester Street, London WC2H 7BL
Tel: 071-437 1528 **£30**
Open: all day, Mon-Sat (closed 3 dys Christmas)
Last orders: 11.15pm
Wind-dried foods – sausage, duck and bacon – and hot pot dishes such as eel with crispy pork and garlic separate this Chinese restaurant from its neighbours. Not to be confused with other restaurants of the same name.

La Poule Au Pot

231 Ebury Street, London SW1
Tel: 071-730 7763 **£50**
Open: lunch Mon-Fri, dinner Mon-Sat
Last orders: lunch 2.15pm, dinner 11.15pm
Dried flowers, breakfast-style plates and paper cloths; generous portions of homely French cooking.

Ragam

57 Cleveland Street, London W1P 5PQ
Tel: 071-736 9596 **£20**
Open: all day, daily (closed Christmas Day + Boxing Day)
Last orders: 11.30pm
Delicious vegetarian and fish specialities from the southern Indian state of Kerala. Small and matey and affordable.

The Red Fort
77 Dean Street, London W1V 5HA
Tel: 071-437 2525 **£45**
Open: lunch + dinner daily (closed Christmas Day + Boxing Day)
Last orders: lunch 3.00pm, dinner 11.30pm
Mogul Indian meat-centred cooking but with some interesting vegetable courses. Service sometimes hard going.

Royal China
3 Chelverton Road, London SW15
Tel: 081-788 0907 **£50**
Open: lunch + dinner daily
Last orders: lunch 2.30pm, dinner 11.15pm
There is a James Bond brand of glamour at this large glittering restaurant in Putney that could have been transported from Hong Kong. The long menu has some original dishes with novel items to try among the first courses. Agreeable staff.

Royal Lancaster Hotel
Lancaster Terrace, London W2 2TY
Tel: 071-262 6737   *Fax:* 071-724 3191 **£60**
Open: lunch + dinner daily
Last orders: lunch 2.30pm, dinner 10.45pm
Good views across Hyde Park from this modern hotel with a luxurious interior and 418 bedrooms.

Royal Garden Hotel
Kensington High Street, London W8 4PT
Tel: 071-937 8000 **£100**
Open: lunch Mon-Fri, dinner Mon-Sat (closed Bank Holidays)
Last orders: lunch 2.30pm, dinner 11.30pm
Enjoy David Nicholl's cooking and rooftop views.

Saigon
45 Frith Street, London W1V 5TE
Tel: 071-437 7109   *Fax:* 071-734 1668 **£40**
Open: all day, Mon-Sat (closed Bank Holidays)
Last orders: 11.30pm
Relatively long established Vietnamese restaurant with taciturn service and quite small portions, but the quality of the food provides compensation. A la carte gets the best out of the menu.

St Ermins Stakis Hotel
Caxton Street, London SW1H 0QW
Tel: 071-222 7888   *Fax:* 071-222 6914 **£65**
Open: lunch Mon-Fri, dinner Mon-Sat (closed 2 wks Dec/Jan, Aug)
Last orders: lunch 2.30pm, dinner 11.00pm
Belgravia location, popular with tourists. 291 bedrooms.

Sala Thai
182 South Ealing Road, London W5 4RJ
Tel: 081-560 7407 **£30**
Open: lunch Mon-Fri, dinner Mon-Sat (closed 1 wk Christmas)
Last orders: lunch 2.30pm, dinner 11.30pm
Long-established popular neighbourhood Thai restaurant with all-encompassing menu.

Salloos
62-64 Kinnerton Street, London SW1X 8ER
Tel: 071-235 4444 **£50**
Open: lunch + dinner Mon-Fri (closed Bank Holidays)
Last orders: lunch 2.30pm, dinner 11.15pm
Family-run Pakistani restaurant utilising first rate ingredients and, unusually, much is cooked to order.

San Frediano
62 Fulham Road, London SW3 6HH
Tel: 071-584 8375 **£45**
Open: lunch + dinner Mon-Sat (closed Bank Holidays)
Last orders: lunch 2.30pm, dinner 11.15pm
Traditional Italian fare, lively atmosphere, booking essential.

Sang Thai
12-14 Glentworth Street, London NW1
Tel: 071-935 4220 **£40**
Open: lunch + dinner daily
Last orders: lunch 3.00pm (2.30pm Sun), dinner 11.30pm (10.30pm Sun)
There is a tradition of female chefs in Thailand and the one here produces notable food. The decor is also above average in stylishness.

San Martino
103 Walton Street, London SW3 2HP
Tel: 071-589 3833 **£50**
Open: lunch + dinner Mon-Sat (closed Bank Holidays)
Last orders: lunch 3.00pm, dinner 11.30pm
Modern Italian food, seasonal produce, busy and bright.

Satay Raya
248 Belsize Road, London NW6
Tel: 071-624 6030 **£25**
Open: dinner Tue-Sun
Last orders: dinner 10.45pm
Packed, inexpensive neighbourhood restaurant serving Malaysian, Singapore and Indonesian food. The mixed satay is well worth ordering.

Scalini
1-3 Walton Street, London SW3 2JD
Tel: 071-581 3591 **£60**
Open: lunch + dinner daily (closed Christmas)
Last orders: lunch 3.00pm, dinner midnight
Modern Italian cooking, up-market setting.

La Seppia
8a Mount Street, London W1Y 5AD
Tel: 071-499 3385   *Fax:* 071-629 5446 **£60**
Open: lunch + dinner Mon-Fri (closed 1 wk Christmas, 1 wk Aug)
Last orders: lunch 2.45pm, dinner 11.00pm
Six-course tasting menu available at this modern Italian restaurant.

Shares
12-13 Lime Street, London EC3M 7AA
Tel: 071-623 1843 **£65**
Open: lunch Mon-Fri (closed Bank Holidays)
Last orders: lunch 3.00pm
Modern style food – rack of lamb, salmon with sorrel – competently cooked for city custom. Sister to Equities.

Sheekey's Restaurant
28-32 St Martins Court, London WC2N 4AL
Tel: 071-240 2565   *Fax:* 071-491 2477   **£60**
Open: lunch Mon-Fri, dinner Mon-Sat (closed Bank
 Holidays)
Last orders: lunch 2.45pm, dinner 11.15pm
Nicky Kerman's long established (1896!)
fish and seafood restaurant.

Sheraton Park Tower
101 Knightsbridge, London SW1X 7RN
Tel: 071-235 8050   *Fax:* 071-235 8231   **£65**
Open: lunch + dinner daily
Last orders: lunch 3.00pm, dinner 11.00pm
Good views of the capital from the circular
tower, luxurious surroundings, 295
bedrooms.

Simpson's-in-the-Strand
100 The Strand, London WC2R 0EW
Tel: 071-836 9112   **£55**
Open: lunch + dinner Mon-Fri (closed Bank
 Holidays)
Last orders: lunch 2.30pm, dinner 9.30pm
Very grand English restaurant featuring
roasts and grills. Edwardian decor, club-
by ground floor, first floor and private
rooms.

Singapore Garden Restaurant
83-83a Fairfax Road, London NW6 4DY
Tel: 071-328 5314   **£35**
Open: lunch + dinner daily (closed 1 wk Christmas)
Last orders: lunch 2.45pm, dinner 10.45 pm
 (11.15pm Fri+Sat)
The Singapore Ambassador eats here,
which should vouch for authenticity and
cooking skills. Seafood dishes are the
ones to go for, especially chilli crab.
There is also a Chinese menu.

Smith's Restaurant
25 Neal Street, London WC2H 9PU
Tel: 071-491 1199   *Fax:* 071-836 8395   **£45**
Open: all day, Mon-Sat (closed Bank Holidays,
 1 wk Christmas)
Last orders: 11.30pm
Christina Smith's individual Covent Garden
restaurant. Modern British menu includes a translation into Japanese!

Smollensky's Balloon Bar & Restaurant
1 Dover Street, London W1X 3PJ
Tel: 071-379 0310   *Fax:* 071-836 3270   **£30**
Open: all day, daily (closed Christmas Day, Boxing
 Day)
Last orders: midnight
Michael Gottlieb's famous American-style
restaurant, great for families.

Soho Soho
11-13 Frith Street, London W1
Tel: 071-494 3491   **£45**
Open: lunch Mon-Fri, dinner Mon-Sat (closed Bank
 Holidays)
Last orders: lunch 3.30pm, dinner 11.30pm
French brasserie, café, wine and piano bar.

The Spice Merchant
130 Bayswater Road, London W2
Tel: 071-243 0197   **£50**
Open: lunch + dinner daily
Last orders: lunch 2.30pm, dinner 11.30pm
New, calm venue for Indian regional spe-
cialities and a good daily lunchtime buffet.

Sri Siam Thai Restaurant
14 Old Compton Street, London W1V 5PE
Tel: 071-434 3544   **£40**
Open: lunch Mon-Sat, dinner daily (closed
 Christmas/New Year)
Last orders: lunch 3.00pm, dinner 11.15pm
 (10.30pm Sun)
A chef formerly at the Blue Elephant (q.v.)
has at last brought success to this Soho
site. Decor is as light as a butterfly.
Vegetarians as well as meat-eaters are
well served from the Thai menu.

Surya
59-61 Fortune Green Road, London NW6 1DR
Tel: 071-435 7488   **£25**
Open: lunch Fri-Sun, dinner daily
Last orders: lunch 2.00pm, dinner 10.30pm
Family-run Indian vegetarian restaurant
featuring food from Uttar Pradesh.
Agreeable decor and sparky chutneys
eliminate thoughts of asceticism.

Sydney Street
4 Sydney Street, London SW3
Tel: 071-352 3433   **£00**
Open: please ring for details
Last orders: please ring for details
New incarnation as we went to press of the
former Les Trois Plats.

Sydney Restaurant
12-14 Battersea High Street, London SW11 3JB
Tel: 071-978 5395   **£40**
Open: lunch + dinner daily
Last orders: lunch 2.30pm, dinner 10.30pm
English cooking, central Battersea location.

Tall Orders in Soho
2 St Anne's Court, Dean Street,
 London W1B 3AW
Tel: 071-494 4941   **£40**
Open: all day, daily
Last orders: 11.30pm (10.30pm Sun)
A second branch of the stack 'em high
basket meals themed restaurant that
opened last year in Fulham.

The Tall House Restaurant
134 Southwark Street, London SE1 0SW
Tel: 071-401 2929   **£40**
Open: lunch Mon-Fri
Last orders: lunch 3.00pm (brasserie open from
 9.00am)
Elizabeth Philip's second venture (after the
Archduke Wine Bar) includes an art
gallery.

Thailand Restaurant

15 Lewisham Way, London SE14 6PP

Tel: 081-691 4040 **£50**

Open: lunch for parties only, dinner Tue-Sun
(closed 1 wk Apr)

Last orders: dinner 10.30pm

A Glaswegian and his Thai wife run this
quaint little restaurant with original and
impressive food, especially the dishes
from Laos. You can finish with a nip of
single malt whisky!

Tampopo

233 Earl's Court Road, London SW5

Tel: 071-373 5400 **£25**

Open: lunch Tue-Fri, dinner Tue-Sun

Last orders: lunch 2.30pm, dinner 11.30pm

They call themselves an Oriental café –
Japanese for the round-eyes at sensible
prices.

Tandoori Lane

131a Munster Road, London SW6

Tel: 071-371 0440 **£30**

Open: lunch + dinner daily

Last orders: lunch 2.30pm, dinner 11.30pm

Hoorays shout, 'Hooray!' for the Indian
food here which is well above average
and even the decor is somewhat out of
the ordinary.

Tatsuso

32 Broadgate Circle, London EC2

Tel: 071-638 5863 **£40**

Open: lunch + dinner Mon-Fri

Last orders: lunch 3.00pm, dinner 9.00pm

Stylish Japanese restaurant fitting neatly
into the Broadgate development. Sushi
and teppan-yaki bars. Take heed of daily
specials.

Thamilan

181-184 Old Kent Road, London SE1

Tel: 071-701 3353 **£25**

Open: lunch + dinner daily

Last orders: lunch 3.00pm, dinner 11.30pm

Perhaps the best place in London to enjoy
Sri Lankan cuisine. Service is caring,
breads and spicing a revelation.

Than Binh

14 Chalk Farm Road, London NW1

Tel: 071-267 9820 **£30**

Open: lunch + dinner Mon-Sat

Last orders: lunch 2.30pm, dinner 11.30pm

Small Vietnamese restaurant with many
Chinese dishes as well. Try crystal
spring roll (steamed rather than fried),
baked squid with garlic and chilli, and the
Vietnamese noodles. Gracious service.

Topsy Tasty

5 Station Parade, Burlington Lane, London W4

Tel: 081-995 3407 **£30**

Open: dinner Mon-Sat

Last orders: dinner 11.00pm

An unpretentious Thai restaurant that is an
off-shoot of the nearby Bedlington Café,
a workman's caff that becomes Thai at
night. Vietnamese and Laotian dishes pad
out the menu. Unlicensed.

Twenty Trinity Gardens

20 Trinity Gardens, London SW9 8DP

Tel: 071-733 8838 **£35**

Open: lunch Mon-Fri, dinner Mon-Sat (closed 1 wk
Christmas)

Last orders: lunch 2.30pm, dinner 10.30pm

Jane Mann's well-established restaurant
serving modern European food.

Vietnam Cottage

65 Old Compton Street, London W1

Tel: 071-439 4658 **£35**

Open: lunch + dinner daily (open all day Sat + Sun)

Last orders: lunch 2.30pm, dinner 11.30pm

The friendly, informative service makes
this restaurant outstanding. The food is
authentic: eel with lemon grass and
peanuts, beef fondue with vinegar, and
the Vietnamese dim sum should be tried.

Wakaba

122a Finchley Road, London NW3 5HT

Tel: 071-586 7960 **£40**

Open: lunch + dinner Mon-Sat (closed 4 dys
Christmas, Easter, 1 wk Aug)

Last orders: lunch 2.30pm, dinner 11.00pm

The architecture announces the cuisine: a
pared-away look, streamlined Japanese
food with some notable vegetarian
options.

The Waldorf

Aldwych, London WC2B 4DD

Tel: 071-836 2400 *Fax:* 071-836 7244 **£90**

Open: lunch Mon-Fri, dinner Mon-Sat (closed Bank
Holidays, 3 wks Aug)

Last orders: lunch 2.30pm, dinner 10.00pm

Famous club-like hotel including the equally
famous Palm Court. 301 rooms.

Water Margin

96 Golders Green Road, London NW11

Tel: 081-458 5815 **£30**

Open: all day, daily

Last orders: 11.15pm

Neighbourhood restaurant with authentic
Cantonese cuisine of Chinatown standard. First rate roast duck and pork, and
fried noodle dishes. Friendly staff and
moderate prices.

The Westbury Hotel

Conduit Street, London W1A 4UH

Tel: 071-629 7755 *Fax:* 071-495 1163 **£70**

Open: lunch + dinner daily

Last orders: lunch 3.00pm, dinner 11.00pm

Thirty-five years old, still going strong.
Take tea in the lounge, dine in the Polo
restaurant. 243 rooms.

Wheeler's

19 Old Compton Street, London W1V 5PJ
Tel: 071-437 2706   **£60**
Open: lunch + dinner daily (closed Christmas Day)
Last orders: lunch 2.30pm, dinner 11.15pm
Near octogenarian restaurant, still going
strong. As popular for the fact that it was
the original Wheeler's restaurant.

White Tower Restaurant

1 Percy Street, London W1P 0ET
Tel: 071-636 8141   **£50**
Open: lunch + dinner Mon-Fri (closed Bank
Holidays, 1 wk Christmas, 3 wks Aug)
Last orders: lunch 2.15pm, dinner 10.15pm
Familiar and homely Greek restaurant,
international menu, new owners.

Whittington's

21 College Hill, London EC4 2RP
Tel: 071-248 5855   **£50**
Open: lunch Mon-Fri (closed Bank Holidays)
Last orders: lunch 2.15pm
Modern English cooking served in base-
ment restaurant.

Wong Kei

41-43 Wardour Street, London W1
Tel: 071-437 8408   **£20**
Open: all day, daily
Last orders: 11.30pm
Unadorned Chinatown restaurant where
you can rely on several things: the
satisfactory quality of a dish of roasted
meat on noodles and greens, the cheap
price, the refusal of cheques or credit
cards and the rudeness of the staff!

Yoisho

33 Goodge Street, London W1
Tel: 071-323 0477   **£25**
Open: lunch Mon-Fri, dinner Mon-Sat
Last orders: lunch 2.00pm, dinner 11.00pm
Ideal place to experiment with Japanese
food choosing from the long list of
smaller, homely dishes. Friendly staff.

You Me

33 Pratt Street, London NW1
Tel: 071-323 0477   **£30**
Open: lunch Mon-Sat, dinner daily
Last orders: lunch 3.00pm, dinner midnight
This family-run Korean restaurant is a
branch of the You Me in Hornsey Road.
With more decoration and a license it
offers similarly good value, especially in
the set price meals.

Young Bin Kwan

3 St Alphage High Walk, London Wall, London EC2
Tel: 071-638 9151   **£50**
Open: lunch + dinner Mon-Fri
Last orders: lunch 3.00pm, dinner 11.00pm
Popular with the Japanese, this Korean
restaurant is handy for the Barbican. The
set meal served in a laquer box (oh jol
pan) would be a good pre-concert choice.

Zazou

74 Charlotte Street, London W1P 1LB
Tel: 071-436 5133   **£60**
Open: lunch Mon-Fri, dinner Mon-Sat (closed Bank
Holidays)
Last orders: lunch 2.30pm, dinner 11.30pm
French/Oriental fish restaurant.

Zen

Chelsea Cloisters, Sloane Avenue, London SW3
Tel: 071-589 1781   *Fax:* 071-437 0641   **£55**
Open: lunch + dinner daily (closed 4 dys
Christmas)
Last orders: lunch 3.00pm, dinner 11.30pm
Considerably gaudier decor and less consis-
tent than Zen Central, this the first of the
Zens has an interesting and varied menu
with many vegetarian dishes.

Zen Central

20-22 Queen Street, London W1
Tel: 071-629 8103   **£60**
Open: lunch + dinner daily (closed Christmas Day
+ Boxing Day)
Last orders: lunch 2.30pm, dinner 11.30pm
Chic, expensive Chinese restaurant with
architect-designed interior. Interesting
menu with classy dishes, some not often
found outside Hong Kong. Salt and pepper soft shell crab, correctly made Peking duck and lobster with tangerine peel
and crushed garlic are rewarding choices.
Slick service.

ZeNW3

81 Hampstead High Street, London NW3
Tel: 071-794 7863   **£50**
Open: lunch + dinner daily
Last orders: lunch 2.30pm, dinner 11.30pm
(11.00pm Sun)
Designer Chinese in look and in the menu
with light, somewhat adapted dishes. Its
clients like to pose both upstairs and
downstairs.

Ziani

45/47 Radnor Walk, London SW3 4BT
Tel: 071-352 2698   **£50**
Open: lunch + dinner daily (closed Bank Holidays)
Last orders: lunch 2.45pm, dinner 11.30pm
Modern Italian food and setting.

AMBERLEY   Amberley Castle

Amberley, Nr Arundel, West Sussex BN18 9ND
Telephone: (0798) 831992   *Fax:* (0798) 831 998
Open: lunch + dinner daily
Last orders: lunch 2.30pm, dinner 10.00pm

£65

Massive 14th-century walls encircle the medieval halls and the
immaculate inner garden. You enter by means of a portcullised gate,
and once inside come face to face with suits of armour and fearsome
weaponry. But you'll also find a cosy library and sitting-rooms with
deep sofas, pretty chintzes and blazing fires. A change in culinary
direction has brought a new chef, Nigel Boschetti, and a more British
slant to the menu. Try breast of pheasant wrapped in a pastry cage,
served with a purée of quince; or medallions of venison with a juniper
sauce and a confit of turnips and chestnuts. The set price lunch menu
at £17.50 (including coffee) is good value. The reasonably priced
wine list is a suitable accompaniment to the food. Stay overnight in
one of the comfortable bedrooms (with jacuzzis), and pretend that
this English castle is your home!

*A new chef at Amberley, but Nigel
Boschetti's British flavours are perfectly
in tune with the surroundings.*

AYLESBURY — Hartwell House

Oxford Road, Aylesbury, Buckinghamshire HP17 8NL
Telephone: (0296) 747444   *Fax:* (0296) 747450
Open: lunch + dinner daily
Last orders: lunch 1.55pm, dinner 9.45pm

£75

The history of this magnificent Jacobean/Georgian stately home includes a period of five years when it was the seat of the exiled court of Louis XVIII. As at Versailles, hundreds of courtiers crammed into the house and even opened shops in the outbuildings. The tone of the beautifully restored interior is set by the splendid plasterwork ceiling and huge fireplace of the Great Hall. The luxurious antique-filled house is staffed with helpful professionalism. This year conference accomodation will be moved from the main house to the restored stables. Chef Aidan McCormack cooks a menu combining traditional and modern British elements: fillet of beef with roast shallots, foie gras and a Hermitages red wine sauce; pan-fried breast of duck with glazed apples, a pudding of summer berries and a bramble sauce. There is a wine list appropriate to the surroundings and the quality of the cooking.

A magnificent stately home run by the Historic House Hotel Group.

Interiors of Hartwell. In the dining room Aidan McCormack's menu combines traditional and modern British elements.

AYLESBURY   Pebbles

1 Pebble Lane, Aylesbury, Buckinghamshire HP20 2JH
Telephone: (0296) 86622
Open: lunch Tue-Sun, dinner Tue-Sat
Last orders: lunch 2.15pm (3.00pm Sun), dinner 11.00pm

£75

Pebbles is situated half-way down a narrow old lane near the church (a dark passage at night). Chef/patron Jeremy Blake O'Connor cooks well but perhaps he needs a larger or different setting in which to display his talents. The pricing which is necessary to turn out the rich style and quality of cooking leads to an incongruity with the low-ceilinged cottage interior. At a recent meal he offered a delicious bouillabaisse tasting strongly of the sea and saffron, a delicate ginger-scented sauce with a steamed fillet of sea-bass filled with a scallop mousse, exquisite banana and cassis sorbets. Bread is good and service is pleasant. An extensive wine list includes several half bottles with some bargains in the Italian section.

BARNSTAPLE   Lynwood House Restaurant

Bishop's Tawton Road, Barnstaple, Devon EX32 9DZ
Telephone: (0271) 43695   *Fax:* (0271) 43695
Open: lunch Mon-Sat, dinner daily
Last orders: lunch 2.00pm, dinner 10.00pm

£45

The Roberts family continue to run their welcoming, pleasant restaurant (now with five rooms) with warmth and enthusiasm. The menu changes little, with seafood terrine and double cream crème caramel remaining popular. Sizzling, crunchy green bean vermicelli adds a novel touch to plump scallops wrapped in bacon and grilled. Vegetables and herbs come from the garden: look for shredded potato cooked with dill. The wine list, annotated with maps and photographs, represents Europe extensively and touches on the New World. Courteous, sometimes formal service. Spacious rooms are comfortable and full of home-from-home extras from shoe-cleaning equipment to real coffee and even stamps.

A friendly family business. The seafood is especially popular.

BASLOW   Fischer's at Baslow Hall

Calver Road, Baslow, Derbyshire DE4 1RR

£60

Telephone: (024 688) 583259
Open: lunch Tue-Sat, dinner Mon-Sat
Last orders: lunch 2.00pm, dinner 9.30pm

Max and Susan Fischer have worked hard at building up a good reputation for their delightful country house style restaurant with rooms. Each of the six prettily decorated bedrooms has its own character, is warm and comfortable, and has a thoughtfully equipped bathroom.

    Dinner is fixed price, offering either a no-choice 5-course menu with coffee, or four courses with choices. Lunch is a short carte, and fixed price on Sundays. Max cooks with an assured hand after a modern European style, offering such delights as baked globe artichokes en croûte with a mushroom duxelle as a starter, beef olives with spätzle noodles served with crisp fresh vegetables from the main courses, and a gratin of exotic fruits for dessert. This dedicated team deserves support.

BATH	The Bath Spa Hotel

Sydney Road, Bath, Avon BA2 6JF
Telephone: (0225) 444424   *Fax:* (0225) 444006
£70
Open: lunch + dinner daily
Last orders: lunch 2.00pm, dinner 10.00pm

The approach is up a winding drive, past a 19th-century grotto. From the hotel there are spectacular views over Georgian Bath. Great attention to detail shows throughout this luxuriously appointed new hotel. There are well-chosen antiques and period furniture everywhere, and the marble and mahogany bathrooms evoke the past but include all modern facilities. There are slippers by your bed and even the inside of the wardrobe is lined with fabric. Standards of housekeeping are exemplary, as are those of general management: someone is always on call and the staff remember your name. It feels much more like a small country house hotel than a 103-bedroom/suite hotel. The health resort includes a good swimming pool (I tried it!). Also a good policy on children – under-10s can dine in the main restaurant before 8.00pm or have high tea. Interconnecting bedroom suites are an advantage.

The Vellore Restaurant is in what used to be the ballroom of the old house. A new Executive Chef, Berndt Meister, was due to be appointed at the beginning of January and at the time of our visit the food was still evolving, although it promises to be first class under his leadership.

Standards of house keeping are excellent at the Bath Spa, and the restaurant augurs well too.

BIRMINGHAM   Sloan's

27-29 Chad Square, Hawthorne Road, Edgbaston, Birmingham, West
Midlands B15 3TQ
Telephone: 021-455 6697
Open: lunch Mon-Fri, dinner Mon-Sat (closed Bank Holidays, 1 wk
Christmas)
Last orders: lunch 2.00pm, dinner 10.00pm

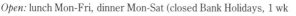
£55

When Roger Narbett became the 1990 Chef of the Year, the
well-deserved award was also a vindication of his customers' loyalty
to this young chef/patron. For since opening his own restaurant in a
modern shopping precinct, the ride has not always been smooth.
Nevertheless, Roger's tenacity seems to be paying off. His level-
headed approach to the competition menu no doubt contributed to his
success: he simply cooked some of the dishes best liked by his
customers. The menu at Sloan's reflects the range of Roger's
cooking skills: mousseline of salmon and lobster served with a lobster
sauce, followed by a rosette of English lamb with a purée of onion and
chives and a wild mushroom sauce, and for dessert a crème brûlée
flavoured with lemon and served with seasonal fruits. It's good to see
a chef/patron establishment of this quality doing well in Birmingham.

*Sloan's, the scene of Roger Narbett's
consistently reliable cuisine.*

BIRMINGHAM   Sir Edward Elgar Restaurant

Swallow Hotel, 12 Hagley Road, Five Ways, Birmingham,
West Midlands B16 8SL
Telephone: 021-452 1144   *Fax:* 021-456 3442
Open: lunch Sun-Fri, dinner daily
Last orders: lunch 2.30 pm, dinner 10.30 pm (10.00 pm Sun)

£45

This new hotel is unashamedly luxurious, with coloured marbles and fine carpets underfoot, crystal chandeliers overhead, and beautiful wallpapers and fabrics overall. Oil paintings and fine furniture add a traditional English elegance. Bedrooms are air-conditioned, double glazed, and fitted with all imaginable facilities.

Despite its name, cooking in the restaurant is French, classically based and modern in style. Chef Idris Caldora is no stranger to challenges: winner of the 1986 RAGB Young Chef of the Year title, his previous post before Birmingham was as head chef of the then newly-opened Bilbrough Manor, where he won much acclaim. Currently, he is cooking well here with precision and style: dodine of duck with its own filling and foie gras, served with an onion confit; fillet of beef garnished with five types of onion in a madeira sauce. Luxury comes at a price but the fixed-price menus offer a cheaper alternative. The wine list is in the middle-to-upper price bracket.

Adam Austin, restaurant manager of the Sir Edward Elgar Restaurant.

BIRTLE	The Normandie Hotel

Elbut Lane, Birtle, Nr Bury, Greater Manchester BL9 6UT
Telephone: 061-764 3869   *Fax:* 061-764 4866   **£50**
Open: lunch Tue-Fri, dinner Mon-Sat (closed Bank Holidays, 1 wk Easter, 2 wks Christmas)
Last orders: lunch 2.00pm, dinner 9.30pm

It's always a good sign when people take the trouble to write to us enthusiastically about a particular place. As one reader put it, she felt she had to do more than just compliment the chef on the spot. There has been a steady stream of letters about the Normandie, the contents of which I heartily endorse. Namely, that beyond the exterior of this jumble of architectural styles lies a friendly personalised atmosphere, and the best restaurant in the Manchester area. Owners Gillian and Max Moussa look after the front of house, while Pascal Pommier cooks some seriously good food. A starter may be a terrine of veal with artichokes, served with an autumnal salad. Then you might choose steamed fillets of rainbow trout with a lemon-balm scented sauce, or maybe some roast woodcock served with green lentils and a port sauce. Desserts and the cheeseboard are both worthy of attention. The helpfully annotated wine list includes a good selection of half bottles, and on the whole is reasonably priced. White clover for cooking.

Pascal Pommier – a young man to watch – earns The Normandie Hotel a white clover for the best cooking at any restaurant in the Manchester area.

Box   Clos du Roy

Box House, Box, Wiltshire SN14 9NR
Telephone: (0225) 744447 Fax (0225) 743971   £65
Open: lunch + dinner daily
Last orders: lunch 2.00pm, dinner 9.30pm (9.00pm Sun)

The success of their restaurant firmly established, Emma and
Philippe Roy have capitalised on the potential of this beautiful
Georgian house, and in August opened it as a country house hotel.
There are now nine individually designed bedrooms, all with private
baths and showers. From the rooms there are fine views over the 7
acres of garden and pasture. A corner of the walled garden shelters a
heated swimming pool. For those who like just to drop in, there's a
helicopter landing pad. The Roys can arrange a variety of special
interest programmes for their guests, ranging from theatre to
ballooning. Devotees of Philippe's excellent cooking will find the
short cookery courses appealing.

In the kitchen, Philippe continues to produce some very good food.
Try arctic shar garnished with baby leeks served with a chervil
sauce, or breast of mallard garnished with kumquats served with a
sherry vinegar sauce, and lemon tartlet with orange ice cream and a
vanilla sauce to finish. All breads and pastries are baked on the
premises, and Emma provides charming service. White clover for
cooking and setting.

BRADFORD	Restaurant Nineteen

Belevedere Hotel, 19 North Park Road, Heaton, Bradford, West Yorkshire
BD9 4NT
Telephone: (0274) 492559
Open: dinner Tue-Sat (closed 1 wk Jun, 1 wk Aug, 1 wk Christmas)
Last orders: 9.30pm (10.00pm Fri + Sat)

£65

This restaurant shines like a beacon in an area not conspicious for
gastronomy, but it would also hold its own in the south-east. The
setting is stylish: a large house overlooking parkland, with a rather
Edwardian dining room in salmon pink and cream with crisp white-
clad tables. Robert Barbour provides attentive, affable service.
Stephen Smith cooks in an accomplished modern style often presenting
the main ingredients cooked in different ways: a salad of roast breast
and leg of quail with a soft quail mousse. The platter of rhubarb desserts
is a favourite. The wine list includes quite a lengthy house selection,
chosen as being typical of their region and also representing good value
for money. Four simply but comfortably furnished rooms make this an
excellent overnight stay. White clover for cooking.

Stephen Smith's cooking makes this a welcome oasis of good food in the Bradford area.

BRAY-ON-THAMES   The Waterside Inn

Ferry Road, Bray-on-Thames, Berkshire SL6 2AT
Telephone: (0628) 20691   *Fax:* (0628) 771966   **£125**
Open: lunch Wed-Sun, dinner Tue-Sun (closed Bank Holidays, 7 wks after
Christmas)
Last orders: lunch 2.00pm, dinner 10.00pm

It's difficult to imagine Bray without the Waterside Inn, just as, in
speaking of the whole British cooking scene, one tends to think of
'before' and 'after' the Roux brothers. It's a point that can be very
enjoyably appreciated by a meal here, particularly on a summer's day
if one is lucky enough to get a table by the window or to take coffee
outside in the summer house. The 5-course menu exceptionnel
(extracts from the à la carte menu but served in smaller portions and
for a minimum of two people) at £48.50 per person is still one of the
best ways really to appreciate the skills of the Waterside brigade, or
you can choose straight from the carte. Crayfish and trout are kept in
a tank and cooked to order. Some dishes (clearly marked on the
menu) need to be ordered twenty minutes in advance but are well
worth the forethought – petit flan d'escargots frais en habit vert, and
tronçonnettes de homard poêlées minute au porto blanc being
examples of these. Desserts are of course legendary – when in doubt
take the péché gourmand selon Michel and indulge all your
sweet-toothed fantasies!

Michel Roux gives his unique interpretation of haute cuisine at the Waterside and demands nothing short of perfection in every department. As a result it remains a focal point of the British restaurant scene.

BROCKENHURST   Le Poussin

57-59 Brookley Road, Brockenhurst, Hampshire SO42 7RB
Telephone: (0590) 23063   *Fax:* (0590) 22912
Open: lunch Tue-Sun, dinner Tue-Sat (closed 2 wks Jan)
Last orders: lunch 2.00pm, dinner 10.00pm

£60

At his own request, Alex Aitken's restaurant did not feature in our
last edition, owing to differing opinions over attention given to a
neighbouring establishment (now closed). Happily, relations are now
mended: good news, as I have always found this a good restaurant.
The comfortable pastel-themed dining room has an elegant French
provincial feel. The cooking, on the other hand, draws much upon the
New Forest and fruits of the sea: chunks of plump wild mushrooms in
a creamy soup; fish soup served with a garlicky rouille; roast teal
prettily set on a confit of cabbage and garlanded by tiny vegetables;
wild salmon with sorrel. Different wines are served by the glass with
each course. Smooth service, they know their regulars well and are
genuinely concerned that you enjoy your meal.

Below: *Alex Aitken with a basket of wild mushrooms from the New Forest.* Above left:
Saddle of sika venison with onions and cabbage confit.

CHELTENHAM Redmond's at Malvern View

Malvern View Hotel, Cleeve Hill, Gloucestershire GL52 3PR
Telephone: (0242) 672017
Open: lunch Tue-Sun, dinner Tue-Sat (closed 1 wk Jan)
Last orders: lunch 2.00pm, dinner 10.00pm

£60

The Haywards have put a great deal of work into improving their restaurant with six rooms, and they deserve support. Menus invariably read well and are changed every six weeks to take advantage of seasonal produce. Saucing and soufflés are strong points. You might choose home-made venison sausages with red cabbage and a juniper berry sauce, or fillet of red mullet sautéed in anchovy oil and served with a tomato sauce; then ballotine of saddle of wild rabbit with a pistachio mousseline and its own juices, or medallions of monkfish with a crab and coriander sauce. If it's available, try the hot ginger soufflé with honey ice cream for pudding. Pippa Hayward supervises the service with efficiency and charm. The wine list is well constructed and reasonably priced.

Saucing, as in this red mullet in a saffron and ginger sauce, is an important aspect of the food at Redmond's.

CHAGFORD   Gidleigh Park

Chagford, Devon TQ13 8HH
Telephone: (0647) 43267   *Fax:* (0647) 432574
Open: lunch + dinner daily
Last orders: lunch 2.00pm, dinner 9.00pm

£105

Shaun Hill's food at Gidleigh Park continues the strong tradition – the
accent is on natural flavours in both meat and fish dishes. His recent
performance as a cookery book writer reflects the careful balance
evident on his menus. Eschewing the 'glamour' approach to cookery
books, Shaun has gone the workaday route of providing some
excellent recipes in a straightforward no-frills style. The book also
reflects his eclectic menu ideas which draw their inspiration from all
over the world, particularly from the Orient and latterly, Italy.
Favourite dishes at Gidleigh Park currently include calf's sweetbreads with basil and olive-oil-mashed potato, a ragoût of wild
mushrooms and baby vegetables, and grilled sea-bass and red mullet
with a lemon and herb sauce. A new pricing policy means that the
best buys on the wine list now are the fine wines. Away from the
delights of the table, the gardens and walks at Gidleigh Park remain a
favourite attraction. Black clover for cooking, decor and location.

Grilled red mullet with tomatoes, ginger and spring onions.

Shaun Hill, a black clover for his cooking as well as for the decor and location of Gidleigh Park.

CLAYGATE Les Alouettes

7 High Street, Claygate, Surrey KT10 0JW

Telephone: (0372) 64882 £75
Open: lunch Mon-Fri, dinner Mon-Sat (closed 2 wks Aug, 11 dys Christmas)
Last orders: lunch 2.00pm, dinner 10.00pm

Pale, dusky pink walls, white-clad tables, comfortable grey upholstered chairs, deep red carpeting and heavy curtains, looped back,
create an elegant French setting. The fixed price menu offers some
accomplished cooking by 1987 MOGB Meilleur Ouvrier de Grande
Bretagne, Michel Perraud. His base remains classical, his style
modern, flavours distinct. Fish features predominently. Daily specials might include a light-textured terrine of langoustine on a lemon
butter sauce. A favourite dish from the main menu remains the roast
loin of young lamb cooked in a crepinette with a farce of black olives,
on a strong red wine sauce. Vegetables depart a little from the norm:
salsify, purée of turnip, celeriac. Excellent cheeses from Philippe
Olivier (£6.00 extra). The largely French wine list is in the medium
price range, and includes an extensive, separate selection of half
bottles. Polite, professional French service.

COLERNE   Lucknam Park

Colerne, Wiltshire SN14 8AZ
Telephone: (0225) 742777
Open: lunch + dinner daily
Last orders: lunch 2.30pm, dinner 9.30pm

Excellent pool + leisure facilities

£70

A long driveway leads to this very grand house. You enter to a
cheery greeting and blazing log fire in one of the huge, beautiful and
classically decorated rooms. New chef Michael Womersley is making
his mark with imaginative, beautifully presented dishes: a warm salad
of char-grilled, steamed and pan-fried Cornish fish served with a red
pepper sorbet; baked breast of teal served on a potato galette with a
madeira sauce, half a baked quince, and a quince purée topped with a
little 'bird's nest' of deep fried celeriac. Desserts match the main
courses – try the stunning hazelnut box. A harpist plays throughout
the evening and a smart young staff provides impeccable service. At
£31.50 the dinner menu is worth every penny. The extensive wine
list is priced in the middle bracket.

*The stunning hazelnut box – it's filled with hazelnut parfait and accompanied
with cherries soaked in kirsch on a sabayan sauce.*

CORSE LAWN   Corse Lawn House Hotel

Corse Lawn, Tirley, Gloucestershire GL19 4LZ
Telephone: (045 278) 479
Open: lunch + dinner, daily
Last orders: lunch 2.00pm, dinner 10.00pm

£70

Corse Lawn's expansion programme is now complete. Nine new bedrooms have been added to the original ten in an extension which blends well with the old Queen Anne house. Two of the new bedrooms are suites and all new bathrooms feature whirlpool baths. The new Regency-style Garden Room with french windows opening onto the lawn is a useful party area. The bar has also been refitted creating a more comfortable area in which to enjoy a drink and perhaps a light dish from the bar menu – a popular option at lunchtime. And if you're planning to indulge in Baba Hine's excellent cooking, perhaps try a bavaroise of smoked trout in smoked salmon; or pigeon breasts with red wine and salad. You can then limber up in the new outdoor swimming pool.

DEDHAM Le Talbooth & Maison Talbooth

Gunhill, Dedham, Nr Colchester, Essex CO7 6NP
Telephone: (0206) 323150 **£70**
Open: lunch + dinner daily
Last orders: lunch 2.00pm, dinner 9.30pm

Chef Steven Blake has underwritten the quality of Maison Talbooth. It must be comforting for Gerald Milsom to have this capable ex-Connaught Hotel chef, trained by Michel Bourdin, in the power house. Typical of his dishes is a salad of lightly browned scallops and crab bound in a sherry vinaigrette; roast cannon of lamb with courgettes and tomato, perfumed with garlic. The dining room enjoys splendid views over the river. It's a peaceful and tranquil 'Old England' establishment with high standards of service.

You can stay at the comfortable ten-roomed Maison Talbooth, about a mile away. Also under the Milsom wing is the cheaper six-roomed Dedham Vale Hotel. The style here is traditional English, although at lunch there's a smorgasbord. The Pier at Harwich, with a simple setting and seafood specialities, completes the group.

The restaurant where Steven Blake's exceptional cuisine may be enjoyed while the eye strays to appreciate, too, the views.

DARTMOUTH   The Carved Angel

2 South Embankment, Dartmouth, Devon TQ6 9BH
Telephone: (0803) 832465
Open: lunch Tue-Sun, dinner Tue-Sat (closed Jan + early Feb)
Last orders: lunch 1.45pm, dinner 9.30pm

£80

Recently published, *The Carved Angel Cookery Book* is a good reflection of Joyce Molyneux's approach to cooking and indeed to her restaurant. She likes her customers to feel comfortable and relaxed, so there are no pretentions or obscure descriptions on her menus, and unnecessary garnish is dismissed. Her cookery book takes the same straightforward approach with a smiling Joyce inviting the reader to open the book. The recipes themselves have been edited by Sophie Grigson to ensure their feasibility in a domestic kitchen, so now you can try for yourself: brill with pistachio mousseline and vegetables, wild duck with blackcurrant and beetroot, geranium and melon ice cream, or even basil ice cream!

The restaurant menu still continues to delight. A recent set lunch comprised goat's cheese grilled on a brioche with pine kernel salad, then Dart salmon grilse with cucumber and sorrel, with an apricot and almond tart to finish. These dishes and many more also appear on the à la carte menu.

Joyce Molyneux's Carved Angel, situated on the riverside, delivers good honest cooking at its very best.

EAST GRINSTEAD	Gravetye Manor

Vowels Lane, East Grinstead, West Sussex RH19 4LJ
Telephone: (0342) 810567   *Fax:* (0342) 810080
Open: lunch + dinner daily (closed Christmas)
Last orders: lunch 2.00pm, dinner 9.30pm

£90

Next time that you're eating at Gravetye and remarking upon the freshness and taste of the salads, vegetables and fruit, you might remember that they come from Gravetye's own garden. The walled 1-acre kitchen garden keeps the restaurant supplied with plenty of fresh, organically grown produce. There are forty types of vegetable, seventeen fruits and twenty-two herbs grown here, and there's also a watercress bed, and chickens that live next to the kitchen garden. In the kitchen, the produce is put to good use by chef Mark Raffan in dishes such as breast of pheasant cooked under a cloche with cocotte potatoes (turned and browned in butter) and thyme, served with fresh horseradish cream; fillet of halibut braised with chicory, apples and cider; timbale of ratatouille with oyster mushrooms and a light celery butter. For dessert perhaps a hot soufflé of cream cheese on a ragoût of strawberries and rhubarb. The outstanding wine list is thoughtfully composed. The fourteen apartments are sumptuously yet restfully appointed, with views over gardens and grounds. Peter Herbert's delightful country house hotel continues to hold its own as one of the best in the country. Black clover for cooking, decor and setting.

The restaurant at Gravetye, a fitting response to the manor's incomparable setting.

Left: *Sautéed medallions of local venison set on a bed of wild mushrooms with poached kumquats and a rich port wine sauce.*

| GILLINGHAM | **Stock Hill House** |

Stock Hill, Wyke, Gillingham, Dorset SP8 5NR
Telephone: (0747) 823626   *Fax:* (0747) 825625
Open: lunch Sat-Sun, dinner Tue-Sat
Last orders: lunch Sat 1.30pm Sun 1.45pm, dinner 8.45pm

£60

Peter and Nita Hauser are dedicated people, constantly striving to improve already high standards at their delightful country house hotel and restaurant. Their dedication has won them not just awards but also an appreciative regular custom. While Nita looks after the hotel side, Peter cooks his heart out in the kitchen – as he says, 'Cooking is my life and love.' He believes that food is only good when it is fresh and well treated, so many of the vegetables and fruit he uses are home-grown. Never keen on nouvelle cuisine, Peter's style tends more to dishes such as home-cured ox tongue braised in a madeira sauce, or roast fillet of lamb cooked with fresh garden herbs. Desserts betray an Austrian weakness for fun and rich indulgence! The wine list is enthusiastically annotated and very reasonably priced. White clover for cooking and friendly approach.

Left: *Peter Hauser – a white clover for cooking and the friendly approach at Stock Hill House.* Right: *Woodland pigeon breast, Jerusalem artichokes with mulberry and hazelnut dressing.*

FAVERSHAM   Read's

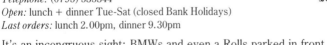

Painter's Forstal, Faversham, Kent ME13 0EE
Telephone: (0795) 535344   **£60**
Open: lunch + dinner Tue-Sat (closed Bank Holidays)
Last orders: lunch 2.00pm, dinner 9.30pm

It's an incongruous sight: BMWs and even a Rolls parked in front of this functional modern brick building. Inside, there's a civilised bar area with sofas and dining room in pale shades of green and pink, and soft background music. David Pitchford's cooking is the draw, including a garlicky brandade of smoked haddock served cold on a bed of chopped green beans and onions with fine olive oil, slivers of black oliver and diamonds of tomato. Best end of lamb with a herb stuffing and an excellent rosemary scented jus simply garnished with a sprig of rosemary. Rona Pitchford and friendly local help provide quietly efficient service.

GRASMERE

Michael's Nook
Country House Hotel

Grasmere, Nr Ambleside, Cumbria LA22 9RP
Telephone: (096 65) 496   *Fax:* (096 65) 765
Open: lunch daily by arrangement, dinner daily
Last orders: lunch 1.00pm, dinner 8.45pm

£75

Ever keen to offer more, Reg Gifford has added another three rooms to his antique-filled country house hotel. Non-residents are also welcome to lunch or to dine here in a room soft with candlelight and fresh flowers. The daily menus allow several options at each course. Excellent fresh produce is the basis of Heinz Nagler's rich and elaborate style. Soups are invariably good. Local produce may feature in dishes such as pan-fried loin of Cumberland pork garnished with black pudding, braised Savoy cabbage and glazed apples, served with a madeira sauce. The British cheeses and fruit-based desserts are as good as ever.

Reg Gifford's beautiful country house hotel at Grasmere.

HERSTMONCEUX — The Sundial Restaurant

Gardner Street, Herstmonceux, East Sussex BN27 4LA
Telephone: (0323) 832217
Open: lunch Tue-Sun, dinner Tue-Sat (closed Christmas – 20 Jan,
    2/3 wks Aug-Sep)
Last orders: lunch 2.00pm (2.30pm Sun), dinner 9.30pm

£65

The Sundial was never intended to set the gastronomic world on fire.
Its aim was, rather, to provide for the local and surrounding area a
reliable, friendly restaurant with competent cooking. In the kitchen,
Giuseppe Bertoli cooks classic French dishes while Laurette looks
after the dining room. Typical dishes might be a breast of chicken
with a calvados sauce, poached Scotch salmon or boeuf marchand de
vin. There's an old fashioned approach to desserts, which the regular
clientele seem to relish. The classic, mainly French wine list starts
with pichets of house wine at £8.25.

GREAT MILTON   Le Manoir aux Quat'Saisons

Church Road, Great Milton, Oxfordshire OX9 7PD
Telephone: (0844) 278881   *Fax:* (0844) 278847
Open: lunch + dinner daily (closed 3 wks Christmas)
Last orders: lunch 2.15pm, dinner 10.15pm

£125

Raymond Blanc's ambitious expansion programme is now complete; the builders have packed up and gone, and he can now revel in his new kitchen, twice the size of the old one. With his brigade of twenty-two chefs, Raymond now opens every day, catering for ninety-five covers in the extended dining room. The conversatory-style extension has a summery pink and white decor and below are the huge new wine cellars. A further thirty covers can also be catered for in the converted stable block, which will be used for receptions. Ten bedrooms and a suite in the old dovecote have been added, bringing the number of rooms to twenty-one.

Raymond's touch at his stove is as assured as ever, and he continues to produce excellent raw ingredients from the grounds of Le Manoir. Try for example his courgettes en fleur de Manoir, au sabayon de truffes et pousses de petits pois. Or, from farther afield, caille des Dombes farcie, jus au vin de Pineau des Charentes et écorces de pamplemousse. Finish with a cassolette fine aux abricots et crème d'amandes amères. Service by Alain Desenclos' team is exemplary, and the wine list of a stature suitable to the surroundings.

The room where Raymond Blanc develops his highly personal, world-renowned cusine.

The blue lounge.

The main lounge.

HAMBLETON   Hambleton Hall Hotel

Hambleton, Oakham, Leicestershire LE15 8TH
Telephone: (0572) 756991   £80
Open: lunch + dinner daily
Last orders: lunch 1.30pm, dinner 9.30pm

Hambleton Hall holds a rather special place in many people's
memories – not just for the approach road flanked by Rutland Water,
nor yet simply for the impressive front entrance to the house itself.
What remains uppermost in memory is the warm greeting, the
friendly, well-informed staff, complemented by the fresh flowers
which spill from room to room. It's the perfect setting for the
accomplished cooking of Brian Baker. What an asset this young chef
is to Hambleton! There are not many more pleasant ways to dine than
gazing out over these gardens to Rutland Water – enjoying, perhaps,
a steamed fillet of sea-bass with an aubergine and mushroom terrine
on a sauce of sweet peppers, or maybe some simple whole lamb's
kidneys roasted in their suet with polenta and baby vegetables.
There are some excellent cheeses, and for pudding an almond milk
blancmange with fresh peaches and a redcurrant coulis. The wine list
includes some annotated personal favourites, for which tasting notes
are available.

Brian Baker (above) *is, with the hotel's setting, Hambleton's greatest asset. Left: Grilled sea-bass on an aubergine and wild mushroom terrine.*

HOPE END   Hope End

Hope End, Ledbury, Hereford & Worcester HR8 1SQ
Telephone: (0531) 3613   *Fax:* (0531) 5697
Open: dinner Wed-Sun (closed mid-Dec to mid-Feb)
Last orders; 8.30pm

£60

Hotel now open 7 days a week

I, for one, am pleased that Patricia and John Hegarty have not gone down the usual country house hotel route. Without any of the frills or fripperies of the traditional country house, this nonetheless rather special house appears almost austere by comparison. But in fact the calm and relaxed feeling of the Scandinavian-influenced interior is the perfect backdrop for Patricia's competent, reliable and flavoursome cooking: cream of mushroom soup, salmi of duckling with juniper stuffing, demerara meringues with black and redcurrant sauces. Flavours are good and earthy, and presentation is simple. John Hegarty assures straightforward service in the plain country-style dining room. Hope End is an excellent place to relax and get away from it all.

The calm and relaxed atmosphere of the Malvern hills provides perfect accompaniment for Patricia Hegarty's cooking at Hope End.

Phase I of beautiful landscaped Georgian gardens now complete with grotto & temple.

ILKLEY   The Box Tree

29 Church Street, Ilkley, West Yorkshire LS29 9DR
Telephone: (0943) 608484
Open: lunch Sun, dinner Tue-Sat (closed Christmas)
Last orders: lunch 2.00pm, dinner 9.45pm

£50

The Box Tree has been around for nearly thirty years and we thought it would be interesting to ask a customer from those early days to report on changes since then. He found the traditions of the over-the-top decor (pictures and ornaments everywhere), pianist and good service, still maintained. The cooking, though, has taken a much more modern stance, with enjoyable dishes such as millefeuille of wood mushrooms and calves' sweetbreads, terrine of mallard with a compôte of redcurrants, or hot raspberry soufflé with a warm raspberry coulis. Such dishes as these should ensure that The Box Tree stays around for another thirty years. Owner Eric Kyte is returning from the States and will be taking a more visible role in 1991, and Andrew Bradley is taking over from Brian Womersley at front of house.

While the 30-year-old traditions of service and style at the Box Tree remain, its cooking has moved with, and helped develop, the tastes of its many customers.

MALVERN WELLS   Croque-en-Bouche

221 Wells Road, Malvern Wells, Worcester WR14 4HF
Telephone: (0684) 565612   **£70**
Open: dinner Wed-Sat (closed Christmas & New Year)
Last orders: dinner 9.30pm

The 1990 Decanter joint award of Wine List of the Year (shared with
Thornbury Castle) to a restaurant with under forty covers must be
doubly gratifying for Robin and Marion Jones. Firstly, of course, it is
a recognition of the undoubted excellence of their wine list, but
secondly it is a personal compliment, for Robin and Marion do
everything for themselves: she in the kitchen, he in the dining room.
That they should also find the time (and energy!) to produce and
constantly improve one of the best wine lists in the country is
testimony to their dedication and enthusiasm. Robin's approach to his
wines encourages advice and experiment. Since prices are reasonable, experimentation by his guests is affordable.

But of course you're not just here for the wines! Marion's cooking
is also some of the best in the area. Her principle is to produce food
as it *used* to be found in provincial France, settling great store by the
quality of her raw ingredients. She does not believe however that
luxury ingredients are necessary to make a good meal. From an
October menu, you might be tempted by a delicious soup of
vegetables and salt cod – vegetables in a broth flavoured with star
anise, and their own salt cod spiced with coriander and ginger. Or a
leg of Welsh lamb, macerated with olive oil and herbs, roast with a
stuffing of garlic and spinach and served with a St Emilion wine sauce.
As ever, the range of salad leaves from their own garden never fails
to astound – accompanying the lamb were red leaves of oak leaf
lettuce, lollo and karibu, red and green parella, little gem and rocket,
all dressed with extra virgin olive oil and balsamic vinegar.

Real provincial French cuisine and an inspired wine list at the Croque-en-Bouche.

NEWCASTLE-UPON-TYNE	Twenty One Queen Street

19-21 Queen Street, Quayside, Newcastle-upon-Tyne, Tyne & Wear NE1 3UG

Telephone: 091-222 0755 **£70**

Open: lunch Mon-Fri, dinner Mon-Sat

Last orders: lunch 2.00pm, dinner 10.45pm (11.00pm Sat)

Terence Laybourne continues to set standards in Newcastle. His accomplished modern cooking shows imagination, with quality and consistency remaining the key notes. Menus are changed quarterly to reflect seasonal produce, supplemented by dishes of the day, which tend to be fish. You might choose a galette of scallops and langoustines with a marmelade of fruits and curry, then fillets of sea-bass and John Dory with red pepper and olive oil sauces. Specialities include a cappuccino of wild mushrooms, and a red mullet and sole terrine; and there are also plenty of well-planned meat dishes. Desserts might include a mango tarte tatin, or a light pear charlotte. The fixed price lunch menu is good value. The smart modern dining room is pale mauve, pink and cream has a '30s feel. Susan Laybourne leads the efficient service.

MELTON MOWBRAY   Stapleford Park

Nr Melton Mowbray, Leicestershire LE14 2EF
Telephone: (057 284) 522   *Fax:* (057 284) 651
Open: lunch + dinner daily
Last orders: lunch 2.30pm, dinner 9.00pm

£65

The lack of stuffiness, so often associated with the grander country
house hotels, is undoubtedly a major contributor to the success of
Bob Payton's Stapleford Park (most of the guests fall into the 30-50
age group). Who else could serve breakfast on Peter Rabbit china and
get away with it?! There have been some fluctuations in the kitchen
but Bob Payton seems to have found kindred spirits in the
husband-and-wife team of Rick Tramonto and Gale Grand from Bob's
home town Chicago. Since he puts his money where his mouth is,
Payton has installed a new kitchen to Tramonto's specification. It's a
kitchen that has to be flexible enough to cope with the demands of a
menu that ranges from home-made pizzas through grills of marinated
fish and meat to a version of bouillabaisse. Gale, a pastry cook, turns
out desserts such as chocolate pecan pie with caramel sauce. The
vegetable garden provides much of their fresh produce, whilst goat's
cheese is made to Rick's specification by a local supplier, and flour is
ground to order at a local windmill. Rooms, designed by the likes of
David Hicks, Nina Campbell and Turnbull & Asser, are elegantly
luxurious. Guests can enjoy a wide range of sporting activities, from
riding to basketball.

*Elegance, well-designed luxury, but there's a welcome lack of self-conscious stuffiness in
the approach of the staff at Stapleford Park. Top right: the Lady Gretton Room. Below
right: the Saloon.*

New Milton   Chewton Glen

Christchurch Road, New Milton, Hampshire BH25 6QS
Telephone: (0425) 275341   *Fax:* (0425) 272310

£95
Open: lunch + dinner, daily
Last orders: lunch 2.00pm, dinner 9.45pm

Standards at Chewton Glen continue in the same professional style
for which it has grown famous over the last twenty-five years. Owner
Martin Skan's commitment to quality is recognised by his peers – he
was named the Hotelier's Hotelier in 1990. Impeccable service and
attention to detail remain the hallmarks here. The conservatory-style
extension to the renowned restaurant is proving popular. The
kitchen continues under the sure hand of Pierre Chevillard with
dishes ranging from sautéed fillet of turbot and langoustines served
with an artichoke-flavoured sauce, or a breast of local duck served on
a bed of provençal olives puréed with potato, to a roast, silver-served
from the trolley. An extensive and in-depth wine list deserves to be
savoured.

Now you can work off the excellent cooking in the newly-built
health club complex which offers everything from reflexology to
tennis, and includes an indoor pool alongside the latest computerised
exercise equipment. I suspect that the only problem in future will be
how to fit all this into the course of your stay – perhaps you'll just
have to stay longer!

Below: *Boeuf Wellington from the kitchens of Pierre Chevillard.*

Above: *the bar.* Below: *the restaurant at Chewton Glen, where owners Martin and Brigitte Skan have now completed their health club complex, predicted in last year's Guide.*

NORTHLEACH   The Old Woolhouse

Market Place, Northleach, Gloucestershire GL54 3EE
Telephone: (0451) 60366
Open: dinner Tue-Sat (lunch by arrangement, closed 1 wk Christmas)
Last orders: dinner 9.30pm

£60

If Jacques Astic ever has time to talk with you, you can bet the main topics will be food, wine and his home-town area, Lyon, and for the traveller, his appraisal of some of the top restaurants there is well worth listening to. This dedicated, hardworking team – Jacques and Jenny – has outlived and outshone, quietly and assuredly, many of its flashier contemporaries. I was reminded on my last visit that it was fifteen years since I first stepped foot in their intimate four or five-tabled restaurant. Over a drink Jenny will take you through the menu and Jacques will cook a distinguished meal of, perhaps, poulet au vinaigre, or fillet of sole with noodles in a Noilly Prat sauce. Game is a speciality in winter, but at any time of the year, this is still one of my favourite places.

Jacques and Jenny Astic follow their own intuitions at The Old Woolhouse. You'll find no preciously followed fashions here.

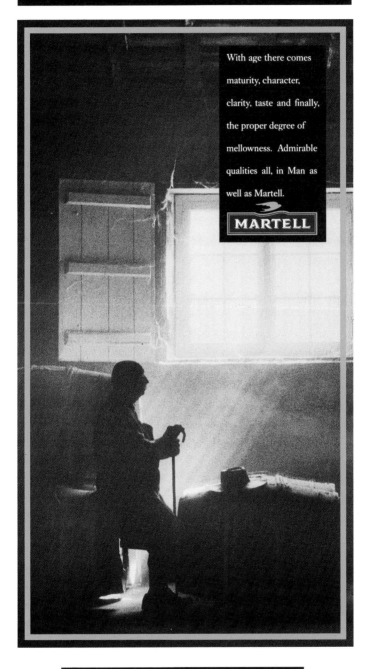

PLYMOUTH | Chez Nous

13 Frankfort Gate, Plymouth, Devon PL1 1QA
Telephone: (0752) 266793
Open: lunch + dinner Tue-Sat (closed Bank Holidays, 3 wks Feb, 3 wks Sept)
Last orders: lunch 2.00pm, 10.30pm

£60

Competitors and followers from the Fastnet and Transatlantic yacht races will invariably be found before departure or after the journey, enjoying Jacques Marchal's reliable straightforward cuisine. But locals (who can usually be relied upon to know a good thing when they see it) form the bulk of his regular customers for dishes such as a blanc de barbue aux chanterelles, and cuisses de canard aux choux verts et pignons de pin. Jacques himself goes to the local fish market and his finds might feature on the menu as le retour de pêche au coulis de poivrons doux. The French wine list has something to suit most pockets. The small team comprising Jacques, his wife Suzanne and one or two staff make this friendly restaurant, with its essentially bistro decor, a must for anyone in the Plymouth area. Don't go expecting a glamorous setting – the restaurant is situated in a shopping precinct, but then so was Raymond Blanc's original restaurant.

Jacques and Suzanne Marchal's illusion of France in a Plymouth shopping mall.

A friendly restaurant and a must for anyone in the Plymouth area.

NORWICH — Adlard's

79 Upper St Giles Street, Norwich, Norfolk NR2 1AB
Telephone: (0953) 603533
Open: lunch Tue-Fri, dinner Tue-Sun
Last orders: lunch 2.00pm, dinner 9.00pm

£60

It's good to see a provincial city such as Norwich with a restaurant such as Adlard's. The welcome from Mary Adlard and her staff is as effervescent as ever. David Adlard has taken on some kitchen staff to ease the pressure on him, and his stylishly simple cooking is consistently enjoyable. Fish and saucing continue to be two of David's fortes on his sensibly short, fixed-price menus. Dishes might include local Brancaster mussels with a basil beurre blanc, followed by breast of wild duck marinaded in honey and soy sauce with a salad of confit of the duck leg and a gratin dauphinois, and ending up with an apple charlotte and cinnamon ice creams. The wine list is wide-ranging and reasonably priced so that one can afford to experiment.

PADSTOW   Seafood Restaurant

Riverside, Padstow, Cornwall PL28 8BY
Telephone: (0841) 532485   *Fax:* (0841) 533344
Open: dinner Mon-Sat (closed mid-Dec – early March)
Last orders: 10.00pm (10.30pm Sat)

£55

Rick Stein excels at his craft and his craft is cooking fish. He feels very strongly about his cooking, preferring food to look utterly fresh and natural (even though it may be the result of much hard work!). Raw fish may be served with soya and Japanese horseradish; sautéed scallops with mange-touts; sea-bass with clams; fruits de mer in the shell, on ice. The harbourside restaurant is light and bright and informal, more relaxed out of season. Booking is essential. A bakery has been added to the delicatessen also run by the Steins, and there are plans to add an oyster bar.

Rick Stein's Padstow restaurant where absolutely fresh fish is the secret.

Fresh fish, landed by local fishermen and cooked the same day in Stein's individual but completely natural style.

POOL-IN-WHARFDALE   Pool Court Restaurant with Rooms

Pool Bank, Pool-in-Wharfdale, Otley, West Yorkshire LS21 1EH
Telephone: (0532) 842288/9   *Fax:* (0532) 843115
Open: dinner Tue-Sat (closed 2 wks summer, 2 wks Christmas)
Last orders: dinner 9.30pm

£50

Consistency and precision set this busy restaurant apart in what is
otherwise a gastronomic wilderness. Its reputation is such that
people will drive miles to eat here. This is a restaurant that
concentrates on attentive service and care for the customer. In the
kitchen, under the watchful eye of Michael Gill, David Watson turns
out some competent, interesting and sometimes innovative dishes,
such as Yorkshire duck pie (a crisp pastry case filled with
mushrooms, onion and braised duck, served with a rich truffle
sauce), oriental salmon with blinis (the salmon marinated with lime,
ginger and coriander, served with tiny Russian pancakes, scallops,
soured cream and salmon caviar), or a lightly curried pumpkin and
saffron soup garnished with toasted almonds and yoghurt. Main
courses include a vegetarian speciality, while puddings are worth
leaving space for. To prolong the pleasure, there are six most
comfortable bedrooms here.

Michael and Hanni Gill's gastronomic oasis – it's worth driving miles to eat here.

PULBOROUGH Stane Street Hollow Restaurant

Codmore Hill, Pulborough, West Sussex RH20 1BG
Telephone: (079 82) 2819
Open: lunch Wed-Fri, dinner Wed-Sat (closed 2 wks May, 2 wks Oct, 2 wks
    Christmas/New Year)
Last orders: lunch 1.15pm, dinner 9.15pm

£50

Consistency is the key word here: you know that when you eat at
René and Ann Kaiser's delightful restaurant you are unlikely to be
disappointed. The greeting is warm – whether you are a regular or a
new face, and the menus, using fresh seasonal produce, offer quite
robust, classically-based dishes. Much of the produce comes from
the Kaisers' own garden, and their own ducks and chickens are also
used. Home-smoked salmon may be available (served with a fresh
horseradish cream), or perhaps kasseler mit weinbirnen (home
smoked loin of port braised in red wine, served with a red wine sauce
and garnished with poached fresh pear), or a canard farci, sauce
groseille. A mainly French wine list is reasonably priced. But, for a
change, why not try a glass of sweet German wine with your dessert?
Set in converted cottages, this is a charming, friendly restaurant
serving good natural food.

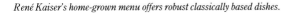

René Kaiser's home-grown menu offers robust classically based dishes.

RIDGEWAY   The Old Vicarage

Ridgeway Moor, Ridgeway, Nr Sheffield, Derbyshire S12 3XW
Telephone: (0742) 475814
Open: lunch Sun, dinner Tue-Sat (closed 1 wk Christmas, 2 wks Aug)
Last orders: lunch 2.30pm, dinner 9.45 pm

£50

At the launch of our 1990 edition, Cliveden chef Ron Maxfield had the task of cooking a menu composed of four specialities from four invited women chefs. The pudding course featured Tessa Bramley's acclaimed baked chocolate pudding with a chocolate fudge sauce and English custard. Afterwards plates were notably empty of crumbs, though Tessa commented that the chocolate could have been more bitter. So, if you want to taste the real thing, a trip to The Old Vicarage is indispensable. What to have before the pudding? Perhaps vine-smoked sea trout with spiced couscous, or pressed beef and calves' foot jelly with wild mushrooms and mustard sauce, or langoustine tempura with oriental dip (Tessa draws her influences from around the globe!); then, as a main course, fillet of lamb served pink, with taglietelli tossed in basil and pine kernels, or fallow deer fillet served with spiced red cabbage and glazed walnuts and a little venison pie, or fillet of brill on a bed of stir-fried sorrel and leek with a crayfish sauce. The extensive wine list has something to suit all pockets and tastes – even chocolate pudding!

Tessa Bramley, whose baked chocolate pudding is infamous.

ROMSEY — The Old Manor House

21 Palmerston Street, Romsey, Hampshire SO51 8GF
Telephone: (0794) 517353
£70
Open: lunch Tue-Sun, dinner Tue-Sat (closed 3 wks Aug, 1 wk Dec)
Last orders: lunch 2.00pm, dinner 9.30pm

Long under-rated by many, the talented Mauro Bregali deserves his white clover. Not just for the care he puts into the production of his food but also for the polished service and style of the establishment, set in an old half-timbered manor house. The little touches applied provide that extra sense of comfort and well-being in his customers. This man is a veritable one-man chain, gathering what he can, hunting what he can, and cooking in an assured and confident fashion. Typical dishes include gratin de cèpes, salamina di ferrara, tresses de saumon à la mandarine impériale, bécasse sur canapé, la poire caramlaisée et sa glace, nougat glacé aux cerises. Excellent cheeses, as always. I'm not sure I don't prefer the old rustic Mauro to the more refined version, but it's well worth making the journey here.

Gatherer, hunter, cook, Mauro Bregoli is the totally integrated restaurateur.

SOUTH MOLTON   Whitechapel Manor

South Molton, Devon EX36 3EG
Telephone: (076 95) 3377   **£65**
Open: dinner daily (lunch daily by arrangement)
Last orders: lunch 2.00pm, dinner 9.15pm

Set high above lush fields and woods, Whitechapel Manor, with its neat terraced gardens, has a friendly, welcoming air. It's a house with character – notice the tilt of the 17th-century panelled ceiling in the lounge. The Shaplands evince a fine sense of hospitality in their attention to detail, such as providing a set of board-games in every bedroom. Antiques enhance the tasteful decor with domestic, rather than 'grand hotel', elegance. In the kitchen, Thierry Leprêtre-Granet continues to substantiate his good reputation for modern French cooking. Local beef, lamb and pork are well-used. But you might try the braised calves' sweetbreads served with celeriac and capers, the Devon crab served between layers of buckwheat pancakes with spinach and crab sauce, or roasted young partridge served with savoy cabbage, bacon and walnuts. To finish, there's caramelized pear with a honey ice cream and chocolate sauce, and some good French and British cheeses.

John and Pat Shapland have mastered the art of easy hospitality at their Elizabethan manor house. Above: Devon crab with buckwheat pancakes, and roast best end of lamb with cous-cous.

John and Pat Shapland and the dining room at Whitechapel Manor.

ST LEONARDS-ON-SEA   Rösers Restaurant

64 Eversfield Place, St Leonards-on-Sea, East Sussex TN37 6DB
Telephone: (0424) 712218
Open: lunch Mon-Fri, dinner Mon-Sat (closed Bank Holidays, 2 wks Jan)
Last orders: lunch 2.00pm, dinner 10.00pm

£60

It is unusual to find good seafront restaurants in this country, which makes Rösers all the more enjoyable. Decor is somewhat reminiscent of an old Wheeler's seafood restaurant, with booth seating around the panelled walls of the room. At a recent lunch, an excellent pike soufflé, served with a smoked salmon and caviar sauce, was alone worth the two-hour journey. A popular choice is a salad of autumn leaves with a slice of warm foie gras, a slice of smoked salmon and avocado – clearly this is intended to satisfy luxury tastes! The main course was beautifully pink roast best end of Romney Marsh lamb, with a tarragon sauce and rösti potatoes. If it's available, a *must* is the apple millefeuille, and the chocolate mousse is good, too. A good wine list with plenty of halves and affordable bottles. Gerald Röser deserves a wider audience. Go there!

SHINFIELD   L'Ortolan

The Old Vicarage, Church Lane, Shinfield, Berkshire RG2 9BY
Telephone: (0734) 883783   **£95**
Open: lunch Tue-Sun, dinner Tue-Sat (closed 2 wks Feb, 2 wks Aug)
Last orders: lunch 2.15pm, dinner 10.30pm

L'Ortolan is now firmly established as one of Britain's top restaurants. John Burton-Race is faced with the same problem as others of this select group, namely to maintain the consistency that such high standards demand. Currently he is succeeding with great style, as may be seen in dishes such as a quail, roasted and sliced, resting on a salad dressed with a walnut oil vinaigrette, spiked with lardons and button mushrooms and croûtons and topped with a quail egg, or baby monkfish tails roasted in a chicken jus, masked with the reduced cooking juices bound with lentils and sweetcorn, then charlotte aux mûres to finish. The wine list is of a depth and range to match the immaculate cooking.

John Burton-Race (left) *maintains the highest standards with his ceaselessly innovative and pleasing cuisine at this 18th-century former vicarage.*

STADDLEBRIDGE   McCoy's

The Cleveland Tontine, Staddlebridge, Nr Northallerton, North Yorkshire
DL6 3JB

Telephone: (060 982) 671

£65

Open: restaurant: dinner Tue-Sun; bistro: lunch + dinner daily (closed 25+26
    Dec, 1 Jan)

Last orders: lunch 2.00pm, dinner 10.00pm (bistro 10.30pm)

This establishment is Yorkshire's answer to Langan's. Downstairs
the noisy, bustling bistro plays to packed houses every night.
Upstairs the restaurant serves its own style of food – a cross
between modern British and a more earthy country style. Try
perhaps flat mushrooms filled with chicken mousse, then sliced duck
breast with spinach stuffing and red wine sauce, and treacle tart with
custard to finish. The wine list offers good value, with very
reader-friendly tasting notes! The McCoy brothers are always in
attendance with their cheerful humour and exuberance. Plans are
afoot to add to the six existing simple bedrooms.

*The McCoy brothers have established a
style unique in the North at their ground-
floor restaurant and basement
bistro.*

Cheerful humour, exuberance even, but Tom McCoy's cooking is seriously good, developing as it does many successful culinary combinations previously unavailable to Yorkshire.

STON EASTON   Ston Easton Park

Ston Easton, Nr Bath, Avon BA3 4DF
Telephone: (076 121) 631   *Fax:* (076 121) 377
Open: lunch + dinner daily
Last orders: lunch 2.00pm, dinner 9.30pm (10.00pm Sat)

£70

This Grade 1 listed Palladian mansion is set within extensive grounds. A golf course will shortly join the list of sporting facilities available here. The formality of this grand house is offset in the main dining room by the use of soft colours and chinoiserie-style chairs. Overall there's good attention to detail, and service is by young, informed staff. At dinner, a fixed-price menu offers four courses of food modern in presentation. You might choose a terrine of maize-fed chicken and foie gras with a light shallot dressing, or a timbale of pike and lobster in a rich cognac cream. For a main course there might be roast partridge on a celeriac galette with baby vegetables and truffle sauce, or medallions of marinated venison with a tartlet of wild mushrooms. There's always a good vegetarian dish available, and good home-made bread. The wine list is extensive and includes a good selection of affordable bottles.

Above left: *Quenelles of lobster wrapped in spinach leaves in a cognac cream sauce.*
Right: *Double chocolate layer cake filled with hazelnut meringue.*

STORRINGTON   **Manleys**

Manleys Hill, Storrington, West Sussex RH20 4BT
Telephone: (0903) 742331   £65
Open: lunch + dinner Tue-Sat (closed Bank Holidays, 2 wks Jan, 2 wks
       Aug/Sep)
Last orders: lunch 2.00pm, dinner 9.30pm

There have been rumours that Karl Löderer is selling up. We hope
they're unjustified, because he is such an asset to this part of the
world. Karl is a talented and capable chef whose essentially classic
cooking has earned him a good reputation since his early days here.
Popular with locals, Manley's also enjoys a clientele drawn as far
afield as London. Those who make the trip to this comfortably
elegant restaurant – whether from near or far – enjoy dishes such as
a millefeuilles de saumon à la sauce langoustine, and noix de St
Jacques à l'encre et tagliatelle miste (made with local scallops and
vegetable tagliatelle). Meat dishes may refer to Karl's Austrian
background: gefüllter rostbraten nach wiener art (grilled sirloin steak
filled with herbs and shallots, served with crisp onions, bacon and
french beans). As an alternative to Karl's renowned salzburger
nockerln, try the kaiser schmarrn mit himbeersaft (a light, hot
sponge with sultanas, soaked in rum and served with raspberry
sauce). The mainly French wine list offers something for most
pockets.

*Karl Löderer attracts custom from as far as London to his Storrington
restaurant.*

STOW-ON-THE-WOLD — Epicurean

* has moved

1 Park Street, Stow-on-the-Wold, Gloucestershire GL54 1AQ
Telephone: (0451) 31613
£85
Open: lunch Tue-Sun, dinner Tue-Sat (closed 2 wks Jan, 2wks Aug)
Last orders: lunch 2.30pm, dinner 11.30 pm

Business is picking up at the Epicurean and this is indeed a restaurant that deserves to succeed. Patrick McDonald is passionate about cooking and he has staked all to elevate the experience of dining at Stow-on-the-Wold. There must be many living in the area who commute to London and appreciate unreservedly his talent for providing good food. Give this restaurant your support – it's worth it. Typically excellent was a recent meal starting with a ravioli of wild mushrooms with a truffle fond riche and salad leaves, followed by pan-fried mullet and scallops with pesto and tomato dressing. Don't be misled by the Cotswold cottage exterior – this is a prettily elegant restaurant with simple bare stone walls offset by immaculate cream cloths, comfortable upholstered chairs and sparkling fire glass and china. Service is courteous and friendly.

* to:-
Cleveland House
Evesham Road
Cheltenham
Tel. 0242 518898

Right: *Patrick McDonald, whose flair in the kitchen is making Epicurean live up to its name.*

Epicurean: a prettily elegant restaurant that deserves to succeed.

STROUD   Oakes

169 Slad Road, Stroud, Gloucestershire GL5 1RG
Telephone: (0453) 759950
£65
Open: lunch Tue-Sun, dinner Tue-Sat (closed 4 wks Dec/Jan, 1 wk Aug)
Last orders: lunch 1.45pm, dinner 9.30pm

Oakes enjoys a simple setting. Although set in a substantial house, Chris Oakes has decided to strip away the swags and plush decor, avoid unnecessary garnish and concentrate on the essential nuances of the food on your plate. This means that produce has to be of the highest quality and freshness, and the menus are short so that he can concentrate on achieving the highest standards throughout. Fish is undoubtedly the strong point of his unpretentious approach, as in a boneless Dover sole filled with a fish mousse and served with a mushroom vermouth and butter sauce. But his treatment of meat is also excellent, as in boneless guinea fowl legs filled with mushrooms and served with a smoked ham and madeira sauce. Good vegetables and desserts, and a short reasonably priced wine list.

TAPLOW   Cliveden

Taplow, Buckinghamshire SL6 0JF
Telephone: (062 86) 68561   *Terrace or Waldo's:*
Open: lunch + dinner daily
Last orders: lunch 1.30pm, dinner 9.00pm

£90

For visitors interested in history and luxury, Cliveden is a must: it has now settled down as a distinguished and important member of the British hotel scene. Much money has been spent on the most sophisticated of equipment for the new boardroom, which boasts more technology than I dare think about. But don't misunderstand me: the house itself remains traditional in both decor and values. From the porters' welcoming greeting and the moment of panic (in my case!) when the maid arrives to unpack your luggage, you know that you have returned to a bygone era of standards and service. The Honourable John Sinclair, a great believer in training and motivation, ensures that all members of his staff make your stay pleasurable.

The traditional said, John Sinclair knows that Cliveden has to move with the times, hence the opening this year of the Pavilion, housing a superbly equipped gym, ozone-treated indoor swimming pool, and virtually every other amenity a leisure centre could contain!

Another innovation in 1990 is the opening of Waldo's, Cliveden's intimate new restaurant that offers Cliveden's chef, Ron Maxfield, an opportunity to display an individualistic approach to modern cookery. Air-conditioned, no-smoking and seating only twenty-four, the new venture offers four courses for £46 or five for £50, inclusive of mineral water (a nice touch), coffee and VAT. No service charge is included or expected. You might choose a warm chicken savarin wrapped in spinach with freshwater crayfish and mussels, and a sauce made from the cooking juices, then saddle of rabbit stuffed with cashew nuts with a tortellini of livers on a St Emilion sauce, infused with cèpes, and to finish, a warm caramelised apple and filo pastry tart on a bilberry sauce with cinnamon ice cream. Cliveden's wine list is all that you would expect in such a setting.

View of Cliveden from the fountain of love.

The Great Hall.

Above: *the dining room.*
Below: *the Pavilion pool and smorgasbord buffet.*

TETBURY   Calcot Manor

Tetbury, Gloucestershire GL8 8YJ
Telephone: (0666) 890391   *Fax:* (0666) 890394
£75
Open: lunch daily, dinner Mon-Sat (daily for residents) (closed 1 wk Jan)
Last orders: lunch 2.00pm, dinner 9.30pm

The Ball family continue to dispense thoughtful hospitality at their attractive converted farmhouse. Once part of Kingswood Abbey, founded in 1158, the outbuildings include a 14th-century tithe barn. Each of the well-equipped bedrooms has its own character, reflecting some aspect of the region. Chef Ray (Ramon) Farthing celebrates his thirtieth birthday this year, and his cooking is modern, assured and extremely enjoyable. Try for example a terrine of marinated rainbow trout layered with sliced vegetables and wild mushrooms, served with a fine ratatouille and sevruga caviar, followed perhaps by loin of fresh rabbit baked in creamed celeriac, spinach and short pastry served with roasted goose liver, home-made noodles and a rabbit sauce, and finish with Calcot's speciality apple dessert – four classical variations on the apple. A meal cooked by Ray is certainly one of the highlights of a visit to Calcot.

Ramon Farthing, Brian and Richard Ball.

THORNBURY   **Thornbury Castle**

Thornbury, Avon BS12 1HH
Telephone: (0454) 418511
Open: lunch + dinner daily (closed 10 days Jan)
Last orders: lunch 2.00pm, dinner 9.30pm

£70

The excellence of owner Maurice Taylor's wine cellars has been recognised in the 1990 Decanter joint award of Wine List of the Year (shared with Croque-en-Bouche) in a restaurant with forty covers. In particular, Maurice is private cellar yields many a fine old wine, resulting in some interesting selections on what he calls the Proprietor's Reserve List. Derek Hamlen is now head chef and continues to turn out reliable specialities such as a crisp salad of smoked chicken with lardons of bacon and toasted croûtons dressed with a hazelnut vinaigrette, fillet of Scottish beef sauté with whole grain Pommery mustard, deglazed with claret and cream, and Thornbury Castle's own butterscotch pudding.

Below left to right: *the Tower Dining Room and the lounge at Thornbury Castle where, in particular, Maurice Taylor's wine choices are well worth savouring.*

ULLSWATER	**Sharrow Bay** **Country House Hotel**

Howtown Road, Lake Ullswater, Cumbria CA10 2LZ
Telephone: (076 84) 86301   *Fax:* (076 84) 86349 £80
Open: lunch Tue-Sun, dinner daily (closed Dec-Feb)
Last orders: lunch 1.30pm, dinner 8.30pm

'Cooking is an art and all art is patience,' proclaims the menu, but Francis Coulson has decided that forty-two seasons is a long enough stint at the stove. Johnnie Martin, Colin Akrigg and Philip Wilson now head the brigade in the kitchen, and the team has been strengthened by the return of Colin White, who cooked here some twenty-five years ago having applied successfully for the job of 'perfectionist young chef'. Radical change in the kitchen is unlikely. White's liking of good honest food is in accord with Sharrow Bay's style, which Coulson admits has barely changed over the years. Indeed, he claims that there would be uproar if certain favourites were removed from the menu! So the famous sticky toffee pudding is safe! Traditional British dishes are mixed with some, more modern, so that roast breast of duckling cooked in the English style may feature on the same menu as a paupiette of smoked salmon filled with a smoked trout mousseline and served with a red pepper sauce. Wonderful, over-the-top bedrooms; and friendly, helpful old-fashioned courtesy.

Sharrow Bay, the prototype country house hotel, retains its pre-eminence.

WARMINSTER | Bishopstrow House

Boreham Road, Warminster, Wiltshire BA12 9HH
Telephone: (0985) 212312   *Fax:* (0985) 216769
Open: lunch + dinner daily
Last orders: lunch 2.00pm, dinner 9.00pm (9.30pm Fri + Sat)

£65

Chris Suter is a talented young man who hasn't let his success as the 1990 Young Chef of the Year go to his head. He is cooking extremely well in his new kitchen with his 'turbo ferrari' stove, as he calls it! If it's available, try his award-winning breast of Bresse pigeon and foie gras cooked en papillote and served on a pool of its own juices, or perhaps a seared salmon supreme served on a raw tomato dressing. Much money has been spent on refurbishing the spacious bedrooms and installing indoor and outdoor swimming pools and an indoor tennis court. This is a hotel determined to lift itself into the top league.

Luxurious facilities, including indoor and outdoor pools, match the high standard of cuisine from Chris Suter, 1990 Young Chef of the Year.

WATERHOUSES   The Old Beams Restaurant

Leek Road, Waterhouses, Staffordshire ST10 3HW
Telephone: (0538) 308254
Open: lunch Tue-Fri + Sun, dinner Tue-Sat (closed 2 wks Jan)
Last orders: lunch 2.00pm, dinner 10.00pm

£60

The best way to appreciate Ann and Nigel Wallis' hospitality and good
food is to book one of the en-suite rooms and stay overnight. Decor is
simple but tasteful and beds immensely comfortable. Ann looks after
you with warmth and enthusiasm. In the kitchen, Nigel uses good
fresh produce, much of it local, in sound, simply presented dishes
such as sauté of calves' sweetbreads on a creamy mustard sauce, or
noisettes of lamb with a ragoût of roast vegetables. The cheeseboard
is well chosen, as is the reasonably priced wine list. It's a pleasure to
have an establishment of this quality in the area.

Above left: *Ann and Nigel Wallis, whose restaurant with rooms is a real pleasure.*
Above right: *Rendezvous of fresh fish in a chervil sauce.*

WINDERMERE   Miller Howe

Rayrigg Road, Windermere, Cumbria LA23 1EY
Telephone: (096 62) 2536   *Fax:* (096 62) 5664
Open: dinner daily (closed early March, early Dec)
Last orders: 8.30pm

£70

The concept of a no-choice set menu is one that goes down curiously
well with the British. Its arch-exponent in the milieu of good regional
British cooking – John Tovey – has had people beating a regular path
to his door for more than two decades. Timings of meals here are
rigid but that doesn't seem to worry anyone, though first-timers
should be aware of this. The resulting pressure on the pre-dinner
drinks area has been relieved by the addition of a conservatory-style
extension. There has been one other change this year – John Tovey
has stepped down as head chef to allow more time for his writing and
broadcasting, and Ian Dutton, who has been here since 1985, is now
in charge of the kitchen. The style of the food remains the same, with
the imaginative five-course menus including a choice of puddings and
a 'simple' cheese plate, as well as an appetiser and coffee with
home-made truffles. You will need to have spent all day walking to
accomodate all this! The views over Lake Windermere remain one of
the other joys of this comfortable Edwardian house.

Rigid schedules, no-choice menus, but John Tovey's style of food is uniquely good.

WINDERMERE	Roger's Restaurant

4 High Street, Windermere, Cumbria LA23 1AF
Telephone: (096 62) 4954
£55
Open: dinner Mon-Sat (closed Christmas)
Last orders: dinner 9.30pm

For many, Roger and Alana Pergl-Wilson's restaurant has become a favourite place for dinner. Alana's friendly, smiling greeting welcomes regulars and newcomers alike. Tables are arranged closely together along the walls in a cosy, modern setting that is a welcome respite from the lakeland norm. Roger's cooking remains the 'raison d'être': his approach is straightforward with a skilful handling of flavours in dishes such as fresh wild Scottish salmon steak with herb butter; fillet steak with a fresh wild mushroom sauce. Service is informal and friendly as befits this good-value, relaxed restaurant.

WOBURN   Paris House

Woburn Park, Woburn, Bedfordshire MK17 9QP
Telephone: (0525) 290692   **£60**
Open: lunch Tue-Sun, dinner Tue-Sat (closed Feb)
Last orders: lunch 2.00pm, dinner 10.00pm

The evolution of menus here seems to mark a gradual change of direction which suggests that they are now catering for a wider range of people. Perhaps try a feuilleté of lambs' tongues in tarragon, or salmon in jelly with baby vegetables; followed by venison stew with port and redcurrant sauce, or hot poached salt beef in consommé. Finish with poached peach and almond glacé, or warn prune tart with armagnac sabayon. Excellent Duboeuf house wines.

This much-travelled house – it went over to Paris and back for the Great Exhibition – enjoys the tranquil setting of Woburn Park. It's as appealing in winter, looking out over the parkland, as it is in the summer to enjoy with a drink in the garden.

Peter Chandler, chef/patron of Paris House.

YORK	Middlethorpe Hall

Bishopthorpe Road, York, North Yorkshire YO2 1QP
Telephone: (0904) 641241   *Fax:* (0904) 620176
Open: lunch + dinner daily
Last orders: lunch 2.00pm, dinner 9.45pm

white clover for decor & style

£65

This classically beautiful William and Mary house continues to delight visitors with either business or leisure in mind; it is situated not far from York racecourse. The interior fulfils the promise of its imposing exterior, with its great hall, open fireplace and grand staircase; and the thirty en-suite bedrooms are comfortably and generously equipped. The kitchen supplies the formal dining rooms with dishes encompassing both the traditional and the modern; the wine list is in the middle to upper price bracket, in keeping with the setting.

Still THE place to stay in the York area.

Bottom left: *the library at Middlethorpe Hall.* Above: *the entrance.*

WORCESTER — Brown's Restaurant

24 Quay Street, Worcester WR1 2JJ
Telephone: (0905) 26263
Open: lunch Sun-Fri, dinner Mon-Sat (closed Bank Holidays, 1 wk Christmas)
Last orders: lunch 1.45pm, dinner 9.45pm (10.00pm Sat)

£65

There's an infectious good humour about this converted riverside cornmill. High cream-painted brick walls are lined with good modern prints and paintings. Pink cloths and cascading green plants add visual warmth. Food is of a good standard. An enjoyable dish was a salmi of duck with lentilles de puy in a red wine sauce. Vegetables may include a casserole of dauphinoise potatoes and cabbage with bacon. Good, mainly British cheeses make up a cheeseboard that is well explained by the helpful, friendly staff. Brown's is as good for a dinner with friends as it is for a quiet meal on your own.

ABERFELDY   Atkins Restaurant

Farleyer House, Aberfeldy, Tayside PH15 2JE

Telephone: (0887) 20332
£60
Open: lunch + dinner daily
Last orders: lunch 1.00pm, dinner 8.30pm

Frances Atkins can turn out some stunning cooking. She is a
compulsive cook, emerging from the kitchen exhausted but inspired.
Tony Heath (ex-Murrayshall) has joined her. Their style is modern
British. A recent meal started with excellent appetisers: a little slice
of foie gras and chicken terrine, scallop mousseline and lobster, an
absolutely delicious combination of textures, flavours and colours. A
tender, moist breast of guinea fowl was served with an excellent
sauce with woodland chanterelles. Essentially French wines appear
on the list, with a sprinkling from other countries. Bedrooms are
fresh and simple in style, and the bar and dining room are furnished
with antiques.

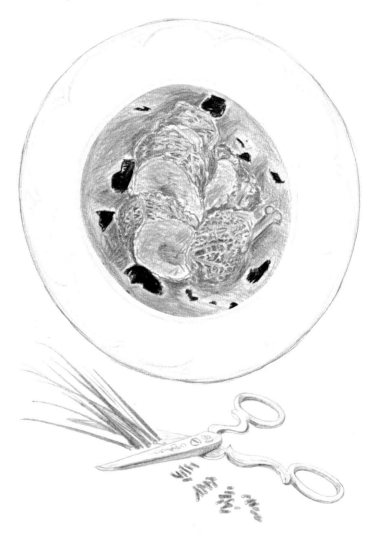

EDINBURGH   **Martins**

70 Rose Street, North Lane, Edinburgh, Lothian EH2 3DX
Telephone: 031-225 3106   **£50**
Open: lunch Tue-Fri, dinner Tue-Sat (closed 4 wks Christmas)
Last orders: lunch 2.00pm, dinner 10.00pm

A back street behind the Rose Street pedestrian precinct is the
unpropitious location for this excellent small restaurant. A simple,
bright decor is offset by tables laid with silver, cut glass and fine
china. An attention to detail is the hallmark of Martin and Gay Irons'
style – from bread to cheese to service – with Gay in the bar and
Martin in the restaurant. Fish remains a prominent feature of the
modern cooking, as seen in sautéed supremes of gurnard with a
yellow pepper and saffron sauce, or poached turbot, halibut and brill
with a cognac and szechuan peppercorn sauce. The selection of
crisply cooked vegetables is organic whenever possible. The concise
wine list includes a good range of halves.

Fish remains a prominent feature at this, one of the best restaurants in Edinburgh.

GLASGOW — One Devonshire Gardens

1 Devonshire Gardens, Glasgow, Strathclyde G12 0UX

Telephone: 041-334 9494   *Fax:* 041-337 1668

£65

Open: lunch Sun-Fri, dinner daily

Last orders: lunch 2.00pm, dinner 11.00pm

For sheer style, this sumptuous town house hotel is hard to beat. Formed out of three adjoining town houses, in an area of graceful Victorian mansions, One Devonshire Gardens was designed to feel like a private home rather than a hotel. Each room, with its clever use of colour – especially deep blues and warm reds, lighting and good furniture, makes a statement of good taste. The well-equipped bedrooms include CD players. A new chef, Roy Brett, produces a menu of understated modern dishes using seasonal produce such as a mussel and onion stew, or breast of wood pigeon in filo pastry, or salt-baked turbot. A simple dessert menu might offer a choice of bread and butter pudding, fresh fruit terrine, and the well-kept cheeseboard. The concise wine list offers something to suit most pockets and palates, including a scattering of half-bottles.

Opulence certainly, but it's made to feel like a private house rather than a hotel.

Bottom left: *the drawing room.*
Above: *one of the well-equipped bedrooms at One Devonshire Gardens.*

FORT WILLIAM　　　　　　　　Inverlochy Castle

Torlundy, Fort William, Highland PH33 6SN
Telephone: (0397) 2177/8　*Fax:* (0397) 2953
Open: lunch + dinner daily (closed mid-Nov to mid-Mar)
Last orders: lunch 1.45pm, dinner 9.15pm

£80

Inverlochy embodies a spirit of professionalism right down to the smallest detail. Our last visit, just days before their annual winter closure, saw no fall-off in standards, even with a well-earned rest almost upon Grete Hobbs' team. Your name is known, remembered and used, room service trays are immaculately laid out, and service in the dining room is polished and not at all starchy.

March 1991 will see the advent of 28-year-old David Whiffen, Connaught-trained, in charge of the Castle kitchens. As hotel manager Michael Leonard explained, his customers are now looking for more traditional food such as oxtail or steak and kidney, and he has every confidence that David will fit the Inverlochy mould well. The wine list is outstanding, and appropriate to the stature of a Castle. Bedrooms are sumptuously appointed.

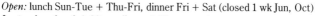

GULLANE   La Potinière

Main Street, Gullane, Lothian EH31 2AA
Telephone: (0620) 843214
Open: lunch Sun-Tue + Thu-Fri, dinner Fri + Sat (closed 1 wk Jun, Oct)
Last orders: lunch 1.00pm, dinner 8.00pm

£55

The setting is an unassuming cottage with a pretty, beamed dining room. The cooking is among the best, north of the border, and Hilary Brown's inspiration is refuelled by annual trips to France. Her style tends to rich, creamy sauces, impeccably dressed salads, stunning dauphinoise potatoes, pigeon with lentils – essentially bourgeois cooking. The no-choice menu changes at each meal, and there's just one (prompt) sitting. David Brown does all the serving. It's worth getting here early to discuss wines with him; the list is magnificent and much of it affordable. Now open for dinner on Fridays also – but booking months ahead is still essential at weekends.

KINGUSSIE   The Cross

25-27 High Street, Kingussie, Highland PH21 1HX
Telephone: (0540) 661166   *Fax:* (0540) 661080   **£55**
Open: dinner Tue-Sat (closed 3 wks May/Jun, 5 wks Nov/Dec)
Last orders: dinner 9.00pm

Plans are afoot for expansion at The Cross (extending the back of the building into a new kitchen and dining room), but meanwhile you can still enjoy the hospitality of Tony and Ruth Hadley in the existing warm and cosy restaurant, each table bearing a welcoming posy of flowers. Tony will go through the menu with you, and there is very much a sense of being a welcome guest in the Hadleys' home. Ruth Hadley's touch is as sure as ever as a recent meal testified: an excellently judged prawn and ginger soufflé with the flavours perfectly balanced, a good contrast to a main course of braised grey partridge with lentils and spiced red cabbage. The pudding was her famous chocolate whisky laird, a meltingly rich marquise slice. The three bedrooms are comfortably furnished without pretention, warm and welcoming and not encumbered by phones or TVs, and Ruth's breakfasts are as delicious as her dinners.

Ruth Hadley's touch is as sure as ever at one of our finest Highland restaurants.

LINLITHGOW   Champanay Inn

Champanay, Linlithgow, Lothian EH49 7LU

Telephone: (050 683) 4532
£80
Open: lunch Mon-Fri, dinner Mon-Sat
Last orders: lunch 2.00pm, dinner 10.00pm

Did you know that beef is not as good in the spring because the cattle
have been feeding on grain all winter, whereas in summer they feed
on grass? That's why the Davidsons (former butchers) use different
cuts of meat according to the season. This unusual restaurant is a
round, former farmhouse milking parlour, accessed by a track.
Freshness is paramount here: you select your meat from a display, or
a lobster from the large sea-water tank. You choose your vegetables
from a large basket; they return excellently cooked, as is the grilled
steak. Start with some smoked salmon from the new smokehouse. A
staggering array of wines is strongest on burgundies.

PEAT INN   Peat Inn

Peat Inn, By Cupar, Fife KT15 5LH
Telephone: (033 484) 206   *Fax:* (033 484) 530
Open: lunch + dinner Tue-Sat (closed 2 wks Jan, 10 days Nov)
Last orders: lunch 1.00pm, dinner 9.30pm

£65

David Wilson says, modestly, that his food reflects the region, but any limitations that imposes on its range are amply compensated for by its quality. The disarming candour of David's approach is one of the secrets of the Peat Inn's success. The Wilsons' aim is to let customers escape from life's pressures, and what more delightful an escape than to savour an aromatic fish soup and, perhaps, breast of wild duck in its juices, flavoured with thyme, followed by a caramelised apple pastry with a caramel sauce. It's worth trying the good value menu, and the outstanding wine list deserves special attention. You can stay in one of the eight suites with their French period furniture and marble bathrooms.

David Wilson treats high quality local ingredients with an inspired touch.

THE·PEAT·INN

ULLAPOOL — Altnaharrie Inn

Ullapool, Highland IV26 2SS
Telephone: (085 483) 230
Open: dinner daily (closed Oct-Easter)
Last orders: dinner 7.45pm

£95

Altnaharrie is, quite simply, a haven of good food. It's accessible only by boat, and it's a tribute to Gunn Eriksen and Fred Brown that so many happily make the crossing. It's a friendly isolation, though, with a warm, bright Scandinavian feel to the interior. Spontaneous inspiration for the food comes from hill walks, what's available that day, and Gunn's imagination. Her cooking is outstanding by any standards, but all the more surprising in this location. Everything possible is made on the premises. The five-course menu offers no choice until the pudding stage, but that is no hardship when offered, for example, a 'soup' of langoustine and squat lobster with a mousseline of scallops wrapped in a leaf of lettuce; then layers of foie gras and asparagus on a bed of crisp potato cake with two sauces, one of veal juices and one of wild sorrel and mushrooms; followed by a main course of wild salmon with a swirl of witch and a filling of crab, leek and ginger in a champagne butter sauce. Cheeses come from Philippe Olivier but the puddings return us to the realm of Gunn's individual imagination: a cranberry cake with hazelnuts, almonds, chocolate and vanilla cream covered with a thin layer of marzipan; or banana baked in a thin shell of pastry with a sauce of cream, orange and cointreau, or a little pastry basket filled with raspberries, strawberries and blueberries with a small heart of ice cream and sauces of raspberries and strawberries. Stay a few days and really appreciate Altnaharrie: eight bedrooms which include a bedside torch and candle for when the generator is switched off.

Below left and right: *the dining room at Gunn Eriksen and Fred Brown's Altnaharrie Inn, where the outstanding cooking, extraordinary views and splendid welcome will dispel any doubts its remoteness may suggest.*

ADARE 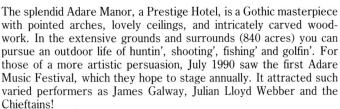 Adare Manor

Adare, Co. Limerick
Telephone: (061) 396566   *Fax:* (061) 396124
Open: lunch + dinner daily
Last orders: lunch 2.00 pm, dinner 10.00 pm

£70

The splendid Adare Manor, a Prestige Hotel, is a Gothic masterpiece with pointed arches, lovely ceilings, and intricately carved wood-work. In the extensive grounds and surrounds (840 acres) you can pursue an outdoor life of huntin', shootin', fishing' and golfin'. For those of a more artistic persuasion, July 1990 saw the first Adare Music Festival, which they hope to stage annually. It attracted such varied performers as James Galway, Julian Lloyd Webber and the Chieftains!

Adare's kitchens are now led by an equally respected name: Ian McAndrew. Ian collected accolades galore at Eastwell Manor then Restaurant 74, then appeared briefly in London's One Sixteen Knightsbridge before settling down at Adare. In between he has had published two books, *A Feast of Fish* and *Poultry and Game.* Such culinary predilections stand him in good stead at Adare, where his robust modern British approach finds an abundance of these products, to the delight of a contented audience. His approach, described as Ian's Irish Dimension, accompanies local lamb or venison with vegetables from the garden, and sends to Cork for oysters. Try a terrine of cauliflower with a sauce of smoked salmon and pearls of salmon caviar, then lamb roasted and served with a parsley mousse and a sauce of carrots and tarragon, and home-made vanilla ice cream in a brandy snap basket with a salad of fruits to complete a meal. A strong wine list, with great depth in the clarets, complements Ian's cooking, as does the service led by his wife Jane.

ADARE   Mustard Seed

Main Street, Adare, Co Limerick
Telephone: (061) 86451
Open: dinner Tue-Sat (closed Feb)
Last orders: dinner 10.00pm

Its isolated location makes the Mustard Seed all the more appreciated. The setting is picturesque: tubs of flowers lead to the
yellow-washed house with its blue-painted woodwork. There's a
friendly welcome from owner Daniel Mullane and young, attentive
and informed staff. The two dining rooms are cottagey and
atmospheric: bric-à-brac and fresh flowers abound. Thomas O'Leary
produces some very competent and enjoyable dishes such as grilled
lambs' kidneys wrapped in bacon and served with a spicy mayonnaise, goujons of monkfish with a saffron and Noilly Prat sauce, and,
to finish, wheels of shortcake on a minted strawberry coulis. The
emphasis is on freshness, and home-made details are good, for
instance the soda bread, and the chocolates served with coffee.
Well-chosen wines.

BLACKROCK — The Park Restaurant

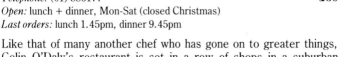

40 Main Street, Blackrock, Co Dublin
Telephone: (01) 886177 £60
Open: lunch + dinner, Mon-Sat (closed Christmas)
Last orders: lunch 1.45pm, dinner 9.45pm

Like that of many another chef who has gone on to greater things, Colin O'Daly's restaurant is set in a row of shops in a suburban shopping centre. The emphasis here is on the food; the rather plain dining room has no frills or furbelows to detract attention from what is on the plate – except perhaps for the single rose on each table. And Colin's food definitely stands out, being soundly based on classical techniques yet not dated: strips of duck breast with an apple and bacon salad; cassoulet of guinea-fowl; and his specialities – steamed lobster, and venison.

DUBLIN   Restaurant Patrick Guilbaud

46 James Place, Off Baggot Street, Dublin, Co Dublin
Telephone: (01) 764192   *Fax:* (01) 601546
Open: lunch Mon-Fri, dinner Mon-Sat (closed Bank Holidays)
Last orders: lunch 2.00pm, dinner 10.15pm

£65

This year sees the tenth anniversary of this, one of Ireland's leading French restaurants. The team is the same, with Patrick Guilbaud as urbane and welcoming as ever, and Guillaume Lebrun continuing to delight with his beautifully presented modern food. Local fish and offal are strong points, while Irish lamb may be cooked with crushed black peppercorns and served with boiled garlic cloves. Excellent cheeses. Service is discreetly efficient. Abstract paintings and plants add colour to the two, light, modern dining rooms. White clover for cooking, decor and style.

KENMARE   Park Hotel

Kenmare, Co Kerry
Telephone: (064) 41200   *Fax:* (064) 41402
Open: lunch + dinner daily (closed 2 Jan – Easter, Nov – 23 Dec)
Last orders: lunch 1.45pm, dinner 20.45pm

£75

As a result of an extensive facelift, thirty-seven of the Park's bedrooms have doubled in size, and include comfortable sitting areas. Antiques complement the restrained decor. Well-equipped bathrooms include a phone (one of three in each suite!), bathrobes and huge towels. The hotel prides itself on its tranquil atmosphere, and high standards of food and service – the porter's greeting, the shoe cleaning service, the turn-down at night – all contribute to the overall sense of ease. In the restaurant, seafood from nearby Kenmare Bay – sea urchins, sole, salmon and turbot – is often a feature of the good modern cooking.

SHANAGARRY	Ballymaloe House

Shanagarry, Co Cork
Telephone: (021) 652531   *Fax:* (021) 652021
Open: lunch Mon-Sat, dinner Sun-Sat (closed 3 dys Christmas)
Last orders: lunch 2.00pm, 9.30pm

£60

Set in 400 acres of farmland, Ballymaloe is a rambling building draped in wisteria, the outbuildings washed a Mediterranean pink. In summer, the swimming pool echoes with the squeals of delighted children. The family atmosphere is warmly welcoming. This is real Irish country house hospitality, with rooms offering simple comforts. Myrtle Allen draws her inspiration from local produce, from the farm, fish landed at nearby Ballycotton, Irish farmhouse cheeses. Myrtle's re-interpretation of traditional Irish cooking produces robust French-influenced country food: Ballycotton fish soup, chicken baked with butter and fresh herbs, lamb provençal. Bordeaux gets pride of place on the wine list.

It's friendly, it's warm, it's a truly Irish country house hotel. Myrtle Allen (above) explores the traditions of Irish cooking in a robust French-influenced style.

PORTRUSH   Ramore

The Harbour, Portrush, Co Antrim BT56 8DN
Telephone: (0265) 822448
Open: dinner Tue-Sat (closed 2 wks Jan/Feb, Christmas + New Year)
Last orders: dinner 10.00pm

£50

George McAlpin's cooking is of a consistently high standard, with dishes ranging from roast quail on a bed of pickled red cabbage, with a potato galette and a cream sauce, to Dover sole meunière. Desserts are a speciality: try hot lemon or chocolate soufflé. The mostly-French wine list includes a separate list of half-bottles as well as good value house wines (white from the Rhône, red from Bordeaux). Mother-in-law Joy Caithness looks after the efficient service in the modern black-and-white themed dining room of this busy harbourside restaurant. Lunch is served in the informal wine bar downstairs.

LLANDEWI SKIRRID   Walnut Tree Inn

Llandewi Skirrid, Abergavenny, Gwent NP7 8AW

Telephone: (0873) 2797

£50

Open: lunch + dinner Tue-Sat (closed 2 wks Feb, Christmas)

Last orders: lunch 3.30pm, dinner 10.30pm

'Plus ça change, moins ça change': the old adage is particularly true of the restaurant business. So I suspect that Franco Taruschio must be chuckling over the current trend towards earthy Italian cooking, since after all that is what he has been serving to his customers for the past twenty-eight years! With time, Franco's repertoire has developed to incorporate Oriental, particularly Thai influences. Thus goujons of sole may be offered alongside an old favourite brodetto (fish stew), Thai pork or porchetta, tagliatella with white truffles in season, sicilian cheesecake and mango ice-cream. Wines from Reid Wines are well balanced to the menu. Ann Taruschio keeps an eye on service in this unique, simple, ever bustling and unpretentious inn.

Mediterranean cuisine in South Wales – a novel idea in 1961 when Franco Taruschio introduced it. Since then his repertoire has extended to incorporate a whole range of far-flung influences that his customers have not found it difficult to appreciate.

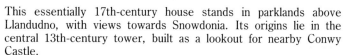

LLANDUDNO   Bodysgallen Hall

Deganwy, Llandudno, Gwynedd LL30 1RS
Telephone: (0492) 584466
Open: lunch + dinner daily
Last orders: lunch 2.00pm, dinner 9.15pm

£55

This essentially 17th-century house stands in parklands above Llandudno, with views towards Snowdonia. Its origins lie in the central 13th-century tower, built as a lookout for nearby Conwy Castle.

The impressive, elegant interior is filled with antiques. The oak panelled entrance hall and first floor drawing room set the tone, with fireplaces, comfortable sofas and fresh flowers. The nineteen bedrooms are well equipped and include Edwardian-style bathrooms. Nine garden cottages provide extra suites. A rare 17th-century knot garden suplies the kitchen with herbs. Other fresh local produce is also featured on Martin James' menus whenever possible, such as Carmarthen ham with tropical fruits, cold poached Conwy salmon served with hot minted new potatoes with a mixed leaf salad, or medallions of Welsh lamb served on an onion marmalade and fresh herbs. Desserts might include a hot lime tart with thick Jersey cream.

England Establishment Reviews

ALDEBURGH   Regatta

171/173 High Street, Aldeburgh, Suffolk IP15 5AN
Telephone: (0728) 452011   *Fax:* (0728) 452011   **£40**
Open: lunch + dinner daily (closed August Carnival Day)
Last orders: lunch 2.15pm (2.00pm Sun), dinner 10.00pm

The Regatta is now well established with both locals and visitors alike. There's a good atmosphere created by the simple setting of pine tables, a huge marine mural, and staff who enjoy their work. Fresh local produce, including fish from Aldeburgh boats, is simply handled: lobster salad with hot potatoes; char-grilled lamb with pan gravy; hot smoked haddock with mushrooms. Simpler dishes at lunch time: soup, pâté, pasta, grilled meat and fish.

AMBERLEY   Amberley Castle

See page 145 – our Clover Award Section.

ASCOT   The Royal Berkshire Hotel

London Road, Sunninghill, Ascot, Berkshire SL5 0PP
Telephone: (0344) 23322   *Fax:* (0344) 27100   **£60**
Open: lunch + dinner, daily
Last orders: lunch 2.00pm, dinner 9.30pm

A member of the Hilton group, this graceful Queen Anne house is a popular business venue. Andrew Richardson has been promoted from sous chef to head chef, ensuring continuity of style and standard. Cooking is accurate and refined: jellied lobster terrine, pan-fried red mullet and watercress sauce; loin of lamb and sweetbreads with a light garlic sauce. The wine list matches the style and price of the menu.

Royal Berkshire Ascot

ASHBURTON   Holne Chase Hotel & Restaurant

Ashburton, Devon TQ13 7NS
Telephone: (03643) 471   *Fax:* (03643) 453   **£55**
Open: lunch + dinner daily
Last orders: lunch 2.00pm, dinner 9.00pm

The large white building sits atop lawns sloping down to the river
Dart and woodlands beyond. The Bromage family continue to run
their friendly hotel. Public rooms are furnished in uncluttered
country-house style with sofas, log fires and light streaming in the
windows. Front facing bedrooms, simply but prettily furnished, enjoy
the same light. Local produce is the backbone of the new Joyce
Molyneux-trained chef, David Beazley. Some interesting Spanish
wines on the wine list.

ASHFORD   Eastwell Manor

Eastwell Park, Boughton Lees, Ashford, Kent TN25 4HR
Telephone: (0233) 635751   *Fax:* (0233) 635530   **£80**
Open: lunch + dinner daily
Last orders: lunch 2.00pm, dinner 9.30pm (10.00 Sat)

Set in sixty-two acres of a 3,000-acre estate, the Jacobean-style
manor dates from 1922. Public rooms feature impressive fireplaces,
plasterwork ceilings, panelling and sofas. Twenty-three spacious
well-appointed bedrooms with period furniture and good fabrics. New
chef Mark Clayton (ex-Turner's in London) seems to be settling in.
Menus cater for the clientele with dishes ranging from Mediterranean red mullet soup to braised knuckle of veal with tagliatelle of
leeks and carrots. A world-wide wine list.

Eastwell Manor.

ASTON CLINTON   The Bell Inn

Aston Clinton, Buckinghamshire HP22 5HP
Telephone: (0296) 630252   *Fax:* (0296) 631250   **£55**
Open: lunch + dinner daily
Last orders: lunch 1.45pm, dinner 9.45pm (9.00pm Sun)

Kevin Cape's menu is still the strong point of this long-established country inn. Its many regular customers appreciate the traditional setting and classically-based cooking such as noisettes of lamb with a herb mousseline. The banqueting suite on the other side of the road is a busy supplement to the main restaurant. Michael Harris's love of wines is reflected in the extensive and affordable wine list. Antiques and paintings add character to the spacious, comfortable bedrooms.

AYLESBURY   Hartwell House

See page 146 – our Clover Award Section.

AYLESBURY   Pebbles

See page 147 – our Clover Award Section.

BARHAM   The Old Coach House

Dover Road (A2), Barham, Nr Canterbury, Kent CT4 6SA
Telephone: (0227) 831218   **£70**
Open: lunch + dinner daily (closed dinner Sun in winter)
Last orders: lunch 2.00pm, dinner 9.00pm

Further improvements here: a smarter re-vamped bar area with armchairs, a bistro-style dining area for snack meals, and a more elegant dining room with pink cloths and silver napkin rings. Building work in the bedrooms is complete, making this a most useful address on the A2 London to Dover road (turn into the BP/Happy Eater service area). As a snack, the garlicky moules are recommended!

BARNSTAPLE   Halmpstone Manor

Bishop's Tawton, Barnstaple, Devon EX32 0EA
Telephone: (0271) 830321   *Fax:* (0271) 830826   **£50**
Open: dinner daily (residents only Sun) (closed Christmas Day + Boxing Day)
Last orders: dinner 9.30pm

Jane and Charles Stanbury's small hotel is run with care and much attention to detail. Bedrooms are well decorated with richly coloured fabrics and good beds. Bedrooms and bathrooms are thoughtfully equipped. Relax in the traditional comfortable lounge and eat in the candle-lit, panelled dining room. Dinner might be soufflé suissesse and roast grouse, then a creamy pud from the trolley. A friendly, relaxed place.

BARNSTAPLE   Lynwood House Restaurant

See page 148 – our Clover Award Section.

BARNSLEY   Restaurant Peano

102 Dodworth Road, Barnsley, South Yorkshire S70 6HC
Telephone: (0226) 244990   **£45**
Open: lunch Tue-Sun, dinner Tue-Sat (closed 2 wks Sep, Bank Holidays)
Last orders: lunch 2.00pm (2.30pm Sun), dinner 9.30pm

A new restaurant with decor still in embryonic state. A huge high
ceilinged room with sunny yellow walls, blue and yellow curtains, a
polished wooden floor, cane chairs and elegantly laid white-clothed
tables. Tracey Davis is an informed hostess. Young chef Michael
Peano (ex-Waterside Inn and Fischer's of Baslow) is half Italian and
half German, an heredity reflected in his cooking: an arborio rice cake
with crustacean seafood; pink and meltingly tender saddle of venison
with a whole fanned pear and reduction sauce of the juices.
Vegetables might include a superb dauphinoise. Good stilton comes
with a bowl of fruit and walnuts; a mille feuille of mint and chocolate
lent a sweet ending to a recent meal. Good Italian wines are the
highlight of the list.

BASINGSTOKE   Audleys Wood Thistle Hotel

Alton Road, Basingstoke, Hampshire RG25 2JT
Telephone: (0256) 817555   *Fax:* (0256) 817500   **£50**
Open: lunch Sun-Fri, dinner daily (closed lunch Bank Holidays)
Last orders: lunch 1.45pm (2.15pm Sun), dinner 9.45pm (10.15pm Sat,
         9.15pm Sun)

This new Victorian mansion hotel offers a high standard of
accommodation (mostly in extensions), geared primarily to the
business person. However, the restaurant, set in the former palm
house, is an attractive showcase for John McGeever's imaginative
cooking. Current trends are apparent in polenta with calves' liver,
deep-fried Japanese dumplings, and cous-cous salad. More mainstream dishes might be a twice-baked cheese soufflé, and salmon
with a sorrel, yoghurt and muscat sauce.

* New chef at Audleys Wood is Terence Greenhouse

Cavendish Hotel, Baslow

BASLOW — Cavendish Hotel

Baslow, Derbyshire DE4 1SP
Telephone: (0246) 582311   *Fax:* (0246) 582312   **£50**
Open: Restaurant: lunch + dinner daily; Garden Room: all day, daily
Last orders: Restaurant: lunch 2.00pm, dinner 10.00pm;
Garden Room: 11.00pm

This mellow stone hotel overlooks the Chatsworth estate. Public rooms are decorated with appealing colours, which offset their formality. Everywhere there are paintings and flowers. The bedrooms are by contrast simple in style, but spacious and well heated; walls are plain, beds comfortable and there are two armchairs – bathrooms similarly simple. There's a formal restaurant and the Garden Room which serves snacks all day from 11.00am. You might be offered a warm salad of mushrooms and coriander with a dressing of black raisin vinegar, followed by pan-fried sea scallops with black noodles and a yoghurt and parsley sauce, then passion fruit tarts with a strawberry sauce, a plate of British cheeses served with fresh dates, nuts and biscuits, and coffee and chocolates to finish. It is still possible to take a table for two in the kitchen and watch Nick Buckingham at work while enjoying his menu surprise at £35 per person. Good staff who work as a team.

BASLOW — Fischer's at Baslow Hall

See page 149 – our Clover Award Section.

BATH — The Bath Spa Hotel

See page 150 – our Clover Award Section.

BATH — Homewood Park Hotel

Hinton Charterhouse, Bath, Avon BA3 6BB
Telephone: (0225) 723731   *Fax:* (0225) 723820   **£75**
Open: lunch + dinner daily
Last orders: lunch 1.30pm (2.00pm Sat), dinner 9.30pm

The new owners have softened the decor, adding warm touches. A framed collection of fans adds interest to sipping aperitifs in the sitting room. An intriguing carte is supplemented by a daily menu of soups, fish and game. A recent enjoyable dinner included tender pan-fried squid and mussels with tomatoes and garlic, and a goat's cheese salad with crunchy croutons and delicious walnut oil dressing. Partridge, sliced over lentils, with bacon and oil, was full of flavour. Home-made vanilla ice cream simply served in a tuile basket was very good. Good vegetables and bread. Coffee and truffles served in the cosy apricot bar was a perfect ending. A good welcome and faultless service.

BATH   The Priory Hotel

Weston Road, Bath, Avon BA1 2XT
Telephone: (0255) 331922   *Fax:* (0255) 448276   **£70**
Open: lunch + dinner daily
Last orders: lunch 2.00pm, dinner 9.15pm

A popular base for visitors near the centre of Bath yet in a quiet
location and country-house in style. Period furniture and attractive
fabrics grace well-equipped bedrooms, mainly with garden views;
bathrooms are spacious. Accurate, well-executed dishes are served
in the three distinctive dining rooms: turban of sole and langoustine
with a spinach mousseline; duck with a sherry and rosemary sauce. A
wine list at popular prices.

BATH   The Queensberry Hotel

Russel Street, Bath, Avon BA1 2XT
Telephone: (0225) 447928   *Fax:* (0225) 446065
Closed: 2 wks Christmas + New Year

The Queensberry Hotel retains the 18th-century character of the
three terraced houses, designed by John Wood, which it comprises.
Contemporary comforts are blended with period furnishings in the
beautifully decorated rooms (some with 18th-century stucco ceilings). No restaurant, but a residents' bar serves lunch-time snacks.

BATH   Royal Crescent Hotel

16 Royal Crescent, Bath, Avon BA1 2LS
Telephone: (0225) 319090   *Fax:* (0225) 339401   **£90**
Open: lunch + dinner daily
Last orders: lunch 2.00pm, dinner 9.30pm (10.00pm Sat)

Celebrated for its unique location at the centre of John Wood's
famous 18th-century crescent, this is a hotel of undoubted elegance.
The Nash architecture forms a distinguished backcloth to period
furnishings and tasteful modern luxuries. The panelled Dower House
restaurant continues the style with professional service. The best
choices from a modern menu include fresh produce lightly handled.

BIGBURY-ON-SEA   The Burgh Island Hotel

Burgh Island, Bigbury-on-Sea, Devon TQ7 4AU
Telephone: (0548) 810514   *Fax:* (0548) 810243   **£65**
Open: lunch + dinner daily
Last orders: lunch 2.00pm, dinner 9.00pm

For the nostalgic, the leisured and the romantic, a stay on Burgh Island provides an evocative glimpse of living in the 1930s. Sufficient time is essential since the island is only accessible by boat, helicopter or the extraordinary sea tractor. The Art Deco interior, lovingly restored by Tony and Bea Porter, offers fourteen individually decorated suites. Public rooms include a Palm Court with leaded glass peacock dome. The Roux-trained chef, Robert Rayney, using fresh local produce, provides (in a manner of speaking) the icing on the cake!

BILBROUGH   Bilbrough Manor
Country House Hotel

Bilbrough, York, Yorkshire YO2 3PH
Telephone: (0937) 834002   *Fax:* (0937) 834002   **£65**
Open: lunch + dinner daily (closed Christmas)
Last orders: lunch 2.00pm, dinner 9.30pm (9.00pm Sun)

The personal touches make Bilbrough stand out: a head waiter, knowledgable and with natural charm, who greets you by name, the blazing log fire, Mrs Bell doing the flowers. Once inside the polished panelled restaurant there's a relaxed, professional atmosphere. Andrew Pressley is the sound, imaginative new chef; a very good lunch offered a firm, well-flavoured galantine de faison, served with quince coulis; roulade de poisson on a bed of seaweed. Stilton soaked in port preceded a light red, sour, cherry fool. Twelve, light, spacious bedrooms with comfortable beds and warm bathrooms complete this unpretentious friendly house.

Bilbrough Manor

BIRDLIP   Kingshead House Restaurant

Birdlip, Gloucestershire GL4 8JH
Telephone: (0452) 862299   **£45**
Open: lunch Tue-Fri + Sun, dinner Tue-Sat (closed 25 + 26 Dec, 1 Jan)
Last orders: lunch 2.00pm (1.45pm Sun), dinner 10.00pm

The setting is rustic: a former 18th-century coaching inn overlooking fields and trees. The unpretentious cooking draws inspiration from France and sometime pre-Victorian England: carré d'agneau tapenade; turkey breast vallée d'Ange. There's always a vegetarian choice, such as a pithiviers aux fromages. Menus are fixed price: £13.00 at lunch, £21.50 at dinner. A well-chosen wine list includes a good selection of ½-bottles.

BIRMINGHAM   Norton Place Hotel

---

180 Lifford Lane, Kings Norton, Birmingham, West Midlands B30 3NT
Telephone: 021-433 5656 *Fax:* 021-433 3048   **£45**
Open: lunch + dinner daily
Last orders: lunch 2.30pm, dinner 10.00pm (9.00pm Sun)

A luxury hotel and restaurant is an unlikely place for a car collection, but why not? After some enjoyable hours among the Patrick Collection, check into one of the well-furnished, luxurious bedrooms with marble-tiled bathrooms. Then enjoy a good dinner in the smart, modern, blue and pink dining room. Cooking is assured: fish soup baked under a pastry lid; duck with braised nectarines and sauternes sauce; praline and pistachio parfait.

BIRMINGHAM   Sloan's Restaurant

See page 151 – our Clover Award Section.

BIRMINGHAM   Sir Edward Elgar Restaurant, Swallow Hotel

See page 152 – our Clover Award Section.

BIRTLE   The Normandie Hotel

See page 153 – our Clover Award Section.

BISHOP'S TACHBROOK   **Mallory Court Hotel**

Harbury Lane, Bishop's Tachbrook, Leamington Spa,
Warwickshire CV33 9QB
Telephone: (0926) 330214 *Fax:* (0926) 451714   **£85**
Open: lunch + dinner daily (closed Christmas Day evening to 29 Dec)
Last orders: lunch 1.45pm, dinner 9.30pm (9.45pm Sat, 9.00pm Sun)

This Edwardian house is set in ten acres of landscaped gardens, with
the rolling Warwickshire countryside as a backdrop. Public rooms
offer comfort. Decor varies from room to room and reflects the
owners' tastes in furniture. Bedrooms and bathrooms are well fitted
and attractive in style. The elegant panelled dining room is the
setting for some good cooking. The fixed-price, 3-course menus are
realistically priced to avoid supplements. A meal here might comprise
warm quail salad with quail egg and foie gras; braised lobster tail with
basil or roast saddle and braised leg of rabbit in tarragon juices, hot
raspberry soufflé. Staff are attentive and professional.

BLACKPOOL   **The River House**

Skippool Creek, Thornton-le-Fylde, Blackpool, Lancashire FY5 5LF
Telephone: (0253) 883497   **£65**
Open: lunch by arrangement, dinner Mon-Sat (closed Bank Holidays,
      2 wks Aug)
Last orders: dinner 9.30pm

Bill Scott is a rare talent in hotelkeeping – from the moment he greets
you, you feel as if you are in the home of a friend. All four bedrooms
now have private facilities, and two have wonderful Victorian hooded
baths which give an all-round shower effect! The rooms are warm
and homely with solid furniture and thoughtful extras: electric
blankets, four varieties of tea and delicious home-made shortbread.
Drinks are served in the new plant-filled conservatory, where Bill
arrives in jeans and butcher's apron to discuss the menu. Pots of
freesias brighten the polished wood tables of the Victorian-style
dining room. The cooking is generous and skilful: rich and creamy
soufflé suissesse, classic roast grouse, good cheeses from a
help-yourself basket, a light-textured steamed ticky-tacky pudding.
Coffee is excellent. Good wines include several Bandols from
Domaine Tempier where Bill once worked. Good cooked breakfasts
and DIY toast! The hotel, situated amidst yachts and jetties, is
difficult to find so ask for directions when booking.

BLACKWATER   Pennypots

Blackwater, Nr Truro, Cornwall TR4 8EY
Telephone: (0209) 820347   **£45**
Open: dinner Tue-Sun (closed Sun winter, 2 wks winter)
Last orders: dinner 10.00pm

Probably the most popular restaurant in the area. Plain cream walls
hung with a few bunches of dried flowers and Pears soap style prints,
pink clad tables – the small cottagey dining room is neat and pleasant.
Simple but well-presented dishes are served with smiles. Ribbons of
crispy deep-fried leek and carrot garnish a brochette of scallops;
duck, lamb and fillet steak are unusually and successfully combined
and served with a peppercorn and black olive sauce with a splash of
cream. Good vegetables. Desserts are a speciality: if it's available
the chocolate temptation is not to be missed! Petits fours served in a
pretty basket round off a good meal.

BOLLINGTON   Mauro's Italian Restaurant

88 Palmerston Street, Bollington , Macclesfield, Cheshire SK10 5PW
Telephone: (0625) 573989   **£45**
Open: lunch + dinner Tue-Sat (closed 3 wks Aug/Sep, Christmas)
Last orders: lunch 1.45pm, dinner 10.00pm (10.30pm Sat)

Mauro's remains popular for Gillian Mauro's welcome, the cheerful
ambience of the pink and white dining room decorated with colourful
plates, and the honesty of Enzo's cooking. The fish and daily specials
(fresh produce from Manchester's markets) are recommended. Good
fresh pasta may be stuffed with artichoke and ricotta cheese, then
tossed with broccoli and garlic butter. Some good bottles on the
Italian wine list.

BOTALLACK   The Count House Restaurant

Botallack, St Just, Penzance, Cornwall TR19 7QQ
Telephone: (0736) 788588   **£55**
Open: lunch Tue-Sun, dinner Tue-Sat (closed Christmas Day, New Year's
         Day, 2 wks Feb; also closed Tue Oct-Easter)
Last orders: lunch 2.00pm, dinner 11.00pm

Situated at the end of a lane on a cliff with spectacular coastal views
and sunsets. Inside the restaurant a plant-filled conservatory leads to
a pretty country-style dining room furnished with antiques. Short
menus (good fresh produce) offer ample portions; dishes might
include duck with a plum and port sauce, John Dory fillet with a
tomato and basil sauce. House wine is £9.95 a litre.

BOTLEY   Cobbett's Restaurant

15 The Square, Botley, Southampton, Hampshire SO3 2EA
Telephone: (0489) 782068   **£60**
Open: lunch Tue-Fri, dinner Mon-Sat (closed 2 wks winter, 2 wks summer)
Last orders: lunch 2.00pm, dinner 9.45pm

The Skipwiths' beamed cottage restaurant continues to provide a
welcome Gallic touch to this corner of England. A no-choice,
fixed-price menu is offered alongside the short carte of competently
prepared dishes: pot-roasted guinea fowl stuffed with goat's cheese,
rib steak marchand de vin. House wine by Lucie Skipwith's great
uncle from his vineyard near St Emilion.

BOUGHTON MONCHELSEA   Tanyard

Wierton Hill, Boughton Monchelsea, Maidstone, Kent ME17 4JT
Telephone: (0622) 744705   **£45**
Open: dinner daily (closed mid-Dec to Mar)
Last orders: dinner 8.30pm

A 15th-century timber-framed building with apple orchards behind
and sweeping views in front. Exposed beams, white walls and uneven
floors characterise the five bedrooms; homely furnishings and light
fabrics. The cosy dining room with its huge fireplace, bare stone
walls, polished oak floor and simple white-clad tables offers residents
straightforward, competently prepared dinner-party dishes: poached
sole fillet with a smoked salmon sauce, saddle of venison with a black
bean sauce. Short wine list and friendly service.

BOX   Clos du Roy

See page 154 – our Clover Award Section.

BRADFORD   Restaurant Nineteen

See page 155 – our Clover Award Section.

BRADFORD-ON-AVON   Woolley Grange

Bradford-on-Avon, Wiltshire BA15 1TX
Telephone: (022 16) 4705   *Fax:* (022 16) 4059   **£60**
Open: lunch + dinner daily
Last orders: lunch 2.00pm (2.30pm Sun), dinner 10.00pm

The Chapmans' two-year-old country house hotel seems to be
succeeding where many apparently established places failed. Chef
Ian Mansfield is making an able replacement for Anand Sastry. His
modern style is similar, and makes use of organically-reared meat
and organic vegetables and fruit from the kitchen garden. A relaxed
and enlightened attitude to children includes a full-time nursery and
nanny, and children's meals. A programme of two-day breaks
includes in the price an activity such as riding or antique hunting, or a
day at a health spa. The 17th-century manor house is attractively
decorated in sunny colours and furnished with some antiques. The
eighteen country-style bedrooms (and two suites) vary in size. Some
have antique beds; all have pretty, personal touches.

BRAMLEY   Le Berger

4A High Street, Bramley, Nr Guildford, Surrey GU5 0HB
Telephone: (0483) 894037   **£55**
Open: lunch Wed-Fri + Sun, dinner Wed-Sat (closed Bank Holidays except
     Easter Sunday, 2 wks Jan)
Last orders: lunch 2.00pm, dinner 9.30pm

A neat, cream-painted shop front leads into two small dining rooms
(one non-smoking). Decor is simple and modern: grey and cream
walls, a few prints, pink cloths. Mary Hirth assures pleasant, efficient
service of Roux-trained Peter Hirth's cooking: guinea-fowl roasted
and served with green chartreuse sauce, émincé of chicken with
tarragon. The style is modern with very subtle flavours. The
no-choice 3-course set menu at £25 is perhaps the best value, as it
includes a ½-bottle of house wine.

BRAMPTON   Farlam Hall Hotel

Brampton, Cumbria CA8 2NG
Telephone: (069 76) 234/357   *Fax:* (069 76) 683   **£55**
Open: dinner daily (closed 1 wk Christmas, Feb)
Last orders: dinner 8.00pm

The grey stone house overlooks mature gardens and a small lake.
Day rooms, with Victorian style wallpaper and masses of fresh
flowers are furnished with antiques and retain a Victorian formality.
The charming owners run an immaculate house, including the
thirteen well decorated, en-suite bedrooms. Long-skirted waitresses
provide efficient service in the elegant dining room. There's just one
sitting for dinner. The menu draws upon local produce: game terrine,
roulade of salmon and lemon sole, local roast grouse. English
cheeses are served before wickedly tempting desserts. The international wine list includes a good number of ½-bottles.

BRAY-ON-THAMES   The Waterside Inn

See page 156 – our Clover Award Section.

BRIDPORT   Riverside Restaurant

West Bay, Bridport, Dorset DT6 4EZ
Telephone: (0308) 22011   **£30**
Open: lunch + dinner daily (closed Sun dinner + Mon out of high season,
        Nov – Mar)
Last orders: lunch 3.00pm (4.00pm Sat + Sun), dinner 8.00pm
        (8.30pm Sat)

At the Watsons' cheap and cheerful restaurant and café fish is the
staple, simple is the approach: grilled lemon sole; West Bay scallops
in wine and garlic; salad of crab, prawns and lobster. Seafood specials
are marked on a blackboard. Book and check opening times as they
vary according to the Watsons' choice of holidays, days off, school
exeunts etc!

BRIGHTON   Le Grandgousier

15 Western Street, Brighton, Sussex BN1 2PG
Telephone: (0273) 772005   **£30**
Open: lunch Mon-Fri, dinner Mon-Sat (closed Christmas + New Year)
Last orders: lunch 1.30pm, dinner 9.30pm (10.45pm Sat)

A long narrow room with tables and banquettes ranged down the
sides is the simple but comfortable setting. The 6-course formula of
crudités, pâté, charcuterie, then a plat du jour, brie, dessert and a
½-bottle of vin de table remains unchanged, and the price (£11.45 +
service) has hardly risen. Typical plats du jour (made with home-
made stocks) are coq au vin or loin of pork in a calvados and apple
sauce. Dessert might be chocolate mousse or crème caramel. Classic
stuff and why not? And at this price you can afford an extra bottle of
wine from the handful listed.

BRIGHTON	Langan's Bistro

1 Paston Place, Brighton, East Sussex BN2 1HA
Telephone: (0273) 606933   *excellent local bistro*   **£50**
Open: lunch Tue-Fri + Sun, dinner Tue-Sat (closed Bank Holidays,
    2 wks Jan, 2 wks Aug)
Last orders: lunch 2.30pm (2.00pm Sun), dinner (10.30pm)

Mark Emmerson has taken over the reins here. He cooks with
competency and care a short menu of dishes such as calves' liver with
sage, seafood terrine, rabbit with mustard sauce, grilled salmon
hollandaise. Good desserts, short wine list, professional service and
of course Langan's distinctive style of decor with its multitude of
pictures on cream walls.

BRIMFIELD	Poppies Restaurant at the Robuck Hotel

Brimfield, Ludlow, Shropshire SY8 4NE
Telephone: (058472) 230   *- best for many milks*   **£60**
Open: lunch + dinner Tue-Sat (closed 2 wks Feb, 1 wk Oct, Christmas)
Last orders: lunch 2.00pm, dinner 10.00pm

Carole Evans' cooking continues to expand. Her imaginative
approach to raw materials locally supplied produces some enjoyable
results: hot spinach soufflé with anchovy hollandaise; fillet of
Herefordshire beef with oyster mushrooms on a red wine sauce.
Don't miss the cheeses described on a separate list. A strengthened
wine list offers some good bottles. The village pub atmosphere is
retained in the bar as a contrast to the light, modern dining room.
The three en-suite bedrooms are comfortable, pretty and thoughtfully equipped.

BRISTOL   Bistro Twenty One

21 Cotham Road South, Kingsdown, Bristol, Avon BS6 5TZ
Telephone: (0272) 421744   **£40**
Open: lunch Mon-Fri, dinner Mon-Sat (closed Christmas + New Year)
Last orders: lunch 2.30pm, dinner 11.30pm

Nothing much seems to change at this ever popular bistro: the
windows still get steamed up (the plants seem to thrive on it!). The
style may now be somewhat anachronistic with its purply-red cloths
on tables jammed together, but it's usually busy, sometimes smoky,
and service is friendly. The menu remains quite long, ranging from
fish soup, spinach and cream cheese pancakes to salmon and
marinaded scallops.

BRISTOL   Howards

1A & 2A Avon Crescent, Hotwells, Bristol, Avon BS1 6XQ
Telephone: (0272) 262921   **£45**
Open: dinner Mon-Sat (closed Christmas)
Last orders: dinner 11.00pm (11.30pm Sat)

A popular bistro situated near the swing bridge, with oak pews,
candles and blackboard menus. Efficient young staff fly up and down
the stairs between the dining rooms. If available try the full of flavour
game terrine with home-made apple chutney, or the hot goat's
cheese parcels with basil and pine nuts. Follow with fillet of salmon
with a cream and vermouth sauce, or breast of pheasant stuffed with
a spinach mousseline and served with a casserole of the legs.
Generous vegetables include a delicious pommes dauphinoise.
Cafetière coffee and good petits fours. Run by an enthusiastic owner,
this is a fun place (mainly young clientele) with generous portions of
good food and a friendly atmosphere. Book.

BRISTOL   Restaurant Lettonie

9 Druid Hill, Stoke Bishop, Bristol, Avon BS9 1EW
Telephone: (0272) 686456   **£60**
Open: lunch + dinner Tue-Sat (closed 2 wks Aug, Christmas)
Last orders: lunch 2.00pm, dinner 9.30pm

Set in a row of shops, the Blunos' tiny restaurant is deceptively
simple: seven tables with banquette seating, pale walls, a few
modern pictures. Siân oversees service by a girl and a helpful French
wine waiter. A good place for a relaxing unhurried dinner. Martin's
cooking – imaginative, skilled and beautifully presented – ranks
among the best. Stars of a recent meal were quail breast wrapped in
ham, then a light chicken mousse and the whole encased in spinach,
lightly steamed and glazed with honey; pan-fried venison served with
a liquorice scented sauce – a startling and successful idea; a chocolate
marquise – richly bitter dark and light with a pistachio nut egg
custard. It's also worth having the selection of goats' cheeses. Coffee
comes in a silver pot with a silver sugar bowl and tongs. Excellent
petits fours. A compact but well-chosen wine list.

BRISTOL	Markwicks

43 Corn Street, Bristol, Avon BS1 1HT
Telephone: (0272) 262658   **£60**
Open: lunch + dinner Mon-Fri (closed Bank Holidays, 10 days Easter,
    2 wks Aug, 10 days Christmas)
Last orders: lunch 2.00pm, dinner 10.30pm

Markwicks (Hunt has left) breaks away from the traditional mould of Bristol restaurants. Booking is now essential to eat in the stylish black, cream and marble basement restaurant. If it's available, try the excellent fish soup, or the ravioli of scallops with spinach and beurre blanc, or noisettes of veal with a selection of vegetables and a fromage blanc sauce. The tarte tatin is worth waiting for. Helpful, willing service and much of interest on a good wine list.

BRISTOL	Michael's Restaurant

129 Hotwell Road, Bristol, Avon BS8 4RU
Telephone: (0272) 276190   **£50**
Open: lunch Sun Oct-Apr, dinner Mon-Sat (closed August Bank Holiday 4
    days, Boxing Day + New Years Day)
Last orders: lunch 2.30pm, dinner 11.00pm (11.30pm Sat)

This cosy local restaurant is still going strong thanks to a fixed price menu with a dependable standard of cooking and warm comfortable surroundings. Everything (from bread to truffles) is made on the premises. A meal here might comprise sole and salmon terrine; roast poussin and tarragon sauce; home-made ice cream then coffee in front of the fire.

BROADWAY	Hunters Lodge

High Street, Broadway, Hereford & Worcestershire WR12 7DT *charming hosts*
Telephone: (0386) 853247   **£50**
Open: lunch Tue-Sun, dinner Tue-Sat (closed 2 wks Feb, 2 wks Aug)
Last orders: lunch 2.00pm, dinner 9.45pm (10.00pm Sat)

A Jacobean house set back from the road is home to Kurt and Dottie Friedli's welcoming restaurant. In winter there's a log fire in the bar; in summer a sheltered garden provides seating. Kurt cooks with the accuracy and knowledge of long experience; it's generous, straight-forward seasonal cooking: sea and shellfish pot-au-feu; guinea fowl with sweet cider and cream; pot roasted rabbit. Good local restaurant.

BROADWAY	The Lygon Arms

High Street, Broadway, Hereford & Worcester WR12 7DU
Telephone: (0386) 852255   **£65**
Open: lunch + dinner daily
Last orders: lunch 2.00pm, dinner 9.45pm

This sixty-six bedroomed hotel, a bastion of traditional English hospitality, is limbering up for the end of another century (it first appeared in 1532!) and offers hunting, shooting, fishing and the hounds meet outside at Christmas. The new leisure complex, due to be completed after we go to press, will include a spa bath, sauna, solarium, gym and swimming pool. After a healthy workout, guests can indulge in a lightly grilled Dover sole or perhaps a sirloin of beef with forest mushrooms and fried celeriac – Clive Howe's menus offer something for most tastes for the international clientele. It is part of the Savoy group.

BROCKENHURST	Le Poussin

See page 158 – our Clover Award Section.

BROMSGROVE	Grafton Manor

Grafton Lane, Bromsgrove, Hereford & Worcestershire B61 7HA
Telephone: (0527) 579007   *Fax:* (0527) 575221   **£60**
Open: lunch Sun-Fri, dinner daily
Last orders: lunch 1.45pm, dinner 9.00pm (7.30pm Sun)

The 16th-century manor (with 18th-century additions) is a warm, family-run house, steeped in history. The Great Parlour with its high, ornate ceiling, and armchairs by an open fire, makes a relaxing day room. The nine bedrooms have open fireplaces and are traditionally furnished. A large herb garden adds subtle flavours to the cooking. Main courses include grouse and sirloin steak pudding with a rich game gravy. Good English cheeses.

BROXTED	Whitehall Hotel

Church End, Broxted, Essex CM6 2BZ
Telephone: (0279) 850603   *Fax:* (0279) 850385   **£65**
Open: lunch Sun (other days by arrangement), dinner Mon-Sat (residents
          only Sun) (closed Christmas + New Year)
Last orders: lunch 1.30pm, dinner 9.30pm (8.30pm Sun)

At the heart of Whitehall is a 600-year-old house with a timber vaulted dining room, and exposed beams in the lounge. Comforts are modern, though, from deep sofas to recessed lighting and well-equipped bedrooms. Chef Jenny Coaker, who succeeded Paula Keane in 1989, cooks accomplished dishes in a modern British style, best seen on her 6-course menu surprise at around £29. The wine list is strong on burgundies; the twenty-five bedrooms are comfortable and well-equipped.

BRUTON	Truffles Restaurant

---

95 High Street, Bruton, Somerset BA10 0AR
Telephone: (0749) 812255 **£45**
Open: lunch Tue-Sun, dinner Tue-Sat (closed 3 wks Sep)
Last orders: lunch 2.00pm, dinner 10.00pm

The Bottrills' restaurant continues to offer good value. Denise looks after the intimate cottage dining room. Martin cooks the monthly menus. His style is French; dishes are well presented: leek and roquefort mousse; duckling with apples and calvados sauce; a rich 'truffles' gateau. A well chosen wine list includes over twenty ½-bottles and six dessert wines by the glass.

BUCKLAND	Buckland Manor

Buckland, Nr Broadway, Hereford & Worcester WB12 7LY
Telephone: (0386) 852626 **£65**
Open: lunch + dinner daily
Last orders: lunch 1.45pm, dinner 8.45pm

-new owners

Adrienne and Barry Berman see their country house hotel as a respite from the stresses of everyday life, modestly minimising their role as hosts. Their caring hospitality however is the soul of Buckland Manor. No large parties or conferences interfere with the enjoyment of this lovely house. For Martyn Pearn, chef of this candlelit restaurant, produces some competent cooking with dishes such as carré d'agneau rôti persillade jus d'estragon. The fully annotated wine list rewards concentrated reading.

BURY	The Village Restaurant

---

16 Market Place, Ramsbottom, Bury, Greater Manchester BL0 9HT
Telephone: (0706) 825070 **£65**
Open: dinner Wed-Sat
Last orders: dinner 8.30pm

Now firmly established two doors up, having moved in 1989, this is a homely setting for some serious food. Ros Hunter cooks a 5-course menu, no-choice except at dessert; there are six courses on Fridays and Saturdays. Guests sit down at 8.30pm and usually rise after midnight! Much fresh, local and organic produce is used. Chris Johnson plays host – his passion is wine, reflected in an extensive and excellent list, on which he will enthusiastically advise.

CALSTOCK   **Danescombe Valley Hotel**

Lower Kelly, Calstock, Cornwall PL18 9RY
Telephone: (0822) 832414   **£55**
Open: dinner Fri-Tue (closed Nov-Easter)
Last orders: dinner 8.00pm

A distinctive Georgian house set on a bank of the Tamar with a steep
wooded hill rising behind. A personal welcome by Martin Smith, deep
comfortable sofas in which to flop down with one of the many books,
and tranquil bedrooms undisturbed by TV, radio or phone. First floor
rooms enjoy the bonus of a verandah. Local produce is the backbone
of Anna Smith's accomplished cooking: Tamar salmon as a fishcake or
with herbs, local beef with fried peppers, vegetables from the valley,
unpasteurised farmhouse cheeses, apple crumble cake. The reasonably priced wine list encourages experimentation and is worth a
careful read. The dining room only seats ten so booking is essential.

— arrange your own country house party

CAMBRIDGE   **Midsummer House**

Midsummer Common, Cambridge, Cambridgeshire CB4 3AE
Telephone: (0223) 69299   **£70**
Open: lunch + dinner Mon-Sat (closed Christmas + New Year)
Last orders: lunch 2.00pm, dinner 9.30pm   *best in the area*

Its location on the banks of the Cam is both an advantage (the view)
and a disadvantage (its distance from the nearest car parking). The
latter is remedied by the welcoming warmth of the decor, with its
brilliant fabrics and deep blue walls. Hans Schweitzer's modern
cooking suits the venue, and continues to impress with specialities
such as ballotine of quail with foie gras and truffle jus, spring lamb
with a herb crust, a mousse of monkfish and spinach. Desserts (from
this former pâtissier) remain a high spot. If you can't choose, try the
composition – a small selection of most of them!

CANTERBURY   Thruxted Oast

Mystole, Chartham, Canterbury, Kent CT4 7BX
Telephone: (0227) 730080
Open: bed & breakfast only

The former oast house is not easy to find at first, so ask for directions
locally. Three twin-bedded guest rooms are spacious, comfortable
and pretty. All have en-suite showers and lots of thoughtful extras,
but no telephone. Breakfast in the farmhouse-style kitchen, with
free-range eggs and home-made preserves. Owners Tim and Hilary
Derouet are sociable, enterprising hosts. No smoking and no children
under fourteen.

CARTMEL   Uplands

Haggs Lane, Cartmel, Cumbria LA11 6HD
Telephone: (053 95) 36248   £55
Open: lunch + dinner Tue-Sun + Bank Holidays (closed 2 Jan – late Feb)
Last orders: lunch 1.00pm, dinner 8.00pm

Diana and Tom Peter's restaurant with rooms continues to offer
short daily menus of food in the Miller Howe tradition. Soups,
invariably good; a warm loaf of bread; main courses such as chicken
breast in cured ham filled with cheese and herbs, a sauce of tomato
and mustard; masses of vegetables; desserts such as banana, walnut
and ginger pie. A compact wine list, simple surroundings and a
relaxed atmosphere.

CASTLE COMBE   Manor House Hotel

Castle Combe, Chippenham, Wiltshire SN14 7HR
Telephone: (0249) 782206   *Fax:* (0249) 782159   £70
Open: lunch + dinner daily
Last orders: lunch 2.00pm, dinner 9.30pm

The village setting is picturesque and much visited, but twenty-six
acres of gardens and parkland provide an effective buffer. The stately
manor house itself has undergone a major refurbishment. A fire burns
in the fireplace of the panelled entrance hall. The sunny coloured
sitting room is attractive with its floral fabrics. Well furnished
spacious bedrooms (cottage bedrooms smaller). The dining room is
formal in style and service. The menu offers competently cooked
dishes such as fillet of beef topped with foie gras served with rösti
potato, and duck on a bed of braised butter beans with endive, tomato
and basil. Desserts such as summer pudding with clotted cream
farmhouse cheeses. The wine list travels the globe.

CHAGFORD   Gidleigh Park

See page 160 – our Clover Award Section.

CHEAM — Al San Vincenzo

52 Upper Mulgrave Road, Cheam, Surrey SM2 7AJ
Telephone: 081-661 9763
—have moved see London listings **£65**
Open: lunch Tue-Fri by arrangement only, dinner Tue-Sat (closed Bank
     Holidays)
Last orders: lunch by arrangement, dinner 9.30pm

Vincenzo Borgonzolo's enthusiastic and skilled modern Italian cooking has always pointed the way to future trends. The set price menu
offers some six choices at each course. Dishes are appetising:
partridge with white puglia grapes, a purée of pumpkin and herbs;
fresh figs with ricotta al caffé. Some lesser known reasonably priced
Italian wines. Simple decor and a warm welcome from Elaine – this
restaurant deserves more local support. Good local restaurant,
which might be moving into London in March 1991.

CHEDINGTON — Chedington Court

Chedington, Nr Beaminster, Dorset DT8 3HY
Telephone: (0935) 89265   **£60**
Open: dinner daily (closed mid Jan – mid Feb, 4 days Christmas)
Last orders: dinner 9.00pm

A poised stone built Victorian house enjoying stunning panoramic
views – you can see both Somerset and Devon from the west
terrace. The interior is formal and calm but comfortable with solid
period furniture. Owners Hilary and Philip Chapman work hard – she
in the kitchen, he in the dining room. The 5-course no-choice menus
(except for starters) offer carefully prepared dishes such as the
excellent loin of lamb with cabbage parcels. The wine list remains
impressive and reasonably priced, with many ½-bottles.

CHELTENHAM — Le Champignon Sauvage

24-26 Suffolk Road, Cheltenham, Gloucestershire GL50 2AQ
Telephone: (0242) 573449   **£60**
Open: lunch Mon-Fri, dinner Mon-Sat (closed Bank Holidays, 1 wk
     Christmas, 2 wks June)
Last orders: lunch 1.30pm, dinner 9.15pm   *good local restaurant*

No 'wild' growth at this husband-and-wife run restaurant, but rather a
steady progression of style in the essentially robust and complex
French-based cooking: slices of pork layered with a purée of black
pudding served with green lentils and a pork sauce; a puff pastry case
filled with fried saddle and braised leg of rabbit with a garlic and
marjoram flavoured sauce. Leave room for the huge array of Philippe
Olivier cheeses. A mainly French wine list includes some New World
bottles and is reasonably priced.

CHELTENHAM	The Greenway

Shurdington, Cheltenham, Gloucestershire GL51 5UG
Telephone: (0242) 862352 Fax (0242) 862780   **£60**
Open: lunch Sun-Fri, dinner daily (closed Bank Holidays, 2 wks from 27 Dec)
Last orders: lunch 2.0pm, dinner 9.00pm

A stone-built country house with light, airy rooms filled with summery colours, chintzes and the solid comfort of antique furniture. Bedrooms, both in the main house and in the converted coach house, are decorated in similar style: spacious, with kingsize beds and warm, well-equipped bathrooms. The conservatory dining room overlooks a sunken garden and lily pond. Traditional fare is offered at lunchtime: caesar salad; grilled liver and bacon. Candlelit dinners include dishes such as roast loin of lamb with a yellow tomato sauce infused with fresh basil, and buttery pastry layers baked with fresh salmon on a lemon balm sauce. The international wine list is fairly priced; Duboeuf house wines.

CHELWOOD	Hunstrete House Hotel

Hunstrete, Chelwood, Nr Bath, Avon BS18 4NS
Telephone: (0781) 490490   *Fax:* (0781) 490732   **£80**
Open: lunch + dinner daily
Last orders: lunch 2.30pm, dinner 10.30pm

The 18th-century house, floodlit at night, now owned by the Clipper Group, looks impressive; you enter through the pretty courtyard with its fountain. There's a warm welcome although the decor is somewhat different from when Thea Dupays was in residence. Aperitifs are served in the beige toned lounge. A favourite room is the library with its bold striped sofas, bookcases and pretty writing-tables. Robert Elsmore is a good chef – a dish of warm ravioli of lobster with mussels, plump scallops and large prawns, trompette de mort mushrooms, surrounded by crisp French beans and a thin but flavoursome tomato sauce, showed the kitchen's potential. A hot caramel soufflé with pecan butter sauce, and a trio of apple desserts were also excellent.

Hunstrete House

CHELTENHAM   Redmond's at Malvern View

See page 159 – our Clover Award Section.

CHESTER   The Chester Grosvenor

Eastgate Street, Chester, Cheshire CH1 1LT
Telephone: (0244) 324024   *Fax:* (0244) 313246   *The place to stay in Chester*   **£100**
Open: lunch Tue-Sat, dinner Mon-Sat (closed Christmas)
Last orders: lunch 2.30pm, dinner 10.30pm

Behind a half-timbered façade lies a hotel of considerable but tasteful luxury. Bedrooms differ in style but are high on comfort from firm beds and air conditioning to well-equipped marble lined bathrooms. Quality is almost tangible in the Arkle restaurant, its polished tables laid with silver and fine glass. Chef Paul Reed's menus offer well-balanced dishes of eclectic inspiration: shellfish with a chowder of mussels; casserole of wild hare with potato gnocchi; fricassée of chicken with morels, cream and asparagus. Good wines strongest on classics. As an alternative, the Brasserie offers cheaper, simpler food in stunning decor and domed glass roof.

CHESTER   Crabwall Manor Hotel

Parkgate Road, Mollington, Chester, Cheshire 6H1 6NE
Telephone: (0244) 851666   *Fax:* (0244) 851400   **£70**
Open: lunch + dinner daily
Last orders: lunch 2.00pm, dinner 9.30pm

An impressive 19th-century Tudor Gothic, castellated manor house set in 11 acres of landscaped gardens. Spacious individually designed bedrooms in a comfortable interior of clean lines and warm colours. Food, which is good modern cooking, continues to live up to its early promise, given the demands of a large hotel dining room. Execution is assured and often imaginative as in a dish of hake with balsamic vinegar sauce and white truffle-flavoured potato purée. Good mid-priced wines.

CHESTER   Francs Restaurant

14 Cuppin Street, Chester, Cheshire CH1 2BN
Telephone: (0244) 317952   *Fax:* (0244) 340690   **£35**
Open: all day daily (closed Christmas + New Year)
Last orders: dinner 11.00pm, (10.00pm Sun)

I suspect the real reason the proprietors personally import all their wines is that they can pop over to France every six weeks! For those less fortunate, this small restaurant may be the next best thing! The decor is simple, the food robust country-style: soupe du jour; assiette de boudin or charcuterie, cassoulet, poulet; fromages. The atmosphere is animated – no doubt helped by the regional French wines; many available by the glass. Santé!

CHIPPING CAMPDEN   Charingworth Manor

Charingworth, Nr Chipping Campden, Gloucestershire GL55 6NS
Telephone: (038 678) 555   *Fax:* (038 678) 353   **£60**
Open: lunch + dinner daily
Last orders: lunch 2.00pm (2.30pm Sat + Sun), dinner 10.00pm (9.30pm Sun)

The allure and charm of an ancient manor house, now owned by Blandy Brothers who also own Bishopstrow, in some 50 acres of Cotswold countryside. Log fires, a beamed library and panelled drawing room exist alongside the comfort of modern amenities in the boldly decorated bedrooms. The cooking continues at a high standard with dishes such as breast of chicken with its own ballotine and beetroot sauce, and fillet of lamb roasted with a tartlet of asparagus on a tomato and basil jus. Lunch is £15.50 for three courses and coffee – dinner is double that. A wide-ranging wine list.

CHIPPING CAMDEN   The Cotswold House Hotel & Restaurant

The Square, Chipping Camden, Gloucestershire GL55 6AN
Telephone: (0386) 840330   *Fax:* (0386) 840310   **£50**
Open: lunch Sun, dinner daily (Greenstocks All-Day Eaterie open all day, daily) (closed 3 days Christmas)
Last orders: lunch 2.00pm, dinner 9.30pm (9.30pm Greenstocks)

Owners Gill and Robert Greenstocks have lent this Cotswold stone house an air of individuality. Period features of the 17th-century building such as the old fireplace in the reception area have been retained; each of the fifteen thematically designed bedrooms has its own distinct character such as a poppy design on the coverlets and cushions in one room and a brass bedstead, wicker chairs and lace in another. A choice of eating styles – informal in what the Greenstock locals call the all-day Eaterie, or formal in the light pink and green dining room – makes this a pleasant, friendly base from which to explore Chipping Camden and the surrounding area.

CLANFIELD   The Plough at Clanfield

Bourton Road, Clanfield, Oxfordshire OX8 2RB
Telephone: (036 781) 222   *Fax:* (036 781) 596   **£70**
Open: lunch + dinner daily
Last orders: lunch 2.00pm, dinner 10.00pm

A sensibly flexible menu makes this a useful place, especially at lunchtime. Eat in the relaxed comfort of the lounge bar, the more formal dining room or the garden, depending on your preference and the weather. If you are in a hurry you can even fax your order in! In the lounge bar you can just have a starter such as a kebab of chicken livers wrapped in bacon grilled and served with garlic butter and some fresh frisée and radicchio. Follow it with some good British cheese and fresh onion granary rolls and a pot of good coffee. Extensive European wine list (also one from England, four from Australia and one low alcohol!) – has helpful tasting notes. Smiling helpful service.

CLAYGATE   Les Alouettes

See page 162 – our Clover Award Section.

CLUN   Old Post Office Restaurant

9 The Square, Clun, Shropshire SY7 8JA
Telephone: (05884) 687   **£30**
Open: lunch Thu-Sun by arrangement, dinner Wed-Sun (closed mid Jan
    mid Mar)
Last orders: lunch 1.30pm, dinner 9.30pm (Sun 8.30pm)

The terrace is a fine place for an aperitif while contemplating the
rooftops of Clun and the fields beyond. The restaurant has a fresh,
pretty air with pale walls, white tables and flowers. Striking
combinations are a feature of Richard Arbuthnot's modern cooking: a
spring onion sauce with red mullet; a whisky and rosemary sauce
with a strudel of lamb's sweetbreads. Fillet of beef with a meaux
mustard sauce is more mainstream. Try a lemon and basil sorbet, or
some of the excellent British farmhouse cheeses. Wines are listed by
price (from £6.75) and include some new ones from Australia and
New Zealand. Anne Arbuthnot provides efficient service. There are
two simple bedrooms.

COLERNE   Lucknam Park

See page 163 – our Clover Award Section.

CORSE LAWN   Corse Lawn House Hotel

See page 164 – our Clover Award Section.

CORSHAM   Rudloe Park Hotel & Restaurant

Leafy Lane, Corsham, Wiltshire SN13 0PA
Telephone: (0225) 810555   *Fax:* (0225) 811412   **£45**
Open: lunch + dinner daily
Last orders: lunch 2.00pm, dinner 9.00pm

Ian and Marion Overend are justly proud of their award-winning wine
list. They spend several weeks each year touring France and
Germany for new additions to their two cellars which already stock
over 560 wines. Unusually, the list includes some fifty or sixty
kabinett German wines. Lone diners are well treated: even if a full
bottle is opened for you, you might only be charged for the half you
drink. Staff knowledge is increased by regular wine tastings.
Accompanying the wine is traditional food aimed at hearty local
appetites. The decor of the house ranges from '60s pubby-bar feeling
to traditional English restaurant style. Check, because extensive
refurbishments are planned for 1991.

CUCKFIELD	Jeremy's Restaurant at The King's Head

South Street, Cuckfield, Hayward's Heath, West Sussex RH17 5JY
Telephone: (0444) 454006 **£45**
Open: lunch + dinner Tue-Fri (closed Bank Holidays)
Last orders: lunch 2.00pm, dinner 10.00pm

Don't expect the Ritz – the restaurant is set in a friendly village pub. Old pine tables, country chairs and fresh flowers complete the scene. The cooking rises above the genre, however, so it's essential to book to enjoy Jeremy Ashpool's cooking. Robust flavours – rabbit with noodles and an aubergine sauce; familiar favourites – sticky toffee pudding.

DARTMOUTH	The Carved Angel

See page 166 – our Clover Award Section.

DARTMOUTH	The Mansion House

2 Mansion House Street, Dartmouth, Devon TQ6 9AG
Telephone: (0803) 835474 **£60**
Open: lunch + dinner Tue-Sat (closed 2 wks Feb, 2 wks Nov)
Last orders: lunch 1.30pm, dinner 9.30pm

The approach, an elegant thickly carpeted staircase, prepares one for the cool modern elegance of the dining room. Cooking is confident and accomplished. Fish is a favourite medium on a regularly changing menu: fillets of Dover sole rolled in sesame seeds, on a sorrel butter sauce; noisettes of lamb with a tarragon mousse, in its own juices with mushrooms. The wine list spans the globe. A new bistro downstairs offers simple, cheaper food with candlelight and music.

DEDHAM   Le Talbooth & Maison Talbooth

See page 165 – our Clover Award Section.

DORCHESTER   Maiden Newton House

Maiden Newton, Nr Dorchester, Dorset DT2 0AA
Telephone: (0300) 20336   **£60**
Open: dinner daily (closed part Dec + Jan)
Last orders: dinner 8.00pm

Maiden Newton House is an imposing manor, built of honey coloured
stone with mullion windows, set in its own grounds. In spring
daffodils flank the banks of the stream which runs through the
garden. Elizabeth and Brian Ferriss are charming and welcoming –
she cooks, he hosts the evenings dinner parties. The elegant house is
comfortably informal and well-kept. Spacious, airy bedrooms are
pretty. Breakfasts are good. Guests sit down together at the
polished mahogany table for a well-prepared no-choice often eclectic
dinner: for example, supreme of chicken punjab preceded by a
French onion flan. Well-chosen wines by the glass.

DORKING   Partners West Street

2, 3 & 4 West Street, Dorking, Surrey RH4 1BL
Telephone: (0306) 882826   **£50**
Open: lunch Sun-Fri, dinner Mon-Sat
Last orders: lunch 2.00pm, dinner 9.30pm

Andrew Thomason and Tim McEntire's new venture unfolds in this
stylishly decorated, 16th-century building. At their previous location
in Sutton, they built up a strong local following for their skilful,
modern cooking. The new restaurant features fixed price menus –
£14.25 at lunch, from £19.95 at dinner. The cooking continues in
familiar style: puff pastry filled with wild mushrooms and shallots,
John Dory and monkfish with basil and garlic. The excellent basket of
cheeses remains a firm favourite.

DORRINGTON   Country Friends

Dorrington, Shrewsbury, Shropshire SY5 7JD
Telephone: (074 373) 707   **£40**
Open: lunch + dinner Mon-Sat (closed Christmas, 2 wks Jul, 1 wk Oct)
Last orders: lunch 1.45pm, dinner 9.00pm (9.30pm Sat)

The setting is an Elizabethan-style house. A huge fireplace and a
large framed piece of quilting provide the focal point of the simple
pink dining room. A good recent meal started with a sole and scallop
mousseline (good texture and flavour). Loin of lamb with a crab
mousse made an unusual and successful main course. Well-flavoured
vegetables included crispy battered cauliflower. Good, ripe British
cheeses. There are four simple bedrooms (one with bathroom)
furnished with antiques. Breakfasts not to be missed!

DREWSTEIGNTON   Hunts Tor House

Drewsteignton, Devon EX6 6QW
Telephone: (0647) 21228   **£40**
Open: dinner daily (closed Nov-Feb)
Last orders: dinner 7.30pm

A charming old house at the centre of a picturesque Dartmoor village.
The four simple bedrooms offer friendly accommodation and good
bathrooms. Sue Harrison only cooks for residents and asks for
twenty-four hours' notice for dinner (which is worth having). Fresh
local produce, including garden herbs, are the basis of the accurate
cooking: timbale of broccoli with fresh tomato sauce and warm shallot
vinaigrette; magret of duck with honey and soy sauce. A short wine
list with Duboeuf house wines. Hearty breakfasts set you up for
Dartmoor treks!

EAST BOLDON   Forsters Restaurant

2 St Bedes, Station Road, East Boldon, Tyne & Wear NE36 0LE
Telephone: 091-519 0929   **£50**
Open: lunch + dinner Tue-Sat (closed Bank Holidays)
Last orders: lunch 2.00pm, dinner 10.30pm

Barry and Sue Forster have finally settled (in July 1990) in the North
East of England after their stint at Longueville Manor in Jersey,
where Barry's cooking gained many accolades. He looks set to repeat
the experience, despite the unlikely setting of this Newcastle
dormitory town. The restaurant seats only thirty but already people
are travelling considerable distances to eat here. On arrival they
might enjoy a set lunch menu (amazing value at £11.00, coffee and
petits fours £1.75 extra) comprising three choices at each of three
courses. The evening carte has five or six choices at each course,
and there are daily changing specials. You might start with mushroom
consommé with tortellini of foie gras, or hot grilled lobster with
ginger, soy and spring onions, then go on to best end of lamb with a
rösti potatoes, and a basil and tomato gravy, or roast fillet of turbot
with red pepper butter and grilled scallops. Puddings might be a hot
apple strudel with calvados custard, or farmhouse cheeses from Alan
Porter in Yorkshire. The wine list is mostly French, with some New
World choices, and is reasonably priced.

EAST GRINSTEAD   **Gravetye Manor**

See page 168 – our Clover Award Section.

EAST BUCKLAND   **Lower Pitt Restaurant**

East Buckland, Nr Barnstaple, Devon EX32 0TD
Telephone: (059 86) 243   *Fax:* (059 86) 243   **£45**
Open: dinner Mon-Sat (closed Christmas Day + Boxing Day)
Last orders: dinner 9.00pm (9.30pm Sat)

The new A361 link road has increased accessibility to this charming small restaurant with three rooms. The white farmhouse sits snug by a stream amidst tubs and flowers. Fresh garden and other local produce form the basis of good food served in ample portions: a casserole of pheasant, guinea-fowl, pigeon breast and venison; loin of pork with apples, shallots, cider and cream. Creamy desserts and English cheeses. Devon cider and reasonable wines.

EDENBRIDGE   **Honours Mill Restaurant**

---

87 High Street, Edenbridge, Kent TN8 5AU
Telephone: (0732) 866757   **£70**
Open: lunch Tue-Fri + Sun, dinner , dinner Tue-Sat (closed 2 wks Jan,
     2 wks Jun)
Last orders: lunch 2.00pm, dinner 10.00pm

The Goodhews' mill is a pristine white-painted, picturesque weatherboarded building. In summer aperitifs may be enjoyed on the terrace. Watch your head on the low timbers of the beamed dining room! Short fixed price seasonal menus, supplemented by daily specials, offer accurate modern cooking well prepared from good materials: escalope of salmon with chives; fricassée of guinea fowl with garlic cloves and morels. Good desserts. The wine list is mostly French with a couple of selections from England and a separate list of ½-bottles.

ELY   **The Old Fire Engine House**

---

25 St Mary's Street, Ely, Buckinghamshire CB7 4ER
Telephone: (0353) 662582   **£40**
Open: lunch daily, dinner Mon-Sat (closed Bank Holidays, 2 wks after
     Christmas)
Last orders: lunch 2.00pm, dinner 9.00pm

An enduring and endearing institution, as much for its friendly warmth as for its refusal to bow to fashion. Hearty lamb and vegetable soup, rabbit with mustard and parsley, then syllabub, are typical of the style. The wine list offers enthusiasts some bargains. A stone-flagged floor and old oak tables provide the simple setting (eat in the garden in the summer). Afterwards, enjoy the art gallery upstairs.

EMSWORTH   36 On The Quay

South Street, Emsworth, Hampshire PO10 7EG
Telephone: (0243) 375592   £60

good local restaurant

Open: lunch + dinner Mon-Sat (closed Bank Holidays, 2 wks Jan, 2 wks
    Aug/Sep)
Last orders: lunch 2.00pm, dinner 10.00pm

A light-filled restaurant by day with views of fishing boats and
seagulls, 36 On The Quay is elegant and romantic by night.
Woodwork is picked out in eau de nil against pale yellow walls, and
there's a low white corniced ceiling. Fresh flowers abound in silver
urns and on immaculate cream-clad tables laid with silver and fine
glass. The chef is Richard Wicks, who was Young Chef of the Year in
1989. Dishes are well executed, unfussily presented, and show
imaginative touches: a sweet glaze on a confit of duck served with
saffron-coloured couscous mixed with chopped red pepper, the
marzipan around a rich chocolate fondant served with amaretto ice
cream. Good hot bread and decent house wines. Pleasant professional service – silver domes are used without theatricality. There are
plenty of ½-bottles on the wine list.

36, On the Quay

EVERSLEY   The New Mill Restaurant

New Mill Road, Eversley, Hampshire RG27 0RA
Telephone: (0734) 732277/732105   *Fax:* (0734) 328780   £60
Open: lunch Sun-Fri, dinner daily (closed 2 wks Jan)
Last orders: lunch 2.00pm, dinner 10.00pm (9.00pm)

A lovely setting for this converted millhouse: the glazed dining room
extension overlooks the river and its resident ducks! Fixed price
menus offer best value, with new chef Robert Allen bringing to them
skills acquired at places like The Dorchester and Hintlesham Hall:
veal terrine, millefeuille of salmon, fillet of beef with braised shallots.
A good wine list, chosen with care.

EVERSHOT   Summer Lodge

Evershot, Nr Dorchester, Dorset DT2 0JR
Telephone: (0935) 83424   **£55**
Open: lunch + dinner daily (closed 2 wks Jan)
Last orders: lunch 1.30pm, dinner 8.30pm

Warm, light and welcoming, Summer Lodge is as appealing as ever.
Pleasant country house with extra bedrooms in a stable block. The
drawing room with its tall french windows, comfortable sofas and log
fires is a favourite retreat. The sunny feeling is carried through in
rattan furnished bedrooms. New chef Roger Jones has added his
stamp to the short fixed price menus, with dishes such as steamed
fillet of turbot with a two pepper coulis; also good pastry and bread. A
new wine list offers some interesting new bottles.

FAVERSHAM   Read's

See page 171 – our Clover Award Section.

FAVERSHAM   Throwley House

Ashford Road, Sheldwich, Nr Faversham, Kent ME13 0LT
Telephone: (0795) 539168   *Fax:* (0795) 535086   **£55**
Open: lunch Sun-Fri, dinner Mon-Sat (closed 3 days Christmas)
Last orders: lunch 2.00pm (1.30pm Sun), dinner 9.30pm

A charming new country house hotel with an appealing eccentric
emblem: a teddy bear! Light, spacious rooms decorated with sunny
colours and furnished with painted reproduction furniture, overlook
surrounding fields. A nursery with full-time nanny is being created.
The elegant deep blue and white dining room is presided over by a
resident teddy bear. Seriously adult food, though, by ex-Hole in the
Wall chef Martin Barratt. If it's available, try the loin of Northdown
lamb served pink with a fresh tarragon sauce, or pheasant casseroled
with local wild mushrooms, pine kernels and red wine. Good
cheeses, but save room for dessert such as a pancake filled with
home-made ice cream topped with ripples of meringue and served
with blackcurrant syrup – well presented and quite delicious! The
wine list is mainly European with some selections from Australia and
America – reasonable prices. Pleasant and willing service.

THROWLEY BEAR

Throwley House, Faversham

FLITWICK · Flitwick Manor

Church Road, Flitwick, Bedfordshire MK45 1AE
Telephone: (0525) 712242 *Fax:* (0525) 712242 ex 55 **£70**
Open: lunch + dinner daily (closed Christmas)
Last orders: lunch 1.45pm, dinner 9.30pm (9.45pm Sat, 9.00pm Sun)

Ownership has changed but manager and chef, Shaun Cook, remain the same. This classic red brick house is as warm and comfortable as ever, from the flagstoned entrance hall with its fireplace and salmon pink walls, to the bedrooms with their period furnishings and bold, unfussy fabrics. Lots of home-from-home extras include games, books and toothbrushes. Oil paintings and old silver adorn the mahogany and salmon pink dining room. The menu emphasis is on fish and the kitchen garden (including a couple of vegetarian dishes). A good classic wine list.

FOWEY · Food for Thought Restaurant

Town Quay, Fowey, Cornwall PL23 1AT
Telephone: (072 683) 2221 **£50**
Open: dinner Mon-Sat
Last orders: dinner 9.30pm

There's a smell of seaweed and a splashing of waves against the quayside as you enter the neat, white, former customs house with its jaunty blue awning. A small bar area leads into the beamed low-ceilinged dining room with its exposed shale walls, carpeting and smart white tables. Food is prettily presented and full of flavours: a smooth deep-coloured fish and shellfish soup; saddle of hare rolled and roasted in a lacy 'net' of pastry, with a pastry basket filled with buttery, turned carrots, apples and swede and a deep blackberry, apple and calvados sauce. For dessert, a trio of home-made sorbets nestling on a swirl of meringue. Friendly efficient service.

GILLINGHAM · Stock Hill House

See page 170 – our Clover Award Section.

GLASTONBURY	Number Three Restaurant & Hotel

3 Magdalene Street, Glastonbury, Somerset BA6 9EW
Telephone: (0458) 32129   **£65**
Open: dinner Mon-Sat (closed Bank Holidays, Christmas)
Last orders: dinner 9.00pm

The Tynans' restaurant in a neat house set back from the road continues to draw a strong local following. Ann Tynan, in her immaculate kitchen, is a competent cook. Fresh produce is the basis of a stable repertoire of dishes prepared with an eye to healthy eating: a charlotte of leeks and walnuts; fat-free loin of new season lamb with fresh rosemary and mint. Indulgence comes in the form of home-made ice creams! John Tynan is a good host in a strongly decorated dining room: deep red walls and carpet, large modern paintings, pastel napery.

GORING-ON-THAMES	The Leatherne Bottel

Goring-on-Thames, Berkshire RG8 0HS   *good local restaurant*
Telephone: (0491) 872667   **£60**
Open: lunch + dinner daily (closed Christmas Day)
Last orders: lunch 2.00pm (2.30pm Sat, 3.00pm Sun) dinner 9.45pm
                        (9.00pm Sun)

The Leatherne Bottel Riverside Inn and Restaurant is establishing itself as a pleasant, comfortable place with its light, airy dining room; and in summer there's alfresco eating while you watch the boats and ducks. Food is unfussy – meat and fish often char-grilled – and herbs abundant. Try rack of lamb marinated with apple mint then char-grilled, or warm poached smoked salmon with lemon grass. A short wine list with house wine at £7.95.

GRASMERE	Michael's Nook Country House Hotel

See page 172 – our Clover Award Section.

GRASMERE	White Moss House

Rydal Water, Grasmere, Cumbria LA22 9SE
Telephone: (096 65) 295   **£55**
Open: dinner Mon-Sat (closed Dec – Feb)
Last orders: dinner 8.00pm

Susan Dixon extends a warm welcome from Wordsworth's former home, and there are lovely views from the comfortable lounge. Guests come to walk, fish or to use the 100-year-old rowing boat, but all enjoy the acknowledged excellence of Peter Dixon's cooking. The 5-course no-choice dinners, one sitting only, draw on regional produce: Coniston Water char and smoked wild salmon in a four fish terrine; Lakeland mallard roasted and served with a fruit and wine sauce. Traditional puddings are a highlight – try the cabinet pudding. Save room for the unusual English cheeses. The main interest of the wine list remains with the bordeaux and burgundies, some New World wines.

GRASMERE   Wordsworth Hotel

Grasmere, Nr Ambleside, Cumbria LA22 9SW
Telephone: (096 65) 592   *Fax:* (096 65) 765   **£55**
Open: lunch + dinner daily
Last orders: lunch 2.00pm, dinner 9.00pm (9.30pm Sat)

Thirty-seven well-kept bedrooms decorated in homely but elegant style. The newly decorated conservatory and lounge bar provide a tranquil retreat, perhaps after a session in the sauna or solarium. The more energetic have the use of an indoor heated pool and keep-fit equipment. There's ample choice also on the restaurant menu which uses local produce: smoked duck in a salad, trout baked in pastry. And in spring, a homage to the poet: crystallised daffodils!

GRAYSHOTT   Woods

Headley Road, Grayshott, Nr Hindhead, Hampshire GU26 6LB
Telephone: (042 873) 5555   **£60**
Open: dinner Tue-Sat (closed 2 wks Aug, 1 wk Christmas)
Last orders: dinner 11.30pm

Set in a row of shops is the neat green-and-cream façade of the Norregens' pleasant little restaurant. White crocheted café curtains screen diners from passers-by. White half-tiled walls and simple wooden tables and chairs form the setting. Gravadlax and blinis are favourites on the short menu. Some good wines on the short list. Escapees from Grayshott Hall are often seen here!

GREAT GONERBY   Harry's Place

17 High Street, Great Gonerby, Grantham, Lincolnshire NG31 8JS
Telephone: (0476) 61780   **£75**
Open: lunch + dinner daily (closed Bank Holidays + Christmas Day)
Last orders: lunch 2.00pm, dinner 9.30pm

Just ten seats at this tiny restaurant in Harry & Caroline Hallam's Georgian house. Pale yellow cloths, white china and silver napkin rings complement pale green walls and a stripped oak fire place. Caroline is a graceful hostess, service well paced and unhurried. Harry uses ingredients beyond reproach, and his cooking is precise in flavour and timing: king scallops and mussels with a creamy sauce and crunchy julienne of leeks and carrots; fillet of sea-bass in a fresh herb crust in a white wine, butter and mustard sauce; apple and calvados soufflé. Supporting elements from nibbles to coffee lived up to the rest. A concise, well chosen wine list.

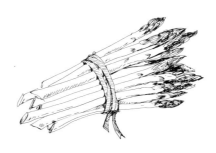

GREAT MILTON   Le Manoir aux Quat'Saisons

See page 174 – our Clover Award Section.

GREAT YARMOUTH   Seafood Restaurant

85 North Quay, Great Yarmouth, Norfolk NR30 1JF
Telephone: (0493) 856009   **£60**
Open: lunch Mon-Fri, dinner Mon-Sat (closed Bank Holidays,
       3 wks Christmas)
Last orders: lunch 1.45pm, dinner 10.30pm

Simple is best, here: lobsters from a tank in the bar, fresh Lowestoft
fish from a display, and local oysters. Reasonably priced wines,
comfortable surroundings (padded banquette seating, frilly swagged
curtains) and friendly service from the Greek owners complete the
picture. Always busy, so book.

GREAT DUNMOW   The Starr Restaurant

Market Place, Great Dunmow, Essex CM6 1AX
Telephone: (0371) 874321   **£65**
Open: lunch Sun – Fri, dinner Mon-Sat (closed 5 dys Christmas)
Last orders: lunch 1.30pm, dinner 9.30pm

Family-run with pride and enthusiasm, the Starr dispenses warm,
relaxed hospitality to regulars and visitors alike. As much as possible
is home-made, from granary bread to ice creams and sorbets. Daily
menus, chalked up on blackboards, are explained in detail. Fish
remains a strong point, especially on Wednesday evenings – a special
fish menu is created from the day's marketing at Billingsgate. A good
wine list including an interesting list of 'second' wines from the great
châteaux. Eight en-suite, well furnished bedrooms. Popular local
restaurant.

GRIMSTON   Congham Hall

Lynn Road, Grimston, King's Lynn, Norfolk PE32 1AH
Telephone: (0485) 600250   **£60**
Open: lunch Mon-Fri + Sun, dinner daily
Last orders: lunch 1.45pm, dinner 9.15pm (9.00pm Sun)

Trevor and Christine Forecast are genuinely welcoming, concerned
hosts. A ground floor garden suite has been added with sympathetic
attention to period detail both inside and out. The Orangery
Restaurant with its glass roof and plants is very pleasant, with
service well directed by Claire Digweed. Chef Clive Jackson cooks in
a modern English style with good use of herbs from the fine herb
garden. Lunch offers excellent value but really to appreciate the
quality of Clive's cooking and the charm of this graceful Georgian
house book to stay in one of the comfortable rooms. Concise wine list
with helpful tasting notes, reasonably priced.

| GUERNSEY | Le Nautique |

Quay Steps, St Peter Port, Guernsey, Channel Islands
Telephone: (0481) 721714 £45
Open: lunch + dinner Mon-Sat (closed Christmas Day to 7 Jan)
Last orders: lunch 2.00pm, dinner 10.00pm

Good views of the harbour from this smart, old-style restaurant, popular with locals and tourists alike. Seafood is the speciality, the style is classic, the cooking accurate and full of flavour. Dishes range from Guernsey lobster grilled then flambéed with Scotch whisky, to a simple grilled Dover sole. Some meat dishes, and a choice of good salads. A short, classic wine list. Book.

| HAMBLETON | Hambleton Hall Hotel |

See page 176 – our Clover Award Section.

| HARROGATE | Betty's Café & Tea Rooms |

1 Parliament Street, Harrogate, North Yorkshire HG1 2QU
Telephone: (0423) 502746   *Fax:* (0423) 565191 £30
Open: all day daily (closed Christmas, phone to check Bank Holidays)
Last orders: 9.00pm

Descendants of Frederick Belmont, the Swiss confectioner who opened Betty's in 1919, still run this family business. There are now sister establishments in York, Northallerton and Ilkley. The menu offers traditional Yorkshire baking – hot buttered pikelets, fat rascals, spiced teacakes . . . plus snacks such as rarebit made with Theakston's ale, salads and omelettes. Some other hot dishes in the evening. Children are welcome (and catered for). Open all day, plus a take-away service.

| HARROGATE | Drum & Monkey |

5 Montpellier Gardens, Harrogate, North Yorkshire HG1 2TF
Telephone: (0423) 502650 £40
Open: lunch + dinner Mon-Sat (closed Christmas + New Year)
Last orders: lunch 2.30pm, dinner 10.15pm

The pub-style decor with its brown and green wallpaper, black marble tables and stuffed fish in glass cases is now well lived-in but still comfortable. Book, even for a place in the bar, although drinks are served to the inevitable queue! Seafood is still the thing – stick to the simpler dishes such as queen scallops with cheese and garlic butter, and grilled hake with salad and new potatoes. Duboeuf house wine. Informal sometimes hectic service.

HARROGATE   Millers

1 Montpelier Mews, Harrogate, North Yorkshire HG1 2TG
Telephone: (0423) 530768   **£70**
Open: lunch Mon-Sat, dinner Tue-Sat (closed 1 wk Aug, Bank Holidays,
        Christmas + New Year)
Last orders: lunch 2.00pm, dinner 10.00pm

Large, contemporary still life paintings add colour to a setting of dark
carpet and walls. This small restaurant is tucked into a smart,
cobbled shopping precinct. Simon Gueller is an accurate chef with
finely crafted presentation dispensing with unnecessary garnish.
Lobster ravioli with leeks, tomato and basil, pig's trotter périgourdine (stuffed with pâté); millefeuille of local rabbit (included foie gras
and truffle!) were much enjoyed at a recent dinner (£27.50 for three
courses). Vegetables included an excellent potato purée scattered
with morels. Good French cheeses and a superb chocolate marquise.
Alert, professional service. Extensions are planned for the New
Year, including inside toilets!

HASLEMERE   Morels

23-27 Lower Street, Haslemere, Surrey GU27 2NY
Telephone: (0428) 51462   **£75**
Open: lunch Tue-Fri, dinner Tue-Sat (closed 2 wks Feb, 2 wks Sep,
        Bank Holidays)
Last orders: lunch 2.00pm, dinner 10.00pm

The low-ceilinged dining room with its pale blue and cream walls,
crisp white cloths, blue undercloths and comfortable wooden chairs,
feels light and summery. Young French staff provide pleasant,
professional service. Jean-Yves Morel's cooking is assured, flavours
subtle yet prominent: an appetiser of ballotine of omelette with
aubergine, red and green pepper and onion; a simple smooth mussel
soup; butter-fried apples and a calvados sauce with loin of pork.
Creamy gratin dauphinois, a sharp palette-cleansing lemon sorbet,
excellent espresso coffee and petits fours. The set lunch menu is a
bargain at around £16.

HASTINGLEIGH   Woodman's Arms Auberge

Hassell Street, Hastingleigh, Nr Ashford, Kent TN25 5JE
Telephone: (023 375) 250   **£60**
Open: dinner daily (closed 1 wk May, 3 wks Sep)
Last orders: dinner 7.30pm

A charming pink painted building with three pretty, comfortable
bedrooms with well equipped private bathrooms (one room even
boasts its own little garden!) One sitting at 7.30pm for just ten guests
(mainly residents). Susan Campion cooks competently to a high
standard, using fresh local produce – Romney Marsh lamb, pheasant,
good vegetables. A copy of the wine list in the bedrooms allows
plenty of time to peruse Gerald Campion's careful selection.

HAWORTH	Weavers

15 West Lane, haworth, West Yorkshire BD22 8DU
Telephone: (0535) 43822   **£50**
Open: lunch Sun in winter, dinner Tue-Sat (closed Bank Holidays, 2 wks
        Christmas, 2 wks Jul)
Last orders: lunch 1.30pm, dinner 9.30pm

Colin, Jane and Tim Rushworth's friendly restaurant with just four
bedrooms caters predominantly for local customers, and takes pride
in using local produce. They make everything on the premises
(stocks, breads, ice creams), and when mushrooms appear on the
menu they will be Yorkshire field mushrooms, not ones from Rungis
in Paris. Local too are the vegetables, cheeses and meat (grass-fed
beef and calves' liver), while fish is from Manchester market.
Inspiration comes from further afield, however, especially the
Orient, with starters like Asia spice chicken salad (strips of chicken
spiced then grilled and served on a salad with a light lemony
dressing), or a main-course crisp roast Gressingham duck, served off
the bone and sliced over a rich plum sauce. Puddings are firmly close
to home – old school pudding with white sauce, traditional raspberry
trifle, and nanny's meringue nest of cream, brown bread ice cream
and a light apricot sauce. A European wine list is moderately priced.

HELFORD	Riverside

Helford, Nr Helston, Cornwall TR12 6JU
Telephone: (032 623) 443   *good local restaurant*   **£60**
Open: dinner daily (closed Nov to mid-Feb)
Last orders: dinner 9.30pm

From the flower bedecked terrace of this whitewashed cottage,
there are fine views over the picture book village and creek. First
class fresh fish remains the chief strength of the imaginative cooking:
hake, for example, may be baked with a crab crust, or cooked with
shallots, mushrooms, grapes and tomatoes. Good puddings and
well-kept cheeses. The Riverside is run with care and enthusiasm.
There are six pretty pine-furnished rooms.

HERSHAM	La Malmaison

By The Green, 17 Queen's Road, Hersham, Walton-on-Thames, Surrey
KT12 5ND
Telephone: (0932) 227412   **£55**
Open: lunch Mon-Fri, dinner Mon-Sat (closed Boxing Day, New Year's Day)
Last orders: lunch 2.30pm, dinner 10.00pm

A dining room in pale pinks, reds and greys with comfortable chairs,
silver and cut glass and classical background music. Lisa Troquet is a
charming, knowledgeable hostess. Natural flavours shine through in
Jacques' classically-based French cooking: a lobster-flavoured tomato sauce served with a smooth-textured gâteau of chicken livers;
steamed chicory in a light cream sauce accompanying a moist fresh
fillet of cod, simply pan-fried. Desserts such as tarte tatin; excellent
coffee.

HERSTMONCEUX — The Sundial Restaurant

See page 173 – our Clover Award Section.

HETTON — Angel Inn

Hetton, Nr Skipton, North Yorkshire BD23 6LT
Telephone: (075 673) 253   **£45**
Open: lunch Sun, dinner Mon-Sat
Last orders: lunch 2.00pm, dinner 9.30pm

excellent local restaurant

I have in the past underrated the Angel Inn and on my last visit came away with a feeling that this was somewhere really special. This has been borne out by others, all unanimous in their praise of Denis Watkins and his team for their ability to turn out the high standard of cooking with dishes such as breast of guineafowl wrapped in parma ham and savoy leaves, baked in the oven and served on a tarragon cream sauce, or best end of Yorkshire lamb, roasted in a herb crust and served in a red wine sauce flavoured with rosemary and garlic, in what was originally a country inn. Excellent service, good value and if you haven't booked and can't get a table, the bar food is a lesson many inns might learn from.

HOCKLEY HEATH — Nuthurst Grange

Nuthurst Grange Lane, Hockley Heath, Warwickshire B94 5NL
Telephone: (0564) 783972   *Fax:* (0564) 783919   **£85**
Open: lunch Sun-Fri (Sat private functions only), dinner daily (closed 2 wks
     Christmas)
Last orders: lunch 2.00pm, dinner 9.30pm

Large picture windows, white table linen and modern black chair frames offset a predominantly pink dining room decor. David Randolph is a skilled chef who clearly enjoys the construction of his dishes based on various skills learned over the years and shown in fixed price 3-course menus. Feuilleté of baby asparagus with lemon butter; duckling with toasted almonds. A well-chosen wine list. Eight spacious bedrooms decorated with pastels and chintzes; en-suite air spa baths. The extended M40 now provides an alternative to the hotel's helipad!

HOPE END — Hope End

See page 178 – our Clover Award Section.

HULL — Ceruttis

10 Nelson Street, Hull, Humberside HU1 1XE
Telephone: (0482) 28501   **£55**
Open: lunch Mon-Fri, dinner Mon-Sat (closed Bank Holidays, 1 wk
     Christmas)
Last orders: lunch 2.00pm, dinner 9.30pm

A friendly, family-run restaurant overlooking the harbour. Fresh fish, listed according to type, on the old style menu, is honestly prepared. Simple is best: grilled Dover sole; monkfish au poivre. A good selection of white wines. This is a useful local restaurant.

HURSTBOURNE TARRANT   Esseborne Manor

Hurstbourne Tarrant, Nr Andover, Hampshire SP11 0ER
Telephone: (026 476) 444   £65
Open: lunch + dinner daily
Last orders: lunch 2.00pm, dinner 9.30pm

This well-kept Victorian house set amidst Wessex downlands is the
Yeos' home; family photographs and ornaments lend an informal air.
The twelve bedrooms (some in an extension) are in striking colours
and pine or period furniture, with carpeted bathrooms. Fixed price
menus offer attractively presented modern English cooking. The
no-choice main course might be pheasant stuffed with foie gras, or
roast loin of lamb with spinach. A choice of desserts and farmhouse
cheeses. House wines from Murray Tyrrell.

ILKLEY   The Box Tree

See page 179 – our Clover Award Section.

IPSWICH   Hintlesham Hall

Hintlesham, Nr Ipswick, Suffolk IP8 3NS
Telephone: (047 387) 334/268   *Fax:* (047 387) 463   £55
Open: lunch Sun-Fri, dinner daily
Last orders: lunch 2.00pm, dinner 9.30pm

Now under new ownership, continuity is assured by the same
management team of Tim Sunderland – hotel manager, Tim O'Leary
– restaurant manager, and Alan Ford in the kitchen. With its
individualistic decor and style, the Hall is as pleasant as ever,
whether staying or just eating. The lovely pine-panelled dining room
hung with oil portraits is warm and comfortable with well-spaced
tables. A good recent meal featured monkfish tails rolled in crushed
black peppercorns with a sharp lime butter sauce; vegetables
included spinach with cream and slivers of mushroom. Dessert was
an elegant rosemary and lemon syllabub with unusual and delicious
tarragon tuiles. Excellent espresso coffee. A wine list that includes a
good selection of ½-bottles and pleasant service. Thirty-three stylish
and well-equipped bedrooms.

JERSEY	Granite Corner

Rozel Harbour, Trinity, Jersey, Channel Islands
Telephone: (0534) 63590
Open: dinner Mon-Sat (closed mid-Dec to mid-Jan)
Last orders: dinner 9.00pm

good local restaurant **£55**

A modest stone cottage overlooking the harbour is the setting for the Robins' small, unpretentious French restaurant. The simple but elegant dining room is dominated by a granite fireplace. Jean-Luc cooks the type of food found in modern restaurants in France but rarely in the Channel Islands, a combination of périgourdine dishes (with ingredients flown in) and some based on local produce: fresh local prawns in their shell, grilled with sea-salt; or a jar of whole home-made duck foie gras; confit de canard; fillets of Jersey sole steamed upon seaweed with a truffle sauce. Execution and judgement are skilled. Jersey needs somewhere like this – go!

JERSEY	Hotel L'Horizon

St Brelade's Bay, Jersey, Channel Islands
Telephone: (0534) 43101   *Fax:* (0534) 46269   **£50**
Open: lunch + dinner daily
Last orders: lunch 2.30pm, dinner 10.30pm

Occupying a prime position overlooking a sandy beach and the bay, this modern 103-bedroomed hotel offers traditional elegance with modern comforts. Sea front rooms have balconies, all are of good size. A programme of refurbishment is gradually improving them. Facilities include an indoor pool, sauna and keep-fit equipment.

JERSEY	Longueville Manor

Longueville Road, St Saviour, Jersey, Channel Islands
Telephone: (0534) 25501   *Fax:* (0534) 31613   **£75**
Open: lunch + dinner daily
Last orders: lunch 2.00pm, dinner 9.30pm

Still the best hotel in the Channel Islands. Parts of the house date from the 13th Century, a setting enhanced by antiques, comfortable sofas by open fires and fresh flowers. Thirty-three plushly decorated rooms with superb bathrooms. The oak panelled dining room is elegant with high-backed chairs and crisp white napery. (A second modern dining room caters for smokers.) The new chef, Andrew Baird, cooks modern, attractively presented dishes: steamed turbot with spinach and langoustine tortellini; grilled duck breast with a king prawn and ginger sauté. Good farmhouse cheeses.

JEVINGTON	The Hungry Monk Restaurant

The Street, Jevington, Nr Polegate, East Sussex BN26 5QF
Telephone: (032 12) 2178   **£50**
Open: lunch Sun, dinner daily (closed Bank Holidays, Christmas + New Year)
Last orders: lunch 2.00pm, dinner 10.00pm

If the monk were to return here, he need not fear going hungry.
Good portions of robust cooking have long delighted the many
regulars, and there's a growing list of favourite dishes. The £16.95
menu includes three courses, home-made bread, vegetables and a
glass of port. Puddings are a feast of indulgence. Always busy (book)
and a good atmosphere in the series of heavily furnished dining
rooms.

KENILWORTH	Restaurant Bosquet

97A Warwick Road, Kenilworth, Warwickshire CV8 1HP
Telephone: (0926) 52463   **£55**
Open: lunch by arrangement, dinner Mon-Sat (closed Bank Holidays, 10 days
        Christmas, 3 wks Jul/Aug)
Last orders: dinner 10.00pm

Bernard Lignier continues quietly and assuredly to produce some fine
cooking. There may be few fireworks and few concessions to the
latest trends, but dependable quality around fixed price and à la carte
menus is the trade-off. A coating of breadcrumbs and truffle for
medallions of lamb with a port and cream sauce; guineafowl cooked
en cocotte; tarte au citron. Some lesser known wines on an extensive
French list. Simple rather homely surroundings. Good local
restaurant.

KINGSBRIDGE	Buckland-Tout-Saints Hotel

Goveton, Nr Kingsbridge, South Devon TQ7 2DS
Telephone: (0548) 853055   *Fax:* (0548) 856261   **£65**
Open: lunch + dinner daily (closed Jan – mid Feb)
Last orders: lunch 1.30pm, dinner 9.00pm

An elegant William and Mary house tucked away in the area with the
mildest climate in Britain. The young staff show a genuine concern
for guests' pleasure. The twelve bedrooms in country house style
(those on the 2nd floor smaller and more modern) enjoy garden
views. The panelled Queen Anne dining room is elegant, with
well-spaced tables. Short modern menus make good use of local
produce, dishes are full of flavour: tagliatelle with fresh crab and
lemon sole; char-grilled Guinea fowl with a local cider and Calvados
sauce; Ashprington and Ticklemore goats' may be among the local
cheeses. Well chosen wines with plenty of choice.

KING'S LYNN   Swinton House

Stow Bridge, King's Lynn, Norfolk PE34 3PP
Telephone: (0366) 383151   **£35**
Open: lunch Sun, dinner Tue-Sat (closed 1 wk Christmas)
Last orders: lunch 2.00pm, dinner 9.00pm

Graham and Alison Kitch have been at Swinton House for three years
now, and have gradually built up a strong local following at their tiny
(only eighteen covers), popular restaurant. Since the House is also
their home, the atmosphere is welcoming and friendly, just as you
would find going to dinner with friends. Graham's cooking (although
he continues to cook on an Aga!) is now modern English with the
occasional exotic influence. He is grateful for his neighbours who are
butcher and market gardener, and thus supply a good proportion of
his needs. From a set menu you might choose baked soft herring roes
with mustard hollandaise, then a rich game pie of pheasant, pigeon,
rabbit, hare and venison, with a selection of British cheeses to finish.

KINTBURY   The Dundas Arms

53 Station Road, Kintbury, Berkshire RG15 0UT
Telephone: (0488) 58263   **£50**
Open: lunch + dinner Tue-Sat, snack lunches available Mon (closed Bank
        Holidays, Christmas + New Year)
Last orders: lunch 1.30pm, dinner 9.30pm

This popular pub is flanked on three sides by water; the garden is a
good spot for duck watching! The simply furnished restaurant serves
fresh, often local, produce in an unpretentious manner: salad of warm
smoked duck breast; saddle of hare with a rosemary scented sauce.
There may be traditional bread and butter pudding. A wine list strong
on burgundies and bordeaux. Five bedrooms with simple bathrooms
in a converted stable block open onto a canal-side terrace.

KIRKBY FLEETHAM   Kirkby Fleetham Hall

Kirkby Fleetham, Northallerton, North Yorkshire DL7 0SU
Telephone: (0609) 748711   **£60**
Open: lunch Sun, dinner daily
Last orders: lunch 2.00pm, dinner 9.00pm

Kirkby Fleetham is a relaxed and informal country house, run by
Roderick Richman and set in its own grounds of 30 acres which
include a Victorian walled kitchen garden (supplying the kitchen with
fruit, vegetables and herbs). Public rooms are elegant and comfortable, as are the twenty-two bedrooms which are not numbered but
named after birds. In the dining room you can try the set-price dinner
menus of modern British cooking, starting perhaps with a timbale of
York ham and Swaledale cheese wrapped in spinach and baked with a
'gathering' of berries, or king scallops seared with a dusting of
nutmeg on a risotto of smoked bacon and sweet pimento with a
tomato and basil coulis. For the main course, perhaps try grey
partridge, pot-roasted with woodland mushrooms on a compote of
red onions with rich game gravy, or canon of lamb with crab apples.
The mostly European wine list has a good sprinkling of half bottles,
and is moderately priced.

KNUTSFORD — La Belle Epoque

60 King Street, Knutsford, Cheshire WA16 6DT
Telephone: (0565) 3060 *Fax:* (0565) 4150 £65
Open: dinner Mon-Sat (closed Bank Holidays, 1 wk Jan)
Last orders: dinner 10.00pm (10.30pm Sat)

Nerys and Keith Mooney's restaurant with five rooms is well established in Knutsford and very popular with locals and travellers alike. The decor is indeed art nouveau, the atmosphere is friendly and the modern British food is cooked from good quality, local produce whenever possible. Stocks are home-made, as are breads, sweets and petits fours, so that you might find on the menu home-made spinach pasta flavoured with wild mushrooms, air-dried ham and spring onions, or snails served Provence style; then fillets of rabbit sautéed with shallots and mushrooms and finished in a madeira sauce, or calves' liver grilled and served on a sauce of port and redcurrants. The wine list includes a special selection of French wines offering the best value at any given moment – these are often interesting alternatives to the main list that are worth perusing.

LACOCK — At the Sign of the Angel

6 Church Street, Lacock, Nr Chippenham, Wiltshire SN15 2LA
Telephone: (024 973) 230 £55
Open: lunch Sun-Fri, dinner Mon-Sat (residents only Sun) (closed 2 wks Christmas + New Year)
Last orders: lunch 1.30pm, dinner 8.15pm (7.00pm Sun)

The combination of the setting – a 14th-century wool merchant's home with beams, fireplaces and oak furniture – and traditional English fare continues to attract visitors. The formula is well-established and simple: a few starters, a traditional roast or a fish dish, a choice of puddings or English cheese, accompanied perhaps by a glass of port.

LANGHO — Northcote Manor

Northcote Road, Langho, Nr Blackburn, Lancashire BB6 8BE
Telephone: (0254) 240555 *Fax:* (0254) 246568 £70
Open: lunch + dinner daily (closed Christmas + New Year)
Last orders: lunch 1.30pm, dinner 9.30pm (10.00pm Sat, 9.00pm Sun)

A friendly welcome to this solid Victorian house and up the fine oak staircase to bedrooms neatly equipped with modern comforts. Bathrooms vary. Chef Nigel Haworth cooks some enjoyable dishes on his daily menus, from simple marinated queen scallops and gravadlax to a breast of wild duckling with a ravioli of girolle mushrooms, and caramelised foie gras, on a sauce of calvados with rösti potatoes. Excellent cheeses. Friendly, professional service in the pleasant bay-windowed dining room.

LAVENHAM   The Great House

Market Place, Lavenham, Suffolk CO10 9QZ
Telephone: (0787) 247431   **£50**
Open: lunch + dinner daily (closed 3 wks Jan)
Last orders: lunch 2.30pm, dinner 10.30pm

Behind a Georgian façade is a 15th-century house with a neat beamed
and panelled interior. Fixed price menus are offered with the addition
of a carte in the evenings. Cooking is classically based: 'cushions' of
cheese fondue, fish soup, pot-roasted pheasant with wild
mushrooms, salmon with hollandaise sauce, crème brûlée. Excellent
bread. French service, and French wine list starting at £12 for house
wine. Four spacious and attractive en-suite bedrooms.

LAVENHAM   The Swan Hotel

High Street, Lavenham, Suffolk CO10 9QA
Telephone: (0787) 247477   *Fax:* (0787) 248286   **£55**
Open: lunch + dinner daily (closed Christmas Day, Boxing Day,
    New Year's Day)
Last orders: lunch 2.00pm, dinner 9.30pm

The main building dates back to the 15th Century, and modernisation
of this group-owned hotel (THF) has been careful and sympathetic.
Walkways overlooking little gardens lead to the traditionally designed
bedrooms, many of them beamed. The restaurant features an
impressive, high-timbered ceiling and an original minstrels' gallery.
Menus cater to an international clientele, and the food is carefully
cooked. The bar is a popular meeting place and the lounge a good
spot for a cream tea.

LEDBURY	The Grove House

Bromsberrow Heath, Ledbury, Hereford & Worcester HR8 1PE
Telephone: (0531) 650584   **£50**
Open: dinner for residents only (closed Christmas & New Year)
Last orders: 8.00pm

The Grove House is Michael and Ellen Ross's home – a lovely old creeper-clad red brick house. Antiques, log fires and fresh flowers complement beams and panelling. Three well-equipped en-suite bedrooms reflect the Rosses' thirty years of professional hotel keeping. Guests can enjoy fresh garden and other local produce (including fish bought at Birmingham central market at 6.00am!) in the 5-course set dinners. Horse riding is a popular activity.

LEEDS	Bryan's of Headingley

Weetwood Lane, Leeds, West Yorkshire LS16 5LT
Telephone: (0532) 785679   **£20**
Open: all day Mon-Sat (closed Christmas)
Last orders: 11.30pm

For a taste of real fish and chips, this is the place! It's a classic northern fish and chip shop and restaurant, but brighter and more modern. Green clad waitresses scurry to and fro. Portions are huge, the fish moist and flakey in superb crisp batter. But watch out for the mushy peas!

LEWDOWN	Lewtrenchard Manor

Lewtrenchard, Lewdown, Nr Okehampton, Devon EX20 4PN
Telephone: (056 683) 256   **£65**
Open: lunch Sun, dinner daily (closed 3 wks Jan)
Last orders: lunch 1.30pm, dinner 9.30pm

A fine 1620 manor house with an impressive, later interior characterised by plasterwork ceilings, beautifully carved panelling, massive fireplaces and leaded windows. Traditionally furnished bedrooms, several with 4-poster beds. The dining room is formal in style and service, with dark wood panelling and crisp white cloths. The cuisine is modern and prepared with skill; dishes are often elaborate, but the simpler ones may be best: asparagus and baby vegetables with hollandaise sauce, grilled sea-bass with lemon and ginger. Owners James and Sue Murray are enthusiastic hosts.

LISKEARD   The Well House

St Keyne, Liskeard, Cornwall PL14 4RN
Telephone: (0579) 42001   **£65**
Open: lunch + dinner, Tue-Sun
Last orders: lunch 1.30pm, dinner 9.00pm

Tranquillity and lovely views of the rolling countryside are guaranteed at this pleasant Victorian house. The ten individually designed
bedrooms offer pretty accommodation, carpeted bathrooms and good
toiletries. Good breakfasts: fresh coffee, freshly squeezed grapefruit
juice, warm home-made brioche and croissant. Comfortable sofas,
log fires warm the lounge, and there's a small bar for drinks. New
chef David Woolfall was settling in well on our last visit, having
moved across from Teignworthy. Pleasant, attentive staff led by
owner Nick Wainford. Tennis court and outdoor swimming pool.

LONGRIDGE   Heathcotes Restaurant

Higher Road, Longridge, Preston, Lancashire PR3 3SY
Telephone: (0722) 784969   **£65**
Open: lunch Fri + Sun, dinner daily (closed Boxing Day, New Year's Day)
Last orders: lunch 2.00pm (2.30pm Sun), dinner 9.30pm (10.00pm Sat)

Chef/proprietor Paul Heathcote was previously executive head chef
at Boughton Park Hotel and Country Club. His partner at front of
house in his solo venture, Deborah Jones, was formerly at Sharrow
Bay, so there is great promise in this new (July 1990) addition to the
Lancashire restaurant scene. The setting is cottagey, with beams;
three rooms on split levels are accessed through archways. Once
inside, everything is very professional, from the Villeroy and Boch
table settings, to Deborah's charming service and Paul's cooking. He
offers a modern British style using the best possible local produce,
and the results can be enjoyed on set lunch menus (three courses
plus coffee for £11.50), a carte, or Paul's gourmet menu at £29.50 for
six courses plus coffee. The gourmet menu is carefully created to
offer a good balance, and thus you might enjoy a warm salad of foie
gras and wild mushrooms, then consommé of game with lentils,
followed by ravioli of lobster served with a light lobster jus and
tarragon. An apple and ginger sorbet clears the palate before fillet of
Aberdeen Angus beef, lightly smoked over oak chippings, served
with a burgundy sauce. The dessert on this menu was deep-fried ice
cream with almond, pistachio and butterscotch sauce. The wine list,
with just seventy bins explores Europe and the New World with
useful tasting notes and a few half bottles. In any setting, Paul
Heathcote would do well. In this part of England he positively shines,
and we wish him well.

LOUGHBOROUGH   Restaurant Roger Burdell

The Manor House, 11/12 Sparrow Hill, Loughborough,
Leicestershire LE11 1BT
Telephone: (0509) 231813   **£55**
Open: lunch Tue-Sat, dinner Mon-Sat (closed Bank Holidays)
Last orders: lunch 2.30pm, dinner 10.30pm

The Restaurant Roger Burdell is now on the first floor of this
building, with Waffles Bistro on the ground floor. Roger however
continues towards French traditional in the bistro (with a blackboard
menu) while modern British predominates upstairs. Unusually,
perhaps, it is the bistro that is the non-smoking room while smoking
is permitted upstairs. From the restaurant menu you might try a
warm salad of pigeon breast with pine kernels and a walnut oil
dressing, followed by noisettes of veal with red pepper, paprika,
chilli, lemon and fromage frais. Puddings could include an unusual
gooseberry and strawberry terrine flavoured with muscat.

LOWER SLAUGHTER   Lower Slaughter Manor

Lower Slaughter, Gloucestershire GL54 2HP
Telephone: (0451) 20456   *Fax:* (0451) 22150   **£75**
Open: lunch + dinner daily
Last orders: lunch 2.30pm, dinner 9.30pm

A shallow brook runs through the picturesque village of Lower
Slaughter; the fine 17th-century manor stands in grounds adjacent to
the church. Inside, ornate plaster ceilings and tall fireplaces are
off-set by sofas, log fires and warm colours. The nineteen en-suite
rooms are restfully decorated in country house style. Croquet,
fishing and an indoor heated pool offer relaxation. Fresh local produce
forms the basis of the elegant cooking served in an equally elegant
dining room.

MAIDENHEAD   Fredrick's Hotel & Restaurant

Shoppenhangers Road, Maidenhead, Berkshire SL6 2PZ
Telephone: (0628) 35934   *Fax:* (0628) 771054   **£80**
Open: lunch Sun-Fri, dinner daily (closed Christmas)
Last orders: lunch 2.00pm, dinner 9.45pm

Fredrick Losel's 37-bedroom hotel caters well to its business
clientele. The decor mixes glitzy luxury with some solid furnishings
and discreet colours. A number of long-serving staff form the nucleus
of the efficient service. The chandeliered dining room is smartly
modern, as is the style of Brian Cutler's cooking: steamed skate with
fresh asparagus and langoustines, noisettes of lamb with rösti and
wild mushrooms. Extensive wine list includes a special reserve from
Fredrick's cellars. Now with a branch in Ireland (see that section).

MAIDSTONE   Soufflé

April Cottage, The Green, Bearsted, Maidstone, Kent ME14 4DN
Telephone: (0622) 37065   **£65**
Open: lunch Tue-Fri, dinner Tue-Sat (closed Christmas to 2nd wk Jan)
Last orders: lunch 1.45pm, dinner 9.30pm

A cry from the heart at this old red brick house by the village green:
We may be in the sticks, and a turbot is a turbot, but lovingly
prepared and served it is a wonderful thing! Daily menus offer
well-executed dishes based on good, fresh produce. Fish (including
turbot!) features strongly with excellent saucing – perhaps a beurre
blanc or saffron sauce. Finish perhaps with an apple soufflé with a
calvados and cider sabayon. A thoughtfully composed wine list.

MALVERN WELLS   Croque-en-Bouche

See page 180 – our Clover Award Section.

MATLOCK   Riber Hall

Matlock, Derbyshire DE4 5JU
Telephone: (0629) 582795   *Fax:* (0629) 580475   **£55**
Open: lunch + dinner daily
Last orders: lunch 1.30pm, dinner 9.30pm

The stone-built Elizabethan manor house is next door to Riber
Castle. An ornately carved fireplace warms the lounge; antiques and
fresh flowers fill the traditional beamed interior. Bedrooms (in
converted stables) feature beams, some 4-poster beds, and warm
bathrooms. In the dining room paintings, flowers and carved period
furniture complement polished tables. The fixed price lunch menu
offers particularly good value: terrine of chicken and spring vegetables, lamb cutlets in a wine, shallot and tarragon sauce, gratin of
strawberries in kirsch. Some good bottles on the classic wine list.

MELTON MOWBRAY   Stapleford Park

See page 182 – our Clover Award Section.

MIDDLE WALLOP   Fifehead Manor

Middle Wallop, Stockbridge, Hampshire SO20 8EG
Telephone: (0264) 781565   *Fax:* (0264) 781400   **£65**
Open: lunch + dinner daily (closed Christmas + New Year)
Last orders: lunch 2.30pm, dinner 9.30pm

The house, set in well-tended gardens, dates back to the 11th
Century. Bedrooms vary in size and amenities, but are comfortable
and light. Good breakfasts. The dining room, in common with the
rest of the house, is traditional and unpretentious in style, and
candlelit in the evenings. A daily table d'hôte and seasonal carte offer
well executed classically-based dishes with good saucing and
imaginative touches: baked quails with a morille sauce; pan-fried tuna
fillet with beetroot and a Noilly Prat sauce. For dessert perhaps a
wedge of Dutch apple pie with cinnamon ice cream and champagne
sabayon. Reasonably priced wines and enthusiastic service.

MILFORD-ON-SEA	Rocher's Restaurant

69-71 High Street, Milford-on-Sea, Lymington, Hampshire SO41 0QG
Telephone: (0509) 642340   **£40**
Open: lunch Sun, dinner Wed-Mon (closed mid-Jan to mid-Feb)
Last orders: lunch 1.45pm, dinner 10.00pm

A smiling welcome from Rebecca Rocher, friendly service and confident, dependably good cooking by Alain Rocher has put this three-year-old restaurant firmly on the map. The simple pink and white cottagey setting emphasises all the more the quality of the food. The base is classic (ex-Chewton Glen): warm leek mousse, pheasant with orange and white wine sauce, crème brûlée. Loire wines provide the main interest of the wine list. No children under sixteen.

MORETON-IN-MARSH	Annie's

3 Oxford Street, Moreton-in-Marsh, Gloucestershire GL56 0AL
Telephone: (0608) 51981   **£50**
Open: lunch Sun, dinner Mon-Sat (closed 28 Jan – 10 Feb)
Last orders: lunch 2.00pm, dinner 10.00pm

A small, unpretentious, softly-lit dining-room with flagstone floors, exposed stone walls, burgundy cloths and country pine chairs. Annie Grady is a friendly host, while chef David Ellis adds his own touches to a classic base: some roasted pistachio nuts with an avocado salad; a smoked salmon, prawn and trout filling for a spinach roulade; almond and orange dumplings with a dish of venison. Wild mushrooms are a favourite ingredient. This is a pleasant and enjoyable local restaurant, well thought of by other chefs in the area.

MOSS NOOK	Moss Nook

Ringway Road, Moss Nook, Greater Manchester M22 5NA
Telephone: 061-437 4778   **£60**
Open: lunch Tue-Fri, dinner Tues-Fri + Sat (closed Bank Holidays except
    Good Friday, 2 wks Christmas)
Last orders: lunch 1.30pm, dinner 9.30pm (10.00 Sat)

A one-bedroomed, attractively decorated and well-furnished cottage now offers accommodation to diners at the Harrisons' long-established restaurant. Given its proximity to Manchester Airport, this is bound to become popular! Service is smooth. The menu is supplemented by daily specials; soups are invariably good. The fish of the day might be halibut in a watercress sauce. Good coffee and petits fours, and a wine list which encourages experiment.

MOULSFORD-ON-THAMES **Beetle & Wedge Hotel**

Moulsford-on-Thames, Oxfordshire OX10 9JF
Telephone: (0491) 651381 *Fax:* (0491) 651376 **£60**
Open: lunch + dinner daily (closed Christmas Day)
Last orders: lunch 2.00pm, dinner 10.00pm

Richard and Kate Smith are most often to be found at the Beetle and
Wedge, although they still have the Royal Oak at Yattendon as well.
In a lovely Thames-side setting you'll find wrought iron garden
furniture outside and a modern wooden-framed boathouse-style
interior. Robert Taylor joins Richard in the kitchen, and turns out
traditional and modern French and British dishes, using whatever is
best from the markets, cooked simply and presented carefully. If it's
available, try the pigeon breast with black pudding.

NAILSWORTH **Flynn's**

---

3 Fountain Street, Nailsworth, Nr Stroud, Gloucestershire GL6 0BL
Telephone: (045 383) 2240 **£50**
Open: lunch Tue-Sat, dinner Mon-Sat
Last orders: lunch 2.30pm, dinner 9.30pm

Go round the back of William's Kitchen Shop. Upstairs, with views
towards hills and trees, is Flynn's. Colourful paintings of food by a
local artist and vases of flowers warm up the modern grey decor.
Good appetisers and home-made bread herald Garry Flynn's modern
cooking. Fish often good, as in a fillet of grey mullet with a red wine
and thyme sauce, topped with strips of deep-fried leek. A well-
chosen, compact wine list. Enthusiastic and helpful service from
Deborah Reid.

NANTWICH **Rookery Hall**

Worleston, Nr Nantwich, Cheshire CW5 6DQ
Telephone: (0270) 626866 *Fax:* (0270) 626027 **£70**
Open: lunch + dinner daily
Last orders: lunch 2.00pm, dinner 9.45pm

A solid 18th-century house, set in some 200 acres; hitherto
traditional elegance has been the style here, especially in the
mahogany panelled dining room with its plaster work ceiling, polished
tables and antique chairs. Major changes are underway though, to
increase the number of bedrooms from eleven to forty-five. A golf
course and conference facilities are also imminent. Christopher
Phillips still heads the kitchen, producing some enjoyable modern
dishes.

NAYLAND	Martha's Vineyard

18 High Street, Nayland, Suffolk CO6 4JF
Telephone: (0206) 262888 £40
Open: dinner Tue-Sat (closed 2 days Easter, 2 wks summer,
 2 wks Christmas)
Last orders: dinner 9.00pm (9.30pm Fri+Sat)

A cream-painted cottage dining room is divided by pale green screens reminiscent of stable partitions; colourful abstract-patterned café curtains, cottagey china, pink cloths and paper napkins. Christopher Warren races around dispensing smiles, advice, and Larkin Warren's good food: bread of the day (dark, moist Irish wholemeal perhaps), goat's cheese soufflé with just a little garlic, on a salad enlivened by fresh garden thyme; venison casseroled with juniper and a bitter chocolate sauce. Vegetables may include puréed fresh beetroot, and tender chopped chard. Puddings may be New Orleans bread and butter pudding with whisky sauce! A short but interesting wine list.

NEWBURY	The Dew Pond Restaurant

Old Burghclere, Newbury, Berkshire RG15 9LH
Telephone: (0635) 27408 £50
Open: lunch Tue-Fri, dinner Tue-Sat (closed 2 wks Jan, 2 wks Aug)
Last orders: lunch 2.00pm, dinner 10.00pm

A family-run restaurant with a warm country house style. A neighbouring farm provides the game which is the speciality here: terrine of chicken and rabbit with home-made brioche and plum compote; saddle of roe deer with a buttery calvados sauce and caramelised apples. Other good dishes on the fixed price menu may include roast best end of lamb with a honey and fresh mint sauce and a tartlet of ratatouille. Duboeuf house wines.

NEWCASTLE-UPON-TYNE	Fisherman's Lodge Restaurant

Jesmond Dene, Jesmond, Newcastle-upon-Tyne, Tyne & Wear NE7 7BQ
Telephone: 091-281 3281 *Fax:* 091-281 6410 £65
Open: lunch Mon-Fri, dinner Mon-Sat (closed Bank Holidays)
Last orders: lunch 2.00pm, dinner 10.45pm (11.00pm Sat)

An elegant refurbished dining room has muted pastel colours and high backed upholstered chairs. Cocktail bar and crockery are also in for an overhaul. Fish is still the raison d'être with a menu of lodge classics alongside a daily menu. From the former, a consommé of lobster with raviolis and fresh herbs; from the latter, escalopes of turbot on puff pastry and creamed leeks. A number of bottles under £10 on the wine list. Efficient service by well trained staff.

NEWCASTLE-UPON-TYNE	21 Queen Street

See page 181 – our Clover Award Section.

NEW MILTON	Chewton Glen

See page 184 – our Clover Award Section.

NORTH HUISH   Brookdale House

North Huish, South Brent, Devon TQ10 9NR
Telephone: (0548 82) 402   **£65**
Open: dinner only (closed 3 wks Jan)
Last orders: dinner 9.00pm

It is rare for restaurants to list their suppliers, rarer still that all produce should be local, additive free and mainly organically grown. Such, though, is the case at Charles Trevor-Roper's small hotel. Chef Terry Rich's straightforward approach allows the quality of his materials to shine through. If available, try the filo parcel of scallops with strips of vegetables and ginger vermouth sauce, or steamed fillet of Dart salmon with cucumber and mint sauce. The wine list is a fine complement with carefully chosen wines from good makers. The house itself, Victorian Gothic, retains the feel of a rectory, and is at its best in the sunshine. The eight bedrooms are homely, and furnished variously with old pine, antiques, and rattan.

NORTHLEACH   The Old Woolhouse

See page 186 – our Clover Award Section.

NORTHLEACH   Wickens Restaurant

Market Place, Northleach, Gloucestershire GL54 3EJ
Telephone: (0451) 60421   **£55**
Open: dinner Tue-Sat
Last orders: dinner 9.00pm

A welcoming restaurant with bare, Cotswold stone walls hung with photos of vignerons and large, well-spaced white-clad tables. Dinner is a leisurely 4-course affair hosted by the friendly, knowledgeable Joanna Wickens. Local produce is the basis of Christopher Wickens' straightforward cooking: char-grilled loin of lamb with a mushroom and aubergine sauce; oxtail cooked with beer and whole-grain mustard. Four or five good well-chosen cheeses precede puddings such as apple and frangipan dumplings and brown bread ice cream. New Zealand and Australian wines are the Wickens' real enthusiasm on the wine list.

NORWICH	Adlard's

See page 189 – our Clover Award Section.

NORWICH	Marco's Restaurant

17 Pottergate, Norwich, Norfolk NR2 1DS
Telephone: (0603) 624044   **£50**
Open: lunch + dinner Tue-Sat
Last orders: lunch 2.00pm, dinner 9.30pm

A smart new decor for Marco Vessalio's enduring restaurant. After twenty years he still enjoys cooking; his enthusiasm is evident in the results. Excellent pasta with porcini and mussels with an aromatic garlicky sauce, are among dishes that have been enjoyed. The wine list encourages experimentation with Italian regional wines.

NOTTINGHAM	Loch Fyne Oyster Bar

17 King Street, Nottingham, Nottinghamshire
Telephone: (0602) 508481   **£40**
Open: all day Mon-Sat (closed Bank Holidays)
Last orders: dinner 9.00pm

This off-shoot of the Argyll original is an asset to Nottingham. It follows the same formula and is, if anything, better. Smoked salmon is served in thick slices with just a wedge of lemon and bread and butter. A seafood platter of beautifully cooked fresh mussels, sweet flavoured queen scallops and plump, creamy oysters, is a real treat in the middle of Nottingham. Finish with a good apple, some Scottish cheese and cappuccino with grated chocolate. Very simple setting and friendly informed service.

OAKHAM	Whipper-In Hotel

The Market Square, Oakham, Rutland, LE15 6DT
Telephone: (0572) 756971   *Fax:* (0572) 757759   **£50**
Open: lunch + dinner daily
Last orders: lunch 2.00pm, dinner 9.30pm

The smartly refurbished 17th-century inn is run with a high standard of friendly, helpful service. Plain and chintz fabrics are tastefully combined with antique furniture in the twenty-four well equipped en-suite bedrooms; size and decor vary. Breakfast and bar food meals are above average. The restaurant offers competent, well-presented dishes such as chicken with a stilton cream sauce, and calves liver with bacon. Good value wine list.

OXFORD	**Bath Place Hotel & Restaurant**

4-5 Bath Place, Holywell Street, Oxford, Oxfordshire OX1 3SU
Telephone: (0865) 791812   **£65**
Open: lunch + dinner Tue-Sun
Last orders: lunch 2.00pm, dinner 10.15pm

Bath Place is a useful and charming city centre hotel. Its location
(down a narrow cobbled alley in a cluster of 17th-century cottages)
ensures tranquillity. There's a friendly welcome, and steep narrow
staircases that lead to eight cosy and pretty en-suite bedrooms. The
rooms' original dimensions add character rather than space! A new
chef, Didier Deville, cooks nouvelle style food.

OXFORD	**Brown's Restaurant & Bar**

5-9 Woodstock Road, Oxford, Oxfordshire OX2 6HA
Telephone: (0865) 511995   **£30**
Open: all day daily (closed 3 days Christmas)
Last orders: 11.30pm

Open all day from 11am, Brown's remains deservedly popular for its
brasserie-style menu, friendly staff and great atmosphere. You could
drop in for elevenses of cappuccino and pain au chocolat, stay on for a
salad or pasta lunch, bring relatives to tea, and return with friends in
the evening for a chef's daily special chosen from the blackboard plus
a bottle of almost philanthropically priced wine!

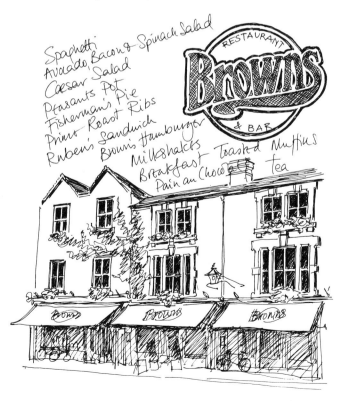

OXFORD   The Cherwell Boathouse

Bardwell Road, Oxford, Oxfordshire OX2 6SR
Telephone: (0865) 52746   **£40**
Open: lunch + dinner Tue-Sat (lunch Sun by arrangement)
Last orders: lunch 2.30pm, dinner 10.00pm

The setting is lovely: a boathouse by the edge of the River Cherwell. The food is simple: a short, weekly menu of just two or three choices; the wines are good, it's inexpensive and it's fun – that, in a nutshell, is the appeal of this old favourite. Eat outside on the terrace in summer or in the warm, friendly interior in winter. Excellent wine list from Anthony Verdin – now in its twenty-second year.

OXFORD   Restaurant Elizabeth

84 St Aldate's, Oxford, Oxfordshire OX1 1RA
Telephone: (0865) 242230   **£60**
Open: lunch + dinner Tue-Sun (closed Christmas + Easter)
Last orders: lunch 2.30pm, dinner 11.00pm

Restaurant Elizabeth is housed in a lovely 15th-century building, and the rooms which comprise the restaurant are actually above the Sheep Shop which featured in Lewis Carroll's *Alice Through the Looking Glass*. Restaurant Elizabeth is much as it was in 1966. The panelled rooms exude an air of constancy, as do classic dishes such as salmon quenelles sauce Nantua and beef stroganoff. As for the excellent, extensive wine list, Alice could have most enjoyably obeyed the instruction, 'Drink Me'!

PADSTOW   The Seafood Restaurant

See page 190 – our Clover Award Section.

PATELEY BRIDGE   The Sportsmans Arms Hotel

Wath-in-Nidderdale, Pateley Bridge, Nr Harrogate, North Yorkshire HG3 5PP
Telephone: (0423) 711306   **£45**
Open: lunch Sun (bar lunches daily) dinner Mon-Sat (Sun residents only)
     (closed Christmas)
Last orders: lunch 2.00pm, dinner 9.30pm (10.00pm Sat, 7.35pm Sun)

Cane-backed chair and pink cloths, an oak dresser and open fire create a homely dining room, but Ray Carter's cooking is quite a cut above the modest trappings. Fresh local produce, including fish from Whitby, is the basis of the menus: Nidderdale trout grilled, with seed mustard butter and hollandaise sauce; lamb (also from Nidderdale) with garlic, olives and tomatoes. Autumn pudding is a popular dessert as are the north country cheeses. A fixed price dinner menu includes a ½-bottle of wine and coffee. Book.

PAULERSPURY	Vine House Restaurant

High Street, Paulerspury, Northamptonshire NN12 7NA
Telephone: (0327) 33267   **£50**
Open: lunch Tue-Fri + Sun, dinner Mon-Sat (closed Bank Holidays,
        2 wks Aug)
Last orders: lunch 2.00pm, dinner 9.30pm

The dining room sets the tone with modern, rusty pink papered walls, modern lightwood chairs and well-spaced white-clad tables. Karen Snowdon is a welcoming hostess. Jonathan Stanbury (ex-Connaught and Inigo Jones) produces well-executed modern dishes. Enjoyable examples have included a salad of red mullet and artichoke with a goat's cheese mousse, a civet of Scottish lobster with baby onions, button mushrooms and smoked bacon, and crème brûlée. As an alternative to the carte, the fixed-price menus offer good value. Six bedrooms offer simple accommodation with comfortable beds and carpeted bathrooms. The Vine House Restaurant deserves support.

PENZANCE	The Abbey Hotel

Abbey Street, Penzance, Cornwall TR18 7QQ
Telephone: (0736) 66906   **£40**
Open: dinner only (lunch for private parties of 10 or more)
Last orders: dinner 8.30pm

The 17th-century blue-painted building stands in a narrow street leading up from the harbour. Guests, who are encouraged to treat the house as their home, enjoy cushion-strewn chintz sofas, log fires and flowers in abundance. Cheerful colours and antiques characterise the bedrooms. Candlelit dining (mainly) for residents and their guests features straightforward, careful cooking: carrot and cardamom soup; fresh Tamar salmon with a sorrel sauce. Good desserts.

PLUMTREE	Perkins Bar Bistro

Station Road, Plumtree, Nottinghamshire NG12 5NA
Telephone: (060 77) 3695   **£30**
Open: lunch + dinner Tue-Sat (closed Christmas Day, Boxing Day, New
        Year's Day)
Last orders: lunch 2.00pm, dinner 9.45pm

As an informal restaurant and bar, the former railway station fulfils its function well. Simple decor – cream walls, a few French prints, country-style wooden tables and chairs. Blackboard menus of dishes such as pork normande and fillet of plaice meunière, and simpler snacks at lunch. House wines from Duboeuf.

PLYMOUTH	Chez Nous

See page 188 – our Clover Award Section.

POOL-IN-WHARFEDALE	Pool Court Restaurant with Rooms

See page 192 – our Clover Award Section.

PULBOROUGH Stane Street Hollow Restaurant

See page 193 – our Clover Award Section.

REMENHAM	The Little Angel

Remenham, Henley-on-Thames, Oxfordshire RG9 2LS
Telephone: (0491) 574165   *Fax:* (0491) 576351   **£55**
Open: lunch + dinner Tue-Sat (closed 25 Dec)
Last orders: lunch 2.00pm, dinner 9.30pm

A perennial Henley week favourite, which is just as enjoyable and less crowded during the rest of the year. The menu has taken a new slant: wok fried chilli prawns and lobster oriental now appear alongside classics such as seafood platter, and Dover sole meunière. The compact wine list is more conventional.

RICHMOND	Black Bull Inn

Moulton, Richmond, North Yorkshire DL10 6DJ
Telephone: (0325) 377289   *Fax:* (0325) 377422   **£50**
Open: lunch + dinner, Mon-Sat (closed 24-31 Dec)
Last orders: lunch 2.00pm, dinner 10.15pm

Some of the best fish in North Yorkshire is to be found at the ever-popular Black Bull. The 1932 Brighton Belle Pullman car has recently been renovated. Classic dishes are well executed and attractively presented: poached turbot served with buttery new potatoes, broccoli and hollandaise sauce, pan-fried scallops and bacon, grilled lobster straight from the tanks. Good wines and pleasant, relaxed service.

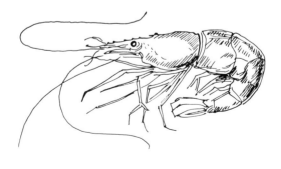

RIDGEWAY   The Old Vicarage

See page 194 – our Clover Award Section.

RIPPONDEN   Over the Bridge Restaurant

Millford, Ripponden, Nr Halifax, West Yorkshire HX6 4DL
Telephone: (0422) 823722   **£50**
Open: dinner Mon-Sat (closed Bank Holidays)
Last orders: dinner 9.30pm

Flower bedecked, converted weavers' cottages are the setting for this long-established restaurant adorned with plants and paintings, situated adjacent to the bridge. Fresh produce forms the basis of the good value menus – four courses plus coffee and truffles for £19.00. A competently prepared meal might include: hot finnan haddock mousse, chilled pea soup, boned roast poussin with a veal and coriander stuffing. The wine list dips into most wine-producing countries.

ROADE   Roadhouse Restaurant

16 High Street, Roade, Northamptonshire NN7 2NW
Telephone: (0604) 863372   **£45**
Open: lunch Tue-Fri, dinner Tue-Sat (closed Bank Holidays)
Last orders: lunch 1.45pm, dinner 9.30pm (10.00pm Sat)

On a chill, dark autumn evening, the Roadhouse's deep pink and green softly-lit drawing room and robust food are of particularly welcome comfort. Rack of lamb is a popular choice – it may be stuffed with a herb forcemeat or cooked with mushrooms and bacon. Good British and Irish cheeses. The wine list looks outside France, including the New World.

ROCHFORD   Hotel Renouf

Bradley Way, Rochford, Essex SS4 1BU
Telephone: (0702) 541334   *Fax:* (0702) 549563   **£50**
Open: lunch Sun-Fri, dinner daily (closed 26 – 30 Dec)
Last orders: lunch 1.45pm, dinner 10.00pm (9.00pm Sun)

Changes are afoot at Derek Renouf's hotel and restaurant. April 1991 will see a new, more upmarket, slimmed-down restaurant under the eagle eye of Derek himself. His restaurant in South Street will become a brasserie. Food will continue very much in the Renouf vein – classically based with modern touches.

ROMSEY — The Old Manor House

See page 195 – our Clover Award Section.

ROYSTON — The Pink Geranium

Station Road, Melbourn, Nr Royston, Hertfordshire SG8 6DX
Telephone: (0763) 260215 *Fax:* (0763) 261936 **£60**
Open: lunch Tue-Fri + Sun (Sat for parties only), dinner Tue-Sat (closed
Bank Holidays)
Last orders: lunch 2.00pm (3.00pm Sun), dinner 10.00pm (10.30pm Sat)

The Saunders' thatched cottage restaurant continues along its
enterprising and sophisticated way. A Jaguar has joined the (un-
leaded) Rolls Royce to chauffeur guests, and crèche facilities are
available (upon request). In the kitchen, organic produce (including
good vegetables) is used as often as possible in the well-prepared
food: free range corn-fed poussin with polenta and muscatel grape
brandy; John Dory fillets cooked en papillote with baby fennel. Good
wines and pleasant service.

RUSHLAKE GREEN — Stone House

Rushlake Green, Heathfield, East Sussex TN21 9QJ
Telephone: (0435) 830553 *Fax:* (082 576) 4673 **£60**
Open: lunch by arrangement, dinner Mon-Sat (closed Christmas + New Year)
Last orders: lunch 2.00pm, dinner 9.00pm

Chintz upholstery, Persian rugs, old English china and books lend a
lived-in effect to the Dunns' ancestral home. Peter and Jane Dunn
like to cosset their guests: making maps of the local area; providing
shooting on the estate, or sophisticated picnics for nearby Glynde-
bourne opera. Menus (residents only) feature produce from the
garden, and from a local butcher and fisherman at Hastings: terrine,
stuffed poussin and date, and apple pie. Good French wines.

RYE — Landgate Bistro

5-6 Landgate, Rye, East Sussex TN31 7LH
Telephone: (0797) 222829 **£40**
Open: dinner Tue-Sat (closed 1 wk Jun, 1 wk Oct, 1 wk Christmas, Bank
Holidays)
Last orders: dinner 9.30pm (10.00pm Sat)

It's ten years since Nick Parkin and Toni Ferguson-Lees – then
inexperienced amateurs – opened this unpretentious bistro. Good
quality fresh seasonal produce, unfussily but imaginatively prepared,
and value for money, is their successful formula. Alongside favourites
such as the fish stew, there may be poached fillet of turbot with a
chervil or watercress sauce, jugged hare or calf's liver sautéed with
apples. A most reasonable wine list.

Rye   Mermaid Inn

Mermaid Street, Rye, East Sussex TN31 7EU
Telephone: (0797) 223065   *Fax:* (0797) 226995   **£40**
Open: lunch + dinner daily
Last orders: lunch 2.15pm, dinner 9.15pm

A former smugglers' haunt on a picturesque cobbled street, the
Mermaid was rebuilt in 1420 when Rye was still a coastal port.
Oozing with character and period features, including Norman cellars,
and roaring log fires in the lounge in winter, is particularly popular
with summer tourists. The beamed dining room offers local produce
– Rye bay fish, Romney Marsh lamb, garden vegetables.

Sark   The Aval du Creux Hotel & Restaurant

Sark, Channel Islands
Telephone: (0481) 832036   *Fax:* (0481) 832368   **£40**
Open: lunch + dinner daily (closed Oct-May)
Last orders: lunch 1.45pm, dinner 8.00pm

This former farmhouse continues to offer simply, homely comfort.
There are six bedrooms in the main house and six smaller ones in an
annex; all but two have showers. There is a swimming pool in the
garden. In the informal restaurant, Peter and Cheryl Tonks are
relaxed, flexible hosts, as happy to serve a simple dish of locally
landed fish as a platter of fruits de mer. Sark lobster and crab are also
popular.

SEAFORD	Quincy's

42 High Street, Seaford, East Sussex BN25 1DL
Telephone: (0323) 895490   **£40**
Open: lunch Sun, dinner Tue-Sat (closed Christmas Day)
Last orders: lunch 2.00pm, dinner 10.00pm

Quincy's is popular and space is limited, so tables are crammed together in the two homely dining rooms decorated with books and pictures. Fixed price menus offer sound, robust cooking, now featured in a cookery book: port and apple terrine with sage and apple jelly, salmon and halibut with pesto in filo pastry, strawberry gluttony! A short, wide-ranging wine list from £5.75.

SEVENOAKS	Royal Oak Hotel

High Street, Sevenoaks, Kent TN14 5PG
Telephone: (0732) 451109   *Fax:* (0732) 740187   **£50**
Open: lunch + dinner daily
Last orders: lunch 2.00pm, dinner 9.30pm

A smart side entrance leads to a pretty conservatory (the ideal place for tea or coffee). Beyond it, through the public bar, lies the newly-elegant dining room with its dark green walls hung with paintings, soft lighting and beige rose chintz covered chairs. Good quality grilled meat and fish are popular main courses, preceded by gravadlax or a soup. A short wine list includes some good New World wines. Refurbished bedrooms feature bold fabrics and some period furniture; neat-tiled bathrooms. Staff are pleasant and helpful.

SHEPTON MALLET	Blostin's Restaurant

29 Waterloo Road, Shepton Mallet, Somerset BA4 5HH
Telephone: (0749) 343648   **£35**
Open: lunch by arrangement only, dinner Tue-Sat (closed 2 wks Jan,
        1 wk Jun, 1 wk Nov)
Last orders: dinner 9.30pm

This friendly, husband-and-wife run bistro attracts its many regulars with very reasonable fixed-price menus. There's a steady but not unchanging repertoire of dishes, supplemented by seasonal specialities: fish soup, smoked duck breast with fresh figs and pine nuts, loin of pork with prunes and armagnac, loin of venison. An equally reasonable wine list.

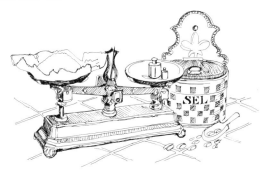

SHIFNAL   Weston Park

Shifnal, Shropshire TF11 8LE
Telephone: (095 276) 201   **£50**
Open: by arrangement

The Earl of Bradford's beautiful 17th-century house offers an opportunity – rare for most people – to stay in a stately home. Parties of a minimum of fifteen and a maximum of thirty-six can be accommodated in the twenty bedrooms. The 1,000-acre estate offers plenty of daytime activities, from archery and horseriding to parascending. In the evening, pre-dinner drinks are served in the library overlooking the Italian gardens. Dinner is served in the stately dining room. Here you might enjoy a pre-set dinner comprising game terrine with Cumberland sauce, or mousse of chicken and exotic mushrooms with a fresh tomato and basil coulis, followed by boned leg of lamb roasted with herbs and served with a mushroom stuffing; and a French peach tart to finish.

SHINFIELD   L'Ortolan

See page 198 – our Clover Award Section.

SISSINGHURST   Rankins' Restaurant

The Street, Sissinghurst, Cranbrook, Kent TN17 2JH
Telephone: (0580) 713964   **£60**
Open: lunch Sun, dinner Wed-Sat (closed Bank Holidays, 1 wk early summer,
    1 wk Oct)
Last orders: lunch 1.30pm, dinner 9.00pm

Hugh Rankins cooks a short modern menu. Main course prices include a starter and vegetables: perhaps a puff pastry of tomato, pesto, mustard and emmenthal, then steamed escalopes of brill and salmon with beurre blanc and herbed tomato sauces. Leonora serves with efficient informality. Cream walls, white cloths and lacey curtains combine to create a light, bright feel to this simple, unprentious restaurant.

SOUTH GODSTONE   La Bonne Auberge

Tilburstow Hill, South Godstone, Surrey RH9 8JY
Telephone: (0342) 893184   *Fax:* (0342) 893435   **£65**
Open: lunch Tue-Fri + Sun, dinner Tue-Sat (closed Bank Holidays)
Last orders: lunch 2.00pm, dinner 10.00pm

A large Victorian house set in its own grounds. Some period features
have been retained in an otherwise modern decor. A log-burning
brick fireplace forms the focal point, and copper pans hang on the
walls. Set menus, including half a bottle of house wine, offer the best
value. A recent meal included a mélodie of mousses of cauliflower,
broccoli and carrot with a chive and champagne sauce, then émincé
de canard sauce bigarade, with a sort of compôte of spiced currants.
Waiters are French.

SOUTHEND-ON-SEA   Slassor's

145 Eastern Esplanade, Southend-on-Sea, Essex SS1 2YH
Telephone: (0702) 614880   **£45**
Open: lunch Tue-Fri, dinner Mon-Sat (closed Bank Holidays)
Last orders: lunch 2.00pm, dinner 9.30pm

As popular as ever, this very simple, old-style family-run restaurant.
It's unlicensed so bring your own bottle (corkage 75p) to enjoy with
the day's fish from Billingsgate, or some local Dover sole which you
might find filleted and served with prawns and a Noilly Prat sauce.

SOUTHWOLD   The Swan Hotel

Market Place, Southwold, Suffolk IP18 6EG
Telephone: (0502) 722186   *Fax:* (0502) 724800   **£35**
Open: lunch + dinner daily
Last orders: lunch 2.00pm, dinner 9.30pm

The Swan retains a traditional feel with its the stone-flagged entrance
hall, the clubby bar, and Nina Campbell-designed drawing room.
Twenty-seven country house bedrooms are located in the main
house; eighteen smaller and simpler rooms are set around the old
bowling green. The airy dining room overlooks the market square.
Set menus offer dishes ranging from foie gras on brioche and Dover
sole to home-cured wild boar and monkfish with saffron sauce. The
Adnams' wine list offers much of interest.

SOUTH MOLTON   Whitechapel Manor

See page 196 – our Clover Award Section.

SPARK BRIDGE — Bridgefield House

Spark Bridge, Ulverston, Cumbria LA12 8DA
Telephone: (0229) 85239   *Fax:* (0229) 85379 **£45**
Open: dinner daily
Last orders: dinner 8.00pm

The Victorian house is well sited in wooded grounds with views over Spark Bridge and the river. Spacious bedrooms offer homely comfort, tranquillity (no televisions!) and large bathrooms. Children are welcome. Polished darkwood tables in a Victorian-style dining room provide the setting for the 5-course (plus a sorbet) dinners. Rosemary Glister cooks singlehandedly with great care, using good raw materials. A meal might start with potted mallard and poached kumquats, then soup, then a main course such as gammon roasted with lager and a spiced damson and port sauce, sorbet, pudding and excellent cheeses – if you can manage them! David Glister is a good host and advises on his wine list.

SPEEN — The Old Plow at Speen

Flowers Bottom Lane, Flowers Bottom, Speen, Buckinghamshire
HP17 0PZ
Telephone: (024 028) 300 **£60**
Open: lunch Tue-Fri + Sun, dinner Tue-Sat (closed Christmas)
Last orders: lunch 2.00pm, dinner 9.30pm

Malcolm and Olivia Cowan continue to dispense some extremely competently cooked food in the setting of their 17th-century inn. This talented chef has managed much larger brigades than he now commands, and he has lost none of his flair. You might choose smoked goose and prosciutto ham with paw-paw and fresh pineapple as a starter, or grilled black pudding with lamb kidneys, bacon, apple and a piquant mustard sauce; and follow it with duck breast marinaded with sage and honey, roasted and served with a red wine marmalade and an apricot confit, or a prime veal cutlet, grilled with rosemary and served with wild mushrooms and chives. A trio of sorbets with a blackcurrant sauce might be just the dessert to complete your meal. A selection of bar meals is also available. Friendly service by local staff – this is a very pleasant, good local restaurant.

STADDLEBRIDGE	McCoy's

See page 200 – our Clover Award Section.

STAFFORD	William Harding's House

Mill Street, Penkridge, Stafford, Staffordshire ST19 5AY
Telephone: (078 571) 2955   **£45**
Open: lunch Sun, dinner Tue-Sat (closed Bank Holidays, Christmas +
    New Year)
Last orders: lunch 1.45pm, dinner 9.45pm

An open fire lends warmth to this small leisurely cottage restaurant.
Fresh seasonal produce is the basis of the short set menus cooked in
a straightforward manner by self-taught chef Eric Bickley: mustard-
flavoured mushroom soup; smoked trout with horseradish and
cucumber mousse. Finish with some British regional cheeses.

STAPLECROSS	Olivers Restaurant

Cripps Corner, Staplecross, Robertsbridge, East Sussex TN32 5RY
Telephone: (0580) 830387   **£50**
Open: lunch + dinner Wed-Sun (closed 3 wks Jan)
Last orders: lunch 1.30pm, dinner 9.30pm

Gary Oliver cooks with confidence and the food is well presented; the
style is modern often with oriental influences. Fixed price 3-course
menus may include a warm terrine of salmon and langoustines;
rosette of lamb in pastry with elderberry and thyme. Vegetables are
often imaginative, desserts and petits fours good. A short French
wine list. Babette Oliver provides courteous service. The setting –
the first floor of a modern detached house – may be unlikely, but
quality is there and the Olivers deserve support.

ST AUSTELL — Boscundle Manor

Tregrehan, St Austell, Cornwall PL25 3RL
Telephone: (072 681) 3557   *Fax:* (072 681) 4997   **£50**
Open: dinner daily (residents only Sun) (closed mid-Oct to mid-Apr)
Last orders: dinner 8.30pm (8.00pm Sun)

Andrew and Mary Flint are enthusiastic hosts who believe in quality over quantity when it comes to accommodation: four of the bedrooms in the old house are being merged to form two larger ones (there are now ten in all). Furnishings are pine or traditional dark wood. Mary's kitchen remains the heart of the house, with fresh produce the mark of the daily set menus: local corn-fed duck with orange sauce, brill baked with breadcrumbs and Noilly Prat. An extensive wine list with Duboeuf house wines.

Boscundle Manor, St-Austell

ST. LEONARDS-ON-SEA — Rösers Restaurant

See page 197 – our Clover Award Section.

STONHAM — Mr Underhill's

Stonham, Nr Stowmarket, Suffolk IP14 5DW
Telephone: (0449) 711206   **£60**
Open: lunch by arrangement, dinner Tue-Sat (closed Bank Holidays)
Last orders: dinner 8.45pm

The decor of Chris and Judy Bradley's small popular restaurant combines wood beams with boldly coloured walls and elegantly clothed tables bathed in pools of light – and it works. Judy provides informed service, and advice on the well-chosen wine list. Chris cooks a no-choice menu (except for dessert) – he feels he cooks better this way – but your personal preferences are discussed when you book. Dishes are straightforward: carrot and orange soup; breast of chicken with a light tarragon flavoured sauce. Cheeses from Androuët precede a choice of dessert.

STONOR   The Stonor Arms

Stonor, Nr Henley-on-Thames, Oxfordshire RG9 6HE
Telephone: (0491) 63345/638866   *Fax:* (0491) 638863   **£60**
Open: lunch daily, dinner Mon-Sat (closed 1 wk Jan)
Last orders: lunch 1.45pm, dinner 9.30pm

You can choose to eat in the bar, in the conservatory or in the dining
room: a warm, softly-lit room with oil paintings, antique chairs and
polished wood tables with fresh flowers and candles. Classical music
plays in the background. Stephen Frost uses local produce in his
cooking, which can be very good indeed, as in a rack of lamb served
with roasted shallots, a creamy celeriac purée and a good clear sauce
well flavoured with rosemary. Good crisp vegetables. Helpful,
friendly service includes (if you're staying) the carrying of cases and
breakfast in your room. The nine rooms are spacious and tastefully
furnished with a mix of antique and modern. Good beds, thick soft
towels and thoughtful extras.

STON EASTON   Ston Easton Park

See page 202 – our Clover Award Section.

STORRINGTON   Little Thakeham

Merrywood Lane, Storrington, West Sussex RH20 3HE
Telephone: (0903) 744416   *Fax:* (0903) 745022   **£75**
Open: lunch daily, dinner Mon-Sat (residents only Sun) (closed 12 days
          Christmas + New Year)
Last orders: lunch 1.45pm, dinner 9.00pm (9.30pm Sat, 8.45pm Sun)

Undoubtedly much of the appeal of a visit to this small manor house
hotel lies in its handsome architecture by Sir Edwin Lutyens, and its
gardens in the style of Gertrude Jekyll. Views of the latter can be
enjoyed from the spacious bedrooms, with their Liberty print fabrics
and thoughtful touches. Fresh produce features in the short, set
4-course menus served in the elegant dining room. You might choose
some boneless quail filled with a pistachio mousse and sliced onto a
bed of red cabbage, followed by noisettes of Southdown lamb with
aubergine, peppers and garlic. Dessert, cheese and coffee are all
included in the price. Hotel facilities include a helicopter pad, tennis
court and swimming pool.

STORRINGTON   Manleys

See page 203 – our Clover Award Section.

STORRINGTON — The Old Forge Restaurant

Church Street, Storrington, West Sussex RH20 4LA
Telephone: (0903) 743402 **£?**
Open: lunch Tue-Fri + Sun, dinner Tue-Sat (closed last wk Sep, 2 wks Oct)
Last orders: lunch 1.30pm, dinner 9.00pm

Clive and Cathy Roberts' restaurant is now into its third year. A neat, small dining room with white walls and black beams is the setting for the imaginative modern cooking. Monthly menus reflect varying influences with resultant dishes competently executed: terrine of Welsh grouse threaded with duck magret, wrapped in vine leaves, with home-made apple and sultana chutney; grilled fillet of fresh halibut on creamed spinach with fresh girolles. A compact and interesting wine list gives equal weight to old and new world. A serious restaurant that is an asset to the area. Good local restaurant.

STOW-ON-THE-WOLD — Epicurean

See page 204 – our Clover Award Section.

STOW-ON-THE-WOLD — Grapevine Hotel

Sheep Street, Stow-on-the-Wold, Gloucestershire GL54 1AU
Telephone: (0451) 30344   *Fax:* (0451) 32278 **£45**
Open: lunch + dinner daily (closed 24 Dec – 10 Jan)
Last orders: lunch 2.00pm, dinner 9.30pm

There's a reason why the breakfast coffee here is unusually good: it was chosen from a tasting conducted among the staff. This involvement is typical of owner Sandra Elliott's approach to hotel-keeping, ever striving to improve standards in not only her own hotel but in the industry as a whole. Service at this individual Cotswold hotel is friendly and helpful. Rooms are simple but cosy and equipped with modern comforts. A 120-year-old vine forms a verdant canopy to the dining room.

STRETTON   Ram Jam Inn

Great North Road, Stretton, Nr Oakham, Leicestershire LE15 7QX
Telephone: (0780) 410776   *Fax:* (0572) 83208   **£35**
Open: lunch + dinner daily
Last orders: lunch 3.00pm, dinner 11.00pm (open for snacks all day, daily)

Open from 7.00am, the Ram Jam is a rarity. It offers travellers decent food throughout the day and doubles as a local brasserie and restaurant in the evening. Pop in for an espresso or some freshly squeezed orange juice, a sandwich, a plate of cheese or a light meal. For more comfort, the attractive dining room offers dishes such as steaks and char-grilled leg of lamb. Simple, comfortable bedrooms with well-fitted bathrooms are fine for an overnight stay.

STROUD   Oakes

See page 205 – our Clover Award Section.

STUCKTON   The Three Lions

Stuckton, Fordingbridge, Hampshire SP6 2HF
Telephone: (0425) 652489   **£60**
Open: lunch + dinner Tue-Sat (closed Bank Holidays, 2 wks Jul-Aug,
      Christmas + New Year)
Last orders: lunch 1.30pm, dinner 9.00pm (9.30pm Sat)

You can just pop in for a drink and a snack but you must book to eat in the restaurant. Blackboard menus offer a dozen or more dishes reflecting both the local and German and Scandinavian influences: grilled Poole Bay sole; haunch of New Forest venison à la Baden-Baden; marinated Swedish herring fillets. Karl is an accomplished chef: sauces are well-flavoured, presentation good. A new wine list will include some Australian wines and more half bottles. The Wadsacks' popular pub-restaurant is an asset to the area. Good local restaurant.

STURMINSTER NEWTON   Plumber Manor

Hazelbury Bryan Road, Sturminster Newton, Dorset DT10 2AF
Telephone: (0258) 72507   *Fax:* (0258) 73370   **£50**
Open: dinner daily (closed Feb)
Last orders: dinner 9.00pm (9.30pm Sat)

This Jacobean house was built for the Prideaux-Brune family in 1665. Richard and Brian are the present generation of that family, and there's a relaxed, friendly atmosphere. This is essentially a restaurant with rooms. Fixed price menus offer generous portions of sound cooking: monkfish with green peppercorns; medallions of beef with red wine and mushrooms; pigeon breast with blackcurrant and cassis. Good desserts. The sixteen en-suite bedrooms are spacious; most in the main house have antique furniture; those in the stable block are more modern.

SUDBURY   Mabey's Brasserie

47 Gainsborough, Sudbury, Suffolk CO10 7SS
Telephone: (0787) 74298   **£40**
Open: lunch + dinner Tue-Sat (closed 2 wks Feb, 2 wks Aug, Bank Holidays)
Last orders: lunch 2.00pm, dinner 10.00pm

Decor is bright and modern, with pine booth seating packed closely together. Customers choose from a blackboard menu and can watch Robert Mabey in his open kitchen preparing their order. The menu caters to the largely local clientele; cooking is straightforward and generous: garlic bread, Japanese giant prawn tempura, gratin of chicken with fresh basil, fat skin-on chips, apple tart. Invariably busy, informal service.

SURBITON   Chez Max

85 Maple Road, Surbiton, Surrey KT6 4AW
Telephone: 081-399 2365   **£60**
Open: lunch Tue-Fri, dinner Tue-Sat (closed Christmas + New Year)
Last orders: lunch 2.00pm, dinner 9.45pm (10.00pm Sat)

Max Markarian continues to turn out the dependably good food that has attracted a strong local following to his well-established restaurant. Inspiration is classic with some modern influences; portions are generous: cheese mousse on a bed of spinach; breast of duck with a pepper and brandy sauce. Well chosen clarets are the highlight of the French wine list. The restaurant, with its conservatory style roof, has a cool, comfortable decor.

SUTTON COLDFIELD   New Hall

Walmley Road, Sutton Coldfield, West Midlands B76 8QX
Telephone: 021-378 2442 *Fax:* 081-378 4637   **£70**
Open: lunch Mon-Fri + Sun, dinner daily
Last orders: lunch 2.00pm (2.15pm Sun), dinner 10.00pm (9.30pm Sun)

This impressive crenellated building with its beautiful mature
gardens, rises proudly from its lily filled moat. The interior retains
many interesting architectural features – panelling, magnificent
ceilings, leaded windows. The hall houses several luxurious suites
but most of the sixty-three spacious and attractive bedrooms are in a
modern extension. New Hall is run mainly as a conference hotel. The
dining room's stained glass windows overlook the gardens. New chef
Glenn Purcell offers dishes such as lamb cutlets with a sweetbread
soufflé on a basil and ratatouille compôte.

TAPLOW   Cliveden

See page 206 – our Clover Award Section.

TAUNTON   The Castle Hotel

Castle Green, Taunton, Somerset TA1 1NF
Telephone: (0823) 272671   **£85**
Open: lunch + dinner daily
Last orders: lunch 2.00pm, dinner 9.30pm

Kit Chapman remains at the helm of the Castle, running and
promoting his excellent hotel with renewed vigour. There has been
one change: Gary Rhodes has left; the new chef is Philip Vickery.
Philip was latterly at the Mount Somerset and has worked at
Gravetye Manor and with Ian MacAndrew; his style is modern, often
inventive. The Castle has been notable in recent years for helping to
bring British food back to centre stage, a cause much nurtured by Kit
Chapman. Vickery's menus continue the theme with dishes such as
braised wild rabbit with turnips, bacon and radishes. Other dishes on
the carte might include grilled fillet of red mullet with bell peppers
and a gewürtztraminer sauce. A traditional British dish, such as
braised beef with chestnuts and celery or spiced lamb pie, is featured
each day on the lunch menu. The excellent wine list shows strength
and depth in all sections, and is in the medium to upper price bracket.
There are thirty-five luxuriously appointed bedrooms.

TETBURY	Calcot Manor

See page 208 – our Clover Award Section.

TETBURY   The Close Hotel & Restaurant

8 Long Street, Tetbury, Gloucestershire GL8 8AQ
Telephone: (0666) 502272   **£65**
Open: lunch + dinner daily (closed 2 wks Jan)
Last orders: lunch 2.00pm, dinner 9.45pm

Menus served in the elegant, Adam-ceilinged dining room are now drawn exclusively from fresh British produce and recipe sources from all round the country. To these, chef Chris Amor brings his skills and a modern approach. The result is sometimes refreshingly different: West Country sea fish cakes of Cornish lobster, sole and red mullet, breast of wild mallard on a sauce of early autumn fruits and berries, damson fool, well-kept British cheeses served with home-made oatcakes and biscuits. The fifteen individually designed bedrooms are in sumptuous traditional or Art Deco style.

THORNBURY   Thornbury Castle

See page 209 – our Clover Award Section.

THORNTON CLEVELEYS   The Victorian House

Trunnah Road, Thornton Cleveleys, Lancashire FY5 4HF
Telephone: (0253) 860619   *Fax:* (0253) 865350   **£45**
Open: lunch Tue-Sat, dinner Mon-Sat (closed 1 wk Mar, 1 wk Nov)
Last orders: lunch 1.30pm, dinner 21.30pm

The show starts when Louise Guérin opens the door, dressed in Victorian costume. Waitresses are similarly attired and the dining room also evokes the period. The 4-course fixed price menus are of traditional French inspiration: terrine de lapin aux pistaches; potage au cresson et laitue; noisettes d'agneau rôties au romarin. Background music ranges from Mozart to Mike Sammes! It's an unusual formula.

TORQUAY   Remy's Restaurant Français

3 Croft Road, Torquay, Devon TQ2 5UN
Telephone: (0803) 292359   **£45**
Open: dinner Tue-Sat (closed 2 wks Christmas + New Year)
Last orders: dinner 9.30pm

Remy Bopp cooks singlehandedly while Dolene Bopp serves. Everything – from bread to pasta and petits fours – is home made. If it's available, try the lapin à la moutarde et aux pâtes fraîches, and the tarte aux amandes, sauce au chocolat. The 3-course fixed price menus offer good value. The setting – candlelit, simple but elegant in a Georgian house – is comfortable. The French wine list starts at £6.00.

TORQUAY	Table Restaurant

135 Babbacombe Road, Torquay, Devon TQ1 3SR
Telephone: (0803) 324292   **£55**
Open: dinner Tue-Sun (closed 2 wks Feb, 2 wks Sep)
Last orders: dinner 10.00pm (9.30pm Sun)

This small restaurant deserves a wider audience: chef Trevor Brooks is talented and turns out some of the best food in the area using quality raw materials. Jane Corrigan serves with informed and infectious enthusiasm. Warm smoked salmon with crisp maize flour pancakes and a sharp lemon sauce may precede grilled sea-bass with an olive and tomato sauce. Well kept cheeses. The setting is the pretty front room of a small terrace house; white napery, candles and fresh flowers add a touch of elegance. Good local restaurant.

TRURO	Long's Restaurant

Blackwater, Truro, Cornwall TR4 8HH
Telephone: (0872) 561111   **£50**
Open: lunch Sun, dinner Wed-Sat, dinner Bank Holiday Mondays (closed 3-4
       wks winter)
Last orders: lunch 1.45pm, dinner 9.30pm

An elegant creeper-clad house is the setting for Ann Long's imaginative and very personal cooking. A typical and enjoyable meal started with crab and shredded courgette in a crab, cream and basil dressing, then best end of lamb rolled in spices and served on an onion marmalade, sliced into a bread box and garnished with a mango and wine sauce. If you have room, the rich desserts, such as crème brûlée on an apple and blackberry base, are worth trying. Menus change daily. Ian Long is host and advised on the short, well-chosen wine list.

TUNBRIDGE WELLS	Cheevers Restaurant

56 High Street, Tunbridge Wells, Kent TN1 1XF
Telephone: (0892) 545524   **£50**
Open: lunch + dinner Tue-Sat (closed 1 wk Christmas, 2 wks Easter,
     1 wk Sep)
Last orders: lunch 2.00pm, dinner 10.30pm

Chef/patron Tim Cheevers continues to draw acclaim at his popular
town centre, modern decor, restaurant, assisted by partner Martin
Miles' professional service at front of house. Modern British cooking
is well demonstrated on menus such as an October one featuring
mousse of crab wrapped in spinach, or terrine of rabbit and pigeon
with toasted brioche from the half-dozen starters, then rack of
Sussex lamb roasted with a mint and almond crust, or mallard
pan-fried with a plum sauce from the main courses. Finish with plum
and greengage sorbets, or a plate of English cheese. The concise
wine list is reasonably priced. Good local restaurant.

TUNBRIDGE WELLS	Eglantine

65 High Street, Tunbridge Wells, Kent TN1 1XX
Telephone: (0892) 24957   **£50**
Open: lunch Tue-Sun, dinner Tue-Sat (closed 1 wk Jan)
Last orders: lunch 1.45pm, dinner 9.30pm (10.00pm Sat)

Light from the large windows reflects in the blue glass of water
bottles on each white-clothed table. Powder blue walls and pink
padded chairs are offset by pink and blue chintz drapes. Young
chef/patron Susan Richardson, ever keen to learn, does stints each
year at places like Roger Vergé's Le Moulin. Her own fixed price
menus reflect her three years with the Roux organisation. Pastry is a
strongpoint: featherlight cheesy nibbles; the puff pastry box with a
dish of poached rabbit; crispy almond tuile pyramid with crunchy
praline ice cream; light petits fours. A vegetarian dish is available;
overall some good ideas and growing confidence in execution. Decent
house claret; pleasant young service.

TUNBRIDGE WELLS   Thackeray's House

85 London Road, Tunbridge Wells, Kent TN11 1EA
Telephone: (0892) 511921   **£50**
Open: lunch + dinner Tue-Sat (closed Christmas)
Last orders: lunch 2.30pm, dinner 10.00pm

Bruce Wass's Thackeray's House (which includes a bistro, Down-stairs at Thackeray's) is a firm fixture on the Tunbridge Wells scene. Bruce claims not to have any particular specialities as he writes his menus daily with the best of what is available seasonally, but fish and desserts regularly draw the highest praise. Midweek set menus are slightly cheaper than those at the weekend. Try perhaps wood pigeon breast salad with lentils, followed by grilled fresh skate with citrus and saffron, and finish with an apricot, walnut and ginger pudding with toffee sauce. The wine list is well thought out and carefully chosen, and starts with a list of Bruce Wass's twelve recommended wines at under £12 a bottle. Good local restaurant.

Thackeray's House, Tunbridge Wells.

TWICKENHAM   Cézanne

68 Richmond Road, Twickenham, Middlesex TW1 3BE
Telephone: 081-892 3526   **£45**
Open: lunch + dinner Mon-Sat (closed 1 wk Sep, Bank Holidays)
Last orders: lunch 2.00pm, dinner 10.30pm (11.00pm Sat)

The signed black awning stands out in a row of shops. The interior is simple, rather café-like, with its plain wooden floor, simply laid tables and prints on the walls. The cooking is several notches above expectations. The approach is simple but with some imaginative touches: squid and grape salad with walnut oil and lemon dressing; calves' liver with spring onion and lime. A short reasonably priced wine list.

TWICKENHAM   McClements

12 The Green, Twickenham, Middlesex TN2 5AA
Telephone: 081-755 0176   **£55**
Open: lunch Tue-Fri, dinner Tue-Sat (closed 1 wk Easter, Bank Holidays)
Last orders: lunch 2.30pm, dinner 10.30pm

Last year John McClements seemed all set to move, but for the
moment seems to be staying put. The two dining rooms in the
two-up, two-down cottage are tiny and elegant. John is a fine
technician. Dishes are often elaborate, always well presented: Dublin
bay prawns with braised red peppers and black olives; lamb with a
charlotte of aubergines. Currently John cooks almost singlehandedly.

UCKFIELD   Hooke Hall

250 High Street, Uckfield, East Sussex TN22 1EN
Telephone: (0825) 761578   *Fax:* (0825) 768025   **£50**
Open: lunch by arrangement, dinner daily (closed 1 wk Christmas)
Last orders: dinner 9.00pm (9.30pm Sat)

The Queen Anne house is filled with pictures, books and objects
collected during owner Alister Percy's travels. There are six,
attractive en-suite bedrooms with names such as Nell Gwynn and
Madame de Pompadour. The recently converted stables offer a
self-contained block of four bedrooms. The restaurant, open to
non-residents on Friday and Saturday evenings, serves Juliet Percy's
cordon bleu cooking.

UCKFIELD   Horsted Place

Little Horsted, Nr Uckfield, East Sussex TN22 5TS
Telephone: (0825) 75581   *Fax:* (0825) 75459   **£60**
Open: lunch Sun-Fri, dinner daily (closed Christmas + first 10 days Jan)
Last orders: lunch 2.00pm, dinner 9.15pm

The stately 19th-century house, former home to the Duke of
Edinburgh's private secretary, is set amidst golf courses and enjoys
views over the Sussex Downs. Not a sign of a reception desk on
arrival: you're greeted and then shown to your room. The nearest
they come to formality is the envelope welcoming you and asking you
to register your details. Chef Allan Garth's food is very good. From
the fixed price menu you might choose a dish of four ravioli set
around a thin tranche of crisply cooked salmon set on capers and
spinach, with a salmon butter sauce or an unusual and moist terrine of
vegetables. Then a generous portion of flavoursome beef daube
garnished with asparagus tips and turned vegetables; or perhaps nine
scallops set in an asparagus sauce with a centre of vegetable
tagliatelle topped with a pastry basket. Vegetables are served in
individual copper pans. The knowledgeable young sommelier is able
and eager to advise on the wine list.

ULLSWATER	Sharrow Bay Country House Hotel

See page 210 – our Clover Award Section.

ULVERSTON — Bay Horse Inn & Bistro

Canal Food, Ulverston, Cumbria LA12 9EL
Telephone: (0229) 53972   **£40**
Open: lunch Tue-Sat, dinner Mon-Sat (closed Jan+Feb)
Last orders: lunch 1.30pm, dinner 9.00pm

The approach is daunting (past grey houses and a huge factory, left and through a car park), but set right on the water, the inn enjoys delightful views across the bay. The quality of the cooking goes way beyond normal pub fare. Last year the inn, owned by John Tovey and Robert Lyons, became a free house, stocking a wider range of beers and strengthening New World wines. At lunch time, food is now also served in the bar lounge: fresh salmon in a wine, herb and cream sauce, Cumberland sausage, steaks (hung for four weeks) with a baked potato and salad. The conservatory restaurant, romantically candlelit in the evenings, continues to serve the very good food that has made the Bay Horse so popular.

UPPINGHAM — The Lake Isle Restaurant

Town House Hotel, 16 High Street, Uppingham, Leicestershire LE15 9PZ
Telephone: (0572) 822951   *Fax:* (0572) 822951   **£40**
Open: lunch Tue-Sun, dinner daily (residents only Sun) (closed Bank Holidays
        but open at Christmas)
Last orders: lunch 1.45pm (2.15pm Sun), dinner 10.00pm (8.30pm Sun)

The ten en-suite bedrooms have recently been refurbished. Well equipped, with thoughtful extras and small carpeted bathrooms. Cooking is straightforward with much use of garden herbs. Set dinner menus are priced at £21 for five courses on Saturdays, while on other evenings you can choose three courses for £17 or five courses for £20. You might be offered a cold tomato and fennel soup, then a mousse of smoked trout served with samphire, and pork fillet with apricots as a main course. Cheeses, a choice of dessert and coffee with petits fours complete the meal. A good French wine list with plenty of half bottles is for many the main attraction here.

WARMINSTER	Bishopstrow House

See page 211 – our Clover Award Section.

WARREN ROW	The Warrener

Warren Row, Nr Wargrave, Berkshire
Telephone: (062 882) 2803   **£80**
Open: lunch Tue-Fri + Sun, dinner Mon-Sat (closed Bank Holidays, 1 wk Jan)
Last orders: lunch 2.00pm, dinner 10.00pm

The setting is two converted cottages; the decor is smart and
predominantly pink. There is clearly talent in the kitchen, although on
busy nights there can be signs of strain. A good dinner included a
quite exceptional mussel and saffron soup served in a demi-tasse. A
good concentrated burgundy sauce with a tournedos owed much to
the oyster mushrooms and tiny morels with the beef. Exquisite,
generous desserts, good bread (home-made poppy seed and walnut),
and excellent coffee.

WATERHOUSES	The Old Beams Restaurant

See page 212 – our Clover Award Section.

WELLS-NEXT-THE-SEA	The Moorings Restaurant

6 Freeman Street, Wells-Next-The-Sea, Norfolk NR23 1BA
Telephone: (0328) 710949   **£35**
Open: lunch Fri-Mon, dinner daily (closed Christmas Day, New Year's Day,
        2 wks Jun, 2 wks Nov/Dec)
Last orders: lunch 1.45pm, dinner 8.45pm

Carla and Bernard Philips' restaurant is, as its name suggests, just
yards away from the fishing boats, and fish remains the strong point
here: a Russian-style salad of smoked kippers, bloaters and
Yarmouth reds with apple, potato and beetroot is an alternative to
the popular gravadlax; cod stockfish-style or for non-fish eaters, a
Norfolk cassoulet with local venison. Cooking and presentation are
simple, as is the restaurant itself. An interesting, good value wine
list.

WEST MERSEA	Le Champenois Restaurant

The Blackwater Hotel, 20-22 Church Road, West Mersea, Colchester, Essex
CO5 8QH
Telephone: (0206) 383338/383038   **£45**
Open: lunch Wed-Sun, dinner Mon-Sat
Last orders: lunch 2.00pm, dinner 10.00pm

Pink and white checked cloths and a mass of exposed beams create a
rustic auberge-style dining room. There's a friendly welcome and a
largely unchanging Anglo-French menu that ranges from pâté or
frogs' legs to steak and kidney pie and chicken chasseur. Choose
your wine by label from a reasonably priced list. A popular and useful
address in the area.

WETHERSFIELD — Dicken's Restaurant

The Green, Wethersfield, Nr Braintree, Essex CM7 4BS
Telephone: (0371) 850723   **£55**
Open: lunch Sun (Mon-Fri by arrangement), dinner Tue-Sat (closed Bank
    Holidays, Feb)
Last orders: lunch 2.00pm, dinner 9.30pm

There's a smiling welcome, then drinks in the tiny front room bar.
The high ceilinged dining room has a gallery at one end (with room for
just two tables) and Suffolk pink walls latticed with exposed beams.
It's a warm room with a fireplace and smart cream-clothed tables.
Maria supervises service with charm and efficiency. John Dicken's
(ex-Connaught and Longueville Manor) dishes are well executed with
delicate flavours and simple presentation: a fricassée of pheasant
with grapes, the sauce unusually flavoured with sancerre rosé;
noisettes of lamb with potato rösti with a touch of garlic, and a light
tomato jus with strands of fresh basil. Good desserts. An enjoyable
new restaurant with a dedicated team who deserve support.

WHIMPLE — Woodhayes Hotel

Whimple, Nr Exeter, Devon EX5 2TD
Telephone: (0404) 822237   **£55**
Open: lunch + dinner by arrangement (residents only)
Last orders: by arrangement

The Rendles have a refreshingly different attitude towards hotel-
keeping. Their tariffs include dinner, bed and breakfast, service,
VAT, morning papers and tea, afternoon teas and other teas or
coffees during your stay! Meals (residents only) are served at times
that suit guests' convenience. Self-taught chef Katherine Rendle
turns out some enjoyable dinner party cooking: tomato bavarois;
fillets of lemon sole in a lemon butter sauce. Excellent local cheddar
to finish. Good house wines head a reasonable list. Newly refurbished bedrooms are spacious and traditionally furnished. Two
lounges and a bar, tastefully decorated in soft warm colours with
comfortable chairs and sofas.

WILLITON — The White House

Williton, Nr Taunton, Somerset TA4 4QW
Telephone: (0984) 32306   **£55**
Open: dinner daily (closed Nov-May)
Last orders: dinner 8.30pm

From the bar, its bark-covered walls hung with wine auction notices,
to the beamed and cosily-lit dining room with its dark wood tables,
the setting is simple. Five-course, fixed price menus of well-
executed dishes start with soup then offer four choices at each
course; for example, lovage soup, soufflé suissesse, boned quail
stuffed with apricots, rice and pine nuts, elderflower and strawberry
sorbet, local cheeses. An enthusiast's wine list offers good value.
Service is as informal and relaxed as the setting. Fourteen bedrooms
in the main house and the coach house.

WINDERMERE	Gilpin Lodge Country House Hotel & Restaurant

Crook Road, Windermere, Cumbria LA23 3NE
Telephone: (053 94) 88818   *Fax:* (053 94) 88058   **£50**
Open: dinner daily
Last orders: dinner 9.00pm

A small, well-run hotel. Cream walls, dark carpets and ample chairs and settees create comfortable public rooms, made homely by fireplaces, magazines and ornaments. A new wing with three en-suite bedrooms and a separate lounge has just been added. Existing bedrooms feature country pine furniture, pretty fabrics and good bathrooms. Five-course dinners offer ample choice and generous portions. Cooking is straightforward and well flavoured in dishes such as salmon with a tarragon butter, and pork with apples and calvados.

WINDERMERE	Miller Howe

See page 213 – our Clover Award Section.

WINDERMERE	Roger's Restaurant

See page 214 – our Clover Award Section.

WINDSOR	Oakley Court Hotel

Windsor Road, Water Oakley, Nr Windsor, Berkshire SL4 5UR
Telephone: (0628) 74141   *Fax:* (0628) 37011   **£80**
Open: lunch + dinner daily
Last orders: lunch 2.00pm, dinner 10.00pm

An impressive Victorian Gothic building with panelling, ornate ceilings and open fires in marble fireplaces. The Thames-side setting is particularly appreciated from the comfort of the yellow and white drawing room. Elegance continues in the dining room. Murdo MacSween's cooking remains consistently good. A mousseline of sole and saffron is a favourite starter, followed perhaps by fillet of lamb with artichokes, tomato or basil and a madeira sauce. Finish with some excellent cheese. An extensive wine list.

WINTERINGHAM | **Winteringham Fields**

Winteringham, Humberside DN15 9PF
Telephone: (0724) 733096   **£65**
Open: lunch Mon-Fri, dinner Mon-Sat (closed 2 wks Mar, 1 wk Aug,
    Christmas, Bank Holidays)
Last orders: lunch 1.30pm, dinner 9.30pm (9.45pm Sat)

Annie Schwab provides a warm welcome to the former 16th-century
manor house. The low-beamed interior retains a homely period feel;
more modern seating in the candlelit dining room. Germain Schwab's
classically based modern food is the best for miles around. Fish,
sparklingly fresh, comes from nearby Grimsby, and is often the star
of the meal: a selection of poached North Sea fish served on
sauerkraut; sea bass with herb and spinach sauce. Game is also
recommended. The outstanding selection of cheeses is not to be
passed over, but save a corner for one of the good desserts. Some
wines from Germain's native Switzerland feature a the wine list.
Annie supervises the young French staff. Four cottagey beamed
bedrooms with well-equipped bathrooms.

WITHERSLACK | **The Old Vicarage
Country House Hotel**

Church Road, Witherslack, Cumbria LA11 6RS
Telephone: (044 852) 381   *Fax:* (044 852) 373   **£55**
Open: dinner daily
Last orders: dinner 8.00pm

Run by two couples with a genuine sense of hospitality, the 'Old
House' retains much of its Victorian character. The new Orchard
House, set between orchards and woodlands, offers five bedrooms
with french windows opening on to private patios and every modern
comfort, including CD music centres. Excellent breakfasts set you up
for the day; the 5-course no-choice dinners are served at 8.00pm
precisely. Cooking is robust and generous: perhaps a fresh salmon
terrine, then a good soup, roast local guinea fowl, a traditional pud
such as treacle tart, British farmhouse cheeses. The wine list offers
plenty of good bottles and a decent number of halves.

WIVELISCOMBE	Langley House Hotel & Restaurant

Langley Marsh, Wiveliscombe, Nr Taunton, Somerset TA4 2UF
Telephone: (0984) 23318 Fax (0984) 24573   **£60**
Open: lunch by arrangement, dinner daily (closed February)
Last orders: dinner 8.30pm

Peter and Anne Wilson work hard to improve and maintain high standards at their delightful 400-year-old house. Their dedication has been recognised by awards for both the interior and garden. Guests feel genuinely welcome and cared for. Bedrooms are warm and pretty; beds comfortable. Anne is a smiling, efficient hostess in the tiny charmingly refurbished dining room with its low beams and fireplaces. Peter's 4/5-course no-choice menus offer good fresh produce (much from the hotel's walled garden), carefully cooked: avocado and orange salad, monkfish medallions, mignons of Angus beef, bread and butter pudding or unpasteurised stilton. The wine list includes a decent selection of half bottles.

WOBURN	Paris House

See page 215 – our Clover Award Section.

WOODSTOCK	Bear Hotel & Restaurant

Park Street, Woodstock, Oxon OX7 1SZ
Telephone: (0993) 811511 Fax (0993) 813380   **£50**
Open: lunch + dinner daily
Last orders: lunch 2.30pm, dinner 10.00pm

This 12th and 16th-century landmark advances slowly to the end of yet another century. Solid oak beams, open log fires, antiques and well-equipped bedrooms. Traditional quality appreciated by both visitors and regulars. A traditional roast of the day carved from the trolley and game in season remain the backbone of the restaurant menu.

WOODSTOCK   The Feathers Hotel

Market Street, Woodstock, Oxfordshire OX7 1SX
Telephone: (0993) 812291   *Fax:* (0993) 813158   **£70**
Open: lunch + dinner daily
Last orders: lunch 2.15pm, dinner 9.30pm (9.15pm Sun)

Under new owners, the 17th-century hotel is undergoing a refurbishment of bedrooms and bathrooms. Its essential character is contained in the panelled lounge and stone-flagged bar, which opens onto a pretty courtyard. Nick Gill is one of three proprietors, and executive chef; the head chef is David Lewis. Menus are fixed price; dishes show skilful combinations of well balanced flavours and textures: a starter of salmon, salmon and salmon which featured that fish as gravadlax, smoked and as tartare; crispy roast breast of duck with apples and calvados. Vegetables come plated on the same dish as the main course. House wines from £9.50 and some decent half bottles. Well-intentioned service.

WORCESTER   Brown's Restaurant

See page 217 – our Clover Award Section.

YATTENDON   Royal Oak Hotel

The Square, Yattendon, Newbury, Berkshire RG16 0UF
Telephone: (0635) 201325   *Fax:* (0635) 201926   **£70**
Open: lunch daily, dinner Mon-Sat (bar meals available daily) (closed
    Christmas Day)
Last orders: lunch 2.00pm, dinner 10.00pm

Perennially popular, so book to eat either in the bar or in the restaurant. (Bar food is similar to that in the restaurant but cheaper.) Dominique Orizet now does most of the cooking, carrying on the tradition of quality with good ingredients, well prepared: calves' kidney with black pudding in a green mustard sauce; crispy duck salad; poached turbot with scallops and crayfish. Cheeses from Patrick Rance. Five bedrooms with king-sized beds, fluffy towels and good toiletries.

YORK	Melton's

7 Scarcroft Road, York, North Yorkshire YO2 1ND
Telephone: (0904) 634341   **£50**
Open: lunch + dinner Mon-Sat (closed Christmas + New Year, Good Friday,
     1 wk Aug)
Last orders: lunch 2.30pm, dinner 9.45pm

A long room with a simple setting – ragged grey walls, grey-blue
carpet and veneer tables set with rush mats. Lucy Hjort serves with
quiet efficiency while husband Michael cooks. He is a skilled chef,
producing generous food with big flavours. A short carte is
supplemented by daily specials. We went on a Tuesday – fish day. A
dark jelly with nuggets of sweet plump langoustine and tomato was
followed by pot-roasted partridge with cabbage, champagne cream
sauce, carrot mousse and new potatoes. The brill and scallop with
wild mushrooms came with potatoes puréed with olive oil and a
featherlight mousse of Jerusalem artichoke. An outstanding meal
ended with a delicious walnut tart with armagnac. The wine list is
small but well chosen. This exciting new restaurant is one to watch.

YORK	Middlethorpe Hall

See page 216 – our Clover Award Section.

YORK	19 Grape Lane

19 Grape Lane, York, North Yorkshire YO1 2HU
Telephone: (0904) 636366   **£45**
Open: lunch + dinner Tue-Sat (closed Bank Holidays, 2 wks Jan/Feb,
     2 wks Sep)
Last orders: lunch 2.00pm, dinner 10.30pm

On a corner of a narrow cobbled lane near the Minster, this
restaurant has been completely refurbished following a fire in 1989.
Michael Fraser remains as chef, turning out some good modern
cooking. The carte and set menus are supplemented by a blackboard
selection of both old favourites and dishes of a limited availability –
these offer good value. Enjoyable meals here have included sautéed
guinea fowl with leeks and wild mushrooms, crunchy vegetables and
a delicious sticky toffee pudding. New World wines now feature, and
there's an improved selection of half bottles.

England Listings

ABBERLEY
The Elms Hotel
Stockton Road, Abberley, Nr Worcester,
 Hereford & Worcester WR6 6AT
Tel: (0299) 896666   *Fax:* (0299) 896804   **£60**
Open: lunch + dinner daily
Last orders: lunch 2.00pm, dinner 9.30pm
Elegant Queen Anne mansion furnished
 with antiques. Twenty-five rooms.

ALDEBURGH
Ye Old Cross Keys
Crabbe Street, Aldeburgh, Suffolk IP15 5BN
Tel: (072 845) 2637   **£30**
Open: lunch + dinner daily
Last orders: lunch 2.00pm, dinner 9.00pm
Picturesque 16th-century pub serving sim-
 ple seafood dishes and local real ale.

ALDERMINSTER
Ettington Park Hotel
Alderminster, Nr Stratford-upon-Avon,
 Warwickshire CV37 8BS
Tel: (0789) 740740   *Fax:* (0789) 450472   **£80**
Open: lunch + dinner daily
Last orders: lunch 1.45pm, dinner 9.30pm (9.45pm
 Sat)
Grade I neo-Gothic house in parkland by the
 Stour. Forty-eight rooms. Fine fur-
 nishings and amenities including indoor
 pool.

ALDERNEY
Inchalla Hotel
The Val, Alderney, Channel Islands
Tel: (048 182) 3220   *Fax:* (048 182) 3551   **£35**
Open: lunch Sun, dinner Mon-Sat (closed 1 wk
 Christmas/New Year)
Last orders: lunch 1.45pm, dinner 8.45pm
Small modern hotel with eleven rooms.
 Fresh local seafood in the restaurant.

Nellie Gray's Restaurant
Victoria Street, St Anne, Alderney, Channel
 Islands
Tel: (048 182) 3333   **£45**
Open: lunch + dinner daily (closed Mon in winter)
Last orders: lunch 2.00pm, dinner 10.00pm
Popular local restaurant. Classic food in
 generous amounts.

ALNWICK
Breamish House Hotel
Powburn, Alnwick, Northumberland NE66 4LL
Tel: (066 578) 266   **£45**
Open: lunch Sun, dinner daily (closed Jan)
Last orders: lunch 1.00pm, dinner 8.00pm
Family-run hotel, useful base for exploring
 the area.

John Blackmore's Restaurant
1 Dorothy Forster Court, Narrowgate, Alnwick,
 Northumberland NE66 1NL
Tel: (0665) 604465   **£40**
Open: dinner Tue-Sat (closed Bank Holidays,
 3 wks Jan, 1 wk Sep)
Last orders: dinner 9.30pm
A small friendly restaurant, with a warm
 atmosphere, in the shadow of the castle.

AMBLESIDE
Rothay Manor Hotel
Rothay Bridge, Ambleside, Cumbria LA22 0EH
Tel: (053 94) 33605   *Fax:* (053 94) 33607   **£35**
Open: lunch + dinner daily (closed early Jan to
 mid-Feb)
Last orders: lunch 2.00pm (1.30pm Sun), dinner
 9.00pm
Eighteen-bedroomed Regency house owned by the Nixon family for twenty-three
 years. Restful atmosphere, 5-course
 dinners.

Sheila's Cottage
The Slack, Ambleside, Cumbria LA22 9DQ
Tel: (0966) 33079   **£20**
Open: all day Mon-Sat
Last orders: 5.30pm
Traditional English and Swiss influenced
 home-cooking.

Wateredge Hotel
Waterhead Bay, Ambleside, Cumbria LA22 0EP
Tel: (053 94) 32332   *Fax:* (053 94) 32332   **£45**
Open: lunch + dinner daily (closed mid-Dec to Feb)
Last orders: lunch 2.00pm, dinner 8.30pm
Converted fishermen's cottages with mod-
 ern extensions. Very comfortable and
 friendly service.

APPLEBY-IN-WESTMORLAND
Tufton Arms
Market Square, Appleby-in-Westmorland,
 Cumbria CA16 6XA
Tel: (076 83) 51593   *Fax:* (076 83) 52761   **£30**
Open: lunch + dinner daily
Last orders: lunch 2.00pm, dinner 9.30pm
Filled with original period furniture and
 paintings, this Victorian building has a
 unique atmosphere.

ASHBOURNE
Callow Hall
Mappleton Road, Ashbourne,
 Derbyshire DE6 2AA
Tel: (0335) 43403   *Fax:* (0335) 43624   **£50**
Open: lunch Tue-Sun, dinner daily (residents only
 Sun+Mon) (closed Christmas Day, Boxing Day,
 2 wks Jan/Feb)
Last orders: lunch 1.15pm, dinner 9.30pm
Large, rather rambling house, set in
 grounds which include a stretch of fly-
 fishing river. Classic, 6-course dinners.

ASPLEY GUISE
Moore Place
The Square, Aspley Guise, Nr Woburn,
 Bedfordshire MK17 8DW
Tel: (0908) 282000   *Fax:* (0908) 281888   **£45**
Open: lunch Mon-Fri, dinner daily (closed 4 dys
 Christmas)
Last orders: lunch 2.30pm, dinner 10.00pm
Georgian mansion furnished to a high
 standard. Conservatory restaurant with
 tented ceiling.

BAGSHOT
Pennyhill Park
Latymer Restaurant, London Road, Bagshot,
Surrey GU19 5ET
Tel: (0276) 71774 *Fax:* (0276) 73217 **£80**
Open: lunch + dinner daily
Last orders: lunch 2.30pm, dinner 10.30pm
Seventy rooms, some in the main house,
others around the redeveloped cour-
tyard. Facilities include fishing, clay-
pigeon shooting and helipad.

BARKSTON
Barkston House Restaurant
Barkston, Nr Grantham, Lincolnshire NG32 2NH
Tel: (0400) 50555 **£40**
Open: lunch Tue-Fri, dinner Mon-Sat (closed Bank
Holidays, 1 wk Christmas, 2 wks Jun)
Last orders: lunch 1.30pm, dinner 9.15pm
Restaurant with two rooms in converted
Georgian farmhouse. Home-baked bread
and traditional English cooking.

BARWICK VILLAGE
Little Barwick House
Barwick Village, Nr Yeovil, Somerset BA22 9TD
Tel: (0935) 23902 **£40**
Open: dinner daily (residents only Sun) (closed
Christmas + New Year)
Last orders: dinner 9.00pm (9.30pm Sat)
Warm welcome, large log fires in the lounge
and dining room. Cooking uses fresh local
ingredients.

BATH
The Circus Restaurant
34 Brock Street, Bath, Avon BA1 2LN
Tel: (0225) 330208 **£60**
Open: lunch daily, dinner Mon-Sat (closed
Christmas + New Year's Day)
Last orders: lunch 2.30pm, dinner 10.30pm (Sat
11.30pm)
Popular restaurant in the centre of Bath.
Light menu at lunchtime and more sub-
stantial in the evening.

Popjoy's
Beau Nash House, Sawclose, Bath,
Avon BA1 1EU
Tel: (0225) 460494 **£60**
Open: lunch Tue-Fri, dinner Tue-Sat (closed Bank
Holidays)
Last orders: lunch 2.00pm, dinner 11.00pm
(11.30pm Sat)
Charming Georgian house with quite formal
dining room and modern food.

Tarts Restaurant
8 Pierrepoint Place, Bath, Avon BA1 1JX
Tel: (0225) 330280 **£50**
Open: lunch + dinner Mon-Sat (closed 4 dys
Christmas/New Year)
Last orders: lunch 2.30pm, dinner 10.45pm
(11.00pm Fri + Sat)
International menu in popular local res-
taurant.

The Theatre Vaults Restaurant
The Theatre Royal, Sawclose, Bath,
Avon BA1 1ET
Tel: (0225) 444080 **£40**
Open: lunch + dinner Mon-Sat (closed Christmas
Day)
Last orders: lunch 2.30pm, dinner 11.00pm
Good venue for pre-theatre suppers.

BATHFORD
Eagle House
Church Street, Bathford, Nr Bath, Avon BA1 7RS
Tel: (0225) 859946
No restaurant but a delightful place to stay.

BATTLE
La Vieille Auberge
High Street, Battle, East Sussex
Tel: (042 46) 2255 **£50**
Open: lunch + dinner daily
Last orders: lunch 2.00pm, dinner 10.00pm
Building constructed from the stones taken
from Battle Abbey. French feel inside.
Good French wine list.

BEANACRE
Beechfield House
Beanacre, Nr Melksham, Wiltshire SN12 7PU
Tel: (0225) 703700 *Fax:* (0225) 790118 **£45**
Open: lunch Sun-Fri, dinner daily
Last orders: lunch 2.00pm, dinner 9.30pm
Twenty-four bedrooms (eight of which are
in the converted coach house) in formal
country house style. Lovely grounds with
open-air swimming pool.

BECKINGHAM
Black Swan Restaurant
Hillside, Beckingham, Lincolnshire LN5 0RF
Tel: (0636) 626474 **£45**
Open: lunch Tue-Sat by arrangment, dinner
Tue-Sat
Last orders: dinner 10.00pm
Popular restaurant with good value fixed
price menus.

BERWICK-UPON-TWEED
Funnywayt'mekalivin'
53 West Street, Berwick-upon-Tweed,
Northumberland TD15 1AS
Tel: (0289) 86437/308827 **£35**
Open: dinner Thu-Sat (closed Christmas Day)
Last orders: dinner 8.00pm
A set meal can last three hours at this
unlicensed restaurant.

BEVERLEY
The Manor House
Northlands, Newbald Road, Beverley,
Humberside HU17 8RT
Tel: (0482) 881645 *Fax:* (0482) 866501 **£75**
Open: lunch by arrangment for groups of 8 or
more, dinner Mon-Sat (closed Bank Holidays)
Last orders: dinner 9.15pm
Small relaxing country house hotel, elegant
drawing room and dining room with
conservatory.

BIRMINGHAM
The Bucklemaker
30 Mary Ann Street, St Paul's Square,
  Birmingham, West Midlands B3 1RL
Tel: 021-200 2515   **£50**
Open: open all day, Mon-Sat
Last orders: 10.30pm
Traditional English dishes.

Chung Ying Garden
Thorp Street, Birmingham,
  West Midlands B5 4AT
Tel: 021-666 6622   **£35**
Open: lunch Mon-Fri, dinner daily (closed
  Christmas Day + Boxing Day)
Last orders: lunch 2.30pm, dinner 11.30pm
Smart, efficient restaurant offering a wide
  range of dim sum and other favourites, all
  served in generous portions.

Chung Ying
16-18 Wrottesley Street, Birmingham,
  West Midlands B5 6RT
Tel: 021-622 5669   **£35**
Open: dinner daily
Last orders: dinner 11.45pm
Original of the two Chung Ying restaurants,
  offering a similar menu.

Henry Wong Restaurant
283 High Street, Harborne, Birmingham,
  West Midlands B17 9QH
Tel: 021-427 9799   **£35**
Open: lunch + dinner Mon-Sat (closed Bank
  Holidays, 1 wk Aug)
Last orders: lunch 2.00pm, dinner 11.00pm
  (11.15pm Sat)
Good Cantonese restaurant at the end of
  the High Street.

Plough & Harrow Hotel Restaurant
135 Hagley Road, Edgbaston, Birmingham,
  West Midlands B16 8LB
Tel: 021-454 4111   **£65**
Open: lunch + dinner daily
Last orders: lunch 2.30pm (2.00pm Sat), dinner
  10.30pm
Red brick Victorian hotel with forty-four
  bedrooms. Classic food is served in the
  formal dining room.

BISHOP'S STORTFORD
Down Hall Hotel
Hatfield Heath, Bishop's Stortford,
  Hertfordshire CM22 7AS
Tel: (0279) 731441   **£50**
Open: lunch + dinner daily (closed New Year)
Last orders: lunch 2.00pm, dinner 9.30pm
Italian-style mansion, elegant pillars and
  frescoed ceiling in the lounge. Thoughtful
  service. Luxurious executive bedrooms.

BLACKPOOL
Il Corsaro
36 Clifton Street, Blackpool, Lancashire FY1 1JP
Tel: (0253) 27440   **£45**
Open: dinner daily (closed Christmas + New Year,
  2 wks May, 2 wks Nov)
Last orders: dinner 11.00pm
Traditional Italian trattoria.

BLANDFORD FORUM
La Belle Alliance
Whitecliff Mill Street, Blandford Forum,
  Dorset DT11 7BP
Tel: (0258) 452842   **£45**
Open: lunch Sun, dinner Tue-Sun (closed 3 wks
  Jan)
Last orders: lunch 2.00pm, dinner 9.30pm
  (10.00pm Sat, 8.30pm Sun)
Relaxed friendly restaurant, frequently
  changing menu according to availability of
  fresh produce.

BODINNICK-BY-FOWEY
Old Ferry Inn
Bodinnick-by-Fowey, Cornwall PL23 1LX
Tel: (0726) 870237   **£40**
Open: lunch + dinner daily (closed Bank Holidays,
  Nov-Mar)
Last orders: lunch 2.00pm, dinner 8.15pm
Useful place to eat whilst waiting for the
  ferry.

BOLLINGTON
Randalls
22 High Street, Old Market Place, Bollington,
  Cheshire SK10 5PH
Tel: (0625) 575058   **£40**
Open: lunch Sun, dinner Tue-Sat
Last orders: lunch 2.30pm, dinner 10.00pm
  (10.30pm Fri+Sat)
Friendly neighbourhood restaurant.

BOLTON ABBEY
Devonshire Arms Country House
Hotel
Bolton Abbey, Skipton, North Yorkshire BD23 6AJ
Tel: (075 671) 441   *Fax:* (075 671) 564   **£50**
Open: lunch + dinner daily by arrangement
Last orders: lunch 2.00pm, dinner 10.00pm
  (9.30pm Sun)
Former coaching inn, much extended, fur-
  nished in traditional style including
  antiques from Chatsworth.

BRIGHTON
The Grand Hotel
King's Road, Brighton, East Sussex BN1 2FW
Tel: (0273) 21188   **£75**
Open: lunch + dinner daily
Last orders: lunch 2.00pm, dinner 10.00pm
Well furnished sea-front hotel where mod-
  ern facilities include a night club and
  health club.

La Marinade
77 St George's Road, Kemp Town, Brighton,
  East Sussex BN2 5QT
Tel: (0273) 600992   **£40**
Open: lunch Tue-Fri + Sun, dinner Tue-Sat
Last orders: lunch 2.00pm, dinner 10.00pm
Classic French food in cosy basement
  restaurant.

The Hospitality Inn
Kings Road, Brighton, East Sussex BN1 2GS
Tel: (0273) 206700   *Fax:* (0273) 820692   **£80**
Open: lunch Mon-Fri, dinner Mon-Sat (closed 2 wks
  Jan)
Last orders: lunch 2.15pm, dinner 10.15pm
Skilled modern cooking and keen profes-
  sional service.

Topps Hotel
17 Regency Square, Brighton,
East Sussex BN1 2FG
Tel: (0273) 729334 *Fax:* (0273) 203679 **£40**
Open: dinner Mon-Sat (closed Christmas)
Last orders: dinner 9.30pm
The restaurant in Topps Hotel is called Bottoms!

BRISTOL
Harveys Restaurant
12 Denmark Street, Bristol, Avon BS1 5DQ
Tel: (0272) 277665 **£50**
Open: lunch Mon-Fri, dinner Mon-Sat (closed Bank Holidays)
Last orders: lunch 2.15pm, dinner 11.15pm
A bastion of tradition, unchanged since the '60s. Extensive and rewarding wine list.

Plum Duff
6 Chandos Road, Redland, Bristol, Avon BS6 6PE
Tel: (0272) 238450 **£50**
Open: dinner Tue-Sat (closed 2 wks Christmas)
Last orders: dinner 8.30pm
Simple but imaginative cooking.

BROADWAY
Collin House Hotel & Restaurant
Collin Lane, Broadway, Hereford &
Worcester WR12 7PB
Tel: (0386) 858354 **£35**
Open: lunch daily, dinner Mon-Sat
Last orders: lunch 1.30pm, dinner 9.00pm
17th-century Cotswold stone house, personally run. English food – duck a speciality.

BROMYARD
The Falcon Hotel
Bromyard, Hereford & Worcester HR7 4BT
Tel: (0885) 483034 **£40**
Open: lunch + dinner daily
Last orders: lunch 2.00pm, dinner 9.00pm
Fourteen en-suite bedrooms. Low beamed ceilings and panelling combine with modern comforts.

BRUTON
Claire de Lune
2-4 High Street, Bruton, Somerset BA10 0EQ
Tel: (0749) 813395 **£45**
Open: lunch Sun (Tue-Fri by arrangment), dinner Tue-Sat (closed 1 wk Jan, 2 wks Aug)
Last orders: lunch 2.30pm, dinner 10.00pm
Homely decor, pleasant welcome, good portions – straightforward dishes are best.

BROUGHTON
Broughton Park Hotel
418 Garstang Road, Broughton, Nr Preston, Lancashire PR3 5JB
Tel: (0772) 864087 **£45**
Open: dinner Mon-Sat
Last orders: dinner 10.00pm
Victorian building, good facilities for businessmen. Classically based cooking.

BURY ST EDMUNDS
Angel Hotel
Angel Hill, Bury St Edmunds, Suffolk IP33 1LT
Tel: (0284) 753926 **£40**
Open: lunch + dinner daily
Last orders: lunch 2.30pm, dinner 9.30pm (10.00pm Sat)
A hotel since 15th Century. Tranquil, a friendly welcome, courteous service. Comfortable spacious rooms.

CAMBORNE
Sarah's Restaurant
109 Trelowarren Street, Camborne, Cornwall TR14 8AW
Tel: (0209) 712927 **£45**
Open: dinner Tue-Sat (closed most Bank Holidays)
Last orders: dinner 10.00pm
Young chef Sarah Heim's new small restaurant; simple decor, modern food.

CAMBRIDGE
Angeline
8 Market Passage, Cambridge, Cambridgeshire CB2 3PF
Tel: (0223) 60305 **£30**
Open: lunch daily, dinner Mon-Sat (closed Christmas)
Last orders: lunch 2.30pm, dinner 11.00pm
Solidly old-fashioned, French bourgeoise cuisine.

Restaurant Twenty Two
22 Chesterton Road, Cambridge, Cambridgeshire CB4 3AX
Tel: (0223) 351880 **£45**
Open: dinner Tue-Sat (closed Christmas/New Year)
Last orders: dinner 9.30pm
Short, fixed price menu which changes monthly according to seasonal produce.

CAMPSEA ASHE
The Old Rectory
Campsea Ashe, Woodbridge, Suffolk IP13 0PU
Tel: (0728) 746524 **£45**
Open: lunch by arrangment only, dinner Mon-Sat (closed Christmas, 3 wks Feb, 1 wk Nov)
Last orders: dinner 9.00pm
Informal atmosphere, classic cooking and extensive wine list in former rectory with conservatory extension.

CANTERBURY
County Hotel
High Street, Canterbury, Kent CT1 2RX
Tel: (0227) 766266 *Fax:* (0227) 451512 **£55**
Open: lunch + dinner daily
Last orders: lunch 2.30pm, dinner 10.00pm
Sully's Restaurant in the County Hotel, a traditional city-centre hotel. Simpler dishes best on modern menu.

CASTLE CARY
Bond's Hotel
Ansford Hill, Castle Cary, Somerset BA7 7JP
Tel: (0963) 50464 **£40**
Open: dinner daily (closed 1 wk Christmas)
Last orders: dinner 9.00pm (8.00pm Sun)
Friendly, family-run hotel with seven bedrooms, informal restaurant.

CASTLE COMBE
Castle Hotel

Castle Coombe, Nr Chippenham,
Wiltshire SN14 7HN
Tel: (0249) 782461   **£50**
Open: lunch Sun-Fri, dinner daily
Last orders: lunch 1.45pm, dinner 9.30pm
Relaxed, homely atmosphere in this eleven-
bedroomed old beamed house.

CHADDESLEY CORBETT
Brockencote Hall

Chaddesley Corbett, Nr Kidderminster,
Hereford & Worcester DY10 4PY
Tel: (0562) 83876   **£60**
Open: lunch Mon-Fri + Sun, dinner Mon-Sat
(closed 3 wks Christmas)
Last orders: lunch 2.00pm, dinner 9.30pm
(10.00pm Sat)
Alison & Joseph Petitjean's lovely old hall
set in parkland – modern French cooking.

CHADLINGTON
The Manor

Chadlington, Oxfordshire OX7 3LX
Tel: (0608) 76711   **£55**
Open: dinner daily
Last orders: dinner 9.00pm
Stone manor house in extensive grounds
tastefully furnished with antiques. Five-
course fixed price menu.

CHELSWORTH
The Peacock Inn

The Street, Chelsworth, Nr Ipswich,
Suffolk IP7 7HU
Tel: (0473) 740458   **£35**
Open: lunch + dinner daily (closed Christmas Day)
Last orders: lunch 2.00pm, dinner 9.30pm
Good pub food with jazz music.

CHELTENHAM
Stones Brasserie

The Montpellier Courtyard, Cheltenham,
Gloucestershire
Tel: (0242) 527537   **£35**
Open: lunch + dinner daily (closed Christmas Day
+ Boxing Day)
Last orders: lunch 2.30pm, dinner 11.30pm
Open-plan bistro offering simple dishes all
day.

CHESTER
Abbey Green

1 Abbey Green, Northgate Street, Chester,
Cheshire CH1 2JH
Tel: (0244) 313251   **£25**
Open: lunch daily, dinner Tue-Sat (closed
Christmas)
Last orders: lunch 3.00pm, dinner 10.15pm
Imaginative vegetarian food.

CHILGROVE
White Horse Inn

High Street, Chilgrove, Nr Chichester, West
Sussex PO18 9HX
Tel: (0243) 59219   *Fax:* (0243) 59301   **£45**
Open: lunch Tue-Sun, dinner Tue-Sat (closed
Christmas, Feb, 1 wk Oct)
Last orders: lunch 2.00pm, dinner 9.30pm
(10.00pm Sat)
Good location for supper during Theatre
Festival season. Excellent wine list,
straightforward cooking, good game
dishes.

CLITHEROE
The Auctioneer Restaurant

New Market Street, Clitheroe.
Lancashire BB7 2JW
Tel: (0200) 27153   **£35**
Open: lunch + dinner Tue-Sat (closed most Bank
Holidays, 2 wks Sep)
Last orders: lunch 1.30pm, dinner 9.30pm (9.00pm
Sun)
Simple setting overlooking cattle market;
seasonal produce, fortnightly French
regional menus.

COCKERMOUTH
Pheasant Inn

Bassenthwaite Lake, Nr Cockermouth,
Cumbria CA13 9YE
Tel: (076 87) 762234   **£45**
Open: lunch + dinner daily (closed Christmas Day
+ Boxing Day)
Last orders: lunch 1.30pm, dinner 8.15pm
Elegant dining room, good service, modern
food in typical Lake District inn.

Quince & Medlar

13 Castlegate, Cockermouth, Cumbria CA13 9EU
Tel: (0900) 823579   **£30**
Open: dinner Tue-Sun (closed Bank Holidays,
3 wks Feb, 10 dys Oct)
Last orders: dinner 9.30pm (9.00pm Sun)
Small vegetarian restaurant in the Close of
Cockermouth Castle. Friendly service.

COGGESHALL
White Hart Hotel Restaurant

Coggeshall, Essex CO6 1NH
Tel: (0376) 61654   **£45**
Open: lunch Sun-Fri, dinner Mon-Sat (residents
only Sun)
Last orders: lunch 2.00pm, dinner 9.00pm
(10.00pm Sat)
Dating from the 1400s this eighteen-
bedroomed traditional hotel is said to
have two ghosts!

COSHAM
Barnards Restaurant

109 High Street, Cosham, Hampshire PO6 3BB
Tel: (0705) 370226   **£40**
Open: lunch Tue-Fri, dinner Tue-Sat (closed Bank
Holidays, 1 wk Christmas, 2 wks Aug)
Last orders: lunch 2.00pm, dinner 10.00pm
Family-run restaurant, traditional and mod-
ern French cooking.

COUNTESTHORPE
Old Bakery Restaurant

Main Street, Countesthorpe,
Leicestershire LE8 3QX
Tel: (0533) 778777   **£40**
Open: lunch Tue-Fri + Sun, dinner Tue-Sat (closed
Bank Holidays + following Tue, Christmas/New
Year)
Last orders: lunch 1.45pm, dinner 9.00pm (9.45pm
Fri+Sat)
Good home-cooking, excellent value.

CROSBY-ON-EDEN
Crosby Lodge Country House Hotel
Crosby-on-Eden, Nr Carlisle, Cumbria CA6 4QZ
Tel: (0228) 73618   *Fax:* (0228) 73428   **£40**
Open: lunch + dinner daily (closed 4 wks
   Christmas/New Year)
Last orders: lunch 1.30pm, dinner 9.00pm (7.45pm
   Sun)
Elegant country house with eleven rooms,
   some in the main house and others in
   converted stable block.

CROYDON
34 Surrey Street Restaurant
34 Surrey Street, Croydon, Surrey CR0 1RJ
Tel: 081-686 0586   **£50**
Open: lunch Sun-Fri, dinner daily
Last orders: lunch 3.00pm, dinner 11.45pm
Cocktail and wine bars and informal res-
   taurant. Specialises in exotic and more
   familiar fish.

CRUDWELL
Crudwell Court Hotel
Crudwell, Nr Malmesbury, Wiltshire SN16 9EP
Tel: (066 67) 7194   *Fax:* (066 67) 7853   **£40**
Open: lunch + dinner daily
Last orders: lunch 2.00pm, dinner 9.15pm (9.30pm
   Sat, 9.00pm Sun)
Comfortable, converted 17th-century rec-
   tory. Modern English cooking.

CUCKFIELD
Ockenden Manor
Ockenden Lane, Cuckfield,
   West Sussex RH17 5LD
Tel: (0444) 416111   *Fax:* (0444) 415549   **£50**
Open: lunch + dinner daily
Last orders: lunch 1.45pm (2.00pm Sun), dinner
   9.30pm (9.45pm Sat, 8.30pm Sun)
Large comfortable public rooms with pretty
   garden views.

DALLINGTON
Little Byres
Christmas Farm, Battle Road, Woods Corner,
   Dallington, East Sussex TN21 9LE
Tel: (042 482) 230   **£55**
Open: dinner Mon-Sat (closed Christmas-Jan)
Last orders: dinner 9.00pm
Four-course, set price menu with four or
   five choices at each course using fresh
   ingredients.

DARLINGTON
Sardi's
196 Northgate, Darlington, Durham DL1 1QU
Tel: (0325) 461222   **£35**
Open: lunch + dinner Mon-Sat (closed Bank
   Holidays)
Last orders: lunch 2.00pm, dinner 10.00pm
Italian restaurant in the centre of town on
   three floors.

Victor's Restaurant
84 Victoria Road, Darlington, Durham DL1 5JW
Tel: (0325) 480818   **£40**
Open: lunch + dinner Tue-Sat (closed Christmas
   Day, New Year's Day)
Last orders: lunch 2.30pm, dinner 10.30pm
Modern British cooking using local produce.

DISS
Weavers Wine Bar & Eating House
Market Hill, Diss, Norfolk IP22 3JZ
Tel: (0379) 642411   **£30**
Open: lunch Mon-Fri, dinner Mon-Sat (closed Bank
   Holidays)
Last orders: lunch 2.00pm, dinner 9.30pm
Good local restaurant now extended to two
   floors.

DULVERTON
Ashwick House
Dulverton, Somerset TA22 9QD
Tel: (0398) 23868   **£45**
Open: lunch Sun, dinner daily
Last orders: lunch 1.45pm, dinner 8.30pm
Good home cooking on the daily changing,
   fixed price, 4-course menus.

EAST BERGHOLT
The Fountain House
The Street, East Bergholt, Nr Colchester,
   Essex CO7 6TB
Tel: (0206) 298232   **£40**
Open: lunch Tue-Fri + Sun, dinner Tue-Sat (closed
   2 wks Aug)
Last orders: lunch 2.00pm, dinner 10.00pm
Flagstoned bar and beamed restaurant
   offering simple dishes using good ingre-
   dients.

EASTBOURNE
Byrons Restaurant
6 Crown Street, Old Town, Eastbourne,
   East Sussex BN21 1NX
Tel: (0323) 20171   **£40**
Open: dinner Mon-Sat (closed Bank Holidays)
Last orders: dinner 10.30pm
Imaginative cooking using mostly free range
   and organic produce.

Grand Hotel
Jevington Gardens, Eastbourne,
   East Sussex BN21 4EQ
Tel: (0323) 410771   *Fax:* (0323) 412233   **£70**
Open: lunch + dinner daily (closed Bank
   Holidays, 2 wks Jan, 2 wks Aug)
Last orders: lunch 2.30pm, dinner 10.30pm
The smart, elegant Mirabelle Restaurant
   within the 64-roomed Grand Hotel offers
   a polished and professional service.

EGHAM
La Bonne Franquette
5 High Street, Egham, Surrey TW20 9EA
Tel: (0784) 439494   **£80**
Open: lunch Sun-Fri, dinner daily (closed Bank
   Holidays)
Last orders: lunch 2.00pm, dinner 9.30pm
French restaurant with three rooms. Oliver
   Hubert cooks in modern French style.

ERPINGHAM
The Ark Restaurant
The Street, Erpingham, Norfolk NR11 7QB
Tel: (0263) 761535   **£40**
Open: lunch Sun, dinner Tue-Sat (closed Oct, also
   Tue in winter)
Last orders: lunch 2.00pm, dinner 9.30pm
Cottage restaurant, above average cooking,
   fresh local produce.

ESHER
Le Petit Pierrot
4 The Parade, Claygate, Esher, Surrey KT10 0NU
Tel: (0372) 465105   **£45**
Open: lunch Mon-Fri, dinner Mon-Sat
Last orders: lunch 2.15pm, dinner 10.30pm
Modern French cooking by Jean-Perre and Annie Brichot, on the site formerly occupied by Read's.

EXETER
White Hart Hotel
South Street, Exeter, Devon EX1 1EE
Tel: (0392) 79897   **£45**
Open: lunch Sun-Fri, dinner daily
Last orders: lunch 2.00pm, dinner 9.30pm
Dating from the 15th Century, this town-centre hotel is built around a courtyard.

FELSTEAD
Rumbles Cottage Restaurant
Braintree Road, Felstead, Essex CM6 3DJ
Tel: (0371) 820996   **£45**
Open: lunch Sun, dinner Tue-Sat (closed Bank Holidays but open Christmas Day)
Last orders: lunch 2.00pm, dinner 9.00pm
Small, popular, local restaurant.

FOLKESTONE
Paul's
2a Bouverie Road West, Folkestone, Kent CT20 2RX
Tel: (0303) 59697   **£35**
Open: lunch Mon-Sat, dinner daily (closed Bank Holidays)
Last orders: lunch 2.00pm, dinner 9.30pm
Well presented, imaginative cooking.

FRESSINGFIELD
The Fox and Goose
Fressingfield, Nr Eye, Suffolk IP21 5PB
Tel: (037 986) 247
Open: please phone for details
Last orders: please phone for details
New venture by Ruth and David Watson from Hintlesham Hall, opening after we went to press. More news in our Taste Update.

GLEMSFORD
Barrett's
31 Egremont Street, Glemsford, Suffolk CO10 7SA
Tel: (0787) 281573   **£55**
Open: lunch Sun, dinner Tue-Sat (closed 10 dys Jan)
Last orders: lunch 2.00pm, dinner 9.30pm
Small local restaurant with regular customers in a small village away from the main routes.

GRASMERE
Lancrigg Vegetarian Country House
Easedale, Grasmere, Cumbria LA22 9QN
Tel: (096 65) 317   **£40**
Open: dinner daily (closed mid-Jan to mid-Feb)
Last orders: dinner 7.30pm
A completely vegetarian, non-smoking Lake District hotel. Ten attractive bedrooms.

GUERNSEY
The Absolute End Restaurant
St George's Esplanade, St Peter Port, Guernsey, Channel Islands
Tel: (0481) 723822   **£40**
Open: lunch + dinner Mon-Sat (closed Jan)
Last orders: lunch 2.00pm, dinner 10.00pm
Sea-front restaurant with the emphasis on seafood although there are meat dishes as well.

La Frégate Hotel & Restaurant
Les Cotils, St Peter Port, Guernsey, Channel Islands
Tel: (0481) 24624   *Fax:* (0481) 20443   **£45**
Open: lunch + dinner daily (closed 3 dys Jan)
Last orders: lunch 1.30pm, dinner 9.30pm (9.00pm Sun)
Lovely views, traditional comfort.

Louisiana
South Esplanade, St Peter Port, Guernsey, Channel Islands
Tel: (0481) 713157   *Fax:* (0481) 712191   **£35**
Open: lunch + dinner Tue-Sat (closed Bank Holidays)
Last orders: lunch 2.30pm, dinner 10.30pm
Smart restaurant with large windows overlooking the sea.

Old Government House
Ann's Place, St Peter Port, Guernsey, Channel Islands
Tel: (0481) 24291   *Fax:* (0481) 31129   **£50**
Open: lunch + dinner daily
Last orders: lunch 2.00pm, dinner 9.15pm
Traditional service and furnishings in the original Governor's residence.

St Pierre Park Hotel
Rohais, St Peter Port, Guernsey, Channel Islands
Tel: (0481) 28282   *Fax:* (0481) 712041   **£50**
Open: lunch Sun-Fri, dinner Mon-Sat (closed Bank Holidays)
Last orders: lunch 2.30pm, dinner 10.30pm
Large modern hotel with extensive leisure facilities.

St Margaret's Lodge Hotel
Forest Road, St Martins, Guernsey, Channel Islands
Tel: (0481) 35757   *Fax:* (0481) 37594   **£30**
Open: lunch + dinner daily
Last orders: lunch 1.45pm, dinner 9.30pm (9.45pm Sat)
Modern hotel close to airport and south coast bays.

GUIST
Tollbridge Restaurant
Dereham Road, Guist, Nr Fakenham, Norfolk NR20 5NU
Tel: (036 284) 359   **£45**
Open: lunch Sun, dinner Tue-Sat (closed 3 wks Jan)
Last orders: lunch 1.15pm, dinner 9.00pm
Sit on the terrace by the river in the warm weather for drinks before your meal or in the comfortable lounge.

HARROGATE
Oliver Restaurant
24 King's Road, Harrogate,
  North Yorkshire HG1 5JW
Tel: (0423) 568600 **£50**
Open: dinner Mon-Sat (closed Bank Holidays, Aug)
Last orders: dinner 11.00pm
Old-style French dishes, popular with
  locals.

HARWICH
Pier at Harwich
The Quay, Harwich, Essex CO12 3HH
Tel: (0255) 503363 **£30**
Open: lunch + dinner daily
Last orders: lunch 2.00pm, dinner 9.30pm
Run by the Milsom family, this is the
  simplest of their establishments and spe-
  cialises in seafood.

HELMSLEY
Monet's
19 Bridge Street, Helmsley,
  North Yorkshire YO6 5BG
Tel: (0439) 70618 **£40**
Open: lunch + dinner Tue-Sun (closed Feb)
Last orders: lunch 2.30pm, dinner 9.30pm (8.00pm
  Sun)
Seasonally changing menu served in a
  relaxed homely dining room.

HEREFORD
Fat Tulip
The Old Wye Bridge, 2 St Martin's Street,
  Hereford, Hereford & Worcester HR2 7RE
Tel: (0432) 275808 **£40**
Open: lunch Mon-Fri, dinner Mon-Sat (closed Bank
  Holidays, 3 wks Christmas)
Last orders: lunch 1.45pm, dinner 9.30pm
Popular restaurant in the centre of town
  with the River Wye at the back.

Restaurant Ninety Six
96 East Street, Hereford, Hereford &
  Worcester HR1 2LW
Tel: (0432) 59754 **£40**
Open: dinner Tue-Sat (closed Bank Holidays, 1 wk
  Christmas, 2 wks summer)
Last orders: dinner 9.30pm
Warm friendly restaurant offering English
  and French dishes using the best local
  seasonal produce.

HERNE BAY
L'Escargot
22 High Street, Herne Bay, Kent CT6 5LH
Tel: (0227) 373876 **£35**
Open: lunch Tue-Fri, dinner Mon-Sat (closed
  Boxing Day, 1st wk Jan, 2 wks Sep)
Last orders: lunch 2.00pm, dinner 10.00pm
Classic and modern dishes using fresh
  produce in a friendly, informal atmos-
  phere.

HIGH ONGAR
The Shoes Restaurant
The Street, High Ongar, Essex CM5 9ND
Tel: (0277) 363350 **£40**
Open: lunch Sun-Fri, dinner Mon-Sat (closed Bank
  Holidays, 1 wk Christmas/New Year)
Last orders: lunch 2.00pm (2.30pm Sun), dinner
  9.30pm (9.45pm Sat)
Eclectic à la carte menu which changes
  every six weeks. Home-made bread,
  pasta, sorbets and ice creams.

HINTON
Hinton Grange Hotel
Dyrham Park, Hinton, Avon SN14 8HG
Tel: (0275) 822916   *Fax:* (0275) 823285 **£45**
Open: lunch + dinner daily
Last orders: lunch 2.15pm, dinner 10.00pm
  (9.30pm Sun)
Converted farmhouse and outbuildings with
  informal atmosphere and friendly service.

HOLDENBY
Lynton House
The Croft, Holdenby, Nr Northampton,
  Northamptonshire NN6 8DJ
Tel: (0604) 770777 **£50**
Open: lunch Tue-Fri + Sun, dinner Tue-Sat (closed
  Bank Holidays, Christmas, 1 wk spring, 2 wks
  Aug)
Last orders: lunch 1.45pm, dinner 9.45pm
Former rectory, smart pink decor, warm
  Italian welcome, competent Anglo-Italian
  food.

HONITON
Combe House
Gittisham, Honiton, Devon EX14 0AD
Tel: (0404) 41938 **£50**
Open: lunch Sun, dinner daily (closed Jan-Mar)
Last orders: lunch 2.00pm, dinner 9.30pm
Elizabethan mansion set in its own park-
  lands. Combines elegance and warmth
  for a friendly atmosphere.

HORNDON-ON-THE-HILL
The Bell Inn
High Road, Horndon-on-the-Hill, Essex SS17 8LD
Tel: (0375) 673154   *Fax:* (0375) 361611 **£40**
Open: lunch Sun-Fri, dinner daily (closed
  Christmas/New Year)
Last orders: lunch 1.45pm, dinner 9.45pm
500-year-old traditional village inn. Five
  starters and six main courses from fresh
  produce written daily on the blackboard.

Hill House
High Road, Horndon-on-the-Hill, Essex SS17 8LD
Tel: (0375) 642463 **£40**
Open: lunch Tue-Fri, dinner Tue-Sat (closed
  Christmas/New Year)
Last orders: lunch 1.45pm, dinner 9.45pm
Lunch menus change daily and dinner
  menus fortnightly. Inventive dishes are
  made with top quality ingredients.

HORTON
French Partridge Restaurant
Horton, Nr Northampton,
    Northamptonshire NN7 2AP
Tel: (0604) 870033 **£50**
Open: dinner Tue-Sat (closed 2 wks Christmas,
    3 wks Jul/Aug)
Last orders: dinner 9.00pm
Family-run restaurant. Monthly changing
    menu combines classic French and mod-
    ern English dishes in friendly surround-
    ings.

HUDDERSFIELD
Pisces Restaurant
84 Fitzwilliam Street, Huddersfield, West
    Yorkshire HD1 5BD
Tel: (0484) 516773 **£40**
Open: lunch + dinner Mon-Sat (closed Bank
    Holidays)
Last orders: lunch 2.00pm, dinner 9.30pm
Good fish dishes, modern setting.

HUNTINGDON
Old Bridge Hotel
1 High Street, Huntingdon,
    Cambridgeshire PE18 6TQ
Tel: (0480) 52681 **£55**
Open: lunch + dinner daily (bar lunches only Sat)
Last orders: lunch 2.00pm, dinner 10.30pm
18th-century house, twenty-seven bed-
    rooms, in grounds leading to the River
    Ouse.

HUNTSHAM
Huntsham Court
Huntsham, Bampton, Nr Tiverton,
    Devon EX16 7NA
Tel: (039 86) 210 **£45**
Open: dinner daily
Last orders: dinner 10.00pm
Victorian Gothic house run in homely style.
    Five-course, no-choice dinners and good
    wines.

HURLEY
Ye Olde Bell Hotel
High Street, Hurley, Nr Maidenhead,
    Berkshire SL6 5LX
Tel: (062 882) 5881 **£65**
Open: lunch + dinner daily
Last orders: lunch 2.00pm (2.30pm Sun), dinner
    9.30pm
Popular since 1135, the hotel has plenty of
    character. Twenty-five bedrooms, some
    (like the dining room) overlook the
    gardens.

IPSWICH
Mortimer's on the Quay
Wherry Quay, Ipswich, Suffolk IP4 1AS
Tel: (0473) 230225 **£40**
Open: lunch Mon-Fri, dinner Mon-Sat (closed Bank
    Holidays, 2 wks Christmas, 2 wks Aug)
Last orders: lunch 2.00pm, dinner 9.00pm
Specialising in seafood the restaurant has a
    nautical theme decor and overlooks
    Ipswich docks.

The Singing Chef
200 St Helen's Street, Ipswich, Suffolk IP3 2RH
Tel: (0473) 255236 **£40**
Open: dinner Tue-Sat (closed Bank Holidays)
Last orders: dinner 11.00pm
A different part of France each month is the
    subject of the menu whose regional
    French dishes are made from fresh,
    quality ingredients. Friendly service from
    the Toyes.

ISLE OF MAN
Harbour Bistro
5 East Street, Ramsey, Isle of Man
Tel: (0624) 814182 **£35**
Open: lunch + dinner daily (closed 4 dys
    Christmas)
Last orders: lunch 2.30pm, dinner 10.30pm
Informal, mainly fish restaurant which is
    fresh daily from the harbour.

La Rosette
Main Road, Ballasalla, Isle of Man
Tel: (0624) 822940 **£65**
Open: lunch + dinner Tue-Sat (closed Christmas to
    mid-Jan)
Last orders: lunch 3.00pm, dinner 10.30pm
Generous helpings of traditional French-
    style food.

Woodford's
King Edward Road, Onchan, Isle of Man
Tel: (0624) 675626 **£45**
Open: lunch Tue-Fri + Sun, dinner Mon-Sat
    (closed 2 wks Jan)
Last orders: lunch 2.00pm (2.30pm Sun), dinner
    10.00pm
Television chef Kevin Woodford's friendly
    local restaurant.

ISLE OF WIGHT
Lugleys
42 Lugley Street, Newport, Isle of
    Wight PO30 5HD
Tel: (0983) 521062 **£40**
Open: lunch by arrangement, dinner Tue-Sat
    (closed 2 wks Feb, 2 wks Nov)
Last orders: dinner 9.30pm
Small restaurant offering seasonal produce,
    especially game in winter.

Seaview Hotel
High Street, Seaview, Isle of Wight PO34 5EX
Tel: (0983) 612711 *Fax:* (0983) 613729 **£45**
Open: lunch + dinner daily (bar meals only Sun
    eve) (closed Christmas Day)
Last orders: lunch 2.00pm, dinner 9.45pm
Friendly owners; attractive homely rooms
    with antiques; lounge overlooking sea.

Winterbourne Hotel
Bonchurch, Isle of Wight PO38 1RQ
Tel: (0983) 852535 *Fax:* (0983) 853056
Open: dinner daily (closed mid-Nov to Mar)
Last orders: dinner 9.00pm (10.00pm by
    arrangement)
Room prices of between £50 and £60
    include dinner and breakfast.

IXWORTH
Theobalds Restaurant
68 High Street, Ixworth, Bury St Edmunds,
Suffolk IP31 2HJ
Tel: (0359) 31707 **£50**
Open: lunch Tue-Fri + Sun, dinner Mon-Sat
(closed Bank Holidays)
Last orders: lunch 2.00pm, dinner 10.00pm
Small cottage restaurant, seasonally chang-
ing dishes using good local produce.

JERSEY
Apple Cottage
Rozel Bay, St Martin, Jersey, Channel Islands
Tel: (0534) 61002 **£40**
Open: lunch Tue-Sun, dinner Tue-Sat (closed Bank
Holidays + following Tue, Jan)
Last orders: lunch 2.15pm (2.30pm Sun), dinner
9.30pm
Traditional French cooking from Settimo
Pozzi.

Château la Chaire Hotel
Rozel Valley, Jersey, Channel Islands
Tel: (0534) 63354 *Fax:* (0534) 65137 **£50**
Open: lunch + dinner daily
Last orders: lunch 2.00pm (2.15pm Sat+Sun),
dinner 10.00pm (9.30pm Sun)
Oak panelled entrance hall, bar and dining
room with chandeliers give a rather grand
impression of the hotel which stands in
seven acres of wooded grounds.

Little Grove
Rue de Haut, St Lawrence, Jersey,
Channel Islands JE3 1JQ
Tel: (0534) 25321 *Fax:* (0534) 25325 **£50**
Open: lunch + dinner daily
Last orders: lunch 1.45pm (2.00pm Sun), dinner
9.30pm
Fourteen bedroomed hotel with great style,
from the Rolls Royce that picks you up on
arrival to the elegant public rooms.

Old Court House Inn
St Aubin, Jersey, Channel Islands
Tel: (0534) 46433 *Fax:* (0534) 45103 **£40**
Open: lunch + dinner daily (closed Christmas,
4 wks Jan/Feb)
Last orders: lunch 2.30pm, dinner 11.00pm
15th-century seaside inn – beamed cellar
bar, nine pretty bedrooms, some overlooking harbour.

Sea Crest Hotel & Restaurant
Petit Port, St Brelade, Jersey,
Channel Islands JE3 8HH
Tel: (0534) 46353 **£65**
Open: lunch + dinner Tue-Sun (closed dinner Sun
in winter)
Last orders: lunch 2.00pm, dinner 9.45pm (9.30pm
Sun)
Traditional menu with French and Italian
specialities. Seven bedrooms.

KILBURN
Foresters Arms Hotel
Kilburn, North Yorkshire YO6 4AH
Tel: (034 76) 386 **£35**
Open: lunch + dinner daily
Last orders: lunch 2.30pm, dinner 9.30pm
Family cooking based on traditional English
and French cooking by Andrew Cussons,
former head chef at Langan's Bistro.

KILDWICK
Kildwick Hall
Kildwick, Nr Skipton, North Yorkshire BD20 9AE
Tel: (0535) 32244 **£50**
Open: lunch + dinner daily
Last orders: lunch 2.30pm, dinner 9.30pm
Jacobean manor house with fine public
rooms and elegant dining room. Modern
British dishes, seventeen bedrooms.

KINGHAM
The Mill House Hotel & Restaurant
Station Road, Kingham, Oxfordshire OX7 6UH
Tel: (0608) 658188 *Fax:* (0608) 658492 **£60**
Open: lunch + dinner daily
Last orders: lunch 2.00pm, dinner 9.30pm (9.45pm
Sat)
A former flour mill, twenty bedrooms,
smart dining room with set price and à la
carte menus.

KINGTON
Penrhos Court Restaurant
Lyonshall, Kington, Hereford &
Worcester HR5 3LH
Tel: (0544) 230720 *Fax:* (0544 230754) **£40**
Open: lunch + dinner daily
Last orders: lunch 1.30pm (2.00pm Sun), dinner
9.00pm
Traditional and modern cooking from chef/
proprietor Daphne Lambert.

KIRBY LONSDALE
Cobwebs Country House
Leck, Cowan Bridge, Kirby Lonsdale,
Lancashire LA6 2HZ
Tel: (05242) 72141 **£40**
Open: dinner Mon-Sat (lunch for residents only)
(closed Jan-Mar)
Last orders: dinner 8.00pm
Six-course menu which changes daily
according to local produce availability.

LECHLADE
Rieunier's Restaurant
6 Oak Street, Lechlade-on-Thames,
Gloucestershire GL7 3AX
Tel: (0367) 52587 **£50**
Open: lunch Sun, dinner Mon-Sat (closed
Christmas Day, Boxing Day, New Year's Day)
Last orders: lunch 1.30pm, dinner 9.30pm
Modern British cooking from René Rieunier
served by wife Sally.

LEICESTER
Woods Restaurant
93 Queens Road, Leicester,
Leicestershire LE2 1TT
Tel: (0533) 708830 **£35**
Open: lunch daily, dinner Tue-Sat (closed Bank
Holidays)
Last orders: lunch 2.30pm, dinner 9.45pm
(10.00pm Sat)
Popular friendly restaurant with live music
at the weekends.

LEOMINSTER
The Marsh Country House Hotel
Eyton, Leominster, Hereford &
   Worcester HR6 0AG
Tel: (0568) 3952   **£40**
Open: lunch + dinner daily
Last orders: lunch 2.00pm (2.30pm Sun), dinner
   9.30pm
Short fixed price menu using fresh ingre-
dients and home-grown herbs.

LEW
University Farm Restaurant
Lew, Oxfordshire OX8 2AU
Tel: (0993) 850297   **£35**
Open: dinner Mon-Sat (closed Christmas + New
   Year)
Last orders: dinner 8.30pm (9.30pm Sat)
Family-run 17th-century farmhouse hotel.
Traditional British cooking.

LIFTON
Arundell Arms Hotel
Lifton, Devon PL16 0AA
Tel: (0566) 84666   **£50**
Open: lunch + dinner daily (closed 5 dys
   Christmas)
Last orders: lunch 2.00pm, dinner 9.00pm
Popular with anglers for the twenty miles of
fishing rights along the Tamar.

LINCOLN
Harvey's Cathedral Restaurant
1 Exchequergate, Castle Square, Lincoln,
   Lincolnshire LN2 1PZ
Tel: (0522) 510333   **£45**
Open: lunch Sun-Fri, dinner Mon-Sat (closed New
   Year's Day)
Last orders: lunch 2.00pm, dinner 9.30pm
Next to the cathedral and castle, you are
warmly welcomed by Bob Harvey.

LIVERPOOL
The Armadillo
20-22 Mathew Street, Liverpool,
   Merseyside L2 6RE
Tel: 051-236 4123   **£35**
Open: lunch + dinner Tue-Sat
Last orders: lunch 3.00pm, dinner 10.30pm
International menu, particularly good value
at lunchtime.

L'Oriel Restaurant
Oriel Chambers, Water Street, Liverpool,
   Merseyside L2 8TD
Tel: 051-236 5025   **£35**
Open: lunch Mon-Fri, dinner Mon-Sat (closed Bank
   Holidays)
Last orders: lunch 2.30pm, dinner 10.30pm
In the centre of the business area it is very
busy at lunchtime but more peaceful in
the evening. Classic French dishes.

Trials
56/62 Castle Street, Liverpool,
   Merseyside L2 7LQ
Tel: 051-227 1021   **£65**
Open: lunch Mon-Fri, dinner Mon-Sat
Last orders: lunch 1.45pm, dinner 9.45pm
Friendly restaurant opposite the law courts.

LONG MELFORD
Chimneys Restaurant
Hall Street, Long Melford, Sudbury,
   Suffolk CO10 9JR
Tel: (0787) 79806   **£60**
Open: lunch Tue-Sun, dinner Tue-Sat
Last orders: lunch 2.00pm, dinner 9.30pm
Good modern and traditional dishes served
in comfy beamed dining room.

LOWER BEEDING
South Lodge
Brighton Road, Lower Beeding,
   West Sussex RH13 6PS
Tel: (0403) 891711   **£70**
Open: lunch + dinner daily
Last orders: lunch 2.30pm, dinner 10.30pm
Set in lovely grounds near the Sussex
Downs this Victorian house offers inven-
tive and well presented cooking.

LOWER BRAILES
Feldon House
Lower Brailes, Nr Banbury,
   Oxfordshire OX15 5HW
Tel: (060 885) 580   **£50**
Open: lunch daily, dinner Mon-Sat, all meals by
   arrangement only (closed 2 wks autumn)
Last orders: lunch 1.30pm, dinner 8.30pm
Dinner party cooking for groups of a dozen
or so in traditional British style.

LUDLOW
The Feathers at Ludlow
Bull Ring, Ludlow, Shropshire SY8 1AA
Tel: (0584) 875261 *Fax:* (0584) 876030   **£50**
Open: lunch + dinner daily
Last orders: lunch 2.00pm, dinner 9.00pm
Forty bedroomed, half-timbered hotel with
ornate plaster work ceilings and panel-
ling.

LYMINGTON
The Stanwell House Hotel
High Street, Lymington, Hampshire SO41 9AA
Tel: (0590) 677123 *Fax:* (0590) 677756   **£50**
Open: lunch + dinner daily
Last orders: lunch 2.30pm, dinner 10.30pm
Modernised hotel with Georgian exterior
and pretty walled garden.

LYMPSTONE
River House
The Strand, Lympstone, Devon EX8 5EY
Tel: (0395) 265147   **£65**
Open: lunch Tue-Sun, dinner Tue-Sat
Last orders: lunch 1.45pm, dinner 9.30pm
   (10.30pm Sat)
Good modern cooking, generous puddings.

MAIDEN NEWTON
Le Petit Canard Restaurant
56 Dorchester Road, Maiden Newton,
   Dorset DT2 0BE
Tel: (0300) 20536   **£45**
Open: dinner Tue-Sat (closed 2 wks Nov)
Last orders: dinner 9.00pm
Four-course, no choice menu served in the
elegant dining room, everyone sitting at
one table. Relaxed, welcoming atmos-
phere.

MALMESBURY
The Old Bell Hotel
Abbey Row, Malmesbury, Wiltshire SN16 0BW
Tel: (0666) 822344 *Fax:* (0666) 825145 **£35**
Open: lunch + dinner daily
Last orders: lunch 2.30pm, dinner 10.30pm
Next to the Abbey, one of the chimneys dates back 800 years. The stable block has been converted more recently to give a total of thirty-six rooms.

MALVERN WELLS
The Cottage in the Wood Hotel
Holywell Road, Malvern Wells,
  Hereford & Worcester WR14 4LG
Tel: (0684) 573487 **£50**
Open: lunch + dinner daily
Last orders: lunch 2.00pm, dinner 9.00pm (8.30pm Sun)
Refurbishment of all bedrooms now complete at this beautifully situated country house hotel.

MANCHESTER
Blinkers
16 Princess Street, Manchester,
  Greater Manchester M1 4NB
Tel: 061-228 2503 **£50**
Open: lunch Mon-Fri, dinner Mon-Sat (Closed Bank Holidays)
Last orders: lunch 2.15pm, dinner 10.15pm
Good value, simple well-cooked food.

Market Restaurant
104 High Street, corner of Edge Street,
  Smithfield City Centre, Manchester,
  Greater Manchester M4 1HQ
Tel: 061-834 3743 **£40**
Open: lunch Tue-Sat (closed 1 wk Christmas, 1 wk spring, Aug)
Last orders: dinner 9.30pm
Lively restaurant, fun atmosphere, friendly service.

Yang Sing
34 Princes Street, Manchester,
  Greater Manchester M1 4JY
Tel: 061-236 2200 **£40**
Open: all day daily
Last orders: 11.00pm
Extremely popular Cantonese restaurant with extensive menu. Booking is essential.

MAWNAN SMITH
Nansidwell Country House Hotel
Mawnan Smith, Nr Falmouth, Cornwall TR11 5HU
Tel: (0326) 250340 **£60**
Open: lunch + dinner daily (closed Jan)
Last orders: lunch 1.45pm, dinner 9.00pm (9.30pm Sat)
Beautiful sea views, comfortable and relaxing atmosphere, competent cooking.

MEVAGISSEY
Mr Bistro
East Quay, The Harbour, Mevagissey,
  Cornwall PL26 6QH
Tel: (0726) 842432 **£45**
Open: lunch + dinner daily (closed Nov-Feb)
Last orders: lunch 3.00pm, dinner 10.00pm
Simple bistro, short menu which changes according to the availability of the fresh fish.

MIDHURST
Maxine's
Elizabeth House, Red Lion Street, Midhurst,
  West Sussex GU29 9PB
Tel: (073 081) 6271 **£40**
Open: lunch Wed-Sun, dinner Wed-Mon (closed 3 wks Feb)
Last orders: lunch 1.30pm (2.00pm Sun), dinner 9.30pm (9.00pm Sun)
Cottagey dining room in pretty half-timbered house. Classic cooking.

MINSTER LOVELL
The Old Swan & Mill Hotel
Minster Lovell, Nr Witney, Oxfordshire OX8 5RN
Tel: (0993) 775614 **£50**
Open: lunch + dinner daily
Last orders: lunch 2.00pm, dinner 9.30pm
600-year-old inn near the river and local cricket pitch.

MITHIAN
The Miners Arms
Mithian, Cornwall TR5 0QZ
Tel: (087 255) 2375 **£35**
Open: dinner daily (bar lunches only) (closed Sun+Mon in winter)
Last orders: dinner 10.00pm
Good home-made food.

MORPETH
Linden Hall Hotel
Longhorsley, Morpeth,
  Northumberland NE65 8XF
Tel: (0670) 516611 *Fax:* (0670) 88544 **£45**
Open: lunch + dinner daily
Last orders: lunch 2.00pm, dinner 9.45pm (10.00pm Sat)
Elegant country house hotel with a pub in the grounds.

NEW BARNET
Mims Restaurant
63 East Barnet Road, New Barnet,
  Hertfordshire EN4 8RN
Tel: 081-449 2974 **£45**
Open: lunch Tue-Fri + Sun, dinner Tue-Sun (closed Christmas Day, Boxing Day, New Year's Day, 2 wks Sep)
Last orders: lunch 3.00pm, dinner 11.00pm
Modern European cooking which is Mediterranean-influenced. Menus change daily.

NEWBURY
Elcot Park Hotel
Newbury, Berkshire RG16 8NJ
Tel: (0488) 58100 **£55**
Open: lunch + dinner daily
Last orders: lunch 2.00pm, dinner 10.00pm
Quality fresh produce in a traditional menu. Facilities include a new leisure centre.

NEWCASTLE-UPON-TYNE
Blackgate Restaurant
The Side, Dean Street, Newcastle-upon-Tyne,
  Tyne & Wear NE1 3JE
Tel: 091-261 7356 *Fax:* 091-261 0926 **£45**
Open: lunch Mon-Fri, dinner Mon-Sat (closed Bank Holidays)
Last orders: lunch 2.30pm, dinner 10.30pm
International cuisine with the main influences from Germany.

NORBITON
Restaurant Gravier
9 Station Road, Norbiton, Kingston-Upon-Thames,
Surrey KT2 7AA
Tel: 081-547 1121 **£60**
Open: lunch Mon-Fri, dinner Mon-Sat (closed Bank
Holidays, 2 wks Christmas, 2 wks Aug)
Last orders: lunch 2.00pm, dinner 10.00pm
(11.00pm Sat)
Traditional French cooking specialising in
fresh fish and shellfish.

NORWICH
Greens Seafood Restaurant
82 Upper St Giles Street, Norwich,
Norfolk NR13 1AQ
Tel: (0603) 623733 **£50**
Open: lunch Tue-Fri, dinner Tue-Sat (closed Bank
Holidays, 10 dys Christmas, 2 wks Aug)
Last orders: lunch 2.15pm, dinner 10.45pm
Simple dishes made with fresh local fish.
Well priced wines.

OCKHAM
The Hautboy
Ockham Lane, Ockham, Surrey GU23 6NP
Tel: (0483) 225355 **£50**
Open: lunch + dinner daily (closed Christmas +
New Year)
Last orders: lunch 2.00pm, dinner 10.00pm
(9.30pm Sun)
Neo-Gothic building dating back to 1864.
Restaurant and brasserie offering inter-
national cuisine, specialising in game and
seafood.

ORFORD
The Butley-Orford Oysterage
Market Square, Orford, Woodbridge,
Suffolk OP12 2LH
Tel: (0394) 450277 **£40**
Open: all day, daily (closed eve in winter except
Sat, closed 2 wks Jan/Feb)
Last orders: 8.30pm
Go for fresh oysters, home-smoked sal-
mon, and a bottle of white wine; coffee-
shop decor, busy on Saturdays.

OSWESTRY
Starlings Castle
Brony Garth, Oswestry, Shropshire SY10 7NU
Tel: (0691) 72464 **£35**
Open: lunch Sun, dinner daily
Last orders: lunch 2.30pm, dinner 9.30pm
Small friendly and informal hotel run by
Antony and Jools Pitt.

OXFORD
Fifteen North Parade
15 North Parade Avenue, Oxford,
Oxfordshire OX2 6LX
Tel: (0865) 513773 **£45**
Open: lunch daily, dinner Mon-Sat
Last orders: lunch 2.00pm, dinner 10.00pm
More informal ambience, chef Stanley
Matthews serving eclectic modern menu.

La Sorbonne
130A High Street, Oxford, Oxfordshire OX1 4DH
Tel: (0865) 241320 **£55**
Open: lunch + dinner daily (closed Bank Holidays)
Last orders: lunch 2.30pm, dinner 11.00pm
Classic French restaurant tucked away just
off the High Street.

Rendezvous Restaurant
100-101 Gloucester Green, Oxford,
Oxfordshire OX1 2DF
Tel: (0865) 793146 **£40**
Open: all day, daily
Last orders: 11.00pm
Useful for a coffee and croissant or snack;
French staff and atmosphere provided by
André Chavagnon.

PANGBOURNE
The Copper Inn
Church Road, Pangbourne, Berkshire RG8 7AR
Tel: (0734) 842244 *Fax:* (0734) 845542 **£50**
Open: lunch + dinner daily
Last orders: lunch 2.00pm (2.30pm Sun), dinner
9.30pm (10.00pm Sat, 9.00pm Sun)
Large smart public rooms with both modern
and antique furnishings.

PAINSWICK
Painswick Hotel
Kemps Lane, Painswick,
Gloucester GL6 6YB
Tel: (0452) 812160
Open: please phone for details
Last orders: please phone for details
Somerset and Hélène Moore's new ven-
ture, opening as we went to press.
Former Georgian rectory, twenty rooms
beautifully furnished with antiques and
fine paintings. Short set menus from
Shaun Cook, shellfish additions from
seawater tank.

PETWORTH
Soanes
Grove Lane, Petworth, West Sussex GU28 0HY
Tel: (0798) 43659 **£65**
Open: lunch Sun, dinner Wed-Sat (closed 1 wk
Feb, 1 wk Oct, New Year's Day)
Last orders: lunch 2.00pm, dinner 10.00pm
Carol Godsmark cooks traditional French
food, husband Derek serves short sea-
sonal good value menus. Changes might
be afoot.

PLYMOUTH
Barrett's of Princess Street
Princess Street, Plymouth, Devon PL1 2EX
Tel: (0752) 221177 **£40**
Open: all day, Mon-Sat (closed Bank Holidays,
1 wk Christmas)
Last orders: 10.30pm
Popular café-restaurant in the city centre.

POLPERRO
The Kitchen at Polperro
The Coombs, Polperro, Cornwall PL13 2RQ
Tel: (0503) 72780 **£40**
Open: dinner Wed-Mon (closed Christmas Day +
Boxing Day)
Last orders: dinner 9.30pm
Interesting menus with the emphasis on fish
– specials depend on the catch of the day.

POOLE
The Mansion House Hotel
11 Thames Street, Poole, Dorset BH15 1JN
Tel: (0202) 685666 *Fax:* (0202) 665702 **£45**
Open: lunch Sun-Fri, dinner daily (closed
    Christmas + New Year)
Last orders: lunch 2.00pm, dinner 10.00pm
Panelled dining room which is a diners club
    – non-members are allowed in at higher
    prices – residents pay club prices.

Warehouse Oyster Bar & Dining
    Rooms
Poole Quay, Poole, Dorset BH15 1HJ
Tel: (0202) 677238 **£55**
Open: lunch Mon-Fri, dinner daily
Last orders: lunch 2.00pm, dinner 10.00pm
    (11.00pm Sat) (oyster bar open all day, daily)
Fresh, simply cooked seafood and views of
    the harbour.

PORLOCK
The Oaks Hotel
Porlock, Somerset TA24 8ES
Tel: (0643) 862265 **£30**
Open: lunch by arrangement dinner daily
Last orders: dinner 8.30pm
Traditional home-cooking using fresh pro-
    duce.

PRESTBURY
The White House
The Village, Prestbury, Cheshire SK10 4DG
Tel: (0625) 829376 *Fax:* (0625) 828627 **£50**
Open: lunch + dinner Tue-Sun (closed Bank
    Holidays, 1 wk Jan, 1 wk Aug)
Last orders: lunch 2.00pm, dinner 10.00pm
Modern British cooking, generous portions,
    using local produce where possible.

PRIOR'S HARDWICK
The Butcher's Arms
Prior's Hardwick, Nr Rugby,
    Warwickshire CV23 8SN
Tel: (0327) 60504 **£45**
Last orders: lunch 2.00pm, dinner 9.45pm
Long-established, popular local inn with log
    fires in the winter and shady garden in
    summer.

PURTON
The Pear Tree
Church End, Purton, Nr Swindon,
    Wiltshire SN5 9ED
Tel: (0793) 772100 *Fax:* (0793) 772369 **£40**
Open: lunch Sun-Fri, dinner daily
Last orders: lunch 2.00pm, dinner 9.30pm
Smart comfortable public rooms with french
    windows on to the gardens from the
    lounge.

REIGATE
La Barbe
71 Bell Street, Reigate, Surrey
Tel: (0737) 241966 **£45**
Open: lunch Mon-Fri, dinner daily (closed Bank
    Holidays, 3 dys Christmas)
Last orders: lunch 2.00pm, dinner 10.00pm
    (10.30pm Sat)
French bistro offering modern cuisine.

RICHMOND, SURREY
Café Flo
149 Kew Road, Richmond, Surrey TW9 2PN
Tel: 081-940 8298 **£35**
Open: all day, daily
Last orders: 11.30pm
Latest of the Café Flo group of brasseries –
    the others are in London.

Prego Restaurant
100 Kew Road, Richmond, Surrey TW9 2PQ
Tel: 081-948 8508 **£30**
Open: lunch + dinner daily (closed Christmas)
Last orders: lunch 3.00pm, dinner 11.30pm
    (10.30pm Sun)
Cheerful friendly restaurant serving good
    pasta.

RIPLEY
Michels Restaurant
13 High Street, Ripley, Surrey GU23 6AQ
Tel: (0483) 224777 **£60**
Open: lunch Tue-Fri + Sun, dinner Tue-Sat (closed
    Christmas Day, Boxing Day, New Year's Day)
Last orders: lunch 1.45pm, dinner 9.00pm (9.30pm
    Sat)
Imaginative, short, fixed price French
    menus.

ROMALDKIRK
The Rose and Crown Hotel
Romaldkirk, Barnard Castle, Durham DL12 9EB
Tel: (0833) 50213 *Fax:* (0833) 50828 **£40**
Open: lunch + dinner daily (closed Christmas Day
    + Boxing Day)
Last orders: lunch 1.30pm, dinner 9.30pm (9.00pm
    Sun)
Daily changing menu using organic veget-
    ables and local game. Specialises in
    British cooking.

ROTHERWICK
Tylney Hall
Rotherwick, Nr Hook, Hampshire RG27 9AJ
Tel: (0256) 764881 *Fax:* (0256) 768141 **£55**
Open: lunch + dinner daily
Last orders: lunch 2.30pm, dinner 9.30pm
    (10.00pm Sat)
Magnificent 19th-century mansion in 66
    acres of estate.

RUSPER
Ghyll Manor
High Street, Rusper, Nr Horsham,
    West Sussex RH12 4PX
Tel: (0293) 871571 **£70**
Open: lunch + dinner daily
Last orders: lunch 2.00pm, dinner 10.00pm
Elizabethan manor and cottages with mod-
    ern extension in 40 acres of grounds.
    Warm, friendly atmosphere.

SANDIWAY
Nunsmere Hall
Tarporley Road, Sandiway, Cheshire CW8 2ES
Tel: (0606) 889100 *Fax:* (0606) 889055 **£65**
Open: lunch daily, dinner Mon-Fri
Last orders: lunch 2.00pm, dinner 9.30pm
    (10.00pm Sat)
Victorian hall on a peninsula of 50-acre lake.
    Organic ingredients are used in the
    cooking.

SENNEN
The State House Hotel
Land's End, Sennen, Cornwall TR19 7AA
Tel: (0736) 871844   *Fax:* (0736) 871812   **£35**
Open: lunch + dinner daily
Last orders: lunch 2.00pm, dinner 9.30pm
Beautiful sea views, friendly staff and a
 peaceful atmosphere at Peter de Savary's
 latest haunt.

SHEFFIELD
The Charnwood Hotel
10 Sharrow Lane, Sheffield,
 South Yorkshire S11 8AA
Tel: (0742) 589411   **£40**
Open: dinner Tue-Sat (closed Christmas Day,
 Boxing Day, New Year's Day)
Last orders: dinner 10.00pm
Hanfrey's Restaurant within the Charnwood
 Hotel offers the traditions of classic
 French with Wayne Bosworth's own
 lighter touch.

Greenhead House Restaurant
84 Burncross Road, Chapeltown, Sheffield,
 South Yorkshire S30 4SF
Tel: (0742) 469004   **£50**
Open: dinner Tue-Sat (closed Christmas/New
 Year, 2 wks May, 2 wks Sep)
Last orders: dinner 9.00pm
Seasonally changing menu using high quality
 ingredients prepared and served simply.

SHERBORNE
The Eastbury Hotel
Long Street, Sherborne, Dorset DT9 3BY
Tel: (0935) 813131   *Fax:* (0935) 817296   **£45**
Open: lunch + dinner daily
Last orders: lunch 2.30pm, dinner 10.30pm
Elegant Georgian town house.

SLAIDBURN
Parrock Head Hotel
Woodhouse Lane, Slaidburn, Nr Clitheroe,
 Lancashire BB7 3AH
Tel: (020 06) 614   **£40**
Open: lunch + dinner daily (closed 1 wk Christmas)
Last orders: lunch 2.00pm, dinner 8.30pm
Well-furnished, comfortable 17th-century
 farmhouse, cheerful dining room,
 straightforward English cooking.

SONNING-ON-THAMES
The French Horn Hotel
Sonning-on-Thames, Berkshire RG4 0TN
Tel: (0734) 692204   **£70**
Open: lunch + dinner daily (closed 5 dys
 Christmas, Good Friday)
Last orders: lunch 1.45pm, dinner 9.30pm
Traditional surroundings and classic menu.
 Excellent clarets on an extensive wine
 list.

SOURTON
Collaven Manor Hotel
Sourton, Nr Okehampton, Devon EX20 4HH
Tel: (083 786) 522   **£50**
Open: lunch + dinner daily (closed 3 wks Jan)
Last orders: lunch 1.45pm, dinner 9.30pm
Spacious rooms, with a miniature decanter
 of sherry to welcome you, well-equipped
 bathrooms and friendly atmosphere.

SOUTHSEA
Bistro Montparnasse
103 Palmerston Road, Southsea,
 Hampshire PO5 3PS
Tel: (0705) 816754   **£70**
Open: dinner Mon-Sat (closed 1 wk Jan, 3 wks
 Nov)
Last orders: dinner 10.00pm
Cheerful popular local restaurant which
 relies heavily upon local fish and game.

SOUTHWOLD
The Crown
90 High Street, Southwold, Suffolk IP18 6DP
Tel: (0502) 722275   **£40**
Open: lunch + dinner daily (closed 1 wk Jan)
Last orders: lunch 2.00pm, dinner 9.45pm
Daily changing, short fixed-price menus.
 Wine list by Adnams.

SPARSHOLT
Lainston House
Sparsholt, Winchester, Hampshire SO21 2LJ
Tel: (0962) 63588   **£80**
Open: lunch + dinner daily
Last orders: lunch 2.00pm, dinner 10.00pm
A taste of gracious living is on offer at this
 magnificent, if rather formal country
 house. Set in 60 acres of grounds which
 includes an 18th-century herb garden.

ST KEVERNE
Laden Table
2 Commercial Road, St Keverne,
 Cornwall TR12 6LY
Tel: (0326) 280090   **£55**
Open: dinner Mon-Sat (closed Aug-Sep)
Last orders: dinner 9.00pm
French influenced cooking renowned for
 quality and generousity.

STOKE BRUERNE
Bruernes Lock
The Canalside, Stoke Bruerne, Towcester,
 Northamptonshire NN12 7SB
Tel: (0604) 863654   **£45**
Open: lunch Tue-Fri + Sun, dinner Tue-Sat (closed
 New Year, 2 wks Feb, 1 wk Sep)
Last orders: lunch 2.00pm, dinner 2.15pm
Modern European and regional British dis-
 hes are on offer in this small popular local
 restaurant.

ST MARGARET'S AT CLIFFE
Wallett's Court Country House Hotel
West Cliffe, St Margaret's at Cliffe,
 Kent CT15 6EW
Tel: (0304) 852424   **£35**
Open: dinner Mon-Sat (closed 4 dys Christmas, 2
 wks Nov)
Last orders: dinner 9.00pm
Short menus offering seasonal produce.
 Gourmet night on Saturdays.

STOKESLEY
Chapters
27 High Street, Stokesley, North Yorkshire
Tel: (0642) 711888   **£35**
Open: lunch daily, dinner Mon-Sat (closed Boxing
 Day)
Last orders: lunch 2.00pm, dinner 10.00pm
Menu with some Middle-Eastern influence.

STONEHOUSE
Stonehouse Court Hotel
Bristol Road, Stonehouse,
Gloucestershire GL10 3RA
Tel: (0453) 825155   *Fax:* (0453) 824611   **£50**
Open: lunch + dinner daily
Last orders: lunch 2.00pm, dinner 9.30pm
(10.00pm Sat)
The magnificent carved stone fireplace is only one of the many features retained in this 17th-century Grade II listed building set in tranquil surroundings.

STORRINGTON
Abingworth Hall
Thakeham Road, Storrington,
West Sussex RH20 3EF
Tel: (0798) 813636   *Fax:* (0798) 813914   **£65**
Open: lunch + dinner daily
Last orders: lunch 1.45pm, dinner 9.00pm
Well presented good quality cooking which changes weekly using seasonal produce.

STOW-ON-THE-WOLD
Wyck Hill House
Burford Road, Stow-on-the-Wold,
Gloucestershire GL54 1HY
Tel: (0451) 31936   *Fax:* (0451) 32243   **£60**
Open: lunch + dinner daily
Last orders: lunch 2.00pm, dinner 10.00pm
(9.30pm Sat)
Modern English cooking.

STRATFORD-UPON-AVON
Billesley Manor Hotel
Billesley, Alcester, Stratford-upon-Avon,
Warwickshire B49 6NF
Tel: (0789) 400888   **£70**
Open: lunch + dinner daily
Last orders: lunch 2.00pm, dinner 9.30pm
(10.00pm Sat)
Oak-panelled restaurant offering dishes made from quality fresh ingredients. Mousses are to be recommended.

The Shakespeare Hotel
Chapel Street, Stratford-upon-Avon,
Warwickshire CV37 6ER
Tel: (0789) 294771   *Fax:* (0789) 415111   **£55**
Open: lunch + dinner daily
Last orders: lunch 2.15pm, dinner 10.00pm
(9.15pm Sun)
Combines traditional charm with modern comfort and a good base for the town. Seventy rooms.

SUTTON
Partners Brasserie
23 Stonecot Hill, Sutton, Surrey SM3 9HB
Tel: 081-644 7743   **£65**
Open: lunch Tue-Fri, dinner Tue-Sat (closed Bank
Holidays)
Last orders: lunch 2.00pm, dinner 10.00pm
Recently refurbished. Modern European cooking.

TARRANT MONKTON
Langtons Restaurant
Langton Arms, Tarrant Monkton, Blandford
Forum, Dorset DT11 8RX
Tel: (025 889) 225   *Fax:* (025 889) 480   **£45**
Open: lunch Sat+Sun, dinner daily (closed
Christmas Day)
Last orders: lunch 2.00pm Sun, 2.30pm Sat, dinner
9.30pm
Good value lunch and dinner.

TAVISTOCK
The Horn of Plenty
Tamar View House, Gulworthy, Tavistock,
Devon PL19 8JD
Tel: (0822) 832528   **£65**
Open: lunch + dinner Tue-Sun (closed Christmas
Day + Boxing Day)
Last orders: lunch 2.00pm, dinner 9.30pm
New owners at the famous Horn – changes envisaged in an evolving menu.

TEDDINGTON
Spaghetti Junction
20/22 High Street, Teddington,
Middlesex TW11 8EW
Tel: 081-977 9199   *Fax:* 081-977 8890   **£50**
Open: lunch Tue-Sat, dinner Tue-Sun (closed Bank
Holidays, 4 dys Christmas, 4 dys Easter)
Last orders: lunch 2.30pm, dinner 11.15pm
Stylish Italian restaurant, good seafood and pasta.

THAME
The Spread Eagle Hotel
Cornmarket, Thame, Oxfordshire OX9 2BW
Tel: (0844) 213661   *Fax:* (0844) 261380   **£45**
Open: lunch (bar snacks only) Tue-Sun, dinner
daily (closed 28th, 29th + 30th Dec)
Last orders: lunch 2.00pm (2.30pm Sun), dinner
10.00pm (9.00pm Sun)
Modern English cooking strongly influenced by traditional French. Much money has been spent on refurbishment. Thirty-three rooms.

Thatchers Hotel & Restaurant
29/30 Lower High Street, Thame, Oxfordshire
OX9 2AA
Tel: (0844) 212146   *Fax:* (0844) 217413   **£60**
Open: lunch Mon-Fri, dinner Mon-Sat
Last orders: lunch 2.00pm, dinner 10.00pm
(10.30pm Sat)
Thatched cottage restaurant with rooms; robust, straightforward cooking: pumpkin soup, pot-roasted spiced chicken.

TRURO
Alverton Manor
Tregolls Road, Truro, Cornwall TR1 1XQ
Tel: (0872) 76633   **£60**
Open: lunch + dinner daily
Last orders: lunch 1.45pm, dinner 9.45pm
Spacious rooms with pretty fabrics; convenient location on edge of town for this former convent.

ULLSWATER
Leeming House
Watermillock, Ullswater, Cumbria CA11 0JJ
Tel: (076 84) 86622   *Fax:* (076 84) 86443   **£70**
Open: lunch + dinner daily
Last orders: lunch 1.45pm, dinner 8.45pm
Six-course dinners. Excellent home-made
breads, jams and chutneys.

UPPER SLAUGHTER
Lords of the Manor Hotel
Upper Slaughter, Nr Bourton-on-the-Water,
   Cheltenham, Gloucestershire GL54 2JD
Tel: (0451) 20243   *Fax:* (0451) 20696   **£70**
Open: lunch + dinner daily
Last orders: lunch 2.00pm, dinner 9.30pm
Former rectory in the beautiful Cotswold
countryside, comfortable rooms and
friendly atmosphere.

VOWCHURCH
Poston Mill
Vowchurch, Hereford & Worcester HR2 0FF
Tel: (0981) 550151   **£40**
Open: lunch Tue-Sun, dinner Tue-Sat (closed Bank
   Holidays)
Last orders: lunch 2.00pm, dinner 9.30pm
Small friendly restaurant serving traditional
and modern food in a relaxed and pleasant
setting.

WANSFORD-IN-ENGLAND
The Haycock Hotel
Wansford-in-England, Peterborough,
   Cambridgeshire PE8 6JA
Tel: (0780) 782223   *Fax:* (0780) 783031   **£40**
Open: lunch + dinner daily
Last orders: lunch 2.00pm, dinner 10.00pm
Classic English dishes in traditional sur-
roundings.

WATERMILLOCK
The Old Church Hotel
Watermillock, Ullswater, Penrith,
   Cumbria CA11 0JN
Tel: (076 84) 86204   *Fax:* (076 84) 86368   **£45**
Open: lunch + dinner daily (closed Dec-Mar)
Last orders: lunch 2.00pm, dinner 8.00pm
House guests rather than visitors is the
approach given by the Whitmores. Su-
perb views of the mountains and lake.

Rampsbeck Country House Hotel
Watermillock, Ullswater, Nr Penrith,
   Cumbria CA11 0LP
Tel: (076 84) 86688   **£40**
Open: lunch + dinner daily (closed 6 wks Jan/Feb)
Last orders: lunch 1.45pm, dinner 8.45pm
Traditional and modern English and French
cooking.

WELLINGBOROUGH
The Flemish House Restaurant
Hinwick House, Hinwick, Wellingborough,
   Northamptonshire NN9 7JE
Tel: (0933) 50012   *Fax:* (0933) 316811   **£55**
Open: lunch daily, dinner Mon-Sat (closed
   Christmas Eve, Boxing Day, New Year's Day)
Last orders: lunch 2.00pm, dinner 10.00pm
Queen Anne house open to the public with
the restaurant in the Victorian wing.
Essentially classic French dishes.

WENSLEYDALE
Simonstone Hall
Hawes, Wensleydale, North Yorkshire DL8 3LY
Tel: (0969) 667255   *Fax:* (0969) 667741   **£45**
Open: lunch + dinner daily (closed 2 wks Jan)
Last orders: lunch 2.00pm, dinner 8.30pm
18th-century stone house with ten cosy
   bedrooms. Attractive white painted
   panelled dining room serving classic
   cooking.

WETHERAL
Fantails
The Green, Wetheral, Nr Carlisle,
   Cumbria CA4 8ET
Tel: (0228) 60239   **£40**
Open: lunch + dinner Mon-Sat
Last orders: lunch 2.00pm, dinner 9.30pm
Family-run popular local restaurant.

WHITLEY BAY
Le Provençale
179/183 Park View, Whitley Bay,
   Tyne & Wear NE26 3PS
Tel: 091-251 3567   **£45**
Open: lunch Tue, Thu+Fri, dinner Mon-Sat
Last orders: lunch 1.45pm, dinner 10.00pm
Generous portions from a menu specialising
   in fish and many classic French dishes.
   Strong regular clientele.

WHITWELL-ON-THE-HILL
Whitwell Hall Country House Hotel
Whitwell-on-the-Hill, York,
   North Yorkshire YO6 7JJ
Tel: (065 381) 554   **£45**
Open: lunch + dinner daily
Last orders: lunch 1.45pm, dinner 8.30pm
Ivy-clad hall in 80 acres of parkland.

WICKHAM
The Old House
The Square, Wickham, Hampshire PO17 5JG
Tel: (0329) 833049   **£50**
Open: lunch Tue-Fri, dinner Mon-Sat (closed 2 wks
   Christmas, 2 wks Easter, 2wks Jul/Aug)
Last orders: lunch 1.45pm, dinner 9.30pm
Georgian town house run by the Skipwiths
   who have been there for around twenty
   years.

WILMSLOW
The Stanneylands Hotel
Stanneylands Road, Wilmslow, Cheshire SK9 4EY
Tel: (0625) 525225   *Fax:* (0625) 537282   **£45**
Open: lunch + dinner daily (residents only Sun eve)
   (closed Bank Holidays)
Last orders: lunch 2.00pm, dinner 10.00pm
Comfortable family-run hotel with mainly
   business clientele. Forty-three tra-
   ditionally furnished bedrooms. New chef
   is Stephen Kitchen.

WRIGHTINGTON
High Moor Restaurant
High Moor Lane, Wrightington, Nr Wigan,
   Lancashire WN6 9QA
Tel: (025 75) 2364   **£55**
Open: lunch Sun, dinner daily
Last orders: lunch 2.00pm, dinner 10.00pm
Popular restaurant, traditional dishes with
   modern approach. Busy on Sundays.

WYLAM
Laburnam House Restaurant
Main Street, Wylam, Northumberland NE41 8AJ
Tel: (0661) 852185 **£40**
Open: lunch by arrangement, dinner Tue-Sat
(closed 2 wks Feb)
Last orders: dinner 9.30pm
Restaurant with four rooms in comfortable
18th-century house.

YORK
The Grange Hotel
Clifton, York, North Yorkshire YO3 6AA
Tel: (0904) 644744   *Fax:* (0904) 612453 **£50**
Open: lunch Sun-Fri, dinner daily
Last orders: lunch 2.30pm, dinner 11.00pm
Elegant interior with period furnishings and
paintings in the public rooms and indi-
vidually designed bedrooms.

Scotland Establishment Reviews

ABERFELDY	Atkins Restaurant at Farleyer House

See page 218 – our Clover Award Section.

ABERFOYLE	Braeval Old Mill

Braeval, By Aberfoyle, Central FK8 3UY
Telephone: (087 72) 711   **£60**
Open: lunch Sun, dinner Tue-Sun (closed Christmas + New Year, 2 wks Feb,
     1 wk Jun, 2 wks Nov)
Last orders: lunch 1.30pm, dinner 9.30pm (8.45pm Sun)

Bare stone walls, simple wooden tables, basic but spotless place
settings – outwardly little has changed at the Nairns' small
restaurant. However, self-taught chef Nick Nairn continues to make
great progress. His cooking is still exploratory, he experiments
interestingly with colour and contrast. A recent dinner confirmed the
quality: parfait of duck livers with foie gras and a Cumberland sauce
dotted with strawberry brunoise; fillet of John Dory with lightly
grilled scallops and a shellfish sauce. Fiona Nairn offers a warm
welcome and supervises service with calm assurance.

ACHILTIBUIE	Summer Isles Hotel

Achiltibuie, By Ullapool, Highland IV26 2YG
Telephone: (085 482) 282   **£60**
Open: dinner daily (closed mid-Oct to Easter)
Last orders: dinner 8.00pm

The hotel is a cluster of buildings decorated in informal homely style.
Neat bedrooms have firm beds and good duvets, and most offer
beautiful views; check when booking. More breathtaking views
towards the Summer Isles from the dining room. The food is the
other reason to come here. Good local produce is the backbone of the
no-choice menus (£28.50 for five courses): mussel soup; moist and
tender roast quail. Saucing is a strong point. Tempting puds and good
cheese. Home-made bread and biscuits. A good selection of New
World wines alongside French.

ALLOA   The Gean House Hotel & Restaurant

Tullibody Road, Alloa, Central FK10 2HS
Telephone: (0259) 219275   *Fax:* (0259) 213827   **£60**
Open: lunch + dinner daily
Last orders: lunch 1.45pm, dinner 9.45pm

The Gean House is a promising new venture in Scotland. Set in its
own grounds with parks, woodland, lawns and a rose garden, the
house has an imposing façade. It was commissioned in 1912 by a
leading industrialist, Alexander Forrester-Paton, as a wedding
present for his son. The current family, grandchildren of Forrester-
Paton, were consulted prior to the 1990 restoration, which has
resulted in a magnificent interior, immaculately decorated. Polished
wood, plants and rugs abound, and there's a crackling log fire in a
hearth big enough to roast a sheep, if you felt so inclined! The overall
ambience is luxurious in a restrained way – nothing is flamboyant. An
imposing leaded window rises to the height of the second storey,
with its gallery corridor. Bedrooms (nine in all) are warm and cosy,
with elegant modern fabrics, big lamps and comfortable bathrooms.

Chef Anthony Mifsud has a sure touch, and a recently enjoyed meal
began with delicious, warm, home-made rolls flavoured with thyme
and sesame, accompanying an unusual and simple sea eel with leek
sauce, followed by sea bream with a red pepper sauce and baby
vegetables. A well-kept cheeseboard preceded a sensational bread
and butter pudding, served in a small soufflé dish – rich, smooth and
delicious. Coffee and petits fours completed the meal. The wine list is
reasonably priced, with helpful notes.

ANSTRUTHER	The Cellar Restaurant

24 East Green, Anstruther, Fife KY10 3AA
Telephone: (0333) 310378   **£60**
Open: lunch Tue-Sat, dinner Mon-Sat (closed 2 wks Christmas/New Year)
Last orders: lunch 1.30pm, dinner 9.30pm

Standards at Peter and Vivien Jukes' little restaurant are consistently high. Vivien is the friendly reigning spirit in the quarry-tiled, stone-walled dining room. Peter's fish is sparklingly fresh, and appears in simple but effective sauces such as his Chardonnay sauce with supreme of turbot and scallops. Soups – perhaps a crayfish and mussel bisque – are intense in colour and flavour. The wine list is remarkable for its scope and quality.

ARISAIG	Arisaig House

Beasdale, By Arisaig, Highland PH39 4NR
Telephone: (068 75) 622   *Fax:* (068 75) 626   **£75**
Open: lunch + dinner daily (closed Nov to mid-Mar)
Last orders: lunch 2.00pm, dinner 9.00pm

The Smithers' aim is that visitors leave refreshed in body and soul. A Victorian house, Arisaig's uncluttered, bright rooms mix modern comforts with antiques and some unusual features: such as an Italian vaulted ceiling in the drawing room. Immaculate housekeeping – even a pair of damp trousers removed for drying! The sober panelled dining room allows concentration on new chef Matthew Burns' cooking: ragoût of local seafood with crab and tarragon; sliced entrecôte of beef with roast garlic on a shallot sauce. Scottish cheeses come with home-made oatcakes and toasted walnut and raisin bread.

AUCHTERADER	The Gleneagles Hotel

Auchterader, Tayside PH3 1NF
Telephone: (0764) 62231   *Fax:* (0764) 62134   **£85**
Open: lunch + dinner daily
Last orders: lunch 2.00pm, dinner 10.00pm

The elegant Strathearn dining room has had a facelift and it's a pleasure to be in the ornate blue and white room with its silver, Wedgwood china and fine glass. Young staff are bright, friendly and take pride in their job. Alan Hill seems to be settling in well as executive chef – our last lunch produced a pretty, marbled vegetable terrine with an onion sauce and good fresh pan-fried turbot with braised endives and garlic. The hotel itself remains as grand as ever, with almost every conceivable leisure activity catered for. Within the 830-acre estate are the Mark Philips Equestrian Centre, the Jackie Stewart Shooting School, the King's and Queen's Golf Courses, five tennis courts (where the coaches include Virginia Wade), croquet, bowling, pitch and putt, and jogging trails; whilst indoors is the Gleneagles Country Club centred around an indoor lagoon-shaped pool, and Champneys The Health Spa. Other facilities available include the hotel's own shops, bank and post office; hairdressing salon; car hire and chauffeur services. As you would expect, public rooms and bedrooms are superbly appointed.

BALLATER	Tullich Lodge

Ballater, Grampian AB3 5SB
Telephone: (033 97) 55406   *Fax:* (033 97) 55397   **£55**
Open: lunch + dinner daily (closed Dec-Mar)
Last orders: lunch 1.00pm, dinner 8.30pm

Neil Bannister and Hector Macdonald run their stylish crenellated
Victorian mansion in a highly personalised way. The relaxed
atmosphere attracts many regular guests who also appreciate the
antiques and fine paintings, high level of care and reliable cooking.
The daily 4-course set menus tend to feature uncomplicated dishes of
game and fish. Simple desserts and Scottish cheeses. Good wines
and an elegant setting with mahogany panelling, silver and fine china.

BANCHORY	Invery House Hotel

Banchory, Grampian AB3 3NJ
Telephone: (033 02) 4782   **£65**
Open: lunch + dinner daily (closed 1 wk Jan)
Last orders: lunch 2.00pm, dinner 10.00pm

Over the river Feugh and through lovely woodland the drive to the
large white house is set amidst lawns and walled gardens. Rooms and
service are of a high standard: you are greeted by name at the car,
there's a friendly voice for an early morning call, papers delivered to
the room, large comfortable beds with good linen, full-size bottles of
bath foam and shampoo. An elegant turquoise, green and white dining
room.

BLAIRGOWRIE	Kinloch House Hotel

Kinloch, Nr Blairgowrie, Tayside PH10 6SG
Telephone:: (025 084) 237   *Fax:* (025 084) 333   **£50**
Open: lunch + dinner daily (closed 2 wks Dec)
Last orders: lunch 2.00pm, dinner 9.15pm

A classic Scottish country house run with old-style formality. No
gimmicks but thoughtful touches in the rooms include an ironing
board and electric blanket. Traditional furnishings include very
comfortable beds. Ties are de rigueur in the wood-panelled dining
room. The short menu of dishes such as loin of lamb with a timbale of
vegetables and madeira sauce, is balanced by a list of supplementary
dishes, such as carpet-bagger steak. Friendly service, and a wine list
strong on clarets.

BUCKIE	The Old Monastery Restaurant

Drybridge, Buckie, Grampian AB5 2JB
Telephone: (0542) 32660   **£50**
Open: lunch + dinner Tue-Sat (closed Bank Holidays, 3 wks Jan, 2 wks Nov)
Last orders: lunch 1.45pm (1.30pm Sat), dinner 9.30pm

Aperitifs are taken in the Cloisters Bar with its views over the Moray
Firth. In the simple, almost austere restaurant – the former chapel –
Maureen Gray is a charming, attentive hostess. Douglas Gray makes
good use of Scottish produce: soups made with Aberdeen Angus beef
stock; venison with redcurrant and port sauce; baked scallop of Spey
salmon. Daughter Sandra is in charge of desserts and petits fours.
Respectable house wines and an admirable selection of half bottles on
a generally good list.

CANONBIE	Riverside Inn

Canonbie, Dumfries & Galloway DG14 0UX
Telephone: (038 73) 71295   **£45**
Open: lunch daily (bar only), dinner Mon-Sat (closed Christmas + New Year,
     2 wks Feb)
Last orders: dinner 8.00pm

A neat cream-walled dining room with simply laid wooden tables and
grey carpeting matching the colours of the stone chimney breast. A
short 4-course menu offers unfussy dishes produced from good
materials: spinach and pine nut ravioli with tomato sauce; some
moist, firm sea trout and turbot. Good vegetables: marrow with a
touch of ginger, baby mangetouts and corn. Well-kept British
cheeses and delicious puddings. A reasonably priced and interesting
wine list. Friendly service.

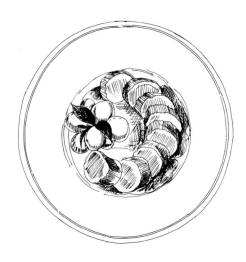

CRINAN	Crinan Hotel

Crinan, Nr Lochgilphead, Strathclyde PA31 8SR
Telephone: (054 683) 261   *Fax:* (054 683) 292   **£75**
Open: dinner Tues-Sat
Last orders: dinner 8.00pm

Don't plan on dining here in rough weather – for if the local fishing boats don't go out, or the catch is unsatisfactory, Lock 16 Restaurant doesn't open. The menu includes a shipping forecast! On good days there may be Loch Craignish mussels, local smoked salmon and the famous jumbo prawns Corryvrechan (landed at 5.30pm!). Small wonder, then, that Nick Ryan wins awards for his fish dishes! The set menu is priced at £35 for five courses and coffee.

Alternatively, you could eat some simply prepared fish downstairs in the Telford Room. Furnishings throughout the hotel are simple but comfortable, the views towards Jura splendid.

CUPAR	Ostlers Close Restaurant

Bonnygate, Cupar, Fife KY15 4BU
Telephone: (0334) 55574   **£45**
Open: lunch + dinner Tue-Sat (closed 1 wk Jan, 1 wk Nov)
Last orders: lunch 2.00pm, dinner 9.30pm (10.00pm Sat)

Situated up an alley off the main street, this casual little restaurant with its cottagey, white plastered walls and simple wooden tables and chairs may not look much. However, Jim Graham's food is good, based on local produce: a selection of seafood with a wine and cream sauce; partridge in a deeply flavoured sauce with home-made rowan jelly. Amanda Graham serves with the help of a young girl.

DRUMNADROCHIT	Polmaily House Hotel

Drumnadrochit, Highland IV3 6XT
Telephone: (045 62) 343   **£55**
Open: dinner daily (closed Nov – Easter)
Last orders: dinner 9.30pm

This delightful Highland house has the lived-in feel and style of a private house. Dinner is a set or limited choice menu – four courses for £22.00. Nicholas Parsons (no, not that one!) glides attentively around the pleasant old-fashioned dining room. Alison cooks good dinner party-style food: soups; grilled brochette of langoustines with garlic butter; honey and cinnamon-glazed roast duckling with olives. Well-kept Scottish cheeses are offered with local oatcakes. Decent house wines and an interesting list of ½-bottles.

DUNBLANE	Cromlix House

Kinbuck, Dunblane, Central FK15 9JT
Telephone: (0786) 822125   **£70**
Open: lunch + dinner daily (closed 2 wks Feb)
Last orders: lunch 2.00pm, dinner 9.30pm

Edward Eden, son of owner Sir Ronald Eden, has taken over as manager. In the kitchen, the classically based cooking has risen well to the setting, with particularly fine sauces: a delicately textured scallop terrine served with a powerful fish sauce; a deep veal stock based sauce with a fresh rosemary flavour served with lamb from the estate. The extensive wine list includes a group of more affordable petits châteaux. Service is formal, in keeping with the style of this grand Victorian house set on its own 5,000-acre estate. Rooms are a mix of period pieces (including, sometimes, a huge Victorian bath tub!) and more modern comforts.

DUNKELD	Kinnaird House

Kinnaird Estate, Nr Dunkeld, Tayside PH8 0LB
Telephone: (079 682) 440   **£70**
Open: lunch + dinner Tue-Sun
Last orders: lunch 2.00pm, dinner 9.15pm

John Webber has now joined as chef

Kinnaird is Mrs Constance Ward's home and it is her personal approach that makes this nine-bedroom country house hotel so special. She is a gracious and caring but unobtrusive hostess who welcomes you as an invited guest into her 9,000-acre estate and beautiful home. Bedrooms retain many original features; tall boys and dressing tables are luxurious without being ostentatious. Bathrooms have huge towels and bathrobes, large baths and very efficient showers. The feeling of wellbeing is as real as ever in the painted panelled dining room with its marble fireplace and large white tables laid with polished silver. Food is generally very good: salad of sweetbreads, chanterelles and shiitake mushrooms dressed with hazelnut and sesame oils; tender pink lamb on creamed leeks; boned braised oxtail wrapped in lettuce. The fixed priced menu is £29.50 for four courses. Service is exemplary.

EDINBURGH — Caledonian Hotel

Princes Street, Edinburgh, Lothian EH2 4LS
Telephone: 031-225 4787   *Fax:* 031-225 6632 **£80**
Open: lunch Mon-Fri, dinner daily
Last orders: lunch 1.45pm, dinner 10.15pm

As ornate and formal as the name implies, from the elaborate plasterwork and huge paintings of flowers to the orchid on each table. Tony Binks now heads the kitchen. Ideas from older Scottish traditions are combined with newer influences: light vegetable dumplings with stir-fried vegetables; boned oxtail stuffed with veal mousseline. George Figuerola leads the polished service in the Pompadour Room. Lunch is a bargain at £15.00.

EDINBURGH — Le Marché Noir

2-4 Eyre Place, Edinburgh, Lothian EH3 5EP
Telephone: 031-558 1608 **£40**
Open: lunch Mon-Fri (Sat by arrangement. dinner daily (closed Christmas + New Year)
Last orders: lunch 2.30pm, dinner 10.00pm (10.30pm Sat, 9.30pm Sun)

As popular as ever for its good value menu (cheaper at lunch). Simply described French dishes (with English translations) range from potage bonne femme to their own charcuterie. Main courses might be pigeon breast pan-fried with red cabbage and baby onions, or some simple moules marinières. An interesting and well-chosen wine list includes vintage notes and some lesser-known regional wines. A great atmosphere – bon appétit!

EDINBURGH — Martin's

See page 219 – our Clover Award Section.

EDINBURGH — Pierre Victoire

10 Victoria Street, Edinburgh, Lothian EH1 2HG
Telephone: 031-225 1721 **£40**
Open: lunch + dinner Mon-Sat (closed 1-10 Jan)
Last orders: lunch 3.00pm, dinner 11.00pm

A facelift has freshened up this busy bistro, but otherwise its appearance is much the same – pictures on white walls, wooden floor, tables crammed together higgledy-piggledy. Straightforward food: roast pigeon breast cooked pink and served warm with frisée and raspberry vinegar dressing; grilled fresh turbot with mussels in beurre blanc. Much of the wine is shipped direct and champagne is only £10.90! Casual service. There are branches too at Grassmarket in Edinburgh, and in Inverness (see listings).

EDINBURGH   The Vintners Rooms

The Vaults, 87 Giles Street, Leith, Edinburgh, Lothian EH6 6BZ
Telephone: 031-554 6767   £30
Open: lunch + dinner Mon-Sat (closed 2 wks Christmas)
Last orders: lunch 2.30pm (2.00pm Sat), dinner 10.30pm (11.00pm Sat)

Tim Cumming has placed this restaurant firmly on the Edinburgh
culinary map. The delightful and ornately plastered former wine
auction room with its candelabra is as atmospheric as ever.
Accomplished and interesting cooking: game terrine with spiced
mirabelles; salmon in pastry with ginger and currants; boudin noir
with spinach and a mustard sauce. Simpler food available also in the
bar room. The wine list includes a good range of house wines.

FORT WILLIAM   Inverlochy Castle

See page 221 – our Clover Award Section.

GLASGOW   The Buttery

652 Argyle Street, Glasgow, Strathclyde G3 8UF
Telephone: 041-221 8188   £65
Open: lunch Mon-Fri, dinner Mon-Sat (closed Bank Holidays)
Last orders: lunch 2.30pm, dinner 10.00pm

Some minor changes: the lighting is now brighter. Otherwise, the
building site location is the same, as are the gloriously Victorian bar
and the style of service: a white glove for changing cutlery and
'Gentlemen, lunch is served' as the silver domes are lifted. Chef
Stephen Johnstone is quite happy to use simple ingredients: bacon
and tuna mixed with fresh salad leaves and a powerful dressing;
stir-fried lamb's liver and sweetbreads. The wine list includes good
house wine. Still *the* place for lunch.

GLASGOW   October Restaurant

128 Drymen Road, Bearsden, Glasgow, Strathclyde G61 3RB
Telephone: 041-942 7272   *Fax:* 041-942 9650   **£60**
Open: lunch daily, dinner Mon-Sat (closed Bank Holidays, Easter, 2 wks Aug)
Last orders: lunch 2.00pm, dinner 10.00pm (Sat 10.30pm)

Changing contemporary Scottish art on the walls, polished mirrors
and vivid blue seating and carpet provide a modern setting for Ferrier
Richardson's excellent food. A recent lunch was typical of the quality:
terrine of rabbit and vegetables, pine nuts and pesto dressing; a
sparkling fresh supreme of wild salmon on a crunchy leek sauce;
chocolate and coffee mousse, espresso crème anglaise. The menu is
backed up by a well-chosen wine list.

GLASGOW   One Devonshire Gardens

See page 220 – our Clover Award Section.

GLASGOW   Ubiquitous Chip

12 Ashton Lane, Glasgow, Strathclyde G12 8SJ
Telephone: 041-334 5007   *Fax:* 041-337 1302   **£50**
Open: lunch + dinner daily (closed Christmas + New Year)
Last orders: lunch 2.30pm, dinner 11.00pm

The Chip comes of age in 1992 but chef/patron Ron Clydesdale says
he doesn't envisage changing much: granny's cooking is 'in'! (Why
was it ever 'out'?) The glassed-in cobbled courtyard, resplendent
with plants and furnished with simple wooden tables, remains a must
in Glasgow. Try a Western Isles lobster salad or perhaps some
Perthshire grouse. The wine list is taken from Ron's adjacent wine
shop, so it's worth perusing the extensive choice.

GULLANE   Greywalls

Muirfield, Gullane, Lothian EH31 2EG
Telephone: (0620) 842144   *Fax:* (0620) 842241   **£65**
Open: lunch + dinner daily (closed Jan – Feb)
Last orders: lunch 2.00pm, dinner 9.00pm

A popular place with golfers who, like the original owner, wish to be
within sight of the Muirfield golf course. The house itself is the only
Scottish example of Sir Edward Lutyen's work; the gardens were
designed by Gertrude Jekyll. Bright, airy and comfortable rooms
furnished in traditional style. New chef Paul Baron cooks skilfully,
always with an eye to the golfing clientele: parfait of chicken livers
with toasted brioche; loin of venison on a celeriac galette and truffle
sauce (the 4-course fixed price menu is £27.00). An exceptional wine
list.

GULLANE   La Potinière

See page 222 – our Clover Award Section.

INVERNESS   Bunchrew House Hotel

Inverness, Highland IV3 6TA
Telephone: (0463) 234917   **£50**
Open: lunch + dinner daily
Last orders: lunch 2.00pm, dinner 9.00pm

Guests arriving by train or plane are picked up in a Rolls Royce. At the house (a 17th-century mansion located on Beauly Firth), a genuinely warm welcome awaits and its comfortable interior combines modernity with period features. A limited choice 4-course dinner menu might include a good leek and potato soup, and poached salmon. The Wilsons are caring, attentive hosts and provide professional, charming service. A further seven rooms will be added in 1991 and a boat is available to cruise the nearby Firth.

ISLE OF SKYE   Kinloch Lodge

Sleat, Isle of Skye, Highland IV43 8QY
Telephone: (047 13) 214   **£70**
Open: dinner daily (closed Dec – Feb)
Last orders: dinner 8.00pm

Lord and Lady Macdonald's home, a 17th-century former farmhouse, has a relaxed, comfortable, homely feel – not at all what one might expect. The dramatic beauty of the Isle of Skye and Lady Macdonald's cooking (assisted by Peter Macpherson) complete the appeal. Local organic produce is the basis of the good home cooking, with wines the domain of Lord Macdonald.

ISLE OF SKYE   Three Chimneys Restaurant

Colbost, Dunvegan, Isle of Skye, Highland IV55 8ZT
Telephone: (047 081) 258   **£50**
Open: lunch + dinner, Mon-Sat (closed Nov – Mar)
Last orders: lunch 2.00pm, dinner 9.00pm

In a remote corner of Skye, by Loch Dunvegan, this old crofter's cottage is a cosy restaurant with its low beamed ceilings and stone walls. Meals are leisurely – dinner may last 3 hours! (No rooms but B&B's will be recommended.) Ample portions of homely cooking: Dunvegan lobster salad; mountain hare with prunes and cognac; superb hot marmalade pudding with whipped cream. Well-kept Scottish cheeses.

ISLE OF MULL	Tiroran House

Isle of Mull, Strathclyde PA69 6ES
Telephone: (068 15) 232   **£60**
Open: lunch (residents only) + dinner daily (closed Oct – May)
Last orders: dinner 7.45pm

The Blockleys' home in a former shooting lodge in 15 acres of woods and gardens – is well decorated and comfortable. There's an abundance of flowers, pictures, and books for rainy days. Rooms (those in the main house are best) provide a warm towel rail, decent sized soap, half a bottle of white wine and a little cheese and biscuits. Robin hosts the house party-style dinners cooked by Sue. With a fixed main course and choice of starters, dinner might be leek and stilton soup then roast lamb. Good cheeses and a short reasonable wine list.

KENTALLEN	Ardsheal House Hotel

Kentallen, Nr Appin, Highland PA38 4BX
Telephone: (063 174) 227   **£70**
Open: lunch + dinner daily (closed Nov to Easter)
Last orders: lunch 2.00pm, dinner 8.15pm

A rough 1½ mile drive leads to the lovely loch-side location. Bob and Jane Taylor are caring hosts, combining Scottish tradition with American relaxedness. Open fires, antiques and easy chairs in the day rooms. Quiet comfort in the bedrooms (no TV or phone). Drinks in a tiny panelled bar then dinner: terrine of sole and sea trout; game consommé; pan-fried scallops; salad with stilton; brandied apricot crêpes (£28 for five courses and coffee with petits fours). Good wines accompany an unhurried meal. Stunning views over Loch Linnhe.

Ardsheal House

KILCHRENAN   Ardanaiseig Hotel

Kilchrenan, Loch Awe, Strathclyde PA35 1HE
Telephone: (086 63) 333   *Fax:* (086 63) 222   **£70**
Open: lunch + dinner daily (closed Nov – mid-Apr)
Last orders: lunch 2.00pm, dinner 9.00pm

A beautifully decorated house surrounded by rhododendrons, by Loch Awe. Jonathan and Jan Brown continue to improve standards here; latterly, bathrooms have been refurbished. Overall, comfortable with the feel of a private house. Diners in the warmly elegant dining room enjoy views of the loch whilst sampling dishes such as chicken liver parfait with Cumberland sauce and lamb cutlets with tarragon mousse. The new chef, Martin Vincent, has brought new zest to the well-presented food, and service is friendly.

KILCHRENAN   Taychreggan Hotel

Kilchrenan, Nr Taynuilt, Strathclyde PA35 1HE
Telephone: (086 63) 211   **£55**
Open: lunch (bar only) + dinner daily (closed end Oct to one wk before
     Easter)
Last orders: dinner 9.15pm

The setting by Loch Awe is beautiful and chef Gail Struthers' food is as good as ever. The quality of her raw materials is evident. The 5-course dinner menus offer limited choices such as grilled whole sea bream with pepper and tomato sauces, or pan fried chicken supreme with lemon and tarragon sauce. Well-kept cheeses and good fresh puddings. New owners, the Tyrells, appear to be settling well into this whitewashed former drovers' inn.

KINGUSSIE   The Cross

See page 223 – our Clover Award Section.

LINLITHGOW   Champanay Inn

See page 224 – our Clover Award Section.

MUIR-OF-ORD   The Dower House

Highfield, Muir-of-Ord, Highland IV6 7NX
Telephone: (0463) 870090   **£55**
Open: lunch (by arrangement only) + dinner daily (closed Christmas Day,
    2 wks March, 1 wk October)
Last orders: dinner 8.30pm

Chintz furniture, decorative plates and flowers add up to a cottagey
effect. Five comfortable rooms with Victorian-style bathrooms and
large, warm towels. A sofa and chairs add to the warmth of the red
dining room with its polished tables. Food is simple but flavours and
presentation are good. Good soups; baked halibut with a mustard
sauce; breast of duck with a caramel sauce. Excellent local
vegetables. The wine list includes a wide range of half bottles.

NAIRN   Clifton House

Viewfield Street, Nairn, Highland, IV12 4HW
Telephone: (0667) 53119   *Fax:* (0667) 52836   **£50**
Open: lunch + dinner daily (closed Dec – Feb)
Last orders: lunch 1.00pm, dinner 9.30pm

An idiosyncratic hotel run along highly personal lines since 1952 by
Gordon MacIntyre. Classical music fills the air; an open fire blazes in
the drawing room filled with antiques, paintings, cushions, books and
objets d'art. Sixteen rooms of character. MacIntyre is a charming
host with discreetly attentive staff. Simply presented good food such
as smoked trout mousse with tabbouleh; fresh scallops in creamy
white wine sauce; delicious crème brûlée. The sounds of opera may
accompany dinner and, in winter, plays and concerts are staged here.

NEWTOWNMORE   Ard-na-Coille Hotel

Kingussie Road, Newtownmore, Highland PH20 1AY
Telephone: (054 03) 214   *Fax:* (054 03) 543   **£50**
Open: dinner daily (closed mid-Nov to late Dec)
Last orders: dinner 7.45pm

A former shooting lodge run by Nancy Ferrier and Barry Cottam.
Seven en-suite rooms have good furnishings and tasteful decor. The
small dining room looks out over the Spey Valley. Self taught (his
friends include David Wilson at Peat Inn and the Hadleys at the
Cross), Barry Cottam cooks a 4-course no-choice dinner. Good
materials are well handled: breast of wild duck with a cassis sauce;
saddle of venison with port and blueberry sauce; warm apricot tart or
crème brûlée for dessert. Take time before dinner to study the
up-graded extensive wine list including ten by the glass.

NORTH BERWICK   Harding's Restaurant

---

2 Station Road, North Berwick, Lothian EH39 4AU
Telephone: (0620) 4737   **£40**
Open: lunch + dinner, Wed-Sat (closed 1 wk Christmas, 4 wks Jan/Feb,
      1 wk Oct)
Last orders: lunch 2.00pm, dinner 9.00pm

Christopher Harding's small restaurant is proving to be a real asset in
the area. Local produce is the basis of the short lunch menu and daily
set dinner menus: pheasant terrine; soups; chicken with rosemary
and madeira sauce; sautéed hare with sherry and green peppercorn
sauce. The wine list is an excellent selection of Australian and New
Zealand wines with a few French. (Harding is Australian.) Also open
for morning coffee.

OBAN   Isle of Eriska Hotel

Ledaig, Oban, Strathclyde PA37 1SD
Telephone: (063 172) 371   *Fax:* (063 172) 531   **£70**
Open: lunch (snacks only), dinner daily (closed Nov – mid-Mar)
Last orders: dinner 9.00pm

The Buchanan-Smiths describe their home as an island sanctuary –
for seabirds, seals, and humans who relish the splendour and
tranquillity of the landscape. The baronial mansion is a proper
country house with comfortable, well equipped rooms, a knowledgeable host and attentive, if sometimes slightly formal, staff. A lovely
Edwardian dining room with silver, crystal and Wedgwood china.
Milk, eggs and vegetables are home-produced and feature in the
traditional cooking. Dinner centres on a trolley-carved roast.
Children are welcome.

OLD MELDRUM   Meldrum House Hotel

Old Meldrum, Grampian AB5 0AE
Telephone: (065 12) 2294   *Sadly, Duff 1990*   **£55**
                               Robin died in
Open: dinner daily (closed mid-Dec to mid-Mar)
Last orders: dinner 9.00pm (8.00pm Sun)

Meldrum has the authenticity of a genuine country house: it has been
home to the Duff family for 700 years. The feeling is reinforced by
family portraits and photos in the drawing room. Bedrooms are warm
and spacious as in a private country house, with good old-fashioned
bathrooms. Breakfast in bed at no extra charge. Daily menus feature
ample portions of straightforward food: well made soups; braised
venison; poached salmon. Well-trained staff.

PEAT INN   Peat Inn

See page 225 – our Clover Award Section.

PORT APPIN   The Airds Hotel

Port Appin, Appin, Strathclyde PA38 4DF
Telephone: (063 173) 236   **£75**
Open: lunch + dinner daily (closed mid-Nov to mid-Mar)
Last orders: lunch 2.00pm, dinner 8.30pm

The Allens seem to have set themselves a high standard and succeed in keeping to it – a consistency that has earned them membership of the Relais & Chateaux group. Behind the modest, whitewashed façade of the former 17th-century drovers' inn is a hotel of understated luxury. Diners enjoy spectacular views over Loch Linnhe, and Betty Allen's good cooking. Scale and location mean just one sitting. The emphasis is on mousses, roasts, poached fish and good saucing: saddle of hare with a port and thyme sauce; mousseline of scallops. Good coffee comes with home-made fudge. Bordeaux and burgundy feature strongly on an excellent wine list.

PORTPATRICK   Knockinaam Lodge

Portpatrick, Dumfries & Galloway DG9 9AD
Telephone: (077 681) 471   *Fax:* (077 681) 435   **£65**
Open: lunch + dinner daily (closed 4 Jan – 15 Mar)
Last orders: lunch 2.00pm, dinner 9.00pm

Tucked away in a remote corner of south-west Scotland, reaching this small hotel is quite a trek, but well worth it. A welcoming handshake, bags carried to your room, queries answered with confidence are typical of the attentive service. The house feels lived in, with lovely old clocks, elegant displays of china, tartan covered chairs, and charmingly comfortable, warm rooms. An elegant dining room with immaculate napery and silver. Marcel Frichot discusses the menu and wines knowledgeably. Daniel Galmiche's cooking is very sound: terrine de foie gras; noisettes de lotte aux épices et filaments de citron au sel; tarte tartin. Cheeses from Philippe Olivier, and a sophisticated French wine list.

SCONE	The Murrayshall

Scone, Perthshire PH2 7PH
Telephone: (0738) 51171 *Fax:* (0738) 52595   **£65**
Open: lunch Sun, dinner daily
Last orders: lunch 2.00pm, dinner 9.30pm

It is a tribute to the overall excellence of Murrayshall's kitchen that a meal in the Old Masters Restaurant on Bruce Sangster's day off proved well worthy of him. A fillet of sole poached to perfection in white wine, and served with a lobster and ginger sauce was the main star in an altogether excellent meal. Canapés (two lots), bread, vegetables and coffee all first class; house wine also good. Relaxed but professional service in this soothing dining room hung with Dutch 16th- and 17th-century oil paintings, where a harpist or pianist plays nightly. Other popular menu choices have been chilled sausage of smoked Tay salmon served on a cucumber, dill and caviar dressing, an unusual soup of prawns perfumed with saffron and a hint of curry, a toast of brioche crowned with creamy scrambled eggs, centred with kidneys and bordered with a port wine sauce, noisettes of local venison served with home-made pasta ribbons. A favourite pudding is the 'orgy of confections created by the Pastry Chef'! The Cellarbook has strength, depth and moderate prices.

STEWARTON	Chapeltoun House Hotel

Stewarton, Strathclyde KA3 3ED
Telephone: (0560) 82696 *Fax:* (0560) 85100   **£60**
Open: lunch + dinner daily (closed 1 wk Jan)
Last orders: lunch 2.00pm, dinner 9.15pm (9.00pm Sun)

A solid, white-painted house, with a sombre traditional interior: lots of dark wood and earth colours. The food is by contrast light and modern with chef Kevin MacGillivray producing some well executed combinations: coddled egg with fennel, topped with creamed spinach; moist breast of chicken run through with a strip of spinach, served on creamed leeks with braised rice. Well trained staff.

ULLAPOOL	Altnaharrie Inn

See page 226 – our Clover Award Section.

ULLAPOOL	The Ceilidh Place

West Argyle Street, Ullapool, Ross & Cromarty IV25 2TY
Telephone: (0854) 2103   *Fax:* (0854) 2886   **£40**
Open: lunch + dinner daily (closed 2 wks Jan)
Last orders: lunch 5.00pm, dinner 9.00pm

For anyone interested in the arts, the Ceilidh, (literally 'Meeting Place') is worth a visit. There are fifteen pretty bedrooms, and reading and writing rooms in which to exchange or jot down ideas! A wide range of events from jazz to Scottish folk singing is staged in the auditorium and there's also a gallery and bookshop. Eat in the café or the restaurant: wild salmon; fresh seafood; steaks and vegetarian dishes simply prepared.

WHITEBRIDGE	Knockie Lodge

Whitebridge, Highland IV1 2UP
Telephone: (045 63) 276   *Fax:* (045 63) 389   **£50**
Open: dinner daily (closed Nov – Apr)
Last orders: dinner 8.00pm

Despite its tranquil setting on a hillside above Loch Nan Lann, Knockie Lodge is easily accessible from Inverness, just twenty-five miles away. Guests walk, sail or fish then return for a candle-lit 5-course set dinner of homely, accurately cooked food centred on a traditional roast. Peace is the by-word here, so there are no TVs or radios in the bedrooms which are neatly furnished, with some antiques.

Scotland Listings

ABERDEEN
Silver Darling
Pocra Quay, Footdee, Aberdeen,
 Grampian AB2 1DQ
Tel: (0224) 576229 **£55**
Open: lunch Mon-Fri, dinner Mon-Sat (closed Bank
 Holidays, 2 wks Christmas)
Last orders: lunch 2.00pm, dinner 10.00pm
French restaurant in former customs
house; fish a speciality.

ABOYNE
Hazlehurst Lodge
Ballater Road, Aboyne, Grampian AB34 5HY
Tel: (033 98) 86921 **£45**
Open: lunch Sun, dinner daily (closed Jan)
Last orders: lunch 2.00pm, dinner 9.00pm
Original food using good, local produce.
Shooting and fishing can be arranged on
request.

ALFORD
Kildrummy Castle Hotel
Kildrummy, Alford, Grampian AB3 8RA
Tel: (097 55) 71288 *Fax:* (097 55) 71345 **£50**
Open: lunch + dinner daily (closed Jan + Feb)
Last orders: lunch 1.45pm (1.15pm Sun), dinner
 9.00pm
Grand country house overlooking castle
ruins. Comfortable, elegant rooms.

ALLOWAY
Burns Byre Restaurant
Mount Oliphant Farm, Alloway,
 Strathclyde KA6 6BU
Tel: (0292) 43644 **£35**
Open: lunch Tue-Sun, dinner Tue-Sat (closed 2
 wks Feb, 2 wks Nov)
Last orders: lunch 2.00pm, dinner 9.30pm
 (10.00pm Sat)
Former cattle byre now a restaurant, situ-
ated within a still-working farm.

AUCHMITHIE
The But 'n' Ben
Auchmithie, by Arbroath, Tayside DD11 5SQ
Tel: (0241) 77223 **£50**
Open: lunch Wed-Mon, dinner Wed-Sat + Mon
Last orders: lunch 2.30pm, dinner 9.30pm
Fresh fish and home made baking are the
specialities at this former fisherman's
cottage.

AUCHTERARDER
Cairn Lodge
Orchil Road, Auchterarder, Tayside PH3 1LX
Tel: (0764) 62634 **£50**
Open: lunch + dinner, daily (closed 2 wks Jan/Feb)
Last orders: lunch 2.00pm, dinner 9.30pm
Elegant country house with five bedrooms.

AUCHTERHOUSE
The Old Mansion House Hotel
Auchterhouse, By Dundee, Tayside DD3 0QN
Tel: (082 626) 366 *Fax:* (082 626) 400 **£50**
Open: lunch + dinner daily (closed Christmas Day
 + Boxing Day, 1 wk Jan)
Last orders: lunch 2.00pm, dinner 9.15pm (8.45pm
 Sun)
Baronial house, splendid views, six com-
fortable bedrooms, welcoming service.

AYR
Fouters Bistro
2a Academy Street, Ayr, Strathclyde KA7 1HS
Tel: (0292) 261391 **£50**
Open: lunch Tue-Sun, dinner Tue-Sat (closed
 Christmas + New Year)
Last orders: lunch 2.00pm, dinner 10.30pm
Small, friendly bistro in a cellar, brasserie
style food.

BALLATER
Craigendarroch Hotel & Country Club
The Oaks Restaurant, Braemar Road, Ballater,
 Grampian AB3 5XA
Tel: (0338) 55858 **£50**
Open: lunch + dinner daily
Last orders: lunch 2.15pm, dinner 10.00pm
Leisure centre and all manner of other
sports facilities. Fifty bedrooms. Oaks
Restaurant serves modern cooking.

BELLOCHANTUY
Putechan Lodge Hotel
Bellochantuy, By Campbeltown,
 Strathclyde PA35 6QE
Tel: (058 32) 323 **£30**
Open: lunch + dinner daily (closed Jan + Feb)
Last orders: lunch 3.00pm, dinner 9.00pm
Local produce is used in simple, well
presented dishes.

BIGGAR
Shieldhill
Quothquan, Biggar, Strathclyde ML12 6NA
Tel: (0899) 20035 *Fax:* (0899) 21092 **£60**
Open: lunch + dinner daily (closed Christmas to 1
 Mar)
Last orders: lunch 2.30pm, dinner 9.30pm
Elegant rooms, named after Scottish bat-
tles, in what was originally a Norman
keep, set in its own grounds.

BLAIR DRUMMOND
Broughton's Restaurant
Blair Drummond, Central FK9 4XE
Tel: (0786) 841897 **£45**
Open: lunch Tue-Sun, dinner Tue-Sat (closed 4
 wks Jan/Feb, 2 wks Mar)
Last orders: lunch 2.00pm, dinner 10.00pm
Little cottage restaurant, meals are cooked
with home grown vegetables and herbs.

BRIDGE OF ALLAN
Kipling's
Mine Road, Bridge of Allan, Central FK9 4DT
Tel: (0786) 833617 **£35**
Open: lunch + dinner Tue-Sat (closed Bank
　Holidays except Good Friday, 2 wks Christmas)
Last orders: lunch 2.00pm, dinner 9.00pm
Popular local restaurant, daily changing
　menus. Chef/patron Peter Bannister.

CAIRNDOW
Loch Fyne Oyster Bar
Clachan Farm, Cairndow, Strathclyde PA26 8BH
Tel: (049 96) 264　*Fax:* (049 96) 234 **£35**
Open: all day, daily (closed 2 wks Feb)
Last orders: 9.00pm
Fresh fish and fabulous views, simple
　setting.

CARRBRIDGE
The Ecclefechan Bistro
10 Main Street, Carrbridge, Highland PH23 3AJ
Tel: (047 984) 374 **£25**
Open: lunch + dinner Wed-Mon (closed 3 wks
　Nov)
Last orders: lunch 4.00pm, dinner 9.45pm
Classic bistro cooking.

CONTIN
Coul House Hotel
Contin, By Strathpeffer, Highland IV14 9EY
Tel: (0997) 21487　*Fax:* (0997) 21945 **£35**
Open: lunch + dinner daily
Last orders: lunch 2.00pm, dinner 9.00pm
Friendly staff and blazing fires add to the
　warmth of the atmosphere at this unique
　twenty-one bedroomed hotel.

CRIEFF
Cultoquhey House Hotel
Crieff, Tayside
Tel: (0764) 3253 **£40**
Open: lunch (snack only) + dinner daily
Last orders: dinner 9.00pm
Warm welcome, homely atmosphere, short
　menu of three choices at each course.

CROMARTY
Thistles
20 Church Street, Cromarty, Highland IV11 8XA
Tel: (038 17) 471 **£50**
Open: lunch Tue-Sun, dinner Tue-Sat (closed 2 dys
　Christmas, 2 dys New Year)
Last orders: lunch 2.00pm, dinner 9.00pm
Former pub now a bar and restaurant.
　Short menu with four choices at each
　course.

DULNAIN BRIDGE
Auchendean Lodge
Dulnain Bridge, Highland PH26 3LU
Tel: (047 985) 347 **£35**
Open: dinner daily (closed Nov to mid-Dec)
Last orders: dinner 9.00pm
Edwardian hunting lodge, well equipped to
　cope with outdoor, wet-weather pur-
　suits. Honest, substantial cooking. Seven
　bedrooms.

DUNKELD
Dunkeld House Hotel
Dunkeld, Tayside PH8 0HX
Tel: (035 02) 771 **£50**
Open: lunch + dinner daily
Last orders: lunch 2.30pm, dinner 10.00pm
Impressive entrance through arched gate-
　way up a long drive with the Tay river
　flowing alongside. Food is interesting and
　well presented.

EAGLESFIELD
The Courtyard Restaurant
Eaglesfield, by Lockerbie, Dumfries,
　Dumfries & Galloway DG11 3PQ
Tel: (046 15) 215 **£30**
Open: lunch + dinner Tue-Sun (bar meals only
　Sun)
Last orders: lunch 2.00pm, dinner 9.00pm
Twenty-eight seater restaurant with four
　bedrooms. Fresh local produce used with
　emphasis on simplicity and good pre-
　sentation.

EASSIE
Castleton House Hotel
Eassie, By Glamis, Forfar, Tayside DD8 1SJ
Tel: (030 784) 340　*Fax:* (030 784) 506 **£45**
Open: lunch + dinner daily
Last orders: lunch 2.30pm, dinner 9.30pm
Small Victorian hotel, six bedrooms, com-
　fortable public rooms. Kitchen produce is
　local, some from hotel gardens.

EDINBURGH
The Alp Horn Restaurant
167 Rose Street, Edinburgh, Lothian EH2 4LS
Tel: 031-225 4787 **£40**
Open: lunch + dinner Mon-Sat (closed local Bank
　Holidays, 2 wks Jan, 2 wks Jul)
Last orders: lunch 2.00pm, dinner 10.00pm
Down-to-earth Swiss restaurant, excellent
　rösti.

Beehive Inn
18 Grassmarket, Edinburgh, Lothian EH1 2JU
Tel: 031-225 7171 **£65**
Open: lunch Mon-Fri, dinner Mon-Sat (closed 2 dys
　Christmas, 2 dys New Year)
Last orders: lunch 2.00pm, dinner 10.00pm
Inn in the heart of the old town dating back
　to the 16th Century.

Café Royal Oyster Bar
17 West Register Street, Edinburgh,
　Lothian EH2 2AA
Tel: 031-556 4124 **£60**
Open: lunch + dinner daily
Last orders: lunch 1.45pm (2.15pm Sun), dinner
　10.15pm
Original turn-of-the-century decor, mainly
　seafood dishes with a few choices of
　game.

Denzlers 121
121 Constitution Street, Leith, Edinburgh,
　Lothian EH6 7AE
Tel: 031-554 3268 **£35**
Open: lunch Tue-Fri, dinner Tue-Sat (closed
　Christmas, New Year, 1 wk Jan)
Last orders: lunch 2.00pm, dinner 10.00pm
Good Swiss cooking.

The Howard Hotel
Number 36 Restaurant, 36 Great King Street,
Edinburgh, Lothian EH3 6QH
Tel: 031-557 3500   *Fax:* 031-557 6515   **£70**
Open: lunch Sun-Fri, dinner daily (closed
Christmas + New Year)
Last orders: lunch 2.00pm, dinner 10.00pm
Three inter-connecting town houses dating
from 18th Century. Sixteen comfortable
en-suite bedrooms.

The Indian Cavalry Club
3 Atholl Place, Edinburgh, Lothian EH3 8HP
Tel: 031-228 3282   **£50**
Open: lunch + dinner daily
Last orders: lunch 2.00pm, dinner 11.30pm
Staff dressed in military-style uniforms,
there are some unusual dishes on the
menu.

Kelly's
46 West Richmond Street, Edinburgh,
Lothian EH8 9DZ
Tel: 031-668 3847   **£45**
Open: lunch Tue-Fri, dinner Tue-Sat
Last orders: lunch 2.00pm, dinner 9.45pm
Good local restaurant with a short set price
menu.

McKirdy's
43 Assembly Street, Edinburgh, Lothian
Tel: 031-553 6363   **£40**
Open: lunch Tue-Fri + Sun, dinner Tue-Sun
(closed Christmas)
Last orders: lunch 3.00pm, dinner 11.00pm
Bar and restaurant specialising in fresh
seafood but also offers a good meat
selection.

Merchants Restaurant
17 Merchant Street, Edinburgh, Lothian EH1 2QD
Tel: 031-225 4009   **£55**
Open: lunch + dinner Mon-Sat (closed 2 dys
Christmas, 2 dys New Year)
Last orders: lunch 2.00pm, dinner 10.00pm
Traditional and modern French dishes with
the menu changing daily.

Negociants
45-47 Lothian Street, Edinburgh,
Lothian EH1 1HB
Tel: 031-225 6313   **£20**
Open: lunch + dinner daily
Last orders: lunch 5.30pm, dinner 11.30pm
Student haunt in the heart of the university
area.

Pierre Victoire
Grassmarket, Edinburgh, Lothian
Tel: 031-226 2442   **£30**
Open: lunch + dinner Mon-Sat
Last orders: lunch 3.00pm, dinner 11.00pm
Pierre Levicky's second Edinburgh outlet.

Sheraton Hotel
1 Festival Square, Edinburgh, Lothian EH3 9SR
Tel: 031-229 9131   **£55**
Open: lunch + dinner daily
Last orders: lunch 2.30pm, dinner 10.30pm
Modern hotel near Edinburgh castle, facili-
ties on offer include a health and leisure
club.

Skippers Bistro
1a Dock Place, Leith, Edinburgh,
Lothian EH6 6UY
Tel: 031-554 1018   **£40**
Open: lunch + dinner Mon-Sat (closed 1 wk
Christmas/New Year)
Last orders: lunch 2.00pm, dinner 10.00pm
Unfussy food, mainly fish, using good
ingredients with great attention paid to
flavours.

La Vinothèque
2-6 Bonnington Road Lane, Edinburgh,
Lothian EH6 5BJ
Tel: 031-554 9113   **£40**
Open: lunch + dinner Mon-Fri (closed Bank
Holidays, 2 wks Jul)
Last orders: lunch 2.30pm, dinner 10.00pm
Simple classic French food, good atmos-
phere for a party.

The Witchery by the Castle
352 Castle Hill, Royal Mile, Edinburgh,
Lothian EH1 1NE
Tel: 031-225 5613   *Fax:* 031-220 4392   **£45**
Open: all day, daily
Last orders: 11.00pm
Wide range of local and international dishes
served in an unpretentious fashion. Proprietor James Thomson takes special pride
in his wine list. Pre- and post-theatre
meals, regular vegetarian dishes.

ELIE
Bouquet Garni Restaurant
51 High Street, Elie, Fife KY9 1BZ
Tel: (0333) 330374   **£40**
Open: dinner Tue-Sat (closed 1 wk Feb, 1 wk Nov)
Last orders: dinner 9.30pm
Family-run cottage restaurant; fish a
speciality.

FALKLAND
Kind Kyttock's Kitchen
Cross Wynd, Falkland, Fife KY7 7BE
Tel: (0337) 57477   **£20**
Open: lunch daily (closed Christmas + New Year)
Last orders: lunch 5.30pm
Traditional homecooking using fresh, local
ingredients.

FIFE
St Andrews Old Course Hotel
Fife, Fife KY16 9SP
Tel: (0334) 74371   *Fax:* (0344) 77668   **£50**
Open: lunch + dinner daily (closed 26-28 Dec)
Last orders: lunch 2.30pm, dinner 10.00pm
125-roomed hotel on the links. Spacious
rooms, marble bathrooms. Golf and other
sports available.

FORT WILLIAM
The Factor's House
Torlundy, Fort William, Highland PH33 6SN
Tel: (0397) 5767   *Fax:* (0397) 2953   **£40**
Open: dinner daily (residents only Mon) (closed
mid-Dec to mid-Mar)
Last orders: dinner 9.00pm
Peter Hobbs' restaurant with rooms in the
grounds of Inverlochy Castle. Whole-
some cooking.

GLASGOW
Bon Chic Bon Genre BCBG
21-29 Ashton Lane, Glasgow, Strathclyde G12 8SJ
Tel: 041-357 4557 **£50**
Open: lunch + dinner daily
Last orders: lunch 3.00pm, dinner 11.00pm
Popular meeting place, live music some nights, good international food.

Brasserie of West Regent Street
176 West Regent Street, Glasgow,
  Strathclyde G2 4RL
Tel: 041-647 5839/248 3801 **£35**
Open: all day Mon-Sat (closed Bank Holidays)
Last orders: 11.00pm (midnight Sat)
Part of the Rogano group. Regency wallpaper, tartan carpet! Good for after-theatre suppers.

The North Rotunda
28 Tunnel Street, Stobcross Quay, Glasgow,
  Strathclyde G3 8HL
Tel: 041-204 1238 *Fax:* 041-226 4264 **£45**
Open: lunch Mon-Fri, dinner Mon-Sat (closed Bank Holidays)
Last orders: lunch 2.30pm, dinner 11.00pm
Complex of two bars and two restaurants. Seasonal local produce used in traditional and modern dishes.

Penguin Café
Princes Square, Off Buchanan Street, Glasgow,
  Strathclyde G1 3JN
Tel: 041-221 0303 **£35**
Open: all day, Mon-Sat
Last orders: 11.00pm
Good modern style bar and brasserie on fourth floor of a busy shopping mall.

Rab Ha's
83 Hutcheson Street, Glasgow,
  Strathclyde G1 1SH
Tel: 041-553 1545 **£50**
Open: lunch Mon-Fri, dinner Mon-Sat (closed New Year's Day)
Last orders: lunch 3.00pm, dinner 11.00pm
Breakfast served in the bar, restaurant in the basement, oyster bar open all day.

Ristorante Caprese
217 Buchanan Street, Glasgow, Strathclyde
Tel: 041-332 3070 **£40**
Open: lunch + dinner Mon-Sat (closed Bank Holidays)
Last orders: lunch 2.15pm, dinner 11.00pm
Good traditional Italian restaurant.

The Rogano
11 Exchange Place, Glasgow, Strathclyde G1 3AN
Tel: 041-248 4055 *Fax:* 041-248 2608 **£55**
Open: lunch + dinner Mon-Sat (closed Bank Holidays) (café open all day, daily)
Last orders: lunch 2.30pm, dinner 10.30pm
Virtually unchanged since 1935, Art Deco ground floor restaurant, basement café. Fish a strong point.

The Triangle
37 Queen Street, Glasgow, Strathclyde G1 3EF
Tel: 041-221 8758 *Fax:* 041-204 3189 **£50**
Open: lunch Mon-Sat (closed Scottish Bank Holidays)
Last orders: lunch 3.00pm, dinner 11.00pm
New owner and chef: bar, brasserie and restaurant; modern food and decor.

Two Fat Ladies
88 Dumbarton Road, Glasgow,
  Strathclyde G11 6NX
Tel: 041-339 1944 **£45**
Open: dinner Tue-Sat (closed Jan)
Last orders: dinner 10.30pm
Plain yellow dining room in two sections, open kitchen, simply cooked fresh seafood.

GOLLANFIELD
Culloden Pottery
The Old Smiddy, Gollanfield, Nr Inverness,
  Highland IV1 2QT
Tel: (0667) 62749 **£15**
Open: all day, daily (closed 10 dys Christmas/New Year)
Last orders: 4.30pm
Small, family-run vegetarian restaurant, menu changes daily.

HADDINGTON
Browns Hotel
1 West Road, Haddington, Lothian EH41 3RD
Tel: (062 082) 2254 **£50**
Open: lunch Sun-Fri by arrangement, dinner daily
Last orders: lunch 2.00pm, dinner 9.00pm (8.00pm Sun)
Smartly decorated hotel with comfortable public rooms. Short menu of mainly classic cooking.

HAWICK
Le Rendezvous
Loughlan Centre, Wilton Path, Hawick, Borders
Tel: (0450) 76653 **£30**
Open: lunch + dinner Mon-Sat (closed Christmas + New Year)
Last orders: lunch 3.00pm, dinner 10.00pm
Informal bistro, international menu with good home-made puddings.

INVERNESS
Culloden House Hotel
Culloden, Inverness, Highland IV1 2NZ
Tel: (0463) 790461 *Fax:* (0463) 792181 **£65**
Open: lunch + dinner daily
Last orders: lunch 2.00pm, dinner 9.00pm
Palladian Georgian mansion of grand proportions, antiques, portrait of Prince Charles Stuart. Restaurant is the Adam Room. Friendly service.

Dunain Park
Inverness, Highland IV3 6JN
Tel: (0463) 230512 **£45**
Open: dinner daily (closed Christmas Day, 1 wk Feb, 1 wk Nov)
Last orders: dinner 9.00pm
Twelve rooms including six luxury suites. Marble bathrooms, private house feeling. Extensive gardens provide much produce for kitchen.

Pierre Victoire
75 Castle Street, Inverness, Highland IV2 3EA
Tel: (0463) 225662   *Fax:* (0463) 713169   **£30**
Open: lunch + dinner Mon-Sat
Last orders: lunch 3.00pm, dinner midnight
   (11.30pm)
Inverness branch of Pierre Levicky's
French restaurants.

ISLE OF IONA
Argyll Hotel
Isle of Iona, Strathclyde PA76 6SJ
Tel: (068 17) 334   **£30**
Open: lunch + dinner daily (closed Oct to Easter)
Last orders: lunch 1.30pm, dinner 7.00pm
Originally built as an inn in 1868 the front
   lawn runs down to the sea. Good home
   cooking.

ISLE OF ISLAY
The Croft Kitchen
Port Charlotte, Isle of Islay,
   Strathclyde PA48 7UD
Tel: (049 685) 208   **£20**
Open: all day daily (closed Oct-Mar)
Last orders: 6.30pm (Sun 7.00pm)
Converted cowshed now a small restaurant
   specialising in baking and fresh organic
   produce.

Kilchoman House & Restaurant
By Bruichladdich, Isle of Islay,
   Strathclyde PA49 7UY
Tel: (049 685) 382   **£30**
Open: dinner Tue-Sat (closed Oct-Dec)
Last orders: 9.30pm
Good home cooking using local ingredients,
   well presented.

Machrie Hotel
Port Ellen, Isle of Islay,
   Strathclyde PA42 7AN
Tel: (0496) 2310   **£35**
Open: lunch + dinner daily
Last orders: lunch 2.00pm, dinner 7.00pm
Smart friendly staff. Close to airport and
   ferry. Own golf course.

ISLE OF LEWIS
Ardvourlie Castle
Aird A Mhulaihd, Isle of Lewis,
   Western Isles PA85 3AB
Tel: (0859) 2307   **£40**
Open: dinner by arrangement
Last orders: dinner by arrangement
Victorian hunting lodge, restored to the
   period with gas and oil lights in the public
   rooms. Relaxed, informal atmosphere.

Baile-Na-Cille
Timsgarry, Uig, Isle of Lewis,
   Western Isles PA86 9JD
Tel: (085 175) 242   **£40**
Open: lunch + dinner daily (closed mid-Oct to
   mid-Feb)
Last orders: lunch 4.00pm, dinner 7.30pm
Comfortable rooms with magnificent views.
   Dining room is gas lit if there's a power
   cut.

ISLE OF MULL
Western Isles Hotel
Tobermory, Isle of Mull, Strathclyde PA75 6PR
Tel: (0688) 2012   **£45**
Open: lunch + dinner daily
Last orders: lunch 1.45pm, dinner 8.30pm
Sit in the conservatory at teatime and
   admire the view over the bay.

ISLE OF SKYE
Ardvasar Hotel
Ardvasar, Sleat, Isle of Skye, Highland IV45 8RS
Tel: (047 14) 223   **£40**
Open: lunch + dinner daily (closed Christmas, New
   Year, Jan+Feb)
Last orders: lunch 2.00pm, dinner 8.30pm
Simply prepared local seafood and good
   home-made bar snacks.

KENTALLEN
The Holly Tree
Kentallen, by Appin, Strathclyde PA38 4BY
Tel: (063 174) 292   **£55**
Open: lunch + dinner daily (closed mid-Nov to
   mid-Mar but open Christmas)
Last orders: lunch 2.00pm, dinner 9.300pm
Converted railway station on the edge of
   Loch Linnhe. Eleven bedrooms.

KILBERRY
Kilberry Inn
Kilberry, by Tarbert, Strathclyde PS29 6YD
Tel: (088 03) 223   **£45**
Open: lunch daily, dinner Mon-Sat (closed Oct to
   Easter)
Last orders: lunch 2.00pm (1.30pm Sun), dinner
   8.30pm
Good home cooking.

KILFINAN
The Kilfinan Hotel
Kilfinan, By Tighnabruaich, Strathclyde PA21 2AP
Tel: (070 082) 201   **£45**
Open: lunch + dinner daily
Last orders: lunch 2.00pm, dinner 9.00pm
Sporting hotel, eleven bedrooms, tradition-
   al food in restaurant.

KILLIECRANKIE
Killiecrankie Hotel
Killiecrankie, By Pitlochry, Tayside PH16 5LG
Tel: (0796) 3220   **£40**
Open: lunch + dinner daily (closed mid-Oct to Apr)
Last orders: lunch 2.00pm, dinner 8.30pm
Small hotel, family run, tartan-clad staff,
   twelve bedrooms.

KILMORE
Glenfeochan House
Kilmore, By Oban, Strathclyde PA34 4QR
Tel: (063 177) 273   **£55**
Open: dinner daily (closed Nov-Mar)
Last orders: dinner 8.30pm
Turretted Victorian house, 350 acres,
   splendid views, non-residents must book
   for dinner.

KINCLAVEN
Ballathie House Hotel
Kinclaven, by Stanley, Tayside PH1 4QN
Tel: (025 083) 268 *Fax:* (025 083) 396 **£50**
Open: lunch + dinner daily (closed Christmas Day,
Boxing Day, 3 wks Feb)
Last orders: lunch 1.45pm, dinner 8.30pm
Well furnished Victorian mansion hotel,
popular with fishing and golfing parties.
Turrets and gables on the banks of the
Tay.

KINLOCHBERVIE
The Kinlochbervie Hotel
Kinlochbervie, by Lairg, Highland IV27 4RP
Tel: (097 182) 275 *Fax:* (097 182) 438 **£50**
Open: lunch by arrangement, dinner daily
Last orders: dinner 8.30pm
Wonderful views of the sea – plenty of fish
on restaurant menu. Also new bistro.

KINROSS
Croft Bank House Hotel
30 Station Road, Kinross, Tayside KY13 7TG
Tel: 0577 63819 **£45**
Open: lunch Tue-Sun, dinner Tue-Sat
Last orders: lunch 2.00pm, dinner 9.00pm
Restaurant with rooms in Victorian house.
Friendly welcome and interesting menu.

MARKINCH
Balbirnie House Hotel
16 Rothesay Mews, Markinch, By Glenrothes,
Fife KY7 6NE
Tel: (0592) 610066 *Fax:* (0592) 660529 **£50**
Open: lunch + dinner daily
Last orders: lunch 2.00pm, dinner 9.30pm
(10.00pm Sat)
Lovely house, 18th-century classical
proportions, gallery with vaulted ceiling,
marble fireplaces, oil paintings, thirty
bedrooms.

MELROSE
Burts Hotel
Market Square, Melrose, Borders TD6 9PN
Tel: (089 682) 2285 *Fax:* (089 682) 2870 **£45**
Open: lunch + dinner daily (closed Christmas +
New Year)
Last orders: lunch 2.00pm (1.30pm Sun), dinner
9.00pm
18th-century inn, family run for over twenty
years. Twenty-one rooms.

Marmion's Brasserie
Buccleuch Street, Melrose, Borders TD6 9LB
Tel: (089 682) 2245 **£30**
Open: lunch + dinner Mon-Sat (closed 2 dys
Christmas, 2 dys New Year)
Last orders: lunch 2.00pm, dinner 10.00pm
Informal family-run brasserie.

MOFFAT
Beechwood Country House Hotel
Harthope Place, Moffat,
Dumfries & Galloway DG10 9RS
Tel: (0683) 20210 *Fax:* (0683) 20889 **£35**
Open: lunch + dinner daily (closed Jan)
Last orders: lunch 2.00pm, dinner 9.00pm
Seven roomed country house hotel set in 2
acres of gardens with lovely views over-
looking the Annan valley.

Moffat House Hotel
High Steet, Moffat,
Dumfries & Galloway DG10 9HL
Tel: (0683) 20039 **£35**
Open: lunch + dinner daily
Last orders: lunch 2.00pm, dinner 8.45pm
Superb Georgian mansion right in the
middle of town.

NEWMILL-ON-TEVIOT
The Old Forge Restaurant
Newmill-on-Teviot, Nr Hawick, Borders TD9 0JU
Tel: (0450) 85298 **£30**
Open: dinner Tue-Sat (closed Christmas/New
Year, 2 wks May, 2 wks Nov)
Last orders: dinner 9.30pm
Former forge, blackboard menu, always a
vegetarian choice.

OBAN
Knipoch Hotel
Oban, Strathclyde PA34 4QT
Tel: (085 26) 251 **£65**
Open: lunch by arrangement, dinner daily (closed
mid-Nov to mid-Feb)
Last orders: dinner 9.00pm
Splendid views across Loch Feochan. Fami-
ly-run Georgian house, comfortable
rooms. Set 5-course dinners. Good
wines and cheeses.

ONICH
Allt-nan-Ros Hotel
Onich, by Fort William, Highland PH33 6RY
Tel: (085 53) 210 *Fax:* (085 53) 462 **£35**
Open: lunch + dinner daily (closed Nov to mid-
Mar)
Last orders: lunch 2.00pm, dinner 8.30pm
On the edge of Loch Linnhe, family run.
Local produce in restaurant.

PEEBLES
Cringletie House Hotel
Peebles, Lothian EH45 8PL
Tel: (072 13) 233 *Fax:* (072 13) 244 **£45**
Open: lunch + dinner daily (closed Jan-Mar)
Last orders: lunch 1.45pm, dinner 8.30pm
Baronial-style mansion in 28 acres of wood-
land and garden. Four-course dinners,
thirteen bedrooms.

PERTH
Number Thirty Three
33 George Street, Perth, Tayside PH1 5LA
Tel: (0738) 33771 **£40**
Open: lunch + dinner Tue-Sat
Last orders: lunch 2.15pm, dinner 9.15pm
Art deco furnishings, simple dishes.

PITLOCHRY
East Haugh House Country Hotel
East Haugh, Pitlochry, Tayside PH16 5JS
Tel: (0796) 3121 **£40**
Open: lunch + dinner daily (closed 3 dys
Christmas)
Last orders: lunch 2.15pm (2.30pm Sun), dinner
10.45pm
Six bedroom hotel, shooting, stalking and
falconry can be arranged.

ST ANDREWS
Lathones Manor Hotel
By Largoward, St Andrews, Fife KY9 1JE
Tel: (0334) 84494 **£40**
Open: lunch + dinner Mon-Sat (closed also Mon
Oct-Mar, closed Bank Holidays, 2 wks Jan/Feb,
2 wks Nov)
Last orders: lunch 2.00pm, dinner 9.30pm
Hotel with old world charm – gas coal fire
and easy chairs and sofas in the bar.
Home-made ice creams and sorbets are a
speciality.

SELKIRK
Philipburn House Hotel
Selkirk, Borders TD7 5LS
Tel: (0750) 20747 *Fax:* (0750) 21690 **£45**
Open: lunch + dinner daily (closed 1 wk Jan)
Last orders: lunch 2.15pm, dinner 9.30pm (9.00pm
Sun)
Original 18th-century house, now a family-
run hotel. Sixteen bedrooms.

STONEHAVEN
Lairhillock Inn & Restaurant
Netherley, Stonehaven, Grampian AB3 2QS
Tel: (0569) 30001 **£45**
Open: lunch daily, dinner Tue-Sat
Last orders: lunch 2.00pm, dinner 9.30pm
Relaxed friendly atmosphere, good home
cooking.

STRACHUR
The Creggans Inn
Strachur, Strathclyde PA27 8BX
Tel: (036 986) 279 *Fax:* (036 986) 637 **£50**
Open: lunch + dinner daily
Last orders: lunch 2.15pm, dinner 9.00pm
On the edge of Loch Fyne – fine views from
the lounges.

STRATHTUMMEL
Port-an-Eilean Hotel
Strathtummel, Tayside PH16 5RU
Tel: (088 24) 233 **£35**
Open: dinner daily (closed Oct-Apr)
Last orders: dinner 8.30pm
Another lochside location for a hunting
lodge. Antiques, six bedrooms.

STRATHYRE
Creagan House
Strathyre, Tayside FK18 8ND
Tel: (087 74) 638 **£40**
Open: lunch Sun (weekdays by arrangement),
dinner daily (closed Feb, 1 wk Oct)
Last orders: lunch 1.30pm, dinner 8.30pm
Homely guest house with comfortable
rooms.

TARBERT
West Loch Hotel
Tarbert, Strathclyde PA29 6YL
Tel: (088 02) 283 **£40**
Open: lunch + dinner daily
Last orders: lunch 2.00pm, dinner 8.30pm
200-year-old coaching inn, open log fires,
simple fresh bedrooms which overlook
the loch.

WALLS
Burrastow House
Walls, Shetland, Highland ZE2 9PD
Tel: (0595) 71307 **£50**
Open: lunch + dinner Wed-Mon (closed Oct-Mar)
Last orders: lunch 2.30pm, dinner 9.00pm
Remote 18th-century house, peat fires,
warm welcome, and home-grown and
local produce.

WEST LINTON
Medwyn House
West Linton, Borders EH45 7HB
Tel: (0968) 60542 **£35**
Open: lunch by arrangement, dinner daily
Last orders: dinner 8.00pm
Small three-bedroomed, friendly and com-
fortable guest house. Good simple
cooking.

Wales Establishment Reviews

CARDIFF   The Armless Dragon

97 Wyverne Road, Cathays, Cardiff, South Glamorgan CF2 4BG
Telephone: (0222) 382357)   **£45**
Open: lunch Mon-Fri, dinner Mon-Sat (closed Bank Holidays, 10 days
    Christmas)
Last orders: lunch 2.15pm, dinner 10.30pm (11.00pm Sat)

The Armless Dragon is not a linguistic pun but a mythical beast
(wyvern) inevitably associated with China as much as Wales, which is
why the menu here combines Welsh and oriental elements: crab soup
with lemon grass; Welsh lamb noisettes paloise. The day's fish is a
good choice, cooked in a variety of six ways from poached to spiced
Barbados-style. A short well-chosen wine list and informal bistro
atmosphere.

CARDIFF   Le Cassoulet

5 Romilly Crescent, Canton, Cardiff, South Glamorgan CF1 9NP
Telephone: (0222) 221905   **£45**
Open: lunch Tue-Fri, dinner Tue-Sat
Last orders: lunch 2.00pm, dinner 10.00pm ·

Chef/patron Gilbert Viader comes from Toulouse. Toulousain (rugby) are therefore the colours of his restaurant – red, white and black;
toulousain is also the style of the cassoulet he makes. It includes
Toulouse sausages specially made in Cardiff! For a lighter meal,
there may be a selection of fish with a lobster sauce, or suprême de
volaille au porto. An accompanying chicory and apple salad is an
unusual touch. Good value plat du jour at lunch.

CHEPSTOW   Beckfords

15-16 Upper Church Street, Chepstow, Gwent NP6 5EX
Telephone: (029 12) 6347   **£55**
Open: lunch Tue-Fri + Sun, dinner Mon-Sat (closed Bank Holidays, 1 wk
    Christmas)
Last orders: lunch 2.00pm (3.00pm Sun), dinner 10.00pm (10.30pm Sat)

This elegant restaurant in a Georgian town house is becoming
increasingly well known, drawing its regular clientele from as far
afield as Bristol and Cardiff. Meals, chosen from fixed price menus,
are leisurely, with dishes such as poached local trout and a cucumber
and lemon sauce, or rack of lamb with leek, honey and orange sauce.
Luscious puddings from chocolate mousse to treacle tart. Some good
bottles on the wine list.

COLWYN BAY · The Old Rectory

Llansanffraid Glan Conwy, Colwyn Bay, Gwynedd LL28 5LF
Telephone: (0492) 580611 **£50**
Open: dinner daily (closed Christmas, Jan)
Last orders: one sitting at 7.30pm

House guests meet for dinner at a large mahogany table in the
Georgian dining room. The routine is precisely timed: drinks at
7.30pm, dinner at 8.00pm. Michael Vaughan plays host, while the
limited menu shows off wife Wendy's understated skills in dishes
such as avocado and leek slice with a tomato vinaigrette, or
medallions of lamb in a red wine sauce served with a fennel and herb
timbale. Non-residents must book, and sit at separate tables. There
are four en-suite bedrooms with period furnishing. 'No smoking' is
the rule.

HARLECH · The Cemlyn

High Street, Harlech, Gwynedd LL46 2YA
Telephone: (0766) 780425 **£45**
Open: lunch by arrangement only, dinner daily (closed mid-Oct to Easter)
Last orders: 9.00pm (9.30pm high summer)

'Cemlyn', it seems, is Welsh for 'frog'. With Harlech Castle visible
through the windows of this charming restaurant, perhaps Ken
Goody is a prince-in-waiting! Certainly he does regal duty as both
competent chef and welcoming host. Closely-typed fixed price menus
offer straightforward dishes in generous portions. Good soups –
perhaps pea with tarragon; local wild salmon with champagne butter
sauce and asparagus, grilled rumpsteak amoureuse à la dijonnaise,
Welsh cheeses. Very reasonable prices on an interesting wine list.

LAKE VYRNWY	Lake Vyrnwy Hotel

Lake Vyrnwy, Llanwddyn, Powys SY10 0LY
Telephone: (069 173) 692   *Fax:* (069 173) 259 £45
Open: lunch + dinner daily
Last orders: lunch 1.45pm, dinner 9.15pm

Much of the appeal at Lake Vyrnwy lies in the truly spectacular views of the lake and the activities available, from fishing to helicopter safaris. Elegant public rooms with soft lighting, rich wood and warm colours, deep sofas and in the lounge, a grand piano. Thirty neat bedrooms combine modern and traditional comforts. The elegant pink dining room offers lake views and table d'hôte menus. Children are welcome.

LLANDEWI SKIRRID	The Walnut Tree Inn

See page 238 – our Clover Award Section.

LLANDUDNO	Bodysgallen Hall

See page 240 – our Clover Award Section.

LLANDRILLO	Tyddyn Llan Country House Hotel & Restaurant

Llandrillo, Nr Corwen, Clwyd LL21 0ST
Telephone: (049 084) 264 Fax (049 084) 264 £50
Open: lunch + dinner daily
Last orders: lunch 2.00pm, dinner 9.30pm

A comfortable country house hotel in prime walking and fishing country. The extended lounge is spacious, the new panelled Georgian style dining room enjoys views through french windows to the croquet lawn. At its heart is the relaxing hospitality of the Kindreds, and chef David Barrett's cooking. His daily menus reflect the seasons and the region; cooking is accurate, quite straightforward and well presented: trio of new season's Welsh lamb cutlets, kidneys and sweetbreads; roast saddle of local rabbit with a thyme-scented gravy. Good vegetables and cheeses. Ten bedrooms with some antiques are neat and airy and have modest en-suite facilities.

LLANRWST	Meadowsweet Hotel

Station Road, Llanrwst, Gwynedd LL26 0DS
Telephone: (0492) 640732 £50
Open: dinner daily
Last orders: dinner 9.30pm (9.00pm Sun)

You have to book to enjoy John Evans' cooking. Based on a short fixed price daily menu, the style is modern, often imaginative: rosé wine in a tomato sauce with a fillet steak of Welsh lamb on garlic croûtons; ginger, honey and white wine combined in a sauce for a sautéed fillet of fresh salmon. An extensive wine list and relaxed service.

LLYSWEN   Llangoed Hall

Llyswen, Brecon, Powys LD3 0YP
Telephone: (0874) 754525   *Fax:* (0874) 754545   **£70**
Open: lunch + dinner daily
Last orders: lunch 2.15pm, dinner 9.30pm

'Functional with a grand feel' was the design brief for Sir Bernard
Ashley's first country house hotel. Edwardian without the clutter,
public areas use fine furniture and Sir Bernard's collection of 19th and
20th-century paintings against plain walls. Bedrooms reflect the best
of Laura Ashley design. Chef Mark Salter (ex-Cromlix House) offers
fixed price menus (lighter at lunch) of his characteristically fine
modern British cooking.

NEWPORT   Cnapan Country House for Guests

East Street, Newport, Nr Fishguard, Dyfed SA42 0WF
Telephone: (0239) 820575   **£35**
Open: lunch + dinner Wed-Mon in summer; lunch Sun, dinner Fri+Sat in
       winter (closed 25+26 Dec, Feb)
Last orders: lunch 2.30pm (2.00pm Sun), dinner 8.45pm (8.00pm Sun)

The Lloyd and Cooper families run this small, friendly house catering
mainly for summer visitors. The house, a listed building, is their
home all the year round and this atmosphere is extended to guests
staying in the five charming bedrooms. The cooking explores a
variety of styles in order to accommodate a broad range of tastes,
and Judith Lloyd uses as much local produce as possible, such as
salmon, sewin, lobster, local cheese and locally grown vegetables,
organic when available. Eluned Lloyd is vegetarian so there is
particular emphasis on the provision of meat and fish-free meals. You
might choose egg noodles served with a spicy mushroom and
tarragon topping, and follow it with some chunks of Welsh lamb,
marinated then grilled and served with a mango sauce. To finish, a
large meringue with chocolate sauce, or perhaps a baked vanilla
cream in a pot served with fresh fruit. The wine list includes a Welsh
wine (produced 2 miles north of Monmouth!) as well as a selection
from around Europe. All choices are very reasonably priced.

BODYSGALLEN HALL

NORTHOP	Soughton Hall

Northop, Nr Mold, Clwyd CH7 6AB
Telephone: (0352) 86811   *Fax:* (0352) 86382   **£60**
Open: lunch Tue-Fri + Sun, dinner daily (closed 2 wks Jan)
Last orders: lunch 2.00pm, dinner 9.30pm (10.00pm Sun)

The impressive early 18th-century bishop's palace is owned and run by the Rodenhurst family. Fabrics and wall-coverings reflect a personal touch, yet with its antiques, marble fireplaces, French tapestries and Persian carpets, this remains very much a stately home in style. A harpist accompanies dinner in the splendid State Dining Room. Food lives up to the surroundings: there's excellent home-made bread, and dishes such as huge scallops, king prawns and turbot with wild mushrooms and asparagus in a champagne sauce. An extensive wine list. Young staff try hard to please.

PWLLHELI	Plas Bodegroes Restaurant with Rooms

Plas Bodegroes, Nefyn Road, Pwllheli, Gwynedd LL53 5TH
Telephone: (0758) 612363   *Fax:* (0758) 701247   **£55**
Open: dinner daily (residents only Sun+Mon) (closed Jan)
Last orders: dinner 9.00pm (9.30pm Sat)

Outstanding value and inspired cooking by Christopher Chown in this pretty manor house restaurant with rooms run by Christopher and his wife Gunna. Prime local ingredients form the basis of the frequently changing 5-course menus, which offer four or five choices at each course except on 'residents only' nights when there is a set menu. You might be offered tiny Welsh rarebits as appetisers, then medallions of guineafowl with pistachio nuts, followed by sautéed sea bream and scallops with samphire. For a main course there might be a char-grilled kebab of lamb with ratatouille and garlic cream. Chris matures his own Welsh cheeses and serves them with home-made walnut bread, before a pudding such as poached pear grilled with pine-nuts and a poire william sauce. A commendable house selection heads a modestly-priced wine list. Friendly, informal service. Five comfortable bedrooms, with a further three planned for 1991.

RUTHIN	Hunters Restaurant

57 Well Street, Ruthin, Clwyd LL15 1AF
Telephone: (082 42) 2619   **£40**
Open: lunch daily, dinner Mon-Sat (closed 25+26 Dec)
Last orders: lunch 2.00pm, dinner 9.30pm (10.00pm Sat)

Robert Hunter is an ambitious – and brave – young man. At twenty, the ex-Miller Howe protégé came home to Ruthin, bought the old steakhouse and turned it into an elegant modern restaurant. He steers a difficult path between local, mainly lunchtime, trade and a more sophisticated evening clientele. At lunch there may be steak and kidney pie or salmon in asparagus cream sauce; at dinner, pan-fried breast of duck with oranges and walnuts and its own jus. Sticky toffee pudding is a popular choice. Home-made bread and petits fours. The wine list has something for most tastes and pockets.

SWANSEA	Annie's Restaurant

56 St Helen's Road, Swansea, West Glamorgan SA1 4BE
Telephone: (0792) 655603   **£35**
Open: dinner Mon-Sat (closed Christmas)
Last orders: dinner 10.00pm (10.30pm Sat)

Pays de Galles and Pays des Gauls come together here in an amicable
alliance of gallic bistro. Ann Gwilym's menus (carte and fixed price),
served in an informal stripped pine setting, range from baked parcels
of green cabbage with chestnut, walnut and lentil stuffing and a sweet
red pepper sauce to poached fillets of brill with baby leeks and oyster
mushrooms. Welsh cheeses and French wines.

TRELLECH	The Village Green Restaurant & Brasserie

Trellech, Nr Monmouth, Gwent NP5 4PA
Telephone: (0600) 860119   **£50**
Open: lunch Tue-Sun, dinner Tue-Sat (closed 1 wk Jan) (open for dinner on
Bank Holiday Mondays)
Last orders: lunch 1.45pm (2.00pm Sun), dinner 9.45pm (10.00pm Sat)

The Evans' agreeable restaurant with two rooms has had some ups
and downs since opening three years ago. Colin Sparks has left and
Bob Evans is now in the kitchen with Jonathan Badham. Good stocks,
fresh herbs and other local produce are well used in the daily soups,
rack of lamb with honey and rosemary, lemon sole with dry vermouth
and sorrel. A sensibly short wine list with house wine at £5.95.

WHITEBROOK	The Crown at Whitebrook

Whitebrook, Nr Monmouth, Gwent NP5 4TX
Telephone: (0600) 860254   *Fax:* (0600) 860607   **£50**
Open: lunch + dinner daily (residents only lunch Mon, dinner Sun)
Last orders: lunch 2.00pm, dinner 9.30pm

A long, white, rather modern looking building in a heavily-wooded
valley above Tintern is the setting for an enjoyable small restaurant
with rooms. From a fixed price menu you might choose an excellent
tartelette alsacienne filled with cheese and onion, followed by
guineafowl cooked in port with wild mushrooms and a filo pastry case
with prunes, accompanied by a large selection of good vegetables.
For dessert perhaps a vacherin aux fruits de saison or some Welsh
cheese. An award-winning wine list and friendly and efficient service.

Wales Listings

ABERDOVEY
Penhelig Arms Hotel & Restaurant
Aberdovey, Gwynedd LL35 0LT
Tel: (065 472) 215   **£40**
Open: lunch + dinner daily (closed 3 dys Christmas)
Last orders: lunch 2.00pm, dinner 9.00pm (8.30pm Sun)
Harbourside inn with eleven rooms. Simple dishes served in the bar and dining room using fresh, local produce.

ABERGAVENNY
The Ant and Rubber Plant
7 Market Street, Abergavenny, Gwent
Tel: (0873) 5905   **£40**
Open: lunch Tue-Sat, dinner Mon-Sat (closed Bank Holidays)
Last orders: lunch 2.00pm, dinner 9.30pm
Exuberant, bistro-style, useful in the area.

ABERYSTWYTH
Conrah Country Hotel
Chancery, Aberystwyth, Dyfed SW23 4DF
Tel: (0970) 617941   **£60**
Open: lunch + dinner daily
Last orders: lunch 2.00pm, dinner 9.30pm
Twenty-two rooms (main house, motel-style and cottage), indoor pool, great views.

Gannets Bistro
7 St James Square, Aberystwyth, Dyfed SY23 1DU
Tel: (0970) 617164   **£30**
Open: lunch + dinner Mon-Sat (closed Christmas)
Last orders: lunch 2.30pm, dinner 9.30pm (10.00pm Sat)
Hearty, home cooking.

ANGLESEY
Tre-Ysgawen Hall
Capel Coch, Nr Llangefni, Anglesey, Gwynedd LL77 7UR
Tel: (0248) 750750   *Fax:* (0248) 750035   **£40**
Open: lunch + dinner daily
Last orders: lunch 2.30pm, dinner 9.30pm
Finely converted Victorian mansion, comfortable and elegant public rooms and bedrooms, modern uncomplicated food.

Ye Olde Bulls Head Inn
Castle Street, Beaumaris, Anglesey, Gwynedd LL58 8AP
Tel: (0248) 810329   *Fax:* (0248) 811294   **£45**
Open: lunch + dinner daily (closed Christmas Day, Boxing Day, New Year's Day)
Last orders: lunch 2.30pm (1.30pm Sun), dinner 9.30pm (9.00pm Sun)
Parts of this coaching inn date back to 1617. Fresh, local produce is served in the bar and dining room.

BARRY
Bunbury's
14 High Street, Barry, South Glamorgan CF6 8EA
Tel: (0446) 732075   **£40**
Open: lunch + dinner Tue-Sat (closed Christmas, 3 wks summer)
Last orders: lunch 2.30pm, dinner 10.00pm
Thirties' decor, short frequently changing menu.

BRECON
Griffin Inn
Llyswen, Brecon, Powys LD3 0UR
Tel: (0874) 754241   **£40**
Open: lunch + dinner daily (dinner Sun residents only)
Last orders: lunch 2.00pm, dinner 9.00pm
Sporting inn with fishing and shooting available for guests.

BRIDGEND
Coed-y-Mwstwr Hotel
Coychurch, Bridgend, Mid Glamorgan CF35 6AF
Tel: (0656) 860621   **£50**
Open: lunch + dinner daily (closed Christmas)
Last orders: lunch 2.30pm (3.00pm Sun), dinner 10.15pm (8.30pm Sun)
Victorian mansion hotel, lovely staircase, dinner four courses and sorbet. Good wines.

CAERNARVON
Seiont Manor Hotel
Llanrug, Caernarfon, Gwynedd LL55 2AQ
Tel: (0286) 76887   **£35**
Open: lunch Sun-Fri, dinner daily
Last orders: lunch 2.30pm, dinner 10.00pm
Thirty-two more rooms planned for 1991 (twenty-eight at present), as well as a golf course. Extensions are sympathetically done.

CAERPHILLY
Le Tricolore Restaurant
25 Ton-y-felin Road, Caerphilly, Mid Glamorgan CF8 1PA
Tel: (0222) 869612   **£30**
Open: dinner Tue-Sat (closed Christmas)
Last orders: dinner 10.00pm
Small, family-run restaurant.

CARDIFF
Blas-Ar-Cymru/A Taste of Wales
48 Crwys Road, Cardiff, South Glamorgan CF2 4NN
Tel: (0222) 382132   **£50**
Open: lunch Mon-Fri, dinner Mon-Sat (closed Bank Holidays, 2 wks Jan)
Last orders: lunch 1.45pm, dinner 11.30pm
Traditional recipes from Wales.

THE ART OF THE XIX CENTURY.

Champers
St Mary Street, Cardiff,
South Glamorgan CF1 1FE
Tel: (0222) 373363 **£40**
Open: lunch Mon-Sat, dinner daily (closed
Christmas Day + Boxing Day)
Last orders: lunch 2.30pm, dinner 11.30pm
Busy, straightforward wine bar and brasserie.

Gibsons
8 Romilly Crescent, Canton, Cardiff,
South Glamorgan CF1 9NR
Tel: (0222) 341264 **£45**
Open: lunch Wed-Mon, dinner Wed-Sat
Last orders: lunch 2.15pm, dinner 9.30pm
French provincial cooking, delicatessen adjacent.

Riverside Cantonese Restaurant
44 Tudor Street, Cardiff,
South Glamorgan CF1 8RH
Tel: (0222) 372163 **£30**
Open: dinner daily (closed Christmas Day +
Boxing Day)
Last orders: dinner 10.30pm
One of the best Chinese restaurants in Wales.

The Trillium
40 City Road, Roath, Cardiff,
South Glamorgan CF2 3DL
Tel: (0222) 463665 **£60**
Open: lunch Sun-Fri, dinner Tue-Sat (closed 5 dys
Christmas)
Last orders: lunch 2.30pm, dinner 10.30pm
Clubby feel, modern British food.

CHEPSTOW
Afon Gwy Restaurant
28 Bridge Street, Chepstow, Gwent NP6 5EZ
Tel: (029 12) 70158 **£45**
Open: lunch daily, dinner Mon-Sat (closed 2-3 wks
Jan)
Last orders: lunch 2.00pm, dinner 10.00pm
Warm Welsh welcome, and Welsh food.

Royal George Hotel
Tintern, Chepstow, Gwent NP6 6SF
Tel: (0291) 689205 *Fax:*(0291) 689448 **£40**
Open: lunch + dinner daily
Last orders: lunch 2.00pm, dinner 9.30pm
(10.00pm Sat)
17th-century inn, fifteen bedrooms.

COWBRIDGE
Basil's Brasserie
2 Eastgate, Cowbridge, South Glamorgan
Tel: (044 63) 3738 **£50**
Open: lunch + dinner Tue-Sat
Last orders: lunch 2.00pm, dinner 10.00pm
Good bistro cooking.

CRICKHOWELL
The Bear Hotel
High Street, Crickhowell, Powys NP8 1BW
Tel: (0873) 810408 **£45**
Open: lunch + dinner daily (closed Christmas Day)
Last orders: lunch 2.00pm, dinner 9.30pm
Former coaching inn, low beams, farm-house furniture, twenty-seven rooms.

Gliffaes Country House Hotel
Crickhowell, Powys NP8 1RH
Tel: (0874) 730371 *Fax:*(0874) 730463 **£40**
Open: lunch + dinner daily (closed Dec to mid-Mar)
Last orders: lunch 2.00pm, dinner 9.15pm
Set in its own grounds, traditional sports facilities, comfortable public rooms.

CWYM
The Blue Lion Inn
Cwym, Dyserth, Clwyd LL18 5SG
Tel: (0745) 570733 **£35**
Open: lunch Tue-Sun, dinner daily
Last orders: lunch 2.00pm, dinner 10.00pm
Large reputedly haunted inn, famous not for the ghost but the collection of chamber pots hanging from the ceiling!

FISHGUARD
Farmhouse Kitchen
Glendower Square, Goodwick, Fishguard,
Dyfed SA64 0BP
Tel: (0348) 873282 **£30**
Open: lunch + dinner daily (closed Bank Holidays,
Mon in winter, 2wks Feb, 1wk Nov)
Last orders: lunch 2.00pm, dinner 9.30pm
On the site of a former farm.

HAVERFORDWEST
Ann Fitzgerald's Farmhouse Kitchen
Mabws Fawr, Mathry, Haverfordwest,
Dyfed SA62 5JB
Tel: (0348) 831347 **£40**
Open: lunch + dinner daily (closed lunch Christmas
to Easter)
Last orders: lunch 2.00pm, dinner 9.00pm
Popular restaurant with take-away service if you phone in advance.

Jemima's
Nash Grove, Freystrop, Haverfordwest,
Dyfed SA62 4HB
Tel: (0437) 891109 **£35**
Open: dinner Tue-Sat
Last orders: dinner 9.00pm
Tiny restaurant using local fish and garden produce.

LLANBERIS
Y Bistro
43-45 High Street, Llanberis, Gwynedd LL55 4EU
Tel: (0286) 871278 **£35**
Open: dinner Tue-Sat (+ light lunches in summer)
(closed Bank Holidays, 1 wk Oct, 3 wks Jan)
Last orders: dinner 9.30pm
Nerys and Danny Roberts' friendly restaurant, local produce used whenever possible.

LLANDEGLEY
Ffaldau Country House & Restaurant
LLandegley, Llandegley Wells, Powys LD1 5UD
Tel: (059 787) 421 **£40**
Open: dinner Tue-Sat (closed Christmas to New
Year)
Last orders: dinner 8.45pm
Family-run, converted farmhouse, three bedrooms, set in an acre of garden.

LLANDUDNO
St Tudno Hotel
The Promenade, Llandudno, Gwynedd LL30 2LP
Tel: (0492) 74411 **£45**
Open: lunch + dinner daily (closed 2-3 wks Christmas)
Last orders: lunch 1.45pm, dinner 9.30pm (8.30pm Sun)
Seafront hotel, friendly owners, twenty-one rooms, fixed price or à la carte meals.

LLANGOLLEN
Gales
18 Bridge Street, Llangollen, Clwyd LL20 8PF
Tel: (0978) 860089 **£30**
Open: lunch + dinner Mon-Fri
Last orders: lunch 2.00pm, dinner 10.15pm
Wine bar in the centre of town. Reasonable prices.

LLANTHONY
Llanthony Abbey Hotel
Llanthony, Nr Abergavenny, Gwent
Tel: (0873) 890487 **£35**
Open: lunch by arrangment, dinner Tue-Sat
Last orders: by arrangement
Atmospheric old abbey – unusual setting.

MACHYNLLETH
Felin Crewi Watermill Cafe
Penegoes, Machynlleth, Powys SY20 8NH
Tel: (0654) 3113 **£25**
Open: lunch + snacks Sun-Fri (closed Oct to Easter)
Last orders: lunch 4.30pm
Traditional home cooking using flour from their own mill as much as possible, free range eggs and organic vegetables.

Ynyshir Hall Country House Hotel
Eglwysfach, Machynlleth, Powys SY20 8TA
Tel: (0654) 781209 **£45**
Open: lunch + dinner daily
Last orders: lunch 1.30pm, dinner 8.30pm
Georgian house and garden offering residential art courses.

MUMBLES
PA's Winebar
95 Newton Road, Mumbles, West Glamorgan SA3 4BN
Tel: (0792) 367723 **£30**
Open: lunch + dinner, Mon-Sat (closed 3 dys Christmas, 3 wks Oct)
Last orders: lunch 2.30pm, dinner 9.30pm
Popular local wine bar, informal atmosphere.

NEWPORT
Celtic Manor Hotel (Hedleys Restaurant)
Coldra Woods, Newport, Gwent NP6 2YA
Tel: (0633) 413000 **£45**
Open: lunch Sun-Fri, dinner daily
Last orders: lunch 2.30pm, dinner 10.30pm
Modernised 19th-century house with seventy-five rooms, sauna and swimming pool.

PENARTH
Walton House Hotel & Restaurant
37 Victoria Street, Penarth, South Glamorgan CF6 2HY
Tel: (0222) 707782 *Fax:*(0222) 711012 **£45**
Open: dinner Mon-Sat
Last orders: dinner 9.00pm
Edwardian villa with thirteen bedrooms.

PENTYRCH
De Courcy's
Tyla Morris Avenue, Pentyrch, Nr Cardiff, South Glamorgan CF4 8QN
Tel: (0222) 892232 *Fax:*(0222) 892232 **£60**
Open: lunch Tue-Fri + Sun; dinner Tue-Sat (closed Bank Holidays, 4 dys Christmas)
Last orders: lunch 2.00pm, dinner 10.00pm
Brought over from Sweden in 1890, the wooden house was re-erected just outside Cardiff.

PONTFAEN
Gelli Fawr Country House
Pontfaen, Nr Fishguard, Dyfed SA65 9TX
Tel: (0239) 820343 **£45**
Open: lunch Mon-Sat, dinner daily (closed 2-3 wks Jan/Feb)
Last orders: lunch 2.30pm, dinner 10.00pm
Unlicensed restaurant (but bring your own) in a large farmhouse with ten bedrooms.

PORTH
G & T's Village Bistro
64-66 Pontypridd Road, Porth, Rhondda, Mid Glamorgan CF39 9NL
Tel: (0443) 685775 **£40**
Open: lunch daily, dinner Mon-Sat
Last orders: lunch 2.15pm, dinner 9.30pm (10.00pm Sat)
Local bistro serving both modern and traditional French dishes.

PORTHKERRY
Egerton Grey Country House Hotel
Porthkerry, Nr Cardiff, South Glamorgan CF6 9BZ
Tel: (0446) 711666 *Fax:*(0446) 711690 **£45**
Open: lunch + dinner daily
Last orders: lunch 2.00pm, dinner 9.30pm
Country house hotel in former rectory – new chef being appointed by the Pitkins as we went to press. Restaurant in former billard room.

PORTMEIRION
Portmeirion Hotel
Portmeirion, Gwynedd LL48 6ER
Tel: (0766) 770228 *Fax:*(0766) 771331 **£50**
Open: lunch + dinner daily (closed mid-Jan to mid-Feb)
Last orders: lunch 2.30pm, dinner 9.30pm (9.45pm Sat)
Fantastic Mediterranean-style village and sumptuous hotel, designed by Sir Clough Williams Ellis. Worth a visit.

REYNOLDSTON
Fairyhill Country House & Restaurant
Reynoldston, Gower, Swansea,
  West Glamorgan SA3 1BS
Tel: (0792) 390139   £45
Open: lunch Sun, dinner daily (closed Christmas +
  New Year)
Last orders: lunch 2.00pm, dinner 9.30pm
Set in twenty-four peaceful acres. 18th-century house, antique furniture.

ROSSETT
Llyndir Hall
Llyndir Lane, Rossett, Nr Wrexham,
  Clywd LL12 0AY
Tel: (0244) 571648   £50
Open: lunch Tue-Fri, dinner Tue-Sat
Last orders: lunch 2.00pm, dinner 10.00pm
Elegant and tasteful hotel, thiry-eight rooms at present, thirty more plus a leisure centre planned for next year. Careful cooking in restaurant overlooking garden.

ST BRIDE'S WENTLOOGE
The Elm Tree
St Bride's Wentlooge, Gwent NP1 9SQ
Tel: (0633) 680225   £50
Open: lunch Sun-Fri, dinner Mon-Sat (closed 2 wks
  Jan)
Last orders: lunch 2.15pm (2.30pm Sun), dinner
  9.30pm (10.00pm Sun)
Eat in either the restaurant or the bistro, both specialise in seafood in summer and game in winter.

ST BRIDE'S SUPER ELY
Bardells
St Bride's Super Ely, South Glamorgan CF5 6EZ
Tel: (0446) 760534   £45
Open: lunch Sun, dinner Tue-Sat
Last orders: lunch 2.00pm, dinner 9.30pm
Thirty-seater restaurant offering a small set menu with a choice of three dishes at each course.

SWANSEA
Green Dragon Bistro
Green Dragon Lane, Swansea,
  West Glamorgan SA1 1DG
Tel: (0792) 641437   £35
Open: lunch Mon-Sat (closed Christmas + New
  Year)
Last orders: lunch 3.00pm
Both modern and traditional dishes are on offer at this good local restaurant.

Keenan's
82 St Helen's Road, Swansea,
  West Glamorgan SA4 1BQ
Tel: (0792) 644111   £45
Open: lunch Tue-Fri, dinner Tue-Sat
Last orders: lunch 2.00pm, dinner 9.30pm
Chris Keenan uses seasonal local produce; short, fixed price lunch menu is good value.

Windsor Lodge
Mount Pleasant, Swansea,
  West Glamorgan SA1 6EG
Tel: (0792) 642158   *Fax:*(0792) 648996   £45
Open: lunch + dinner, Mon-Sat (closed Christmas
  Day + Boxing Day)
Last orders: lunch 1.30pm, dinner 9.30pm
Grade II listed Georgian building with twenty bedrooms. Good, satisfying dishes.

TALSARNAU
Maes-y-Neaudd
Talsarnau, Nr Harlech, Gwynedd LL47 6YA
Tel: (0766) 780200   *Fax:*(0766) 780211   £50
Open: lunch + dinner daily (closed 2 wks
  Christmas)
Last orders: lunch 2.00pm, dinner 9.00pm (9.15pm
  Sat)
Wonderful views from Georgian rooms – additional bedrooms this year now total sixteen.

THREE COCKS
Three Cocks Hotel & Restaurant
Three Cocks, Nr Brecon, Powys LD3 0SL
Tel: (049 74) 215   £50
Open: lunch Mon-Sat, dinner Wed-Mon
Last orders: lunch 2.00pm, dinner 9.00pm
15th-century building with seven bedrooms. Food is generous with a Belgian influence.

USK
Nag's Head Inn
Twyn Square, Usk, Gwent NP7 1HO
Tel: (029 13) 2820   £30
Open: lunch + dinner daily
Last orders: lunch 2.00pm, dinner 10.00pm
Unpretensious home cooking in traditional inn.

WELSH HOOK
Stone Hall
Welsh Hook, Nr Haverfordwest,
  Dyfed SA62 5NS
Tel: (0348) 840212   *Fax:*(0348) 840815   £40
Open: dinner daily (closed Mon Nov-Mar, 1wk
  Dec)
Last orders: dinner 9.30pm
French-style restaurant in typical Welsh manor house. Martine Watson cooks, Alan serves. Five bedrooms.

LLANTHONY ABBEY HOTEL

Northern Ireland Establishment Reviews

BELFAST — The Crown Liquor Saloon

46 Great Victoria Street, Belfast, Co. Antrim BT2 7BA
Telephone: (0232) 249476   **£60**
Open: lunch + dinner daily (closed Christmas Day)
Last orders: lunch 3.00pm (2.30pm Sun), dinner 11.15pm (10.00pm Sun)

This Victorian pub has had no real alterations since it was built in the 1800s – it is still lit by gas lamps – although it is now owned by the National Trust and leased to Bass. It's a great tourist attraction because of its infectiously happy atmosphere – and the possibility of seeing a famous face. It was, quite recently, used as a setting in the film *Odd Man Out.* The High Victorian Art interior boasts stained glass, ceramics, gold leaf and ornate mirrors. You can close the door to your snug and enjoy in peace an excellent pint of Guinness, with Strangford oysters, or Irish stew, or champ; or else sit in the lounge bar and be part of the atmosphere!

BELFAST — Roscoff

Lesley House, Shaftesbury Square, Belfast, Co. Antrim
Telephone: (0232) 331532   **£40**
Open: lunch Mon-Fri, dinner Mon-Sat (closed Bank Holidays, 2 wks Jul)
Last orders: lunch 2.30pm, dinner 10.30pm

Roscoff is a new star in Northern Ireland's firmament. Paul Rankin has returned to his home territory after stints with the Rouxs at Le Gavroche and also some work experience in the States, and his pedigree shows in the assured touch of his modern European cooking. Set price menus are available at both lunch and dinner. The simply decorated dining room is a perfect backdrop to this young man's skills. We think you might hear more of him!

COLERAINE	MacDuff's Restaurant

Blackheath House, Blackhill, Coleraine, Co. Londonderry BT51 4HH
Telephone: (0265) 868433 **£40**
Open: dinner Tue-Sat (closed Christmas Day + Boxing Day)
Last orders: dinner 9.30pm

MacDuff's Restaurant is to be found within Blackheath House, a lovely converted rectory with just five bedrooms in which fresh fruit and home-made biscuits await you. Joseph and Margaret Erwin are welcoming hosts, and although Margaret supervises the kitchen, Head Chef Alan Wade makes a considerable contribution to the menus. Richly varied influences are apparent – spiced salmon and prawn puffs with savoury Indian dip, medallions of pork véronique, and Jamaican bananas can whip you round the globe in the space of a meal! The wine list is similarly expansive, while the house selection is more familiarly Georges Duboeuf's cuvée Paul Bocuse.

HOLYWOOD	Culloden Hotel

Craigavad, Co. Down BT18 0EX
Telephone: (023 17) 5223   *Fax:* (023 17) 6777 **£35**
Open: lunch Sun-Fri, dinner daily
Last orders: lunch 2.30pm, dinner 9.45pm (10.00 Sat, 8.30pm Sun)

The Culloden began life in baronial style but there are now modern extensions. The mature grounds sweep down to the lough, encompassing secluded gardens and woodland. The original parts of the hotel are quite splendid, with great arched windows, ornate balustrades and plasterwork ceilings. The dining room enjoys views over the gardens. Here residents and visitors can sample local produce carefully cooked and served – Irish lamb, fish, and good crisp vegetables.

Northern Ireland Listings

BELFAST
La Belle Epoque
103 Great Victoria Street, Belfast,
  Co Down BT2 7AG
Tel: (0232) 323244   **£50**
Open: dinner Mon-Sat
Last orders: dinner 12.45am (11.30pm Sat)
French restaurant with good modern cooking.

Branigans Restaurant
11a Stranmills Road, Belfast, Co Down BT9 5AS
Tel: (0232) 666845   **£30**
Open: lunch + dinner daily
Last orders: lunch 3.00pm, dinner 11.45pm
Simple bistro-type dishes. No licence so bring your own wine.

Nick's Warehouse
35-39 Hill Street, Belfast, Co Antrim BT1 2LB
Tel: (0232) 439690   **£30**
Open: lunch + dinner Mon-Fri
Last orders: lunch 3.00pm, dinner 6.30pm
Fifty seater restaurant with wine bar downstairs.

Restaurant 44
44 Bedford Street, Belfast, Co Antrim BT2 7FF
Tel: (0232) 244844   **£45**
Open: lunch Mon-Fri, dinner Mon-Sat (closed Bank Holidays)
Last orders: lunch 3.00pm, dinner 10.30pm
Friendly welcome to the intimate, candle-lit restaurant.

The Strand Restaurant
12 Stranmillis Road, Belfast, Co Down BT9 5AA
Tel: (0232) 682266   **£30**
Open: lunch Mon-Sat, dinner daily
Last orders: lunch 2.00pm, dinner 11.00pm
Bustling bistro serving generous portions, conservatory bar.

CRAWFORDSBURN
The Old Inn
15 Main Street, Crawfordsburn,
  Co Down BT19 1JH
Tel: (0247) 853255   *Fax:* (0247) 852775   **£35**
Open: lunch + dinner daily (closed Christmas)
Last orders: lunch 2.30pm, dinner 9.30pm (8.00pm Sun)
Thatched inn in pretty village setting. Gas lighting. Garden.

DUNADRY
Dunadry Inn
Dunadry, Co Antrim BT41 2HA
Tel: (084 94) 32474   *Fax:* (084 94) 33389   **£35**
Open: lunch + dinner daily (buffet only Sat+Sun)
  (closed 3 dys Christmas)
Last orders: lunch 1.45pm, dinner 9.45pm
Close to Belfast airport; leisure complex; garden access from ground floor bedrooms.

PORTAFERRY
The Portaferry Hotel
10 The Strand, Portaferry, Co Down BT22 1PE
Tel: (024 77) 28231   **£45**
Open: lunch + dinner daily (closed Christmas Day)
Last orders: lunch 2.30pm, dinner 9.00pm
  (10.00pm Sat)
Convenient for the ferry, the large menu has an emphasis on seafood.

STRANGFORD
The Lobster Pot
11 The Square, Strangford, Co Down BT30 7ND
Tel: (039 686) 288   **£45**
Open: lunch + dinner daily
Last orders: lunch 2.30pm, dinner 9.30pm (9.00pm Sun)
Restaurant and bar specialising in seafood.

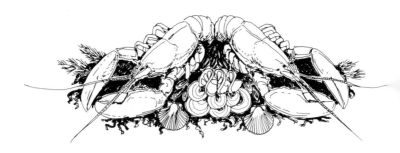

THE ART OF DINING.

Republic of Ireland
Establishment Reviews

ADARE   Adare Manor

See page 228 – our Clover Award Section.

ADARE   Mustard Seed

See page 230 – our Clover Award Section.

BALLINA   Mount Falcon Hotel

Ballina, Co. Mayo
Telephone: (096) 21172   **£40**
Open: dinner daily (closed 5 days Christmas, Feb + Mar)
Last orders: dinner 8.00pm

Mount Falcon is one of the many turretted castles now enjoying a new lease of life as a hotel. Mrs Constance Aldridge has supervised all aspects of the hotel and kitchen for over fifty years. She presides over dinner, substantial meals cooked in traditional style, served at one long table in the dining room.

BLACKROCK   The Park Restaurant

See page 231 – our Clover Award Section.

CORK   Arbutus Lodge Hotel

Montenotte, Cork, Co. Cork
Telephone: (021) 501237   *Fax:* (021) 502893   *An ordinary bar leads into a warm friendly restaurant* **£50**
Open: lunch + dinner Mon-Sat (closed 1 wk Christmas)
Last orders: lunch 2.00pm, dinner 9.30pm

Arbutus Lodge, a town house converted into a hotel, was once the home of the Lord Mayor of Cork and is now the home of the Ryan family. Visitors to Arbutus feel equally at home staying in any of its twenty bedrooms. In the restaurant you can enjoy a high standard of Irish and French specialities, such as pigs' trotters, bacon and cabbage Arbutus-style, fresh lobsters from a tank, a mousseline of salmon and pike, a pine kernel and almond tart to finish. A good wine list complements the cooking.

Marlfield House – see opposite

DINGLE   Doyle's Seafood Bar and Townhouse

John Street, Dingle, Co. Kerry
Telephone: (066) 51174   *Fax:* (066) 51816   **£50**
Open: lunch + dinner Mon-Sat (closed mid-Nov to mid-Mar)
Last orders: lunch 2.15pm, dinner 9.00pm

The dolphin is still in Dingle Bay, and John and Stella Doyle are still at the Seafood Bar, so there are at least two reasons for you to smile when in Dingle! The cosy, simply decorated restaurant, seating just forty-five, is the setting for Stella's delicious mostly fish menus. Try a millefeuille of warm oysters in Guinness sauce, or hot trout smokies, then perhaps fillets of black sole stuffed with crab and served with a chive sauce, or perhaps mouclade, or for carnivores roast rack of lamb served pink. Complete the meal with Irish farmhouse cheeses, or you might like an almond meringue with apricot purée. Not surprisingly, the wine list is particularly strong on white burgundies, and is also enlivened by some very amusing cartoons! If, by the end of dinner, you still haven't seen the dolphin, stay overnight in one of the eight rooms of the adjoining Townhouse, and try again after a nourishing breakfast.

DUBLIN   Restaurant Patrick Guilbaud

See page 232 – our Clover Award Section.

GOREY   Marlfield House

Gorey, Co. Wexford
Telephone: (055) 21124   *Fax:* (055) 21572   **£55**
Open: lunch + dinner daily (closed Dec)
Last orders: lunch 2.15pm, dinner 9.15pm (9.30pm Sat, 8.15pm Sun)

Marlfield is a fine Regency house set in 14 hectares of woodland and gardens, and when an extension and conservatory were added, matching brick and stone ensured a sympathetic blending of old and new. The nineteen bedrooms (and five state rooms) are lavishly decorated with period furniture and marble fireplaces. The public rooms are also gracious and hospitable.

Mary Bowe is equally gracious and hospitable as hostess, and at her table you might enjoy some of her specialities such as a hot wholemeal pancake topped with smoked salmon and served with a warm horseradish sauce; or perhaps pan-fried breast of chicken stuffed with home-made tomato and apple chutney, served on a madeira sauce. Mary now controls the kitchen herself too, as well as everything else, Steven Doherty having left for southern climes.

KANTURK	Assolas Country House

Kanturk, Co. Cork
Telephone: (029) 50015   *Fax:* (029) 50795   **£60**
Open: dinner daily (closed Nov to mid-Mar)
Last orders: dinner 8.30pm

Another house that has been in the same family for generations, the Bourkes' Assolas enjoys a peaceful setting in grounds stretching down to the River Blackwater – boating, angling and feeding swans are just some of the outdoor pursuits on offer here. Head-of-the-family Joe Bourke explains that he shares his home with his guests, offering hospitality and simple but good quality service. Nine well-equipped and comfortable bedrooms.

Hazel Bourke's menus offer sound cooking in plentiful quantities. An October menu offered West Coast scallops and prawns with a beurre blanc sauce; then cream of carrot soup; a main course of monkfish strips, with mushrooms and leeks flamed in brandy to create the sauce, served with ratatouille, florets of broccoli and cauliflower, and dauphinoise potatoes; and, to finish, a black-and-white chocolate truffle cake served with home-made ice cream.

KENMARE	Park Hotel Kenmare

See page 233 – our Clover Award Section.

MALLOW	Longueville House

Mallow, Co. Cork
Telephone: (022) 47156   *Fax:* (022) 47459   **£50**
Open: lunch + dinner daily (closed Christmas-Mar)
Last orders: lunch 2.00pm, dinner 9.00pm

Michael and Jane O'Callaghan are still in charge at Longueville, and son William oversees the cooking. Much of the produce used comes from the estate which comprises a farm as well as a kitchen garden. Fish comes from the River Blackwater. The sixteen bedrooms, fully equipped with modern amenities but antique furnishings, make Longueville a delightful place to stay.

MOYCULLEN   Drimcong House

Moycullen, Co. Galway
Telephone: (091) 85115/85585   **£40**
Open: dinner Tue-Sat (closed Christmas-Mar)
Last orders: dinner 10.30pm

Gerry and Marie Galvin are happily into their sixth year at Drimcong, which is first and foremost a locals' restaurant, serving Galway and its environs. The customers are a mixture of business people, families, couples and generally anyone with a keen interest in contemporary food. Thus the Galvins have a wide appeal in an area not very heavily populated.

Gerry's cooking, which uses the finest ingredients available, draws inspiration from many sources – even if he has to go to the European mainland for them! His food is uncomplicated, clean-tasting and presented with the minimum of fuss. Try perhaps a rabbit terrine served with a rowanberry preserve, then perhaps roast guineafowl with red wine, mushrooms and bacon, and, to finish, marinated summer fruits in a sweet geranium sauce. The wine list is helpfully divided into bottles at under or over £13, with bargains all round.

NEWPORT   Newport House Hotel

Newport, Co. Mayo
Telephone: (098) 41222   *Fax:* (098) 41613   **£60**
Open: dinner daily (closed early Oct to mid-Mar)
Last orders: dinner 9.30pm

Newport House, Georgian, ivy-clad and situated by the River Newport where it flows into Clew Bay, was for 200 years home to the O'Donel family. For the past five years it has been run by Kieran and Thelma Thompson, although chef John Gavin joined in 1983, and restaurant and hotel manager Owen Mullins has been a pillar of this particular establishment since 1946! Newport loves longevity, and there is a timelessness in the graceful staircase (principal feature of the main hall), the gracious public rooms and the twenty comfortable bedrooms.

Specialities from the kitchen include wild salmon and other seafood from their own waters (some of the salmon is destined for home-smoking), and vegetables from the walled garden. Noisettes of lamb might be served with a rosemary and pink peppercorn sauce, while for pudding try a damson tartlet, or some home-made ice cream. The wine list includes a couple of pages of house recommendations.

OUGHTERARD   Currarevagh House

Oughterard, Connemara, Co. Galway
Telephone: (091) 82312/82313   **£40**
Open: dinner daily (closed Oct/Nov-Apr)
Last orders: dinner 8.00pm

Harry and June Hodgson have lived at Currarevagh for over twenty years, and are the fifth generation of the Hodgson family to do so. The house was built for the family over 150 years ago, situated beside Lough Corrib and set in 150 acres of woodland. It is run as a private country estate and the international clientele enjoys total privacy.

A 5-course dinner is served promptly at 8.00pm and might comprise Criterion soup, scallops and prawns mornay, then stuffed leg of veal with lemon sauce, roast potatoes, courgettes and tomatoes, white chocolate mousse with marinated fruits, Irish cheeses and a good strong pot of Kenya coffee to finish.

PORTRUSH   Ramore

See page 236 – our Clover Award Section.

RATHNEW   Tinakilly House Hotel

Wicklow, Co. Wicklow
Telephone: (0404) 67806   *Fax:* (0404) 69274   **£60**
Open: lunch + dinner daily
Last orders: lunch 2.00pm (2.30pm Sun), dinner 9.00pm

William and Bee Power celebrate seven years at Tinakilly, a Victorian house restored to its former splendour, in both decor and furnishings. Fourteen comfortable bedrooms enjoy all modern amenities. Bee makes the bread daily in the kitchen, and also makes full use of fresh local produce whenever possible – Wicklow lamb, local oysters in a pie, vegetables from the garden.

SHANAGARRY   Ballymaloe House

See page 234 – our Clover Award Section.

YOUGHAL   Aherne's Seafood Restaurant

163 North Main Street, Youghal, Co. Cork
Telephone: (024) 92424   **£40**
Open: lunch + dinner daily (closed 4 days Christmas, Good Friday)
    (bar lunch Sun)
Last orders: lunch 2.15pm (1.50pm Sun), dinner 9.30pm

Youghal is tiny – only 6,500 inhabitants – so the Fitzgibbon family has
to draw custom from the surrounding area. They therefore plan to
expand the 45-seater restaurant by the addition of some bedrooms.
Meanwhile, go to the pretty green-and-cream building with its floral
terrace on the sea front for lunch or dinner, cooked by David
Fitzgibbon. He emphasises locally caught fish, preparing and
presenting it as simply as possible to enhance the natural flavours.
Try grilled flounder with parsley butter, baked sea-bass with white
wine and fennel, mussels, drabs, prawns, brill, monkfish, lobster . . .
Some meat dishes for carnivores, homely desserts or Irish farmhouse cheeses and a good list of predominantly white wines.

Republic of Ireland Listings

(Prices are quoted in Irish punts) `

ADARE
The Dunraven Arms
Adare, Co Limerick
Tel: (061) 396209   *Fax:* (061) 396541   **£50**
Open: lunch + dinner daily
Last orders: lunch 2.00pm, dinner 9.00pm
Friendly welcome at this 47-bedroomed hotel. Large function facilities.

AHAKISTA
Shiro Japanese Dinner House
Ahakista, Nr Bantry, Co Cork
Tel: (027) 67030   **£65**
Open: dinner daily (closed Jan-Feb)
Last orders: dinner 9.00pm
Charming restaurant, delicate Japanese cuisine by Kei Pilz and service from husband Werner.

BALLYLICKEY
Ballylickey Manor House
Ballylickey, Bantry Bay, Co Cork
Tel: (027) 50071   *Fax:* (027) 50124   **£50**
Open: lunch + dinner daily (residents only Wed) (closed Nov-Apr)
Last orders: lunch 2.00pm, dinner 9.15pm
Former 17th-century shooting lodge; views over Bantry Bay. Eleven bedrooms, antique furniture.

BALLYVAUGHAN
Gregans Castle Hotel
Ballyvaughan, Co Clare
Tel: (065) 77005   *Fax:* (065) 77111   **£50**
Open: lunch + dinner daily (closed Nov-Easter)
Last orders: lunch 2.30pm, dinner 8.30pm
Once the home of the Prince of Burren, now a comfortable hotel. Sixteen bedrooms, set 4-course dinners.

BRAY
The Tree of Idleness Restaurant
Seafront, Bray, Co Wicklow
Tel: (01) 863498   **£60**
Open: dinner Tue-Sun (closed Bank Holidays, 1 wk Christmas, 2 wks Aug/Sep)
Last orders: dinner 11.00pm (10.00pm Sun)
Originally a Greek/Cypriot restaurant but now owner Akis Courtellas cooks a more international menu, served by his wife Susan.

BUNRATTY
MacCloskey's
Bunratty House Mews, Bunratty, Co Clare
Tel: (061) 364082   **£60**
Open: dinner Tue-Sat (closed Christmas to Feb)
Last orders: dinner 10.00pm
Restaurant in the cellars of Bunratty House. Five-course, fixed price menus.

CASHEL, Co Galway
Cashel House Hotel
Cashel, Co Galway
Tel: (095) 31001   *Fax:* (095) 31077   **£55**
Open: lunch + dinner daily (closed Nov-Christmas, 4 wks Jan/Feb)
Last orders: lunch 2.00pm, dinner 8.45pm (8.00pm Sun)
Thirty-five acres of grounds, comfortable public rooms, thirty-two luxury bedrooms, private beach. Restaurant with conservatory. Menus use local produce whenever possible.

CASHEL, Co Tipperary
Cashel Palace Hotel
Cashel, Co Tipperary
Tel: (062) 61411   *Fax:* (062) 61521   **£60**
Open: lunch + dinner daily
Last orders: lunch 2.15pm, dinner 9.15pm
Palladian brick-built mansion which was still the bishop's palace until 1960. Twenty en-suite bedrooms.

CASTLEDERMOT
Doyle's School House Country Inn
Main Street, Castledermot, Co Kildare
Tel: (0503) 44282   *Fax:* (0503) 43653   **£45**
Open: lunch Sun, dinner Tue-Sat (closed Feb)
Last orders: lunch 2.00pm, dinner 10.30pm
Traditional British cooking for local clientele.

CASTLETOWNROCHE
Blackwater Valley Castle
Castletownroche, Co Cork
Tel: (022) 26333   *Fax:* (022) 26210   **£60**
Open: lunch by arrangement, dinner daily
Last orders: dinner 9.00pm
Small 12th-century castle overlooking valley. Comfortable public rooms and bedrooms. Fixed-price, 4-course dinner menus.

CLONES
Hilton Park
Scotshouse, Clones, Co Monaghan
Tel: (047) 56007   *Fax:* (047) 56033   **£50**
Open: dinner daily, residents only (closed Oct-Apr)
Last orders: dinner 8.00pm
In the same family (the Maddens) for 250 years – full of their personal touches. Popular with sporting parties.

CONG
Ashford Castle
Cong, Co Mayo
Tel: (092) 46003   *Fax:* (092) 46260   **£80**
Open: lunch + dinner daily
Last orders: lunch 2.00pm, dinner 10.00pm
Dating from 13th Century but resembling a French château. Magnificent castle and grounds. Large panelled restaurant serving set-price dinners. Also the smaller Connaught Room restaurant.

CONNEMARA
Boluisce Seafood Bar & Restaurant
Spiddal Village, Connemara, Co Galway
Tel: (091) 83286 **£30**
Open: lunch Tue-Fri, dinner daily (closed Bank
 Holidays)
Last orders: lunch 2.00pm, dinner 10.00pm
John and Margaret Glanville's restaurant –
 she cooks, he serves. Simple dishes are
 best.

Rosleague Manor
Letterfrack, Connemara, Co Galway
Tel: (095) 41101   *Fax:* (095) 41168 **£50**
Open: lunch + dinner daily (closed Nov-Easter)
Last orders: lunch 3.00pm, dinner 9.30pm (8.30pm
 Sun)
Overlooking Connemara National park,
 family-run in friendly manner. Antique
 furnishing, fishing available.

CORK
Clifford's Restaurant
23 Washington Street West, Cork, Co Cork
Tel: (021) 275333 **£50**
Open: lunch Tue-Fri, dinner Mon-Sat (closed Bank
 Holidays, 1 wk Aug)
Last orders: lunch 2.30pm, dinner 10.30pm
Michael Clifford's seasonally changing
 menus, now in larger premises. Set lunch
 £10, set dinner £22.

DUBLIN
Le Coq Hardi
35 Pembroke Road, Ballsbridge, Dublin 4,
 Co Dublin
Tel: (01) 689070 **£70**
Open: lunch Mon-Fri, dinner Mon-Sat (closed 2
 wks Aug)
Last orders: lunch 2.30pm, dinner 11.00pm
Gracious Georgian building, traditional
 comforts in a 50-seater restaurant. Fish a
 speciality.

King Sitric The Fish Restaurant
East Pier, Harbour Road, Dublin, Co Dublin
Tel: (01) 325235   *Fax:*(01) 392442 **£55**
Open: dinner Mon-Sat (closed Bank Holidays,
 10 dys Christmas)
Last orders: dinner 11.00pm
Celebrating twenty years of producing
 excellent fresh local fish dishes.

Shay Beano
St Stephen's Green, Dublin, Co Dublin
Tel: (01) 776384 **£50**
Open: lunch + dinner Mon-Sat (closed Bank
 Holidays)
Last orders: lunch 2.30pm, dinner 10.30pm
Intimate French restaurant, good pâtisserie
 and wines.

The Shelbourne Hotel
St Stephen's Green, Dublin, Co Dublin
Tel: (01) 766471   *Fax:* (01) 616006 **£55**
Open: lunch + dinner daily
Last orders: lunch 2.00pm, dinner 10.00pm
Classical façade, 164 bedrooms, famous
 Horseshoe Bar.

Whites on the Green
119 St Stephen's Green, Dublin 2, Co Dublin
Tel: (01) 751975 **£55**
Open: lunch Mon-Fri, dinner Mon-Sat (closed Bank
 Holidays)
Last orders: lunch 2.30pm, dinner 10.45pm
 (11.00pm Sat)
Set menus of French cooking in this tradi-
 tional Dublin restaurant.

DUNDERRY
Dunderry Lodge Restaurant
Robinstown, Navan, Dunderry, Co Meath
Tel: (046) 31671 **£60**
Open: lunch + dinner, Tue-Sat (closed Bank
 Holidays, Jan)
Last orders: lunch 2.00pm, dinner 7.00pm
New owners this year at this well-known
 restaurant.

DURRUS
Blair's Cove House Restaurant
Blair's Cove, Durrus, Nr Bantry, Co Cork
Tel: (027) 61127 **£55**
Open: lunch Sun, dinner Tue-Sat (closed Nov-Feb)
Last orders: lunch 2.00pm, dinner 9.30pm
Restaurant with rooms – or rather a self-
 contained flat with cooking facilities. Not
 that you need these with plenty of fish
 dishes to choose from the restaurant
 menu. Views over Bantry Bay.

KILLARNEY
Aghadoe Heights Hotel
Aghadoe, Killarney, Co Kerry
Tel: (064) 31766   *Fax:*(064) 31345 **£65**
Open: lunch + dinner daily
Last orders: lunch 2.00pm, dinner 9.30pm
Splendid views from the heights. Sixty
 well-equipped bedrooms and bathrooms.

Gaby's Seafood Restaurant
17 High Street, Killarney, Co Kerry
Tel: (064) 32519   *Fax:*(064) 32747 **£40**
Open: lunch Tue-Sat, dinner Mon-Sat (closed
 mid-Dec to mid-Mar)
Last orders: lunch 2.30pm, dinner 10.00pm
In fact, Geert Maes's seafood restaurant!
 Live lobsters await their fate in a tank.
 Good wines, especially white burgundies.

MOYGLARE
Moyglare Manor Hotel
Moyglare, Maynooth, Co Kildare
Tel: (01) 6286351   *Fax:* (01) 6285405 **£50**
Open: lunch Sun-Fri, dinner daily (closed
 Christmas, Easter)
Last orders: lunch 2.30pm, dinner 10.30pm
Georgian house, traditional furnishings in
 bedrooms, public rooms and restaurant
 which serves traditional food.

RATHMULLAN
Rathmullan House
Rathmullan, Co Donegal
Tel: (074) 58188   *Fax:*(074) 58200 **£40**
Open: lunch Sun, dinner daily (closed 10 dys
 Christmas, Jan to mid-Mar)
Last orders: lunch 2.00pm, dinner 8.30pm
Georgian house overlooking Lough Swilly,
 in peaceful countryside. Nineteen bed-
 rooms.

THOMASTOWN
Mount Juliet Hotel
Mount Juliet, Thomastown, Co Kilkenny
Tel: (056) 24455   *Fax:* (056) 24522   **£55**
Open: lunch + dinner daily
Last orders: lunch 2.30pm, dinner 9.30pm

18th-century creeper-clad hotel in 1,400-acre estate. Luxurious interior, international golf course designed by Jack Niklaus.

WATERFORD
Waterford Castle
The Island, Ballinakill, Waterford, Co Waterford
Tel: (051) 78203   **£60**
Open: lunch + dinner daily
Last orders: lunch 2.00pm, dinner 10.00pm

18th-century castle, 310-acre estate, reached by private ferry! Baronial splendour in public rooms and nineteen bedrooms.

WICKLOW
The Old Rectory Country House & Restaurant
Wicklow, Co Wicklow
Tel: (0404) 67048   *Fax:* (0404) 69181   **£50**
Open: dinner daily (closed Oct-Easter)
Last orders: dinner 8.00pm (9.00pm Sat)

Paul and Linda Saunders' friendly restaurant with five rooms has a private-house feel. Pretty rooms, thoughtful extras. Linda's set dinner menus use local organically-grown produce when possible.

The Maps

1. SOUTH-WEST ENGLAND & WALES

The maps show only those villages, towns and cities where recommended hotels and restaurants may be found.

Liverpool

Moss Nook

Sheffield SOUTH
YORKSHIRE

Knutsford Wilmslow

Prestbury Bollington

Ridgeway

Linc

Chester Sandiway

CHESHIRE

Baslow

Rossett Nantwich

Waterhouses

DERBY-
SHIRE

Matlock

NOTTINGHAM-
SHIRE

Beckingh

Ashbourne

Bilbrough

Nottingham

Barks

Great
Goner

STAFFORD-
SHIRE

Plumtree

Stafford

Melton
Mowbray

Stre

Loughborough

Oakham

Hamble

SHROPSHIRE

Shifnal

LEICESTERSHIRE

Leicester

Uppingham

Dorrington

WEST
MIDLANDS
Birmingham

Sutton
Coldfield

Countesthorpe

Ludlow

Bromsgrove

Hockley
Heath

Kenilworth

NORTHAMPTON-

Brimfield

Abberley

WARWICKSHIRE

Holdenby

Wellingborough

HEREFORD

Bromyard

Stratford-
upon-Avon

Bishop's
Tachbrook

SHIRE

Horton

Leominster

Worcester

Alderminster

Priors
Hardwick

Stoke
Bruerne

Roade

AND WORCESTER

Paulerspury

Aspley Guise

Malvern Wells

Lower
Brailes

Woburn

Hereford

Ledbury

Broadway

Moreton-in-Marsh

Fli

Vowchurch

Hope
End

Buckland

Upper
Slaughter

Stow-on-the-Wold

Kingham

Corse
Lawn

Cheltenham

Lower
Slaughter

Chadlington

Aylesbury

Whitebrook

GLOUCESTER-
SHIRE

Birdlip

Northleach

Minster
Lovell

Woodstock

Aston Clinton

BUCKINGHAM-

Usk

Trellech

Stonehouse

Stroud

OXFORD-
SHIRE

Lew

Oxford

Great
Milton

Thame

SHIRE

Speen

WENT

hepstow

Nailsworth

Clanfield

Lechlade

Stonor

Thornbury

Tetbury

Crudwell

Remenham

Hurley

Maiden

AVON

Malmesbury

Purton

Moulsford-
on-Thames

Warren Row

Tap

Bristol

Castle Combe

Goring-on-Thames
Yattendon

Sonning-
on-Thames

Bray-
on-
Thames

W

Colerne

Corsham

Pangbourne

Bathford

Box

Lacock

Kintbury

BERKSHIRE

Ascot

E

Chelwood

Bath

Beanacre

Newbury

Shinfield

Bags

Ston Easton

Bradford-
on-Avon

WILTSHIRE

Eversley

Rotherwick

R
S

Shepton
Mallet

Warminster

Basingstoke

Bramley

Graysho

astonbury

Middle Wallop

HAMPSHIRE

Haslemere

SOMERSET

Bruton

Gillingham

Sparsholt

Pet

Castle Cary

Romsey

Midhurst

Chilgrove

W

Barwick
Village

Sherborne

Sturminster
Newton

Stuckton

Botley

Wickham

Pulboro
Amber

Evershot

Tarrant Monkton

Brockenhurst

Cosham

Emsworth

Storri

Chedington

Blandford Forum

DORSET

Lymington

Southsea

Bridport

Maiden Newton

Poole

New Milton

Dorchester

Milford-
on-Sea

Isle of Wight

COLNSHIRE

Wells-next-the-Sea

Erpingham

Grimston

Guist

King's Lynn

NORFOLK

Norwich

Great Yarmouth

CAMBRIDGE-

Ely

Diss

Fressingfield

Huntingdon

Ixworth

Southwold

SHIRE

Bury St Edmunds

SUFFOLK

Cambridge

Stonham

Campsea Ashe

Lavenham

Chelsworth

Woodbridge

Aldeburgh

Glemsford

Sudbury

Ipswich

Orford

Royston

Nayland

East Bergholt

Broxted

Wethersfield

Dedham

Harwich

Great Dunmow

Coggeshall

Bishop's Stortford

Felstead

RTFORD-

ESSEX

West Mersea

HIRE

High Ongar

New Barnet

Rochford

GREATER

Horndon-on-the-Hill

ton

London

Southend-on-Sea

enham

hmond

LONDON

biton

rbiton

Herne Bay

on-Thames

gate

Faversham

utton

Croydon

Maidstone

Canterbury

South Godstone

Sevenoaks

KENT

Barham

Reigate

Boughton Monchelsea

Hastingleigh

St Margaret's at Cliffe

Edenbridge

Ashford

sper

Tunbridge Wells

Sissinghurst

Folkestone

ower

East Grinstead

eding

Staple Cross

eld

Uckfield

EAST

Dallington

Rye

X

Rushlake Green

Battle

SUSSEX

Herstmonceux

Brighton

Jevington

St Leonards on Sea

Seaford

Eastbourne

3. NORTHERN ENGLAND

Isle of Man

Berwick-on-Tweed

Alnwick

NORTHUMBERLAND

Morpeth

Whitley Bay
Wylam
TYNE AND WEAR
Newcastle-upon-Tyne
East Boldon

Brampton
Crosby-on-Eden

Wetheral

Cockermouth

Watermillock
Romaldkirk
DURHAM
Darlington
CLEVELAND

CUMBRIA
Ullswater
Appleby-
in-Westmorland
Stokesley

Grasmere
Ambleside
Staddlebridge

Windermere
Wensleydale
Kirkby Fleetham

Spark Bridge
Witherslack
Kilburn
Helmsley

Cartmel
Ulverston
NORTH YORKSHIRE
Whitwell-
on-the-Hill

Kirkby
Lonsdale
Pateley
Bridge

Hetton
Bolton
Abbey
Harrogate
York

Slaidburn
Kildwick
Ilkley
Wansford-
in-England

Thornton Cleveleys
Clitheroe
Haworth
Pool-in-
Wharfedale
Beverley

Blackpool
Longridge
WEST
Leeds
HUMBERSIDE

Broughton
Langho
Bradford
Hull

LANCASHIRE
YORKSHIRE
Ripponden
Winteringham

Wrightington
Huddersfield

Bury
Birtle
GREATER
MANCHESTER
Barnsley

MERSEYSIDE
Manchester
SOUTH
YORKSHIRE
LINCOLNSHIRE

Liverpool
Moss
Nook
Sheffield

4. SCOTLAND

Walls

ORKNEY
ISLANDS

Kinlochbervie

Isle of Lewis

Ullapool

Contin
Cromarty
Nairn
Muir-of-Ord
Gollanfield
Inverness
Buckie
Drumnadrochit
Carrbridge
Old Meldrum
GRAMPIAN
Whitebridge
Dulnain
Bridge
Alford
HIGHLAND
Kingussie
Aboyne
Banchory
Aberdeen
Newtonmore
Ballater
Stonehaven
Isle of
Skye
Arisaig
Fort
William
Killiecrankie
Onich
Pitlochry
TAYSIDE
Kentallen
Aberfeldy
Strathtummel
Port Appin
Blairgowrie
Eassie
Kilcheran
Dunkeld
Auchmithie
Isle of
Oban
Kinclaven
Auchterhouse
Isle of Iona
Mull
Kilmore
Strathyre
Crieff
Perth
Scone
Cupar
Peat Inn
Auchterarder
St Andrews
Cairndow
Tarbert
Dunblane
Falkland
FIFE
Anstruther
Strachur
Aberfoyle
Kinross
Elie
Crinan
Blair Drummond
Alloa
Markinch
North Berwick
CENTRAL
Kilfinan
Bridge of Allan
Gullane
Linlithgow
Edinburgh
Haddington
Kilberry
Glasgow
LOTHIAN
Isle of Islay
West Linton
Melrose
Biggar
Peebles
Selkirk
Bellochantuy
STRATHCLYDE
BORDERS
Ayr
Hawick
Alloway
Moffat
DUMFRIES
AND
Holywood
Canonbie
Eaglesfield
GALLOWAY
Portpatrick
Stewarton

5. IRELAND

THE ART OF SOPHISTICATION.

The best of France...

MARTELL

COGNAC. L'ART DE MARTELL.

SINCE 1715.

Pot Luck in Europe

I promised some ten years ago that every time I went on a journey, I would keep a pictorial notebook of the various places I stayed at and ate in, and this summer was no exception. August 1990 took me on a varied journey down through the Dordogne region of France, on to the Algarve in Portugal, and then to Tuscany in Italy.

I was lucky to have the photographer Leigh Simpson travelling with me on this particular foray. (He was there shooting stills for a film we were making for OSL Villas.) So, I came back from this trip with a bundle of menus, jotted notes of meals and places enjoyed – and a stack of photos taken by Leigh, which have been reproduced in this section.

The establishments we visited range from grand hotels and castles to small, family-run places. I hope you will enjoy some of the pleasures we experienced as we delved into colourful local markets and afterwards indulged our sharpened appetites in restaurants great and small.

Also included in this section are some recent 'jottings' on eating in Paris and Brussels.

Invariably, wherever I stay, one of my first ports of call is the local market – fruit, vegetables or fish (in the Mediterranean, often landed straight from the boat). I usually watch what the locals are buying, as particularly in France and Italy they tend to buy what is in season at the best price. Even in cities such as Paris the daily habit of shopping at street stalls and markets persists, and in rural communities the tradition is even more marked. There, it's especially interesting to see what local restaurateurs choose at the morning markets.

Pick of the Paris Bistros

A meal in a Parisian bistro remains one of the delights of a visit to this city, but prices and quality can vary alarmingly. The following is a selection of bistros (and a couple of brasseries) where a 3-course meal (even chosen from the carte) and ½-bottle of wine will not usually cost more than 200F per person, and very often a good deal less.

Lescure
PLACE DE LA CONCORDE
7 rue de Mondovi, 75001   *Telephone:* 42.60.18.91
Open: lunch Mon-Sat, dinner Mon-Fri (closed Aug, 10 days Christmas)
Last orders: 10.00pm

Just off Place de la Concorde, nestling in the corner of rue Mondovi and rue du Mont Thabor. A small dining room with rustic decor and cuisine de ménage: confit, poule au riz etc. Established in 1919 and the best value in the area. Terrace in summer. Book.

Chez André
CHAMPS-ÉLYSÉES
12 rue Marbeuf, 75008   *Telephone:* 47.20.59.57
Open: lunch + dinner Wed-Sun (closed 3 wks Aug)
Last orders: 11.45pm

Traditional bistro fare. Packed out, elbow to elbow, by locals. Rapid service. Totally authentic but you pay a little more for the location. Ask for a table outside on the pavement. Interior is almost as old as the bistro (over fifty years!).

L'Assiette Lyonnaise
CHAMPS-ÉLYSÉES
21 rue Marbeuf, 75008   *Telephone:* 47.20.94.80
Open: lunch + dinner daily (closed Aug)
Last orders: 11.30pm

New alternative to Chez André: simple, rustic style decor with red checked cloths, simple 'bouchon lyonnais'. Short typical menu might include quenelles de brochet or andouillettes.

Au Roi du Pot-au-Feu
CHAMPS-ÉLYSÉES

40 rue de Ponthieu, 75008   *Telephone:* 43.59.41.62
Open: lunch + dinner Mon-Sat
Last orders: 10.00pm

Two tiny dining rooms on ground and first floors. Simple decor with wooden chairs and red and white checked cloths. A newcomer; run by the daughter-in-law of the owner of long-established Le Roi du Pot-au-Feu in rue Vignon (9th arr). Speciality: pot-au-feu!

La Poule au Pot
LES HALLES/CHATELET

9 rue de Vauvilliers, 75001   *Telephone:* 42.36.32.96
Open: daily 7.00pm – 6.00am

Archetypal bistro open all night, 365 days a year! Tiled floor, brown vinyl banquette seating, stucco ceiling, real old bar counter, waiters in long white aprons.

Le Chatelet Gourmand
LES HALLES/CHATELET

13 rue des Lavandières, 75001   *Telephone:* 40.26.45.00
Open: lunch + dinner Tue-Sat (closed Aug)
Last orders: 10.30pm

A real 'find', this recently opened bistro, with good cooking by a stalwart of the bistro tradition. Wine bar decor belies the quality of the food: gigot de jeune mouton des Pyrénées, contre-filet de boeuf, terrines etc. Set menus from 120F – including wine!

Le Rond de Serviette

OPÉRA

16 rue Saint-Augustin, 75002   *Telephone:* 49.27.09.90
Open: Mon-Fri
Last orders: 11.00pm

New (and cheaper) 'annexe' of the classic Chez Pauline. Modern decor in cream and wine red, with Daumier drawings on the walls, and the dishes of the day chalked up on blackboards. Pleasant service and classic cooking: blanquette, terrines etc.

Le Troumilou

SOUTHERN MARAIS/HÔTEL DE VILLE

84 Quai de l'Hôtel-de-Ville, 75004   *Telephone:* 42.77.63.98
Open: Tue-Sun
Last orders: 11.00pm

Huge, old riverside bistro serving good, cheap, classic food: canard aux pruneaux; ris de veau grand-mère; truite aux amandes. Crammed with locals oblivious to its station waiting room decor.

L'Oulette

PLACE DES VOSGES/BASTILLE

38 rue des Tournelles, 75004   *Telephone:* 42.71.43.33
Open: lunch Mon-Fri, dinner Mon-Sat (closed 3 wks Aug)
Last orders: 10.30pm

Tiny, pretty restaurant, in tones of beige and cream, serving very good food of south-western inspiration from ex-pupil of Alain Dutournier (Carré des Feuillants): caneton rôti et confit aux petits pois frais; selle d'agneau au four avec ragoût de fèves tendres. Some of the best value in Paris. Book.

Le Temps des Cerises

PLACE DES VOSGES/BASTILLE

31 rue de la Cerisaie, 75004   *Telephone:* 42.72.08.63
Open: lunch only Mon-Fri (closed Aug)

Popular lunchtime bistro with menu at 48F: eg oeufs mayo, pâté, côtes d'agneau, pintade rôti. Get there early.

Les Fontaines

LA RIVE GAUCHE

9 rue Soufflot, 75005   *Telephone:* 43.26.42.80
Open: lunch + dinner Mon-Sat
Last orders: 10.00pm

Deceptively bland, modern café – decor belies very good food and amazingly reasonable prices; some fish and seasonable game. Good Loire wines. Book. Situated between the Panthéon and Jardins Luxembourg.

Le Bistro de la Maube

LA RIVE GAUCHE

17 rue Frédéric-Sauton, 75005   *Telephone:* 43.29.40.72
Open: daily
Last orders: 10.30pm

Tiny beamed dining room and good cuisine bourgeoise: boeuf en daube, truite aux amandes. A charming husband-and-wife-run place.

Le Bistro de la Grille
LA RIVE GAUCHE
14 rue Mabillon, 75005   *Telephone:* 43.54.16.87
Open: all day, daily from 8.00am
Last orders: 00.30am

Elbow-to-elbow old bistro on two floors, with walls covered in filmstars' photos. Good bistro cooking: saucisson chaud, pavé de morue, oysters. Eat outside on the pavement in summer.

Chez Ribe
LA TOUR EIFFEL
15 Avenue de Suffren, 75007   *Telephone:* 45.66.53.79
Open: lunch + dinner Mon-Sat (closed 2 wks Aug, Christmas + New Year)
Last orders: 10.30pm

148F fixed price menu (plenty of choice) is best value in the area. Art Deco brasserie decor, with etched glass mirrors and comfortable banquette seating.

Brasserie de la Poste
TROCADERO
54 rue de Longchamp, 75016   *Telephone:* 47.55.01.31
Open: lunch + dinner daily
Last orders: 1.00am

Attractive, characteristic brasserie decor – mirrors and banquette seating – and cooking of a reliable standard: filet de hareng, pied de porc pavé, steak tartare.

Bistro du Petit Bedon
PLACE DE L'ÉTOILE
1 rue Pergolèse, 75016   *Telephone:* 40.67.10.67
Open: lunch + dinner daily
Last orders: 11.00pm

Sister establishment to Petit Bedon, with traditional dishes served in modern grey-and-red setting: pot-au-feu, tête de veau etc.

A NOTRE DAME DES VICTOIRES

·1· EPICERIE P. LEGRAND CONFISERIE ·1·

Wepler

MONTMARTRE

14 Place de Clichy, 75018   *Telephone:* 45.22.53.24
Open: lunch + dinner daily
Last orders: 1.00am

Classic huge old brasserie with attentive service. Choose a plate of seafood and a glass of wine, or a simple brasserie dish.

Le Bistrot des Deux Théatres

MONTMARTRE

18 rue Blanche, 75009   *Telephone:* 45.26.41.43
Open: lunch + dinner daily
Last orders: 00.30am

Not actually in Montmartre but easily accessible by métro. 145F fixed price menu includes apéritif, wine and coffee, with a good choice of dishes.

Paris Favourites

It's difficult to select favourites among restaurants in Paris as there are always newcomers vying for position. Indeed the overwhelming choice across the board is what makes this one of my favourite cities to visit. My short list is based on the following criteria: consistently excellent food, a warm welcome and courteous, informed service, an elegant setting and, since the best does not have to cost the moon, value for money. Instead of opting for obvious choices, I have been on the look-out for talent that is tipped for the top – visit these now while table availability and prices still permit! But first, a general round-up of Paris favourites.

In the same breath as 'best' is the name **'Robuchon'**, but few people get an opportunity these days to see for themselves, since the restaurant is always full of regulars. Pity too that he has decided to withdraw his cheaper fixed price menu, opting instead for one at 790F . . .

It is advisable to book well in advance for any of the restaurants mentioned here.

Jules Verne, Eiffel Tower, 75007, (*Telephone:* 45.55.61.44). Chef Louis Grandard has left the Jules Verne for the Drouant. The new chef here is Alain Bariteau and the Jules Verne (on the 2nd floor of the Eiffel Tower) remains a favourite Paris restaurant.

Les Ambassadeurs, 10 Place de la Concorde, 75001, (*Telephone:* 42.65.24.24). Christian Constant is still at the Crillon's Les Ambassadeurs restaurant. However, chefs never seem to stay long here, so don't dally, enjoy his excellent cooking served, as always, by one of the best brigades in Paris. Go for lunch and revel in the splendour.

Le Grand Véfour, 17 rue de Beaujolais, 75001, (*Telephone:* 42.96.56.27). Le Grand Véfour has survived the razzmatazz of its re-opening and is now settling down to being a very good restaurant – but let's be honest, it's the exquisite setting and romance of the Palais Royal that really makes it a place worth visiting.

Jacques Cagna, 14 rue des Grands Augustins, 75006, (*Telephone:* 43.26.49.39), **Faugeron**, 52 rue de Longchamp, 75016, (*Telephone:* 47.04.24.53) and **Michel Rostang**, 20 rue Rennequin, 75017, (*Telephone:* 47.63.40.77). Jacques Cagna, Henri Faugeron and Michel Rostang remain three of the best chefs in Paris, each offering superb cooking in comfortably elegant surroundings with good service.

Olympe, 8 rue N Charlet, 75015, (*Telephone:* 47.34.86.08). Last but not least, two women: first, Dominique Nahmias, chef-patronne of Olympe. If the 15th arrondissement is too far for dinner, go there for her excellent value-for-money lunch at 200F.

Le Bourdonnais, 113 Avenue de la Bourdonnais, 75007, (*Telephone:* 47.05.47.96). Also maintaining a good reputation in this city of male chefs is Micheline Coat at Le Bourdonnais (Le Cantine des Gourmets): exemplary for its warmth of welcome, service and good value for money food.

Now, in no particular order, my Top Ten choice is:

Lucas-Carton
MADELEINE/RUE ROYALE
9 Place de la Madeleine, 75008 *Telephone:* 42.65.22.90
Open: lunch + dinner Mon-Fri (closed 27 Jul – 20 Aug, 2 wks Christmas)
Last orders: 10.30pm

Alain Senderens has made a point of offering lunchtime menus at 350F and 400F, thus bringing this, the other best restaurant in Paris, just about within reach of non-expense account diners. Some cheaper wines are also listed. Perhaps, therefore, a small point scored over Robuchon?!

L'Ambroisie
LE MARAIS
9 Place des Vosges, 75004 *Telephone:* 42.78.51.45
Open: lunch + dinner Tue-Sat (closed 2 wks Feb + 3 wks Aug)
Last orders: 10.15pm

We mentioned Bernard Pacaud's new restaurant in our meander through Paris in 1989. Two years on, Pacaud is snapping at the heels of the 'big two' and 'le tout Paris' has not been slow to adopt this elegant restaurant in the newly-restored Place des Vosges. Danièle Pacaud assures attentive service of the perfectly executed food which needs only a touchpaper to put it into the orbit of his starry rivals. L'Ambroisie is not cheap, but inevitably it will become more expensive, so book now!

Le Vivarois
RUE DE LA POMPE
192 Avenue Victor Hugo, 75016   *Telephone:* 45.04.04.31
Open: lunch + dinner Mon-Fri (closed Aug)
Last orders: 9.45pm

Claude Peyrot is generally considered to be one of the best chefs of his generation. In the curious way that these things go, after some twenty-five years he has been 'rediscovered' and his ratings have shot up. Classically based food and good service from long-serving staff. Ignore the curious modern decor which remains a touch off-putting.

Guy Savoy
PLACE DE L'ÉTOILE
18 rue Troyon, 75017   *Telephone:* 43.80.36.22
Open: lunch Mon-Fri, dinner Mon-Sat (not Sat Easter – Oct),
(closed 14 Jul – 5 Aug)

The last few years have seen a discernible drift of good restaurants into the 17th arrondissement, such that it must surely be in danger of becoming overcrowded! Guy Savoy was one of the earlier arrivals. The lighthearted classicism of his unique personal style and the restrained elegance of his restaurant have kept this 'star' at the top of the ratings. The sommelier can sometimes be over-enthusiastic with his recommendations!

Apicius
PEREIRE/WAGRAM
122 Avenue de Villiers, 75017   *Telephone:* 43.80.19.66
Open: lunch Mon-Fri, dinner Mon-Sat (not Sat Easter – Oct),
(closed 14 Jul – 5 Aug)

Jean-Marie Vigato is shy and good-looking and a talented chef; his
wife Madeleine is charming and smiling; between them they have
endeared this restaurant to clients and critics alike. Vigato's forte is
in aigre-doux or sucré-salé while his purée de pommes de terre is
said to be worthy of Robuchon!

Amphycles
PALAIS DES CONGRÈS/TERNES
78 Avenue des Ternes, 75017   *Telephone:* 40.68.01.01
Open: lunch Mon-Fri, dinner Mon-Sat (closed 3 wks August),
Last orders: 10.30pm

Another new restaurant for the 17th arrondissement! Chef-patron
Philippe Groult (Meilleur Ouvrier de France 1982) has moved in just
down the road from his former employers, Le Manoir de Paris. He
has also worked with Robuchon and has already gained a good
reputation. Summery garden decor, well-spaced tables and professional service. Good value lunch menu.

L'Arpège
LES INVALIDES
84 rue de Varenne, 75007   *Telephone:* 45.51.47.33
Open: lunch Mon-Fri, dinner daily (closed 3 wks Aug)
Last orders: 10.30pm

Another persistent candidate for the top is Alain Passard's restaurant. His lunch menu at 150F remains one of the best bargains in
Paris – and the waiters will produce it unprompted! Passard might be
advised to improve the decor, but the food is reason enough to go.

Carré des Feuillants
TUILERIES/PLACE VENDÔME
14 rue de Castiglione, 75001   *Telephone:* 42.86.82.82
Open: lunch Mon-Fri, dinner Mon-Sat (closed dinner Sat July + Aug)
Last orders: 10.30pm

If Alain Dutournier had been overstretching himself, he has now returned to the essentials – his 'terroir'. A certain theatricality has gone, although Slavik's decor remains. Dutournier is at his best when remaining true to his roots, his inspiration, and seems more at ease now. Lunch is good value, and the excellent sommelier is always on the look-out for fresh additions to the wine list.

Goumard
MADELEINE
17 rue Duphot, 75001   *Telephone:* 42.60.36.07
Open: lunch + dinner Tue-Sat
Last orders: 10.30pm

Jean-Claude Goumard stakes his reputation on fish – so he himself goes nightly to Rungis to ensure the pick of the best and freshest fish in Paris, which is then cooked simply and well by his chef. The first floor dining room with its Portuguese-style azulejos (blue-and-white tiles) lends charm to the restaurant, which also has a reputation for excellent service.

Miravile
HÔTEL DE VILLE
72 quai Hôtel de Ville, 7500   *Telephone:* 42.74.72.22
Open: lunch Mon-Fri, dinner Mon-Sat

Young chef Gilles Epié is one to watch. He has rapidly gained a good reputation for this left bank restaurant. Muriel Epié looks after the restrainedly elegant dining room. The food is imaginative – Epié is not afraid to be audacious!

En Route through France

These are some of the places I found while meandering through the Dordogne.

Restaurant le Centenaire
LES EYZIES-DE-TAYAC

Le Rocher de la Penne, 24620   *Telephone:* 53.06.97.18
Open: lunch daily (except Tue), dinner daily (closed Nov – Mar)
Last orders: 9.30pm

My favourite hotel and restaurant in the area. Alain Scholly has been running this charming hotel for about twenty years, and each season brings a new sparkle to the hotel. Recently added facilities include a swimming pool and mini-gym. The excellent cooking is by chef Roland Mazère who, in his own way, transforms food traditional to Périgord into light modern dishes, yet retains a style still firmly rooted in the cuisine of the region.

Hôtel Cro-Magnon
LES EYZIES-DE-TAYAC

24620 *Telephone:* 53.06.97.06
Open: lunch Thurs-Tue, dinner daily (closed mid Oct – Mar)
Last orders: 9.00pm

More rustic in style than Le Centenaire, this is a delightful, well-kept hotel. Ask for a room overlooking the garden (and heated pool). M and Mme Leyssales are charming hosts and the food here is good. Specialities include an effeuillé d'artichaux aux cailles confites, and a jambonnette de volaille au foie gras et morilles. In summer, eat on the pretty flowered terrace.

Les Glycines
LES EYZIES-DE-TAYAC

Route de Périgueux, 24620 *Telephone:* 53.06.97.07
Open: lunch + dinner daily (closed Nov – mid Apr)
Last orders: 9.15pm

The kitchen garden provides some of the ingredients for the competent cooking here. Service is atttentive, and a terrace for summertime eating adds to the charm.

Relais Soleil d'Or
MONTIGNAC

16 rue du 4-Septembre, 24290 *Telephone:* 53.51.80.22
Open: lunch + dinner daily (closed mid-Jan – mid-Feb)
Last orders: 10.00pm

Set in pleasant grounds (with heated pool), close to the river Vézère, this typical French provincial hotel is establishing a good gastronomic reputation. Recently it has expanded, and renovated its rooms. The cuisine draws its inspiration from the region – duck, foie gras and truffles feature prominently. Madame presides – somewhat fiercely – over a helpful, friendly staff.

Au Vieux Moulin

LES EYZIES-DE-TAYAC

24620   *Telephone:* 53.06.93.39
Open: lunch + dinner daily (closed mid-Nov – Jan)
Last order: 9.30pm

Old milling implements and artefacts in the large beamed dining room recall the original use of this well-restored building. Good value menus offer classic regional cuisine. Staff are friendly and helpful.

Moulin de l'Abbaye

BRANTÔME

1 route de Bourdeilles, 24310   *Telephone:* 53.05.80.22
Open: lunch + dinner Tue-Sun (closed mid-Oct – May)
Last orders: 9.30pm

A Relais et Châteaux member. The old mill enjoys a riverside location and views of old Brantôme. To enjoy the excellent cooking, stick to the fixed-price menus which offer value for money. Attentive and charming service.

L'Oisin

PERIGUEUX

31 rue St Front, 24000   *Telephone:* 53.09.84.02
Open: lunch daily, dinner Tue-Sat (closed mid-Feb – mid-Mar)
Last orders: 9.30pm

The best of a host of restaurants here. Chef Régis Chiorozas's star is rising, so it's advisable to book in order to enjoy dishes such as a fondant de saumon et foie gras de canard or a panaché de poissons au beurre d'aromates. Uninspiring exterior belies the talent within.

Moulin de Roc

CHAMPAGNAC DE BELAIR

Lieu-dit Moulin du Roc, 24530   *Telephone:* 53.54.80.36
Open: please phone for details
Last orders: please phone for details

This is a favourite restaurant in the area. The simpler, regional dishes and fixed price menus offer the best value, and the former 17th-century oil mill by the river, a charming setting. Attentive service and superb cooking by Mme Solange Gardillou, who has become one of the foremost women chefs in France.

Château de Monbazillac

MONBAZILLAC

24240   *Telephone:* 53.57.06.38
Open: 9.00am – noon, 2.00pm – 6pm

The Renaissance château, belonging to a wine co-operative, houses a museum devoted to two areas of local interest – wine and protestantism. The Monbazillac vines were originally planted in the 11th Century by monks, prospering under the patronage of Bergerac merchants and exiled Protestants. In recent times, like its famous rival Sauternes (which it pre-dates), Monbazillac has suffered from the modern preference for dry wines; but both are now beginning to make a comeback.

Restaurant du Château de Monbazillac

MONBAZILLAC

24240   *Telephone:* 53.58.38.93
Open: lunch + dinner, Tue-Sun
Last orders: please phone for details

After a visit to the museum you can enjoy a summer meal on the terrace or eat in the grand dining room run by Mons Alvarez. It's a place that tends to be used for special occasions, presentations, weddings or gourmet gatherings.

Closerie St Jacques
MONBAZILLAC
Le Bourg, 24240   *Telephone:* 53.58.37.77
Open: lunch Tue-Sun, dinner Tue-Sat (closed Jan + out in season)
Last orders: 9.30pm

The starred restaurant, with its blue and white dining room, offers modern dishes such as a pâté de bar served with a sauce aux pointes d'asperges et aux boules de melon.

Les Ruines
MONBAZILLAC
24240 Monbazillac   *Telephone:* 53.57.16.37
Open: lunch Tue-Sun, dinner Tue-Sat (closed Feb)
Last orders: 9.30pm

A stone fireplace is the focal point of the simple rustic dining room of this new restaurant. Seafood is a speciality, the fixed price menus are good value, and the wines reasonably priced.

Hôtel de la Cité
CARCASSONNE
Place Eglise, 11000   *Telephone:* 68.25.03.34
(no restaurant)

Steeped in history, this well-kept hotel has some superb public rooms and exquisite gardens as well as comfortable modernised bedrooms. Among the charms of its location in the city are the walled garden and, from the upper floors, views over both old and new Carcassonne.

Hôtel Aragon
CARCASSONNE
15 Montée Combéléran, 11000   *Telephone:* 68.47.16.31
(no restaurant)

This is a useful 'budget' place to stay, and is situated just outside the medieval city. Simple rooms have en-suite bathrooms, and a swimming pool in the courtyard.

Dinner in Valladolid

Lying on the route from France to Portugal, the city of Valladolid in Spain makes a convenient stop. Here, Ferdinand and Isabella, the Catholic rulers of Castile and Aragon, were married, a union which ultimately led to the defeat of the Moors in 1492. The city has retained some buildings of note, such as the 15th-century university and the cathedral.

Hotel Mozart
VALLADOLID
Menéndez Pelayo 7   *Telephone:* (983) 29.77.77
Open: all year (no restaurant)

A good place to stay that is stylish though modern. Simple marble rooms, good reception, café-style breakfast.

Meson la Fragua
VALLODOLID
Paseo de Zorrilla 10   *Telephone:* (983) 33.87.85
Open: daily (except Sun lunch)
Last orders: please ring for details

Don't miss a visit to this marvellous restaurant. Situated in a row of shops, you pass a range of fish tanks as you enter, then a friendly bar where distinguished-looking waiters serve tapas with wines and sherries by the glass, or by the bottle. Thence past the open grill and charcoal burners into the dining room. Your meal kicks off on a light-hearted note with hysterically funny English translations of the menu, such as 'veal from the inner upper arm burnt in the fire to your liking'! Language aside, the food is very good. Stick to the simple grills and fish dishes, and try the local cheeses. There's a very good wine list and charming helpful service. The best for many miles.

THE ART OF INTIMACY.

A moment, a glance, a glass of Martell VSOP - Intimacy to be shared.

MARTELL

COGNAC. L'ART DE MARTELL.

SINCE 1715.

Long Weekend in the Algarve

Portugal was once described as being like a patchwork counterpane upon which a box of toys had been emptied.

The low white houses of the Algarve (especially at Olhão) are a legacy of the Moors who occupied the area from the 8th to 13th Centuries. They gave the Algarve its name – Al Gharb – 'land of the setting sun'. The Moors also introduced irrigation systems, and the fig and the almond – favourite Portuguese ingredients.

Bacalhau, the smell of sardines grilling over charcoal fires, fish split open and threaded onto lines drying by harbour walls: sole, sea bream, eels, clams, octopus, prawns, crayfish . . . The gleaming hauls of the sea are one of the Algarve's most characteristic sights.

Fishermen still live in the old part of the ever-expanding town of Quarteira and it's worth visiting the lively fish market here. Fish is nearly always grilled, or poached in a court-bouillon, and often served with cabbage, green beans and boiled potatoes.

Alfonso
QUARTERIA
Centro Comercial Abertura Mar   *Telephone:* 089-346-14

After a visit to the fish market, you could try this place for lunch. Eat on the terrace or in the air-conditioned dining room.

The cataplana, a hinged copper cooking vessel, is unique to Portugal and has given its name to a number of dishes. Try ameijoas (clams or mussels) na cataplana. At Loulé, where there is a large regional market on Saturdays, watch craftsmen hammering out cataplanas around the Avenida area, then go to the **Avenida** restaurant, upstairs above the petrol pumps!

The formal gardens and fountains of the 18th-century palace at Estoi are one of the Algarve's jewels, as is the church of S. Lourenço, also near Faro: its simple white exterior belies an interior completely covered in azulejos (the blue and white tiles so typical of Portugal – 'azul' is Portuguese for blue).

The majority of people here appear either to own villas or to rent from reputable villa holiday companies such as OSL, Horizon Holidays, Five Ways, Edgbaston, Birmingham B15 1BB Telephone: 021-643 2727.

Alternatively, the Quinta Park Apartments offer well-furnished self-catering accommodation.

Pergola Lago
ALMANCIL

This is conveniently situated for the Quinta Park and makes a change from the beach bars. The inland lake offers wind surfing and other sporting activities. An open-air grill and barbeque are run by the same team as Shepherd's.

Shepherd's
QUINTA DO LAGO
Casa Velha   *Telephone:* 089-94541
Open: Tue-Sat

For those self-imposed exiles whiling away the year in the Algarve sunshine, Shepherd's provides a nostalgic return to London with its decor and style the hallmarks of Richard Shepherd (co-proprietor of Langan's). The menu offers roast rib of beef, roast potatoes and horseradish sauce alongside more local dishes such as grilled tuna fish with a tomato and onion sauce. Concise Portuguese wine list.

There is also a club adjacent to Shepherd's, with its internal courtyard open to the skies.

Passos Beach Bar
QUINTA DO LAGO
Telephone: 089-396435

Passos is the prince of the beach bars here and Joao Passos rules this most stylish of them with a casual but firm hand. As its name implies it is right on the beach, and is little more than a huge wooden shack with a platform at the front where people vie for the best tables. The kitchen equipment consists merely of a series of open grills, but the food that is produced on them is truly wonderful. No doubt it wouldn't taste as good in a city away from the coast, but the atmosphere here is magical and the fish is collected every morning by Joao. This is the Portuguese equivalent of Club 55 in St Tropez.

There are two interesting places in Almancil, **Casa da Torre Ermitage**, (*Telephone:* 089-943-29). Situated on the road to Vale do Lobo. An attractive, elegantly decorated, large farmhouse recently opened as a restaurant. Pleasant terrace.

Bistro da Praca, Vale do Lobo, (*Telephone:* 089-944-44 x 5412). Cosy, traditional Portuguese style bistro decor, with hanging bunches of garlic.

En route through Italy

English 19th-century aristocrats, attracted to the region's mild climate and beautiful lush landscape, were the first to frequent the Riviera, followed by their Russian and German counterparts. The Genoese nobility also left their mark – exquisite villas which perch regally on hillsides overlooking sparkling blue bays and long beaches of fine sand.

The countryside around San Remo is covered with flowers – roses, carnations, jasmine, narcissi – intensively cultivated for San Remo's flower market, the most important in Italy and open each weekday from October to June from around midnight to 8am.

Royal Hotel
SAN REMO
Corso Imperatrice 80, 18038 Imperia   *Telephone:* 0184-7991/5391
Open: daily (closed mid-Sep – mid-Dec)
Last orders: please phone for details

Since 1872, members of the Bertalini family have been welcoming guests to this famous hotel a gracious neo-classical building with skilfully designed extensions. Ask for a sea-side room with a private balcony. Set in its own park sloping up to the hotel, the Royal is a haven of calm and its salt water swimming pools are wonderful. It's impossible to sink – I proved it by dozing off in the water! Some good dishes on the menu including pasta and veal. You can eat either outside on the terrace or in the brightly lit main dining room. If hotel cuisine doesn't appeal, San Remo has a number of good restaurants.

La Broche
SAN REMO
Corso Imperatrice 112   *Telephone:* 0184-33901/667871
Open: daily (closed Wed + Nov)
Last orders: please ring for details

Just along the Corso from the Royal. Ignore the busy main road in front and enjoy the sea view. It's a friendly restaurant with a marvellously eccentric owner who greets you with a slap on the back even if he happens to be holding a trout at the time! He also enjoys (in equal quantities) practising his English and shouting at the staff. Try the excellent pasta and seafood dishes but avoid the table directly in front of the television – where customers have been known to fight for their favourite programme!

Grand Hotel dei Castelli
SESTRI LEVANTE
Via alla Peninsola 26, 16039 Genova   *Telephone:* 0185-41044
Open: 15 May – 10 October
Last orders: please ring for details

Hans Christian Andersen once described the bay at Sestri Levante as a 'fairy tale bay', and who could resist falling under its spell when seen from this splendid location?

Easy to approach from the sea-front, follow the neon sign on top of the castle, and after a steep winding climb you will emerge into a walled garden with not one, but two castles situated inside – one in which you stay and the other in which you eat. What a setting for a restaurant! Certainly for any romantic the setting is outstanding, with views of the setting sun over the harbour and the curve of the bay. The food is either from the set menu or from the carte, with very good pasta and fish dishes. The castle hotel itself has some suites actually overlooking the sea, but even if you can't book one of them, the views on all sides are attractive, and each suite has its own individual touches. Mine had a sunken bath set in a mosaic, arched and domed bathroom. Charming staff for whom nothing is too much trouble. A walk through the gardens leads you via a private lift to a hidden beach.

The hills of the Tuscan interior provide a tranquil summer retreat, while La Maremma, once a malarial coastal swamp, is now rich agricultural land producing fruit, cereals and vines.

Ristorante Il Bugiale
GUARDISTALLO

Via Palastro, 56050 Pi *Telephone:* 0586-655123
Open: lunch + dinner, Fri – Wed
Last orders: please ring for details

Il Bugiale serves very good country fare beautifully presented in a much lighter and more modern manner than its rustic setting would imply. A summer lunch comprised excellent crostini (large croûtons garnished with fegato – a Tuscan speciality), then a selection of parma hams with slices of fragrant orange melon. A salad of arugola, with shavings of grana padama cheese, came with a whole bottle of the most delicious local olive oil which, in true Italian-child style, you can also pour onto the warm bruschetta and ciabbatta breads. The main course was freshly made whole egg linguine served with sautéed wild boar meat (game and wild boar are local specialities); then came a selection of desserts including the most delicious tiramisu. Friendly, helpful owners. This place is worth a detour – I would certainly return if I found myself within twenty miles of here – and that's saying something on these roads.

Where better to raise a glass of Vernaccia di San Gimignano, accompanied by a platter of cheese or ham, than in one of the cantines in San Gimignano itself, such as the Enoteca il Castello, via del Castello (0577-940878). Some enjoy stunning views over archetypal, medieval Tuscan, hilltop towns. If the view should move you to poetic thought, you'll be in good company, for Dante lived here.

Hotel Cisterna

SAN GIMIGNANO
53037 Siena   *Telephone:* 0577-940328
Open: lunch Thur-Mon, dinner daily (closed mid-Nov – mid-Mar)
Last orders: please ring for details

Lunch in Le Terrazze restaurant for views over the red-tiled rooftops and to the Val d'Elsa beyond. The 15th-century dining room is part of the hotel that is situated in a former medieval convent on a pretty square named after its 14th-century cisterna (well). Good regional cuisine and wines.

Chianti is classically produced in a small area barely thirty miles long and twenty miles wide, at Barberino Val d'Elsa, San Casciano Val di Pesa, Greve in Chianti and Tavernelle Val di Pesa – touring routes through the area are signposted. There are no fewer than three highly rated restaurants in the area.

Arnolfo

COLLE DI VAL D'ELSA
Piazza Sta Caterina 2, 53034 Siena   *Telephone:* 0577-920549
Open: lunch + dinner, Wed-Mon (closed Oct-10 Feb)
Last orders: please ring for details

Offers seasonal specialities such as terrina di coniglio alle erbe aromatiche and piccione brasato al Chianti. Small and well-known, so book.

Antica Posta

SAN CASCIANO VAL DI PESA
Piazza Zannori 1, 50026 Firenze   *Telephone:* 055-820116
Open: lunch + dinner, Tue-Sun (closed Aug)
Last orders: please ring for details

Offers accommodation as well as a menu with dishes such as raviolo di patate con crema di formaggi e pepperoni and sella di capriolo al brunello. Book.

La Tenda Rossa

CAERBAIA

50020 Firenze   *Telephone:* 055-826132
Open: lunch Fri-Tue, dinner daily (closed 3wks Aug)
Last orders: please ring for details

Offers equally good food – if it's available try the carpaccio di scampo, or the petto di piccione ai due fegati. Book.

———————————◇———————————

Several wine-producing estates offer on-the-spot tastings of Chianti wines; or wait until Siena where the Fortezza Medicea houses the Enoteca Italica Permanente exhibition of wines from all over Italy. (Tastings possible, open 3.00pm – midnight.) On Wednesdays, Siena's weekly market is held in this area.

Ai Marsili

SIENA

Via del Castoro 3, 53100   *Telephone:* 0577-47154
Open: Tue-Sun
Last orders: please ring for details

Near the Duomo, it is generally considered Siena's best restaurant. It's set on the ground floor and in the vaulted cellars of the 15th-century Palazzo Marsili. Ceci (chick peas with garlic and rosemary), contrefilet Marsili and roast guineafowl are typical of the Tuscan cuisine served here.

Al Mangia

SIENA

Piazza del Campo 42   *Telephone:* 0577-281121
Open: Tue-Sun (closed Feb)
Last orders: lunch 2.00pm, dinner 11.00pm

If your priority is the Piazza del Campo, this is also a useful place for a meal or an ice cream and coffee – especially if you braved the 503 steps to the top of the Torre del Mangia for the wonderful view! Very crowded in the tourist season.

Le Campane
SIENA

Via delle Campane 6   *Telephone:* 0577-284035
Open: Mon-Sat, Jun-Sep (closed Mon Oct-May; closed Nov)
Last orders: please ring for details

This is a small trattoria with tables outside in good weather. Fresh fish features alongside soups, grilled meats and crostini.

Osteria le Logge
SIENA

via del Porrione 33   *Telephone:* 0577-48013
Open: lunch + dinner, Mon-sat (closed mid-Nov – mid-Mar)
Last orders: please ring for details

A popular, informal restaurant with specialities such as Sienese bean soup, and meat dishes. Get here early to be sure of a table. No credit cards.

Mariotti da Mugolone
SIENA

Via dei Pellegrini 8   *Telephone:* 0577-283235
Open: lunch daily, dinner Fri-Sat + Mon-Wed)
Last orders: please ring for details

Traditional in style, this restaurant is popular for its good Tuscan cooking.

Most good hotels are situated outside the old town.

Park
SIENA

Via di Marciano 18   *Telephone:* 0577-44803
Open: lunch + dinner, Thurs-Tue
Last orders: please ring for details

Siena's leading hotel (part of the Ciga group) is a 15th-century building, set in its own grounds. It has been furnished with some good antiques and the rooms are air-conditioned. The garden restaurant and terrace overlook Siena – most beautiful at sunset or in the early morning. The menu reflects the international clientele – stick to the Italian dishes. Enthusiastic bar and restaurant staff.

Other hotels include:

Certosa di Maggiano
SIENA
Strada di Certosa 82   *Telephone:* 0577-288180
Open: lunch + dinner, Wed-Mon
Last orders: please ring for details

Sophisticated, elegant and expensive, this hotel is set in a former 13th-century monastery.

Palazzo Ravizza
SIENA
Piano dei Mantellini 34   *Telephone:* 0577-280462
Open: Mar-Nov

A converted 17th-century building with its own garden just within the city walls.

Montepulciano is a dignified and beautiful Renaissance city whose steep streets culminate in the Piazza Grande. Recover from the climb in the café on the square and look into the wine shops on the way back down. On Thursdays, a market is held in the lower part of the town.

Porta di Bacco
MONTEPULCIANO
1OO Via Graciano nel Corso, 53045 Montepulciano   *Telephone:* 0578-716907
Open: daily (closed Fri in winter)
Last orders: please ring for details

Housed just by the city gate – regional cooking served in rustic dining rooms. A wine shop and museum are attached to this picturesque restaurant.

Other recommended restaurants in the Siena area:

La Chiusa
SIENA
Montefollonico, 35040   *Telephone:* 0577-669668
Open: 16 Mar – 4 Nov + 6 Dec – 1 Jan (closed lunch July + Aug)
Last orders: please ring for details

Located in a lovely, tiny hilltop village. Book to eat in this starred restaurant: a converted farmhouse serving specialities such as conchiglio marinato and colle d'oca ripieno con salsa di pecorino.

Locanda dell'Amorosa
SINALUNGA
53048 Siena   *Telephone:* 0577-679497
Open: lunch Wed-Sun, dinner Tue-Sun (closed 20 Jan – 28 Feb)
Last orders: please ring for details

Situated some distance from Sinalunga, at the end of an impressive cypress-lined avenue. The lovely old whitewashed buildings are recorded as existing as far back as 1300, and are now the setting for the sophisticatedly 'rustic' restaurant. The menu reflects the style with dishes such as risotto ai fiori di zucca and rombo di ricci di mare alongside grilled meats, vegetables from the kitchen garden or market and local cheeses. Smart service. End a romantic meal by staying in one of the rooms. (Market at Sinalunga on Tuesday mornings.)

Osteria delle Grotta
SINALUNGA
53048 SIENA   *Telephone:* 0577-630269
Open: Thu-Tue

Picturesque location on steep, terraced hillside planted with olive trees and flowering plants. Good value 6-course dinner menu – bring a good appetite and start early – dinner is a lengthy affair!

Il Conte Matto
TREQUANDA
Trequanda

Park in the square below the ramparts and walk up the hill to the tiny square behind which is this trattoria-style restaurant. Good home-made pasta – try their pici (fat spaghetti) served with duck sauce. Crostini served with local truffle sauce. Try the wild boar casseroled with funghi porcini, or pigeon with black olives. Good vegetables and fresh local fruit.

La Romita
MONTISI
53020 Siena   *Telephone:* 0577-824186
Open: Thu-Tue

Small chef-patron restaurant open by reservation only. Three charming tiny dining rooms are the setting for antica cucina toscana – all recipes are inspired by the cooking of the ancients using fresh local produce, including herbs from the garden.

San Gimignano
-opposite

Short stop in Brussels

If there is a problem with eating out in Brussels, it is that there is too much choice, and you really need a week if you are going to eat your way through the plethora of Michelin-starred restaurants in Belgium's capital.

Almost every taste is catered for, and there are many cafés and bars you can try around the centre of Brussels. Whilst deciding where to eat, drop off for a drink or a coffee at an open-air café such as La Chaloupe d'Or on the Grand'Place, and at the same time take in the colourful flower market which is held there every day except Monday.

Villa Lorraine

75 avenue du Vivier d'Oie, 1180
Telephone: (2) 374.31.63
Open: Mon-Sat (closed Jul or Aug)
Last orders: 9.30pm

A place which is a must, especially in the summer, situated about fifteen minutes from the centre of town overlooking parkland in a wealthy suburb. It's as lovely to sit outside on the terrace as inside the large, light and airy dining room. The waiters glide around as if on casters, ably guided by Henri Van Ranst. Freddy Vandecasserie in the kitchen produces some outstanding dishes in the classic style. The menu offers a wide choice and caters for most tastes. If it's available, try the petit homard à la nage au beurre de Sancerre, or the escalopes de foie de canard sur une salade de pourpier. Game in season is a speciality. Leave room for one of the delicious desserts, such as a chocolate soufflé with a green walnut sauce.

The cuisine at Villa Lorraine is elegantly presented but substantial in portion – classic cuisine with nouvelle overtones. There is also a sister restaurant, the equally famous L'Ecailler du Palais Royal.

Comme Chez Soi

23 place Rouppe, 1000 *Telephone:* (2) 512.29.21/(2) 512.36.74
Open: Tue-Sat (closed Jul, Christmas + New Year)
Last orders: 10.00pm

Comme Chez Soi is very different in size and style to Villa Lorraine. Housed in an elegant building, its Art Nouveau decor reflects the fact that it was founded in 1926. Owners Pierre and Marie-Thérèse Wynants watch proudly over their intimate restaurant – Marie-Thérèse from her vantage point behind the elegant glass doors that divide the restaurant from the kitchen, and Pierre from his domain, the beautifully equipped and spotless kitchen. Pierre Wynants has a dedicated following from all over the world, and it's easy to see why, as you relax and read the menu with anticipation. Usually three fixed-price menus plus an à la carte are offered. The waiting staff are attentive and arrive at the very moment you want them, perhaps to bring, as an amuse-gueule, a tartlet of creamed herring and apple garnished with a slice of radish.

Dishes are pictures on a plate: coquilles Saint-Jacques, lightly smoked, on a stunning salad of green beans, leeks, cauliflower, asparagus and a slice of tête de veau; fillets of sole with a riesling-scented mousseline and crevettes grises; a wonderful pigeon à la royale de truffes. Desserts, such as an apple tart with a green apple sorbet, are a fitting conclusion to the meal. The wine cellar, under the expert eye of René Goriseen, yields some real treasures.

Index

Discount Offers to Readers of

THE
ACKERMAN
MARTELL
GUIDE
1991-92

All offers subject to availability at the time of booking – discounts to be claimed when booking.

ANNIE'S RESTAURANT
MORETON-IN-MARSH
Tel 0608 51981
A complimentary bottle of house wine for 4 people when taken with dinner from Monday to Thursday inclusive – valid to 31/07/91.

ARDSHEAL HOUSE
KENTALLEN OF APPIN
Tel 063 174 227
10% off a meal for 2 or more people
– valid to 31/07/91.
10% off accommodation for 2 people
– valid to 31/07/91.

AT THE SIGN OF THE ANGEL
LACOCK
Tel 024 973 230
15% off the total bill for food and wine on all pre-booked weekday lunches – valid to 30/11/91.

ATKINS RESTAURANT AT FARLEYER HOUSE
ABERFELDY
Tel 0887 20332
10% off food and/or accommodation bills (not including service) – valid to 15/05/92.

THE BEAR HOTEL & RESTAURANT
WOODSTOCK
Tel 0993 811511
A complimentary bottle of house wine for 2 people when taken with a set or à la carte meal – valid to 31/08/91.

LE BERGER RESTAURANT
BRAMLEY
Tel 0483 894037
A complimentary half-bottle of champagne for 2 people eating a 3-course meal from the à la carte menu – valid to 30/09/91.

BISHOPSTROW HOUSE
WARMINSTER
Tel 0985 212312
10% off a meal for 2 or more people –
valid to 31/12/91.
10% off accommodation for 2 people
against quoted rates, including break
rates but excepting Bank Holidays –
valid to 31/12/91.

LA BONNE AUBERGE
SOUTH GODSTONE
Tel 0342 892318
£10 off a meal for 2 people, any day except Saturday – valid to 30/11/91.

THE CASTLE AT TAUNTON
Tel 0823 272671
25% off normal accommodation rates for 2 people – valid to 31/12/91.

CÉZANNE CAFÉ/RESTAURANT
TWICKENHAM
Tel 081-892 3526
A complimentary bottle of of house wine for 2 people eating a 3-course meal from Monday to Thursday inclusive – valid to 30/04/92.

CHARINGWORTH MANOR
NR CHIPPING CAMDEN
Tel 038 678 555
10% off accommodation for 2 people – valid to 23/12/91.

CORSE LAWN HOUSE HOTEL
CORSE LAWN
Tel 045 278 479
10% off accommodation for 2 people in one twin or double room for one night or more – valid to 31/08/91.

THE COUNT HOUSE
BOTALLACK
Tel 0736 788588
A complimentary bottle of house wine for 2 people with dinner or Sunday lunch – valid to 30/11/91.

CLOS DU ROY
BOX
Tel 0225 744447
A complimentary half-bottle of champagne for 2 people with dinner – valid to 31/08/91.
20% off accommodation for 2 people on any nights from Monday to Thursday – valid to 31/08/91.

THE CROWN AT WHITEBROOK
NR MONMOUTH
Tel 0600 860254
Free accommodation for a 3rd night after a 2-night stay on demi-pension terms from Mondays to Thursdays inclusive but excluding Bank Holidays – valid to 15/05/92.
20% off accommodation for 2 people when dining, from Mondays to Thursdays inclusive but excluding Bank Holidays – valid to 15/05/92.

EGLANTINE
TUNBRIDGE WELLS
Tel 0892 24957
15% off a meal for 2 or more people – valid to 30/09/91.

FLITWICK MANOR
FLITWICK
Tel 0525 712242
25% off accommodation for 2 people – valid to 15/05/92.

HEATHCOTE'S RESTAURANT
LONGRIDGE
Tel 0772 784969
A complimentary half bottle of champagne for 2 people with dinner on any evening from Sunday to Thursday inclusive – valid to 31/08/91.
A complimentary bottle of champagne for 4 people with dinner on any evening from Sunday to Thursday inclusive – valid to 31/05/91.

HILAIRE
LONDON SW7
Tel 071-584 8993
15% off a meal for 2 or more people – valid to 31/05/91.

HOPE END
LEDBURY
Tel 0531 3613
10% discount on room and meal charges for any 3-night stay – valid to 31/12/91.

HUNTERS RESTAURANT
RUTHIN
Tel 082 42 2619
A complimentary bottle of house wine for 4 people when taken with a 3-course table d'hôte meal – valid to 16/07/91.

KINGSHEAD HOUSE
BIRDLIP
Tel 0452 862299
£2.50 taxi voucher for the journey home per person when taking dinner – valid to 30/11/91.

THE LAKE ISLE
UPPINGHAM
Tel 0572 822951
Special Break rate of £90 per couple per night for dinner, bed and breakfast on any night from Friday to Sunday inclusive – valid to 31/10/91.
Special Break rate of £96 per couple per night for dinner, bed and breakfast on 2-night stays from Monday to Friday inclusive – valid to 31/10/91.

LEITH'S RESTAURANT
LONDON W11
Tel 071-229 4481
Any first-growth claret on the wine list will be offered at the prevailing auction price as quoted in Decanter magazine (plus VAT and 15% service). Offer extends to Petrus and Château d'Yquem – valid to 31/08/91 and again from 01/01/92 to 30/04/92.

LOWER PITT RESTAURANT WITH ROOMS
EAST BUCKLAND
Tel 059 86 243
10% off accommodation for 2 people on Tuesday, Wednesday or Thursday nights – valid to 30/09/91.
10% off a meal for 4 or more people on Tuesday, Wednesday or Thursday – valid to 30/09/91.

LA MALMAISON
HERSHAM
Tel 0932 227412
A complimentary bottle of wine for 4 people with their meal – valid to 31/07/91.

MANLEY'S
STORRINGTON
Tel 0903 742331
20% off accommodation for 2 people – valid to 16/07/91.

LE MANOIR AUX QUAT'SAISONS
GREAT MILTON
Tel 0844 278881
A complimentary bottle of champagne for 2
people with any meal, plus a signed copy of
the menu – valid to 31/08/91.
20% off accommodation for 2 people when
taken on any night(s) from Sunday to
Thursday inclusive – valid to 31/08/91.

MELTON'S RESTAURANT
YORK
Tel 0904 634341
£10 off wine on any Tuesday, Wednesday or Thursday – valid to 30/11/91.

MICHAEL'S NOOK
GRASMERE
Tel 096 65 496
50% discount on the 3rd night of a 3-night stay, excluding Bank Holidays – valid to
22/08/91.

MURRAYSHALL COUNTRY HOUSE HOTEL
SCONE
Tel 0738 51171
10% of accommodation for 2 people at any
time plus a complimentary round of golf –
valid to 31/03/92.
A complimentary bottle of champagne for 2
or more people with dinner – valid to
31/03/92.

NEW HALL
SUTTON COLDFIELD
Tel 021-378 2442
£25 off room rate at any time – valid to 15/05/92.

THE NEW MILL
EVERSLEY
Tel 0734 732277
A complimentary glass of champagne on arrival in the Restaurant or Grill Room –
valid to 30/06/91.

NORMANDIE HOTEL & RESTAURANT
NR BURY
Tel 061-764 3869
50% off accommodation for 2 people on Friday night, when dining – valid to
30/09/91.

NORTON PLACE HOTEL
BIRMINGHAM
Tel 021-459 9111
10% off lunch or dinner in the Lombard Room Restaurant when staying at the hotel –
valid to 15/05/92.

NUTHURST GRANGE
HOCKLEY HEATH
Tel 0564 783972
20% off accommodation for 2 people on a
Friday, Saturday or Sunday night – valid
to 15/05/92.
10% off a meal for 2 or more people – valid
to 15/05/92.

THE OLD FORGE RESTAURANT
STORRINGTON
Tel 0903 743402
A complimentary bottle of house wine for 2 people taking a 3-course meal in the evening – valid to 21/09/91.

THE OLD VICARAGE
RIDGEWAY
Tel 0742 475814
Free private meeting facilities in the boardroom for people or Companies booking lunch or dinner – valid to 30/09/91.
A complimentary bottle of gold-medal winning white Alsace wine, served as an aperitif to 4 people with lunch or dinner – valid to 30/09/91.

THE OLD COACH HOUSE
BARHAM
Tel 0227 831218
Discount-inclusive package for 2 people of dinner (excluding wines), bed and breakfast plus tickets as foot passengers to Boulogne in France: one night £70, 2 nights £112 – valid to 15/05/92.

THE OLD PLOW AT SPEEN
NR AYLESBURY
Tel 0494 488300
15% off a meal for 2 people (not including wine) when dining in the main à la carte dining room on Tuesday, Wednesday or Thursday evening – valid to 30/11/91 and from 01/01/92 to 15/05/92.

PARTNERS RESTAURANT
DORKING
Tel 0306 882826
A complimentary bottle of house wine for 2 people with lunch or dinner – valid to 15/05/92.

THE PLOUGH AT CLANFIELD
Tel 036 781 222
20% off accommodation for stays of 5 nights or more on bed-and-breakfast terms – valid to 31/08/91.
10% off accommodation for 2 people staying a minimum of 2 nights, midweek, on bed-and-breakfast terms – valid to 31/08/91.

POLLYANNA'S RESTAURANT
LONDON SW11
Tel 071-228 0316
A complimentary glass of champagne per person as an aperitif – valid to 31/08/91.

POMEGRANATES RESTAURANT
LONDON SW1
Tel 071-828 6560
15% off a meal for 2 or more people – valid to 31/08/91.

POPPIES RESTAURANT AT THE ROEBUCK
BRIMFIELD
Tel 058 472 230
15% off accommodation for 2 people for a minimum of 2 nights – valid from 01/07/91 to 30/09/91.

THE PRIORY HOTEL
BATH
Tel 0225 331922
15% off a meal for 2 or more people – valid to 31/08/91.

RESTAURANT PEANO
BARNSLEY
Tel 0226 244990
A complimentary bottle of wine for 2 people taking an à la carte meal – valid to 30/09/91.

RUDLOE PARK
CORSHAM
Tel 0225 810555
A superior de luxe room at the standard room price – valid to 31/03/92.

SLASSORS RESTAURANT
SOUTHEND
Tel 0702 614880
No corkage charge, saving 75p per bottle on all wines and spirits – valid to 30/11/91.

STAPLEFORD PARK
NR MELTON MOWBRAY
Tel 057 284 522
Special set menu price of £19.91 – normally £30 – valid to 31/12/91 excluding Bank Holidays.
3 nights' accommodation for the price of 2 for 2 people – valid to 31/12/91 excluding Bank Holidays.

SWINTON HOUSE
KING'S LYNN
Tel 0366 383151
15% off a meal for 2 people – valid to 30/11/91.

THIERRY'S
LONDON SW3
Tel 017-352 3365
A complimentary bottle of champagne for 4 people with lunch or dinner – valid to 31/08/91.

THIRTY SIX ON THE QUAY
EMSWORTH
Tel 0243 375592
A complimentary bottle of wine for 2 or more people with dinner – valid to 15/07/91.

THORNBURY CASTLE
THORNBURY
Tel 0454 418511
Complimentary 4th night's accommodation after a 3-night stay – valid to 30/11/91.

THROWLEY HOUSE
FAVERSHAM
Tel 0795 539168
A complimentary bottle of house wine for 2 people at dinner on Friday or at lunch on Sunday – valid to 30/11/91.

VERONICA'S RESTAURANT
LONDON W2
Tel 071-229 5079
A complimentary bottle of house wine for 2 people when taken with 2 main-course meals – valid to 30/11/91 and from 01/02/92 to 30/04/92.